The Making of a Consciousness Leader in Business:
An Integral Approach

BOOKS BY MARIANA BOZESAN, Ph.D.

*Diet for a New Life: An 8-step Integral Solution to
Weight Loss and Wellbeing* (2007)

*Diet for a New Life Anthology:
Expert Advice on Weight Loss and Wellbeing* (2005)

The Making of a Consciousness Leader in Business

An Integral Approach

Mariana Bozesan, Ph.D.

SageEra

San Franscico & Munich

2010

Published by SageEra Institute LLC, 434 Quartz St., Redwood City, CA 94062, USA, www.SageEra.com. SageEra and the SageEra logo are trademarks of SageEra Institute LLC.

Book design by Lewis Agrell. Cover design by Derek McDavid.

Library of Congress Cataloging-in-Publication Data

Bozesan, Mariana

The Making of a Consciousness Leader in Business – An Integral Approach

Includes bibliographical references.

ISBN 978-0-9746102-5-2[MB1]

Library of Congress Control Number: 2009932739

1. Leadership—psychological aspects. 2. Business, management, and executive ability—psychological aspects. 3. Adult Development. 4. Emotional intelligence. 5. Consciousness. 6. Spirituality.

THE MAKING OF A CONSCIOUSNESS LEADER IN BUSINESS:

AN INTEGRAL APPROACH

by

Mariana Bozesan

A dissertation submitted

in partial fulfillment of the requirements

for the degree of Doctor of Philosophy

in Psychology

Institute of Transpersonal Psychology

Palo Alto, California

March 5th, 2009

I certify that I have read and approved the content and presentation of this dissertation:

_____   _____
Mark L. McCaslin, Ph.D., Committee Chairperson   Date   4/28/09

_____   _____
Ruth H. Judy, Ph.D., Committee Member   Date   5/5/09

_____   _____
Russell W. Volckmann, Ph.D., Committee Member   Date   5/9/09

Abstract

The Making of a Consciousness Leader in Business:
An Integral Approach

by

Mariana Bozesan

This dissertation explores the phenomenon of becoming a consciousness leader within a business environment. Consciousness leaders are people who have evolved to postconventional levels of interior development and are engaged in globally sustainable wealth creation for the benefit of all. The present research employs Ken Wilber's All Quadrant All Lines (AQAL) map of consciousness and the newly designed qualitative method named heuristic structuralism. The nature, meaning, and cause of transformative experiences of 8 female and 8 male top business executives is investigated along with the structural impact over time. The research question is the following: What are the most significant emotional, physical, cognitive, spiritual, or other extraordinary experiences that characterize the interior transformation of consciousness leaders within a capitalistic environment? The research results have multiple dimensions and include (a) the evolutionary journey of becoming a consciousness leader; (b) the lines of development involved in the transformation including the egoic, cognitive, emotional, physical, moral, and psycho-spiritual; and (c) the potential structural changes that occurred over the course of transformation. It can be expected that the exploration of becoming a consciousness leader will not only reveal the interiority of exceptional leaders, but it will support a paradigm shift in leadership, business, and capitalism in general. This understanding will also provide encouragement, inspiration, and hope to those who are actively involved with wealth creation in a business environment as well as to those who struggle to live a life of meaning within the same context.

Dedication

I dedicate this work
to my extraordinary parents,
Maria and Grigore Bozesan,
who are my role models for parenting,
unconditional love, compassion, and service in the world;
to Tom Schulz, the love of my life, amazing husband,
and best father in the world;
and to Albert Bozesan, our brilliant son and
greatest accomplishment, whose humor, creativity,
and joie de vivre have always been my shining light.
I love you all more than you will ever know.

Acknowledgements

This dissertation would not have been possible without the many exceptional people who directly or indirectly have contributed with their content, support, love, and dedication. I wish I could name you all. Thank you.

Mark McCaslin, how could I thank you enough for your unconditional love, potentiating leadership, and tireless support? Your wisdom, unconditional love, and friendship made all the difference in my life especially during the darkest hours in my dissertation process. Without you, I would still be analyzing my data. You have always believed in me more than I believed in myself. My gratitude to you is infinite.

Thank you from the bottom of my heart, Ruth Judy for accompanying me through my entire Ph.D. program at ITP. Your mentorship, wisdom, love, friendship, and unconditional support mean everything to me. Russ Volckmann, you have been instrumental in helping me grow beyond myself through this dissertation. This work is much better because of you. I thank you for your friendship, kindness, wisdom, and for bringing your gifts into my world.

My gratitude goes especially to all consciousness leaders who despite your busy schedules have been kind enough to participate in and contribute to my research. Without you, this dissertation would not exist. I cannot mention your names, but you know who you are and I am deeply humbled by your presence in my life. I am honored to know you and thank you from the depths of my heart for everything you are and do to make this world a better place.

Furthermore, I am profoundly obliged to Wendelin Küpers for your expert advice on the research method for this study. Despite the time difference between San Francisco and New Zealand, you have taken the time to speak with me and make excellent recommendations on conducting a successful research interview. Your selflessness is highly appreciated. Thank you and thank you Russ for introducing us.

I am also deeply indebted to all ITP professors including Rosemarie Anderson, William Braud, Ruth Judy, Marius Koga, Ana Perez Chisti, Kartik Patel, Henry Poon, Nancy Rowe, and Judy Schavrien for believing in me and for trusting, supporting, and encouraging me to look beyond the appearance of the day-to-day reality. Your friendship, deep caring, and tireless support during the past 5 years have been instrumental in giving me the strength and confidence to grow.

Thank you also to the members of my ITP co-heart—too many to mention—over the past 5 years. Your loving presence in my life has long been nectar for my soul and without your loving embrace over the years my doctoral journey would have been a much bumpier ride. Thank you. I am especially grateful to Wendy Peters for your authentic friendship, unconditional love, and support. How could I ever show you my endless gratitude for becoming such an integral part of my life, dear sister?

My profound gratitude goes also to my editors, the late Vera Lind and Kelly Lynch. Your thoroughness and endless patience are highly appreciated. A well-deserved thank you also to the administrative staff and dissertation team at ITP including Ryan Rominger, Allison Perry, and many others who helped me tirelessly along the way. You have given me everything I asked for without expecting anything in return. Thank you.

Many thanks go also to you, Curtis Turchin, my chiropractor and healer. Thank you for taking care of my back and for keeping me healthy, vital, and in good spirits. Without your loving support and shining presence in my life, I would not have been able to finish this dissertation in a timely fashion.

I do not have enough words to express my appreciation and gratitude to Ken Wilber, one of the most brilliant minds in the world today. The theoretical foundation of my dissertation is based on your outstanding work, yet the shining lights in my life were also your humor, innate joy, and beautiful spirit. Thank you for being who you are.

For their presence in my life, as well as friendship, encouragement, contributions, endorsements, and ongoing support, I am deeply indebted to His Holiness the Dalai Lama, Susanne Cook-Greuter, Ram Dass, Riane Eisler, Stephen LaBerge, George Leonard, Edgar Mitchell, Stephen Mitchell, Michael Murphy, Marilyn Schlitz, Lynne Twist, Neale Donald Walsch, and many others whom space does not permit to mention. Thank you.

Finally, I would like to express my deep gratitude to Tom Schulz, my husband, the love of my life, and friend of three decades. Without you, I would never have finished this work. Your unconditional love, curiosity, generosity, and tireless support during some of the darkest hours in this dissertation process have given me the love and strength needed to complete this journey. Also, I could not have completed my doctoral program without the unconditional love and support of the best parents in the world, Maria and Grigore Bozesan. You have unconditionally loved, guided, and supported me ever since I can remember. Thank you for your selfless giving, flexibility and youthful attitude, and for being our guardian angels. Endless thanks go also to our son Albert. You are my best teacher and supporter. You have given me the love, room, and time to study and write. Your creativity, joy, and humor have often reminded me of my true nature. Thank you. I love you all beyond measure.

May all our journeys continue to be blessed and divinely guided!

Table of Contents

LIST OF FIGURES

Figures   **Page**

CHAPTER 1

INTRODUCTION

The notion of the consciousness leader in business has gained personal relevance since 1995. That year, I left my successful high-tech career in Corporate America to start my own company because I began missing the joy of life. Time had arrived to integrate what had more heart and meaning not only professionally, but also personally, mentally, emotionally, physically, spiritually, culturally, and ecologically. I sought an environment that would nourish not only my intellect but also support my interior transformation including that of my soul and spirit. I desired to create an atmosphere that would enable the integration of personal and professional values, as well as maintain the development of an ecosystem for wealth creation at all levels of human existence, not only monetary or materially. Eventually, I succeeded in creating my vision and my life changed significantly. In the meantime, the idea of the consciousness leader became a reality that was worth exploring because it seemed to have become a contemporary trend.

To further research this phenomenon, this dissertation explored the emotional, spiritual, egoic, and other structural characteristics of business people who have already made a significant shift in consciousness and who are now serving the greater good. The term consciousness leader was chosen to indicate that these extraordinary individuals have evolved to higher stages of consciousness and human development (Alexander et al., 1990;

Commons, Richards, & Armon, 1984; Commons, Armon, Kohlberg, Richards, & Grotzer, 1990; Cook-Greuter, 2005, 2008; Koplowitz, 1984, 1990; Torbert et al., 2004; Wilber, 2000c). Consciousness leaders continue to lead themselves and others to higher levels of consciousness and are furthermore outstanding personalities who have established a new paradigm in business by aligning their individual goals with global collective goals (Kofman, 2007; Ray & Rinzler, 1993). They engage in integral wealth creation, monetary and otherwise, and do it in a sustainable fashion for the benefit of all.

Within this context, it is important to note that the main focus of this dissertation was the phenomenon of the *interior* transformation and process of becoming a consciousness leader. The *exterior* dimensions such as the aspects of leading others as well as the function of leadership with its cultural and social context are analyzed from the perspective of the impact resulting from the interior evolution.

Statement of Problem

In the light of today's increasing financial, ecological, and geopolitical crisis and challenges it is obvious that individual dissatisfaction within the business world has also increased (Kofman, 2007; Ray & Rinzler, 1993; Secretan, 2006). Money seems to have ceased keeping its promise for security, and a growing number of business people are becoming aware of the separation between the material world and a meaningful life (Klein & Izzo, 1999). For these people, financial abundance appears to stop being the ultimate goal because the promise of happiness was not fulfilled by material prosperity (Ricard, 2003). In fact, the opposite seems to be the case (Blanchflower & Oswald, 2004, p. 1366).

An additional cause for the overall discontent seems to be rooted in the fact that the majority of today's businesses are still operating primarily from outdated corporate values (Kofman, 2006) including (a) short-term monetary profit-orientation (Collins & Lazier, 1992, pp. 67-69), (b) tough competition (Collins, 2001), (c) hierarchical organization structures

(Eisler, 2007, pp. 182-183), (d) dominating management styles (Eisler, 2002), (e) disregard for individual human values (Toms, 1997), (f) inability and/or unwillingness to look at the shadow side of business (Senge, Scharmer, Jaworski, & Flowers, 2005, p. 229), and (g) fear and mistrust (Secretan, 2006). All of these attitudes, actions, and outdated values run counter to or are rejected by the consciousness leader.

The economic and geopolitical challenges such as financial crisis, terrorist attacks, or ongoing wars are exacerbated by large-scale climate changes such as natural catastrophes including hurricanes, droughts, and tsunamis. Addressing these challenges in an integral fashion requires not only massive capital but also higher levels of consciousness (Capra, 1993; Harman & Hormann, 1993; Senge et al., 2005; Soros, 2004, 2008; Wilber, 2000a). The challenges faced by any leader are perennial and vary in an infinite degree yet it appears that the integral approach taken by the consciousness leader makes the ultimate difference to their success. Thus, given the evidence, the consciousness leader recognizes that change has become inevitable and the only question is not *if* it will happen but *how*, *when*, in *which* direction, and with *which* consequences for humanity. In offering solutions, both Friedman (2005) and Nobel Peace Prize laureate Albert Gore (2006) argued that we should all be motivated to change or we will not survive either economically, geopolitically, or environmentally.

Yet, what is required is not the trivial change required by everyday life, but "*significant* changes of mind" (Gardner, 2004, p. 2) such as represented in people who become change agents and who are predestined to become consciousness leaders of humankind. These are people who operate from later stages of development such as Wilber's (2000c) *vision logic* (pp. 262-272), the *turquoise altitude* within the Spiral Dynamics (Beck & Cowan, 1996, pp. 287-294), the *Alchemist* level in Torbert's (2005) *action logic* (pp. 177-193), or Cook-Greuter's (2005) *Unitive* level as the highest stage of her Ego development stages (pp. 32-35). According to research, these people represent less than 1% of the U.S. population (Cook-Greuter, 2004, p. 1) and 1% of the research sampling business leaders (Rooke & Torbert, 2005, p.3).

Leadership in general and business leadership in particular have been researched and documented thoroughly (Collins, 2001, 2005; Collins & Lazier, 1992; Kouzes & Posner, 2003, 2007; Porras, Emery, & Thompson, 2007; Senge et al., 2005). In analyzing existing literature, it became obvious that the business world is changing in the following directions:

1. From the *outside-in*, in response to the overall globalization (Friedman, 2005), the need to address the current economic crises (Sachs, 2008; Soros, 2008), environmental and energy crises (Brown, 2006; Gore, 2006), as well as geopolitical challenges (Eisler, 2007; Porras et al., 2007; Soros, 2004);

2. From the *inside-out* through awakening individuals at all levels of an organization and in both directions, bottom up and top down (Covey, 1989; Goleman, Boyatzis, & McKee, 2002; Lietaer, 2001; Porras et al., 2007; Ray & Myers, 1989 Renesch, 2002; Senge et al., 2005);

3. Through newly born organizations that are often being lead by consciousness leaders and their integral teams (Wilber, 2003). These organizations are based on new (i.e., renewable energies) and disruptive technologies (i.e., electromotors replacing the old internal combustion engines) that will replace old and inflexible ones.

Yet, literature that goes beyond the external aspects of leadership in business and focuses more on the interior transformation of the leader by addressing questions such as *why, how,* and *when* the transformation took place is relatively rare (Adams, 2005; Boyatzis & McKee, 2005; Goleman et al., 2002; Kouzes & Posner, 2003; Marques, Dhiman, & King, 2007; Mitroff & Denton, 1999; Pauchant, 2002; Renesch, 2002; Senge et al., 2005; Taylor, 2005).

Therefore, in analyzing the current state of the art in business leadership, this dissertation calls for a more integral approach that (a) complements and expands existing research in this field by adding a heuristic structuralism perspective (Cook-Greuter, 2004; Goleman et al., 2002; Rooke & Torbert, 1998, 2005); (b) considers the phenomenological interiority aspects of the leader; and (c) includes cultural, social, and sustainability components from a transpersonal psychology perspective.

In mapping Wilber's (2000a) integral model of consciousness, the problems addressed by the current study are the following:

1. The apparent separation and conflict between the interiority of the individual (including soul, emotions, values, needs) and the dissatisfaction with the exterior, or the material world (Goleman et al., 2002; Marques et al., 2007; Mitroff & Denton, 1999; Pauchant, 2002; Renesch, 2002; Senge et al., 2005; Taylor, 2005).

2. The demand for a paradigm change that provides the integration between the interior and exterior aspects of a human being and accommodates the latest neuroscientific discoveries (Beauregard & O'Leary, 2007; Damasio, 2006; Lipton, 2005; McCraty, 2003), such as questioning the current mechanistic worldview as well as the scientific understanding of reality.

3. The lack of cultural and social infrastructure to support awakening business individuals to "come out of their closets," address their inner conflicts, and extend group values and beliefs in a significant way (Porras et al., 2007; Ray & Myers, 1989; Secretan, 2006; Toms, 1997).

4. The need for (a) a radical systemic change and social structures with respect to the globalization of businesses; (b) the overarching call for consciousness leaders and leadership tools for sustainable change; and (c) the necessity for systemic wealth creation, especially as it relates to the role of capital and global resources (Beck & Cowan, 1996; Capra, 2002; Eisler, 2007; Friedman, 2005; Renesch, 2002; Senge et al., 2005; Twist, 2003).

Purpose Statement

With insights from having lived through this transformative process myself, the proposed study concentrated on *what* brings consciousness into the heart of capitalism through the business leaders themselves. The intention was to identify what exactly has the power to transform capitalism into what could be named either as conscious capitalism, spiritual capitalism, or integral capitalism. Why focus on capitalism? Because, it could be argued that conscious capitalism lies at the core of integral wealth creation and has the power to trigger significant transformation at all levels of human existence, especially beginning with the interior dimensions of the leader. In my worldview, capitalism is at the foundation of wealth creation where almost everything is measured by its monetary value (Eisler, 2007; Lietaer, 2001; Soros, 2004, 2008; Twist, 2003; Yunus, 2007).

By employing Wilber's (2000a) All Quadrant All Level (AQAL) Integral Theory of Consciousness, as well as Wilber's (2006) Integral Methodological Pluralism (IMP), the purpose of this heuristic structuralism research was to:

1. Deconstruct the societal myths regarding business people by uncovering the integral transformation of extraordinary business leaders toward higher levels of human development and consciousness.

2. Identify, analyze, understand, and portray in detail the transformative experiences of business leaders. The research and analysis hereto has occurred not only from the *inside-out* view of the participants themselves but also from the *outside-in* perspective to identify the "patterns or structures [that] actually govern the phenomena" (Wilber, 2006; p. 55). The transformational path was demonstrated following the framework used by Campbell's (1949/1968) in his book *The Hero with a Thousand Faces*. Thus, the process of becoming a consciousness leader is called the *Hero's Journey*.

3. Extract and represent the essence of the transformation toward consciousness leadership along various lines of development (cognitive, emotional, physical, ethical, spiritual, and egoic) that are involved in the studied transpersonal phenomena.

4. Contemplate, evaluate, and reveal how transpersonal states of consciousness have been integrated into the lives of the participants over time (*state stages*) and how these state stages have been translated into permanent structures of higher levels of consciousness (Cook-Greuter, 2005; Wilber, 2006).

5. Comprehend, elucidate, and assess *how* the participants have been able to translate their interior transformation into exterior transformation of (a) their inter-subjective, cultural environment; (b) their behavior and the interdependent coherence of the people they lead; and (c) the inter-objective, social and organizational coherence of their businesses, industry, and the environment.

6. Consider, illuminate, and appraise the global consequences of the interior transformation as it relates to its implications with respect to social structures, intergenerational coherence, social responsibility, as well as the long-term viability and health of the planet

The transformative experiences researched here have been variously termed *peak* or *transcendent experience* (Maslow, Stephens, & Heil, 1998), *flow* (Csikszentmihalyi, 1990; *Kjaer et al.*, 2002), *states of* or *unity consciousness* (Wilber, 2003), *exceptional human experience* (White, 1998), *transpersonal experience* (Grof, 2006), and *spiritual emergency* (Vaughan, 2000). Regardless of its name, this transformative experience can be triggered by external circumstances, a nonordinary ordinary state of consciousness, an emotional or physical trauma, or a spiritual experience. Furthermore, the experience has a significant impact both with respect to the interiority of the participant and with regard to its long-term positive effect manifested through the congruent social action of the percipient (Beauregard & O'Leary, 2007; Goleman, 1995; Goleman et al., 2002; Maslow et al., 1998; Mitroff & Denton, 1999; Saron & Davidson, 1997; Toms, 1997; Wilber, 2000a, 2006).

In addition, the current research intended to contribute to the redefinition of the word capitalism and its most significant driving force, money (Twist, 2003). Since its invention, money has become one of the most treasured, if not the most important, driving forces in human life, the world economy, and politics. In general, we have forgotten that money is a human creation made to serve us. Instead, we have arrived at a point in human history where we are serving it. Because we often misunderstand it, we seem to have succumbed completely to it as a source of absolute power and authority. In *The Soul of Money*, Twist (2003) argued that money has become the measure for "our competence and worth as people" (p. 6) and is rarely a "place of genuine freedom, joy, or clarity" (p. 9). Through our collective unconscious behavior, we have elevated money to an almost divine-like status that seems to make us sometimes lose our most sacred values to the point of self-destruction. For the sake of making money, we seem to be ready to sacrifice our planet, poison our bodies, environment, and food, send our own children to war, and are even ready to kill for it (Secretan, 2006, p. 22). However, the time of significant change is a "precarious [one] because we are experiencing simultaneous action, reaction, counter action, and conflict" (Beck & Cowan, 1996, p. 104). It is a time that requires a redefinition of leadership, a redefinition that must come from higher levels of consciousness.

As a dot-com serial entrepreneur, I have participated in and experienced firsthand how through the Internet, humanity has entrance to information, free human resources, free telephony, free virtual businesses, and most important, free communication. Through cyberspace, the world has truly become a global village. For the first time in human history, Internet users have access to free virtual human capital, virtual land, and virtual currency. Human consciousness has evolved beyond the information age (Wilber, 2000b). The Internet is now providing us not only with the possibility of an open society, resources and information, but also with an infrastructure that is bypassing old and inflexible monetary structures (Lietaer, 2001). The newly born and unofficial currency is now that of the Internet.

This development can give us all more hope for a better world, a world in which Internet access brings down boundaries between countries, the rich and the poor, the privileged and the underprivileged, as well as between race and gender. It is a world that gives access to people regardless of their location, cultural environment, social status, skin color, or education. In this so-called "flat" world (Friedman, 2005, p. 5), we are able to connect, exchange ideas, share our intellectual capital and even start companies without one single penny except for internet access. In a wider sense, the additional purpose of the present study was to contribute to creating a new era of true wealth creation, an era of conscious capitalism, an era that is outgrowing the traditional moneymaking paradigm.

Research Questions

Consciousness leaders can presumably be found everywhere including business, education, politics, religion, and social work. They can have different types of education and positions in their organizations. However, they all are driven by an insatiable thirst for making the world a better place. Some of them are loud, charismatic, and intense, and others are calm, gentle, and quiet Nonetheless, most of them are resourceful, courageous, creative, and playful (Beck & Cowan, 1996). What they have in common is the fact that they honor, appreciate, and cultivate the wealth of their souls for the benefit of all because they are able to transcend their own challenges and grow beyond themselves. Although they represent the business world, these leaders are people like Rosa Parks (Hansen 2003, pp. 5-8) who had the courage to break traditional rules by refusing to cede her seat to the whites; people like Gandhi (1977), who questioned authority and changed himself to serve others; people like Nelson Mandela (1994) and His Holiness The Dalai Lama (Dalai Lama, 1999), who transcended hatred to serve the greater good and unify people; and leaders like the educator Marva Collins (Porras et al., 2007), who encouraged her students to create a life of meaning and helped them see that without the contribution of every single one of us "the world would be a darker place" (p. 3).

Triggered by my own life experience, the current research focused on identifying, researching, and analyzing the transformational experiences of consciousness leaders within the business world. These are people involved with systemic wealth creation, monetary and otherwise (Aburdene, 2005; Goleman et al., 2002; Gore, 1992; Covey, 1989; Hendricks & Ludeman, 1996; Lietaer, 2001; Porras et al., 2007; Ray & Myers, 1989; Renesch, 2002; Robbins, 1986; Senge et al., 2005). The heuristic inquiry of the current study is tightly connected with my own personal growth and spiritual transformation after growing up poor in communist Romania and my subsequent career as a high-tech entrepreneur.

Therefore, the main question for this research is: What are the most significant emotional, physical, cognitive, spiritual, or other transpersonal experiences that characterize the structural interior transformation of consciousness leaders in business? Secondary questions include the following:

1. What are the triggers, the context, and process of their transformation into a consciousness leader or, in other words, what are the causes of their *peak* or *transcendent experiences* (Maslow et al., 1998), experiences of *flow* (Csikszentmihalyi, 1990; Kjaer et al., 2002), *states and stage development* (Wilber, 2003), *exceptional human experiences* (White, 1998), *transpersonal experiences* (Grof, 2006), or *other spiritual emergencies* (Vaughan, 2000)?

2. What is the structural impact that can be deduced from the researched transpersonal phenomena over time—hence the term *heuristic structuralism*?

3. How do people become the integral change agents required for a paradigm shift in business?

4. What facilitates and what may inhibit the change of their minds?

5. How do these consciousness leaders keep evolving to higher levels of consciousness in a hostile environment dominated by less-conscious investors, stakeholders, tough competition, and a litigation-friendly environment?

6. What is the future of business and how can new business structures be created in the light of awakened and awakening consciousness leaders?
7. What is the future of capitalism within the context of global sustainability?

Key Term Definitions

Consciousness

There are many meanings of consciousness and each discipline involved in consciousness research has its own definition. For instance, within the field of social psychology, consciousness is considered to be embedded in and viewed as the result of the existing cultural and social systems (Wilber, 1997, p. 72). Neuropsychology views consciousness as part of the anatomical structure of the human body (Beauregard & O'Leary, 2007), and according to psychologist Csikszentmihalyi (1990) "it is understood that whatever happens in the mind is the result of electrochemical changes in the central nervous system, as laid down over millions of years by biological evolution" (p. 26).

For the scope of this research, consciousness is defined using Wilber's (2000a) AQAL map of consciousness that draws on the strengths of most major definitions of consciousness "and attempts to incorporate and integrate their essential feats" (Wilber, 1997, p. 72). Furthermore, the present research also emphasizes a nondual worldview, which regards *unity consciousness* as the highest form of human consciousness (Wilber, 1996, p. 173). In unity consciousness, boundaries disappear all together and there are no opposites, no good or evil, no positive or negative, and no pain or pleasure. Within the nondual worldview, instead of manipulating opposites against each other in the search for peace and a better world, we transcend them both (Wilber, 2001, pp. 102-105).

Leader, Leading, and Leadership

There are many ways to define leader, leading, and leadership. However, for the scope of this research, a leader is understood as an individual who fulfills the role of motivating and/or influencing a group of people towards the achievement of common goals. Leading is seen as the sum of all activities and behaviors of a leader. Within the context of the underlying integral approach of this dissertation that employs Wilber's (2000a) AQAL as a theoretical foundation, the term leadership "involves the role (leader), the behaviors (leading) and the context. . . that includes culture, as well as systems, processes, technologies and artifacts" (R. W. Volckmann, personal communication, February 25, 2009). However, it is important to emphasize again that the research in this dissertation was mainly focused on the phenomenological components related to the *interior* transformation of the leader. The *exterior* dimensions are thus analyzed as a result and within the context of the *interior* evolution.

Consciousness Leadership

Although the term consciousness leadership has not yet been established it represents—from the perspective of the current study—an integral evolution of leadership that affects all "states, structures, memes, types, levels, stages, and waves of human consciousness" (Wilber, 2000a, p. 7) with consciousness being the space in which all evolution manifests; it is "the emptiness, the openness, the clearing in which phenomena arise" (Wilber, 2006, p. 68). It is to be expected that consciousness leadership will enable not only the development of the interior and exterior aspects of the leader but also those of society and culture in an ecologically sustainable way. This kind of leadership acts with a global perspective in mind and "must be forged in the social and technological crucibles that result in business, religion, education, and politics" (Beck & Cowan, 1996, p. 104).

The Consciousness Leader

Consciousness leadership requires as its agent a consciousness leader, yet another new concept. A consciousness leader is a different kind of leader that would possess the ability, insight, wisdom, and personality to address interior and exterior levels of complexity that have rarely before been encountered in the known history of humanity (Torbert et al., 2004). Consciousness leaders would be pioneers of change who break new grounds and have the wisdom, power, and skill to transcend stale situations and develop more evolved ones for the benefit of all. Consciousness leaders would have the insight that human life is continuously evolving to later stages of consciousness whereby each stage transcends and includes the previous one and only represents a transition to the next stage (Wilber, 2006, p. 29).

Consciousness leaders would be holistic problem solvers, honor people at their own stage of evolution, and would be able to flow naturally and comfortably within each stage with appreciation, understanding, and compassion. They are alchemists of change management who naturally recognize and transcend their own weaknesses for the benefit of all (Porras ct al., 2007, p. 242). They would possess not only emotional intelligence but also existential intelligence as the "capacity to pose and ponder the biggest questions: Who are we? Why are we here?" (Gardner, 2004, pp. 40-41).

Within the business context of the present research, consciousness leaders would be considered to have reached mature levels of ego-transcendence through significant transformational processes and events (Cook-Greuter, 2008). They would have also reached emotional and moral maturity, high levels of cognitive development, and high spiritual development through regular transformative practices (Wilber, 2006, pp. 201-205). The interior transformation of the consciousness leader would be accelerated by transformative experiences (defined below), would occur in stages and along several lines of human development (Wilber, 2000c, p. 13) including the cognitive, emotional, moral, physical, and spiritual (Cook-Greuter, 2005, pp. 3-4). Thus, consciousness leaders would have the ability to move beyond rational thought and dual reality (p. 29), and could see through the mind-constructed world (Cook-

Greuter, 2005, pp. 28-31). Therefore, they would be able to live in the present moment, accept what is and the paradoxes inherent in the world (pp. 35-36). They would be able to let go of control because they can connect with and unleash their unlimited potentials, identify with the source of all creation, and realize the futility of objective self-identification and materialistic attachment (Cook-Greuter, 2004; Torbert et al., 2004). Through their new understanding and structural changes, consciousness leaders would have become passionate contributors to the business world. They would get involved with and create conscious businesses (Kofman, 2006) by continuing to be deeply anchored within themselves and by leading others to higher levels of consciousness through presence, trust, hope, humility, and humor (Senge et al., 2005). They would be able to expand our understanding of money by opening up new vantage points for creating sustainable wealth (Yunus, 2007).

Transformative Experiences

The transformative experiences observed here and that can serve as significant catalysts for the evolution of consciousness leaders are known in the literature for instance as *transcendent* or *peak experiences* (Maslow et al., 1998), *flow* (Csikszentmihalyi, 1990; Kjaer et al., 2002), *state or unity consciousness experiences* (Wilber, 2003), *exceptional human experiences* (White, 1998), *transpersonal experiences* (Grof, 2006), and *spiritual emergency experiences* (Vaughan, 2000).

We seem to reach higher levels of consciousness when we can become the observer, the witness of life, and begin to honor the truth in all there is (Walsh, 1999). Peak experiences, meditation, contemplation, near-death experiences, and other states of awe can accelerate this evolutionary process (Maslow et al., 1998, p. 1; Vaughan, 2000, p. 31). Through such states, we seem to be able to move beyond duality, the good and the bad, the beautiful and the ugly, and realize that "the point is not to separate the opposites and make 'positive progress,' but rather to unify and harmonize the opposites, both positive and negative, by discovering a ground which transcends and encompasses them both" (Wilber, 2001, pp. 27-28).

As will become apparent through the present research, such transformational experiences played a key role in the lives of the business leaders studied because they seem to transform over time from temporary states of consciousness into permanent traits or stages of consciousness. Therefore, it is important to note the difference between a state of consciousness and a stage of consciousness. Apart from the peak experiences, meditative states, and the nonordinary states of consciousness discussed above, there are familiar states of consciousness such as "waking, dreaming, and deep sleep" (Wilber, 2006, p. 4). States of consciousness are temporary and can partially be identified using brain-wave measuring devices available today (pp. 164-167). From the perspective of developmental psychology (Cook-Greuter, 2008), stages of consciousness refer to the center of gravity out of which "people make sense of experience. Thus, stage is a purely abstract, psychological construct that has no correlate in the brain" (p. 7). Within the context of the Wilberian (2000a) AQAL employed in this research, there are "8 to 10 stages of consciousness development" (p. 5). Wilber (2006) argued, "Where states of consciousness are temporary, stages of consciousness are permanent. Stages represent the actual milestones of growth and development" (p. 5). The phenomenological research in the current dissertation aimed at finding significant interior or transformational experiences (extraordinary states of consciousness) in business leaders and identifying the patterns or structures that control these phenomena and that possibly led to higher stages of consciousness.

Delimitations and Limitations

A practical delimitation of this research was transferability of the research findings. This has to do with the fact that the research participants are top leaders who have undergone a process of extraordinary transformation that took place over many decades. They have evolved along several lines of human development and have presumably reached higher levels of consciousness. Such extraordinary transformations occur sometimes spontaneously and are often not replicable. Therefore, it is difficult to transfer the research findings to other people unless the tools, circumstances, and means of transformation could also be made available. Yet, knowing that such significant changes are possible provides already deep hope.

One of the limitations of the current study is that the extraordinary individuals researched are highly visible people and therefore difficult to reach a second time. Furthermore, whereas a heuristic structuralism approach to this research seemed to be the ideal method of inquiry, it is deep, time consuming, and cumbersome. Consequently, although the qualitative research findings may be transferable they may not be generalized to other leaders.

Significance of the Study

The exceptional phenomenon of becoming a consciousness leader and how it occurs may not only enhance our definition and understanding of the notion of leader, leading, and leadership in general, but also provide more qualitative data regarding the meaning of transformative experiences (states of consciousness) as it translates into permanent traits of consciousness over time (Cook-Greuter, 2008, p. 7; Wilber, 2006, p. 4).

Moreover, this research can contribute to a more pluralistic mode of inquiry, named here *heuristic structuralism*, in which each point of view is honored as a potential source of insight. The *heuristic structuralism* mode of inquiry was born out of a combination between Moustakas' (1990) heuristic research method and Wilber's (2006) Integral Methodological Pluralism, which "involves, among other things, at least eight fundamental and apparently irreducible methodologies, injunctions, or paradigms for gaining reproducible knowledge or verifiable repeatable experiences" (p. 33). These methods are explained in more detail in chapters 2 and 3.

Additionally, Waldron (1998) argued that transcendent experiences have the powerful potential to help people (a) become change agents, (b) increase their psychosocial effectiveness, (c) accomplish social change, and (d) enhance their psychological function by taking "the recipients way beyond 'adaptation' into the hard work of integration and manifestation in the world" (p. 129). This dissertation study may demonstrate how this transformation can occur within the business world. Furthermore, it could offer not only inspiration, hope, but also a concrete transformational path to make a change, seek peer groups, and begin to live a life of more meaning within the business context. In addition, this research may contribute to a new characterization or expansion of the current understanding of capitalism, business leadership, and money. Thus, the geopolitical, social, cultural, and individual implications of a paradigm change may be substantial.

Chapter Summary

This dissertation represents the heuristic structuralism exploration of the phenomenon of consciousness leadership in a capitalistic environment. In mapping Wilber's (2000a) map of consciousness (AQAL), the current study analyzed, synthesized, and presented the emotional, spiritual, and other structural characteristics of consciousness leaders on their paths to higher levels of consciousness (Cook-Greuter, 2008; Kegan, Lahey, & Souvaine, 1990; Torbert et al., 2004; Wilber, 2006). Furthermore, this research was also concerned with the impact of the interior transformation with respect to the exterior transformation of the research participants such as their leadership abilities within the context of their cultural and social environment. The transformational path of consciousness leaders, which occurred between 1 and 4 decades via significant transformational experiences (Boorstein, 1996), is called *Hero's Journey* and is demonstrated using Campbell's (1949/1968) process described in his book *The Hero with a Thousand Faces*. Following their transpersonal transformation, consciousness leaders are presumably rooted in oneness rather than separation, gratefulness rather than deprivation, abundance rather than scarcity, and love rather than fear.

CHAPTER 2

LITERATURE REVIEW

By employing a qualitative heuristic structuralism research design, the current study explored the interior aspects of exceptional emotional, spiritual, and other transformative experiences of consciousness leaders who were actively involved in the business world. Consciousness leaders are defined as outstanding leaders who have evolved to higher levels of consciousness through transpersonal experiences and who are now leading others toward higher levels of consciousness.

The problems addressed by this research are (a) the apparent separation between the interiorities of business people and their exteriorities; (b) the lack of appropriate business infrastructure to support awakening and awakened business individuals; (c) the necessity for appropriate and holistic leadership tools and skills; (d) the need for a radical systemic change in the business world in the light of current financial, environmental, and geopolitical crisis; and (e) the demand for a paradigm change that accommodates the unification and integration of transpersonal experiences within the scientific paradigm.

Theoretical Views

There is an enormous amount of information and research that focuses on leadership, success, achievement, and business in general. From the integral perspective that underlies the focus of the current research, namely Wilber's (2000a) AQAL, it could be argued that many theories address some aspects and neglect others. For instance, the exterior aspects and manifestations of success and leadership, as defined earlier, seem more attractive and easier to replicate than the interiority transformation of the leader (Porras et al., 2007). It appears that the lines along which the interior development (Wilber, 2006, pp. 23-25) took place and the questions on *how, when,* and *why* the business leaders transformed still need to be researched in more depth. Such a line of development is spirituality (Wilber, 2006, p. 101). Although spirituality in business appears to have become a megatrend (Aburdene, 2005), the phenomenological investigation on the interior transformation of the leader, which also includes spirituality or the transpersonal realm, is relatively rare but is increasing (Adams, 2005; Boyatzis & McKee, 2005; Cook-Greuter, 2004; Goleman et al., 2002; Hendricks & Ludeman, 1996; Jaworski, 1996; Lietaer, 2001; Marques et al., 2007; Mitroff & Denton, 1999; Pauchant, 2002; Paulson, 2002; Ray & Myers, 1989; Renesch, 2002; Rooke & Torbert, 1998, 2005; Senge et al., 2005; Taylor, 2005).

Consciousness and Leadership

Over time, there have been many attempts to comprehend and define consciousness. As the understanding of consciousness has expanded, the definition of it has changed as well. In his paper, *An Integral Theory of Consciousness,* Wilber (1997) provided an overview of 12 major concepts of consciousness including those used in cognitive sciences, neuropsychology, developmental, and social psychotherapy, nonordinary states of consciousness, and quantum consciousness. As expected, there is no common understanding of what consciousness is. Therefore, Wilber (2000a) developed an integral map of consciousness, the *All Quadrant All Level* (AQAL) model, which attempted to honor the "strengths of each of these approaches" (p. 3). Wilber's map is arguably one of the most comprehensive maps of consciousness evolution available today and is increasingly applied in business, politics, science, education, medicine, and spirituality (Wilber, 2000a).

Wilber's (2000a) model of consciousness has been chosen as the foundation for the heuristic structuralism research proposed in the current study because it appears to provide an integral holding tank for consciousness evolution and how it could be associated with consciousness leadership. Therefore, the following literature review is mapped to correlate with Wilber's model.

All Quadrant All Level Model (AQAL)

Wilber's (2000b) definition of consciousness is based on humanity's indivisible value spheres called by William James the Great Chain of Being (Lovejoy, 1942, pp. 67-98). *The Great Chain of Being*, also called the *Value Spheres of Humanity*, or the *Big Three*, has three components: the *Beautiful*, the *Good*, and the *True* (Plato, 1938/1961). The next figure represents the *Big Three* as it relates to Wilber's AQAL.

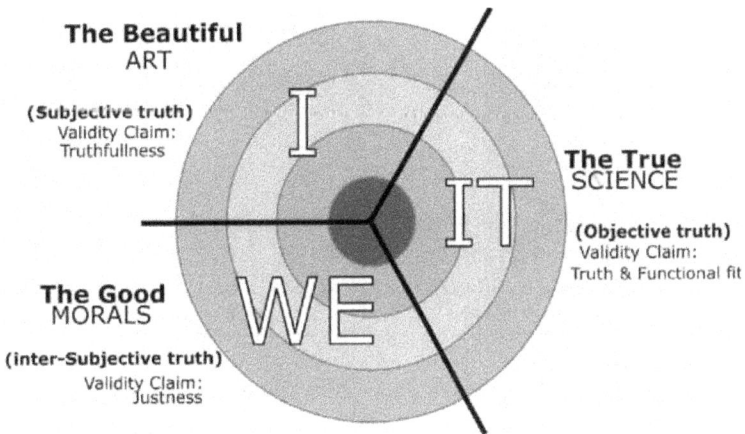

Figure 1. Value spheres of humanity, the *Big Three* (Wilber, 2000c, p. 64).

Wilber (2000b) associated the definition of consciousness with various pronouns, which we usually use to relate to each other and make sense of the world. He connected the first person pronoun, the I, also referred to as the self, or subjective truth, with the *Beautiful*. The pronoun WE that represents the intersubjective truth, the morals, and the culture in which we live is associated with the *Good*. Finally, Wilber correlated the pronoun IT with the *True*, or objective truth.

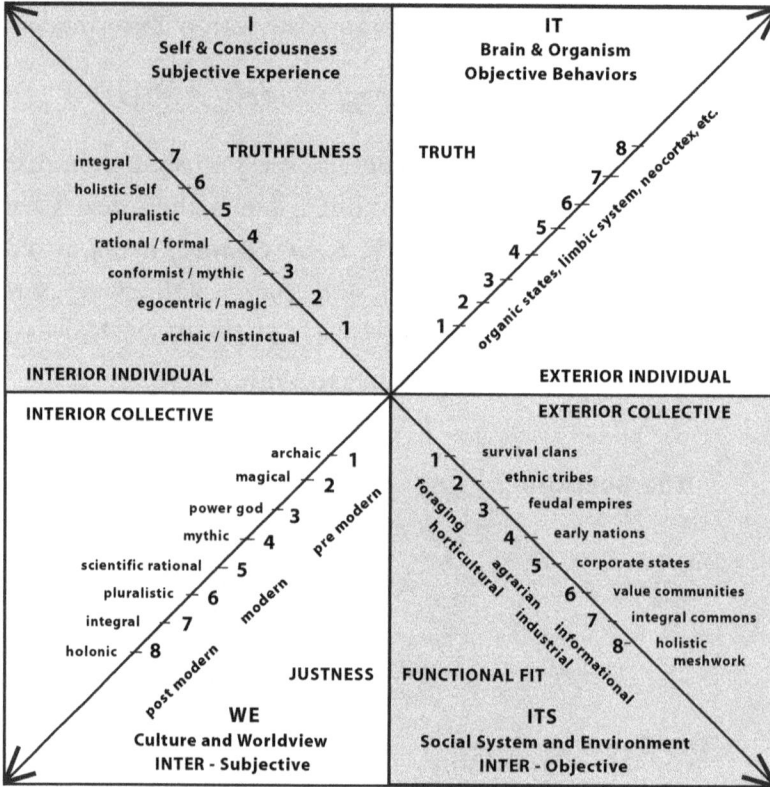

Figure 2. The *Big Three* and Wilber's four quadrants adapted from Wilber (2006, pp. 20-22).

To achieve a higher granularity and inclusiveness for the consciousness map, Wilber (2000c) expanded the *Big Three* to include a fourth component, the Lower Right quadrant that is represented in Figure 2. This quadrant, which he associated with the pronoun *ITS*, is the exterior collective quadrant and represents the social, the global, and the ecology realms. This quadrant can be best understood from a systems theory perspective. Being an interdisciplinary field of science, systems theory studies the nature of complex systems such as nature, society, and science, and provides a framework through which complex systems can be better understood, analyzed, and influenced (Capra, 2002). All quadrants are equally important for the consciousness leadership paradigm discussed here, however the fourth quadrant is significant, because it expands the common definitions of both consciousness and leadership to include the global perspective and to address the financial, geopolitical, ecological, and environmental impact of collective actions (Capra, 1993).

Self and Consciousness (I)

The Upper-Left quadrant in Wilber's (2000a) AQAL or Integral model refers to the personal subjective and the inner life of the individual. It "includes the entire spectrum of consciousness as it appears in any individual, from bodily sensations to mental ideal to soul and spirit" (Wilber, 2000c, pp. 62–63) and contains several lines of interior or self-development as represented in Figure 3.

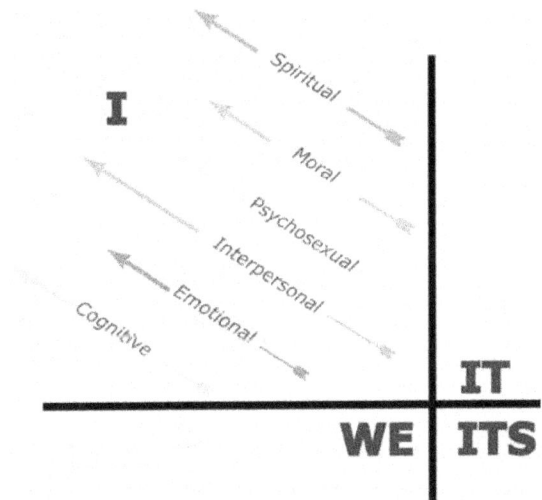

Figure 3. Upper Left quadrant and lines of development (Wilber, 2005, p. 36).

All lines of the internal or personal growth are significant, however, within the consciousness leadership concept discussed here, and it is important to highlight the emotional and spiritual lines of development. Most advanced leadership theories focus on the cognitive (Gardner, 1993), moral (Gilligan, 1982/1993; Kegan et al., 1990), value (Beck & Cowan, 1996), and emotional lines of development (Goleman et al., 2002). Yet, the spiritual line, or transpersonal line of development is rarely addressed within the definition of leader, although there is a strong indication that spirituality has become an important trend in business (Aburdene, 2005; Cook-Greuter, 2005; Hendricks

& Ludeman, 1996; Pauchant, 2002; Rooke & Torbert, 1998, 2005; Secretan, 2006; Torbert et al., 2004).

To lead consciously within the new paradigm, consciousness leaders would have to be deeply fulfilled and self-actualizing individuals who live an integral life (Fadiman & Frager, 2002; Maslow et al., 1998, Wilber, 2000a). When taking their responsibilities seriously, they would have to have a well-developed sense of humor and live joyous lives (Dalai Lama, 2002; Ricard, 2003; Saron & Davidson, 1997). Furthermore, they would recognize the need for self-care as a premise for caring for others (Leonard & Murphy, 1995; Mandala Schlitz, Vieten & Amorok, 2007; Murphy, 1993; Wilber, 2006). The assumption made here is that consciousness leaders are committed to and consider interior development as one of the primary tasks in their lives. However, this is to be differentiated from narcissism, which is concerned only with the ego self (Secretan, 2006).

Within Wilber's (2000a) Upper Left quadrant, a consciousness leader would have to be integrally informed (Wilber, 2003) and address all areas pertaining to his or her inner and therefore subjective aspects of life. Based on personal experience and as outlined by both Wilber's (2006) Integral Life Practice (p. 102) and the Integral Transformative Practice developed by Leonard and Murphy (1995), the transpersonal practices of consciousness leaders within this quadrant would include:

1. Daily spiritual practice such as meditation, prayer, yoga, or other mystical practices (Walsh, 1999). By being in spirit, a consciousness leader would also be in-spired to lead in a more conscious way (Burkan, 2001).

2. Recognizing the importance and practice of humor, joy, and laughter (Ricard, 2003).

3. Practicing gratitude as a daily-cultivated emotion (Saron & Davidson, 1997).

4. Practicing forgiveness with themselves and others (Welwood, 1985).

5. Focusing on love as one of the most significant emotions to enable the feeling of oneness with all there is (Welwood, 1985).

6. Keeping a conscious balance between the feminine and the masculine aspects of his or her psyche by consciously honoring both energies (Secretan, 2006).

Brain and Organisms (IT)

Whereas Wilber's (2000a) Upper-Left quadrant relates to the interior and subjective aspects (lines, states, stages, structures) of the individual consciousness, the Upper-Right quadrant refers to the exterior or the more objective states of being and behavior. These are more easily measurable with the scientific methods available today, and include "the brain mechanisms, neurotransmitters, and organic computations that support consciousness" (Wilber, 2000c, p. 63). Paulson (2002) argued, "This is the domain of empirical science and technology, which bases its findings on dispassionate standards of observation to discover objective truth" (p. 22). Csikszentmihalyi (1990) contended furthermore that it is in this artificial separation and "differentiation that has produced science, technology, and the unprecedented power of mankind to build up and to destroy its environment" (p. 241). Building upon Maslow's (Maslow et al., 1998) notion of "self-actualizing" people (p. 1), Csikszentmihalyi (1990) offered moreover the possibility of growth in consciousness through the process of flow, as joy, creativity, and the "total involvement with life" (p. xi). He was able to prove his theory of flow over 4 decades of empirical research and to show how it can be applied within the context of the evolving leader, leading, and leadership.

Within the Upper Left quadrant (Wilber, 2000a), the following characteristics may contribute to the making of a consciousness leader as they add to the cultivation of an empowering belief system and personal growth supporting behaviors (Collins & Lazier, 1992; Covey, 1989; Leonard 1991; Leonard & Murphy, 1995; Robbins, 1986):

1. Extraordinary problem solving capabilities. Consciousness leaders would spend most of their time focusing on the solution rather than on the problem at hand (Ray & Rinzler, 1993).

2. Thriving on challenges (Collins, 2001).

3. Perseverance. Consciousness leaders never give up (Harman & Hormann, 1993).

4. Knowing their personal strengths and weaknesses (Ray & Myers, 1989).

5. Having a clear mission in life and being servant–leaders who are conscious and aware of the impact of their actions, both at an interpersonal and material level (Secretan, 2006). They are driven by the need to provide a work environment filled with meaning, clear vision, and joy (Taylor, 2005).

6. Being aware of the impact of their actions, operations, and products with respect to levels of sustainability in the world (Paulson, 2002).

7. Acknowledging and honoring differences in personalities and desires of different individuals, organizations, and industries (Boyatzis & McKee, 2005).

8. Keeping a healthy balance between innovation and stability, between inspiration and reality, and between creativity and its manifestation (Goleman et al., 2002).

9. Cultivating the ability to embrace and live with nonduality and paradoxes in a world that is mostly driven by fear and the need for control (Watts, 1989).

Like Kouzes and Posner (2003, p. 150), Secretan (2006) summarized the behavior of the consciousness leader from the perspective of this quadrant by emphasizing the importance of love and by stating: "If we truly want to inspire people, then we should communicate the love that we have for them" (p. 152).

Culture and Worldview (WE)

Wilber's (2000a) Lower-Left (p. 43) quadrant, the cultural domain, enlarges the definition of consciousness to include the interpersonal subjective, justness, goodness, and moral areas of culture. Wilber (2000b) defined this quadrant as "the values, meanings, worldviews, and ethics that are shared by any group of individuals" (p. 63). The cultural context in which businesses, politics, science, education, and so on occur, are at the heart of humanity; it gives our existence meaning, we become almost inseparable from it, and it turns into our "absolute reality" (Paulson, 2002, p. 22).

From the consciousness leadership perspective discussed here, it is important to note that whereas it is possible to become impatient with the slow rate of cultural or social change, it must also be acknowledged that culture provides the necessary stability for evolution. In business, Paulson (2002) maintained, "cultural values are not, then, niceties; they are life's blood for humans" (p. 23), for they include and refer to the moral values of culture. It is in the culture where collective emotions show up as rituals, customs, ceremonies, and rites such as indigenous dances and traditions. They carry significant meaning for the respective culture and must therefore be part of a more complete definition of consciousness. To prevent further global degradation, both Osterberg (1993) and Twist (2003) contended that we must redefine not only our understanding of the leader, but our entire economic system that reduces our culture to a culture of consumerism. This might be the reason why a major characteristic of a consciousness leader must be the cultivation of awareness with respect to group values and beliefs.

Social Systems and the Environment (ITS)

Together with the Upper Right quadrant, the Lower-Right quadrant is the area of the external objective *ITS* in which institutions, businesses, and geopolitical organizations are traditionally operating (Wilber, 2003). Similar to the Upper Right (IT) quadrant, this is the domain in which science has conventionally been active, but in a social context. One of the reasons why we are facing the current challenges may have to do with the fact that since Descartes (Secretan, 2006), we have focused mostly on these two (external or right) sides of the AQAL and often neglected the internal development of both the individual (I) and collective levels (WE). This quadrant further expands the definition of consciousness by adding the aspects of social and ecological sustainability for our planet. Capra (2002) argued "the causes of most of our present environmental and social problems are deeply embedded in our economic systems . . . [that are] ecologically and socially unsustainable, and hence politically unviable in the long run" (p. 211). If the human race and our civilization are to survive, the new leadership paradigm must implement a radical systemic change at this level—a change that brings the intelligence of the heart together with the understanding of the brain in our collective awareness (Klein & Izzo, 1999).

In summary, Wilber (2003) defined leaders in consciousness as "integrally informed" (CD 1) people who address all growth areas pertaining to their inner and therefore subjective aspects of life, including emotions, values, needs, and spirituality, as well as how subjective aspects relate to all other three quadrants (Wilber, 2003, CD 1). Furthermore, Wilber also noted how difficult it is to be a well-rounded integrally informed person, but emphasized that integral consciousness is achievable within the context of an integrally informed team (Wilber, 2003, CD 2).

The assumption made here is that the journey of consciousness leaders begins with interior growth and continues with the integration of the inner world with the outer world. As such, the values at the core of a consciousness leadership model may have to do with and include the following list that came out of a weekend session with my own leadership team: (a) joy and playfulness, (b) fulfillment and creativity, (c) love and connection, (d) freedom and stability, (e) inspiration and courage, (f) abundance and honesty, (g) growth and contribution, (h) humanity and sustainability, (i) cooperation and individuality, and (j) transparency and integrity. Businesses that would embrace a new paradigm based on consciousness leadership could provide to their managers, employees, and other stake-holders an integral platform that would combine the personal and professional realms in a holistic manner. Thus, corporations practicing consciousness leadership values could enhance not only their efficiency and effectiveness due to a dedicated and empowered workforce, they could also become preferred providers of goods within a trusted community of businesses and customers worldwide (Paulson, 2002).

In other words, in order to develop the ability to take action in the right direction, a consciousness leader would have to not only know what is currently creating the contemporary need for change, but would have to move beyond the individual (ego-centric), the corporation, the industry, and expand outside the borders of nations (ethno-centric). They must create change that is sustainable and world-centric.

The Transpersonal Approach

A transpersonal approach can contribute to existing leadership theories by providing additional evidence for the evolution of the interiority of the leader along various lines of development including the *cognitive, moral, interpersonal, value, emotional*, and *spiritual* (Alexander et al, 1990; Commons et al, 1990; Cook-Greuter, 2004; Gilligan, 1982/1993; Goleman, 2000; Goleman et al., 2002; Kegan et al., 1990; Loevinger, 1977).

From a transpersonal psychology point of view, Maslow et al. (1998) maintained that deeply fulfilled and self-actualizing individuals lead from the heart. In this characterization, leaders recognize the need for self-care as a premise for caring for others. They are committed to self-growth as one of the primary tasks in their lives (pp. 20-42). This characterization is very different from narcissism as defined in Stage 1 of Kohlberg's (Kohlberg & Ryncarts, 1990) or Gilligan's (1982/1993) moral levels of development. Unfortunately, narcissism, low morals, and greed have been the predominant components in the old leadership practice (Harman & Hormann, 1993, pp. 16-27). In his book, *One: The Art and Practice of Conscious Leadership*, Secretan (2006) referred to conscious leaders as "servant leaders" and warned about the danger of narcissism by illustrating the importance of "working more from our souls rather than our egos" (p. 188). Yet, as they evolve toward unity consciousness (Cook-Greuter, 2008), consciousness leaders seem even to transcend the idea of self-renunciation that Greenleaf (1977) discussed in his book entitled *Servant Leadership*.

Other researchers such as Stanford professor Michael Ray (Ray & Rinzler, 1993) indirectly supported Wilber's (2000a) model and confirmed that a new leadership must include and operate from "our most profound inner awareness and in connection with the connection of others and the earth" (pp. 4-5). In Wilberian terms, this new leadership paradigm would be integral and relate to all quadrants. As we evolve as human beings, we seem to develop the ability to live at several levels of consciousness concomitantly (Ram Dass, 1989, CD 1). That means that an awakened being is able to become increasingly more aware of the *physical, mental, emotional, soul,* and *spiritual* realms (Wilber, 2000a, p. 46) at the same time. This seems to be a transpersonal characteristic of an integrated human being (Vaughan, 2000, 2005; Walsh, 1999; Walsh & Vaughan, 1993; Watts, 1989, 2003; Wilber, 2006).

This might be the reason why ethics, morals, and spirituality appear to be increasingly more important in a business environment (Aburdene, 2005; Hendricks & Ludeman, 1996; Klein & Izzo, 1999; Kofman, 2006; Pauchant, 2002; Rooke & Torbert, 1998, 2005; Secretan, 2006; Toms, 1997; Torbert et al., 2004; Wilber, 2006). Therefore, at this stage of human development, it seems that a consciousness leadership practice must include the transpersonal aspects such as spirituality, which will be addressed next.

A New Understanding of Spirituality

It appears that most people associate spirituality with religion as "an inner feeling that there *is* a God" who takes care of us (Armstrong, 1993, p. 389). Like religion, the terms atheism, but also fundamentalism, mysticism, and so on, are terms with which many postmodern people struggle. As we begin to seek a deeper meaning in life, we appear to prefer using the term spirituality to avoid possible quarrels simply because it has not yet been as overused as the word religion. Yet, even spirituality seems to be perceived as a private matter possibly because "mainstream religions have not developed an ethic appropriate for the age of globalization" (Capra, 2002, p. 19) to help humanity open up to the new reality. Wilber (2006, pp. 100-102) may provide much needed clarification about the four various meanings of the word spirituality.

Spirituality as the highest of any of the lines of development. Wilber (2006) argued that we perceive "the highest levels in any of the [24] lines" (p. 101) of development as spiritual. For instance, nobody would consider an impulsive, ego-driven person as being spiritual. However, we would consider (a) a highly developed moral person (Gilligan, 1982/1993), (b) a person with the highest form of consciousness (Kegan et al., 1990), or (c) a transpersonally developed human being such as the Dalai Lama as a spiritually evolved leader in consciousness.

Spirituality as a separate line of development. Researcher James Fowler (1995), for instance, looked at faith as a separate line of development and was able to show that people evolve spiritually along several stages of faith: undifferentiated, intuitive, mythic, synthetic-conventional, individuative-reflective, conjunctive, and universalizing (p. 290). For Fowler, "faith and religion, in this view, are reciprocal" (p. 9).

Spirituality as a nonordinary state of experience. This definition is contained in all spiritual traditions such as shamanism, meditative, and contemplative religions. These religious practices support seekers in inducing peak-states of spiritual experience where glimpses of the divine can be obtained (Wilber, 2006, pp. 101-102). This type of spirituality requires special emphasis within the present context because of its potential contribution to the transformation of altered states of consciousness into permanent traits of character. *States* of consciousness can accelerate the transpersonal transformation of the leader by facilitating the *structural* evolution of their development (Pauchant, 2002; Torbert et al., 2004; Vaughan, 2000, 2005; Walsh & Vaughan, 1993; Wilber, 2006).

Spirituality as an attitude. To this interpretation of spirituality, Wilber (2006) included the attitude of love, compassion, wisdom, and other qualities, which can be present at every stage or state of human development (p. 102).

No matter how we split the definition of spirituality, what seems to be very important within a new consciousness leadership paradigm is authentic spiritual growth that supports leaders on the path. Vaughan (2005) argued that authentic spirituality is holistic because it includes "body, emotions, mind, soul and Spirit" (p. 3) and, in its healthy form, it ultimately leads to self-realization and self-actualization. In her view, the spiritual path begins with the glimpse of the soul, which can be awakened through peak and mystical experiences, and can often be triggered by spiritual emergencies (Grof, 2006; Vaughan, 2005).

This view seems to be supported by Einstein (1954) who stated that "The most beautiful experience we can have is the mysterious. It is the fundamental emotion which stands at the cradle of true art and true science" (p. 11). He maintained that "the cosmic religious feeling" is "the strongest and noblest motive for scientific research," which inspires the scientists and gives them "strength to remain true to their purpose in spite of countless failures" (pp. 39-40).

Whereas Wilber's (2000a) map of consciousness is comprehensive and may seem overwhelming at first, it is important to note that it represents the map of consciousness, not the territory. Reality shows that due to the speed of change even the territory is not the territory and the only constant is the change itself. Therefore, all quadrants, lines, levels, and stages are only constructs designed to help us make sense of our world. These elements are fingers pointing at the moon and not the moon itself.

Applied Consciousness Leadership

The concept of consciousness leadership is relatively new whether it is called consciousness leadership, conscious leadership, integral leadership, transpersonal leadership, or simply leadership in the 21st Century. Therefore, much more empirical research is needed to gain a more complete understanding of its characteristics and nature. The current discussion, however, focuses on individual aspects of the Wilberian (2000a) AQAL model as they relate to various lines of development represented in the Upper Left quadrant including their impact on the other quadrants.

Quantitative Instrumentation for Measuring Leadership Development

In response to the need for a more profound and rapid change, various researchers including Cook-Greuter (2004), Rooke & Torbert (2005), Torbert et al. (2008), and Wilber (2000a) were making the case for a developmental perspective in leadership that goes beyond Loevinger's (1977) most widely used validity tested instruments in psychometrics WUSCT, Washington University Sentence Completion Test of Ego Development. In supporting Wilber's (2000a) integral map of consciousness (AQAL), the leading developmental theorist and methodologist Cook-Greuter (2004), expanded Loevinger's WUSCT and called such ego development "full-range" (p. 3). In her model and the Sentence Completion Test (STC) that she developed, Cook-Greuter considered both the horizontal—the acquisition of new skills and knowledge at a certain stage—but also the vertical or structural transformation in human development. She concurred with the fact that "development in its deepest meaning refers to transformation of consciousness" (p. 3). According to Cook-Greuter, such an internal transformation in consciousness does not happen through learning or knowledge acquisition alone—horizontal growth—because "only long term practices, self-reflection, action inquiry, and dialogue" (p. 4) have shown to cause lasting, structural, and vertical transformation.

The Sentence Completion Test and the Leadership Development Profile

Based on research of business leaders and in collaboration with Cook-Greuter, the creator of the Sentence Completion Test, Torbert (1987) built the Leadership Development Framework (LDF). LDF is a quantitative instrument designed to measure the mental profile and adult egoic development from egocentric action to world-centric action logic. The Leadership Development Framework (LDF) has the following major stages:

1. *Opportunist and below*, 5% of sampled leaders, characterized as must-win, self-oriented, and manipulative but who are good in emergency situations and in sales positions;
2. *Diplomat*, 12% of sampled leaders characterized as conflict avoiders but who help unify people;
3. Expert, 38% of sampled leaders, ruled by logic and expertise and who are good as individual contributors;
4. *Achiever*, 30% of sampled leaders, who mostly meet strategic goals, are good team leaders, who are action and goal-oriented;
5. *Individualist*, 10% of sampled leaders, who have the ability to combine very well competing personal and professional goals and who are effective in venture and consulting positions;
6. *Strategist*, 4% of the overall sampled leaders, who are very effective at initiating and generating both organizational and personal transformations;
7. *Alchemist and above*, 1% of sampled leaders, who are integral leaders who excel at bringing about and leading social transformations by integrating all areas of life.

Most developmental theories also use the terms preconventional, conventional, postconventional, and transpersonal to describe the full spectrum trajectory of human consciousness development, which also applies to leaders, of course (Cook-Greuter, 2004, p. 5). According to Cook-Greuter, "only about 10% to 20% of adults demonstrate postconventional action logics. Transpersonal ways of meaning are even rarer" (p. 5). The transformational process of business leaders into transpersonal action logic (beyond postconventional) is of special interest within the context of the research addressed in this paper.

Of the 10 organizations researched over several years, five were headed up by leaders at the postconventional/strategist level and five at conventional level or below (Torbert et al., 2008). All five organizations lead by the CEOs at the postconventional or strategist level succeeded in transforming their organization into successful businesses, but only two of the conventionally-led organizations transformed successfully to meet the needs of the changed business paradigm (p. 14). The current study complements the quantitative results of such research by adding the qualitative and in-depth phenomeno-logical aspects that deal with the internal transformation of leaders that have the ability to transform themselves, the culture of the organizations they lead, as well as the social and environmental aspects in a sustainable fashion.

The Spiral Dynamics

In addition to the ego development perspectives on leadership by Cook-Greuter (2004), and the action logic by Torbert et al. (2004), Beck and Cowan's (1996) Spiral Dynamics model deserves special attention. Within the context of applied transpersonal leadership, the concept of large-scale psychology is significant because it includes the aspects of larger populations that must be taken into consideration by any leader let alone a consciousness-driven one.

Based on Graves' (as cited in Beck and Cowan, 1996) value system, Beck and Cowan (1996) have developed the Spiral Dynamics model, which represents the evolutionary structures of the *value* line of development (see Figure 4). This model has successfully been applied in several transformational interventions performed around the world including the Netherlands, Palestine, Mexico, and South Africa (p. 318). The Spiral Dynamics lends itself to significant strategic applications in leadership because it provides two major tiers of consciousness definition and development: Tier 1, which contains six stages of human development from ego-centric, to ethno-centric, to world-centric, and Tier 2, which begins with a spirit-centric view and goes to higher stages, including the transpersonal and others that have not yet been developed (Wilber, 2000a).

The current dissertation focused mainly on the late first tier and second tier leaders, which were also addressed by Pauchant, professor and Chair in Ethical Management at the University of Montreal, who initiated in 2002

9. **Integral-Holonic**
   (is slowly emerging)

8. **Whole View**
   synergize & macromanage

7. **Flex Flow**
   integrate & align systems

6. **Human Bond**
   explore inner self, equalize others

5. **Strive Drive**
   analyze & strategise to prosper

4. **Truth Force**
   find purpose, bring order, insure future

3. **Power Gods**
   express impulsively, break free, be strong

2. **Kin Spirits**
   seek harmony & safety in a mysterious world

1. **Survival Sense**
   sharpen instincts & innate senses

coral

turquoise

yellow

green

orange

blue

red

purple

beige

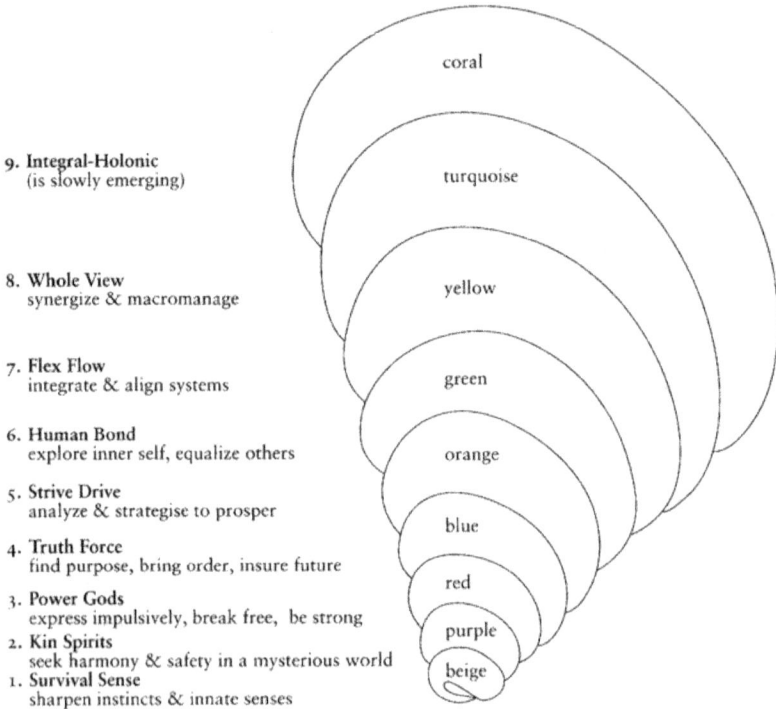

Figure 4. The Spiral of development (Wilber, 2000b, p. 8)

the Great Consciousness Leadership project (Horibe, 2003). The goal of this project was to identify and examine 100 consciousness leaders who have changed the world. The results of the research is supposed to be published in a series of 100 books that will be complemented by other materials such as audio and visual information (Volckmann, 2007).

In a different empirical study on ethics and spirituality at work, Pauchant (2002) recommended Wilber's (2000a) AQAL as the appropriate framework to provide proper support for top executives in need of more meaning in their working environment. In his research, Pauchant referred to a forum of studies on international management, ethics, and spirituality, the first of its kind to be held at an internationally recognized business school, and represented the views of 6 CEOs and 6 scholars of ethics and spirituality from all over the world including Australia, Canada, the United States, and

Switzerland. With case studies from five organizations in finance, nutrition, health, education, and politics the research strongly suggested that there is a true search for meaning going on in today's organizations, and that this quest leads inevitably to a search for ethics and spirituality. The study clearly revealed the need for spirituality in the workplace and outlined the benefits and dangers associated with it. However, the study did not focus on the internal transformative aspects of the leaders.

One of the most recent empirical studies on leaders and leadership was performed at Stanford University (Porras et al., 2007). However, it focused mainly on the changing definition of success from the perspective of accomplished human beings. Spirituality and the transpersonal realms were not addressed.

Chapter Summary

Despite the enormous amount of research performed in the area of leadership it becomes obvious that a transpersonal approach using Wilber's (2000a) integral map of consciousness (AQAL) could provide significant phenomenological data around both the interior development of the leader as well as its impact on the exterior dimensions. Through its heuristic structuralism approach, this dissertation research attempted to complement existing research and literature in this field (Adams, 2005; Beck & Cowan, 1996; Boyatzis & McKee, 2005; Cook-Greuter, 2005; Goleman et al., 2002; Kouzes & Posner, 2003, 2007; Marques et al., 2007; Mitroff & Denton, 1999; Pauchant, 2002; Porras et al., 2007; Renesch, 2002; Senge et al., 2005; Taylor, 2005; Torbert et al., 2004). The next chapter addresses the research method used in the present study.

CHAPTER 3

RESEARCH METHOD

Based on Wilber's (2000a) All Quadrant All Level (AQAL) integral map of consciousness, the present research addressed the following main question: What are the most significant emotional, physical, cognitive, spiritual, or other transpersonal experiences that characterized the structural interior transformation of consciousness leaders in business? Secondary questions include the following:

1. What are the triggers, the context, and process of their transformation into a consciousness leader, or in other words, what are the causes of their *peak* or *transcendent experiences* (Maslow et al., 1998), experiences of *flow* (Csikszentmihalyi, 1990; Kjaer et al., 2002), *states and stage development* (Wilber, 2000a), *exceptional human experiences* (White, 1998), *transpersonal experiences* (Grof, 2006), or *other spiritual emergencies* (Vaughan, 2000)?

2. What is the structural impact that can be deduced from the researched transpersonal phenomena over time?

3. How do people become the integral change agents required for a paradigm shift in business?

4. What facilitates and what may inhibit the change of their minds?

5. How do these consciousness leaders keep evolving to high levels of consciousness in a hostile environment dominated by less-conscious investors, stakeholders, tough competition, and a litigation-friendly environment?

6. What is the future of business and how can new business structures be created in the light of awakened and awakening consciousness leaders?

7. What is the future of money and capitalism within the context of global sustainability?

Heuristic Structuralism

The conclusion of the previous chapter was that despite the enormous amount of research performed in the area of leadership, a phenomenological approach that focuses more on the interior evolution of the leader could significantly contribute to existing literature (Adams, 2005; Beck & Cowan, 1996; Boyatzis & McKee, 2005; Cook-Greuter, 2005; Goleman et al., 2002; Kouzes & Posner, 2003, 2007; Marques et al., 2007; Mitroff & Denton, 1999; Pauchant, 2002; Porras et al., 2007; Renesch, 2002; Senge et al., 2005; Taylor, 2005; Torbert et al., 2004). Such research could complement the external, behavioral, cultural, social, or so-called objective characteristics of success (Porras et al., 2007) by including the transpersonal, subjective, interiority, and self-growth aspects of becoming a leader (Alexander et al., 1990; Commons et al., 1984, 1990; Cook-Greuter, 2005, 2008; Koplowitz, 1984, 1990; Torbert et al., 2004; Wilber, 2000c). By employing a qualitative *heuristic structuralism* method, this research is studying not only the nature and the meaning of transpersonal experiences of consciousness leaders (the state stages discussed in the previous chapter), but also the structural (stages addressed before) impact thereof over time. But, what is *heuristic structuralism*? Heuristic structuralism is a term that was born out of the requirements posed by the research in the current dissertation and will be explained next.

Driven by my own transformational experiences, this investigative approach sought to illuminate the development, meaning, description, essence, and understanding of the phenomenon of becoming a consciousness leader. It upheld the objective to discover the intrinsic nature of consciousness leadership from "the first person account" (Moustakas, 1990, p. 38). However, as much as my previous scientific (computer science) education required an objective separation between me, my own experiences, and those of the research participants, a clean division could not occur. In fact, my own transformation turned into an asset that enabled me to relate to my research participants and have the necessary compassion, deep understanding, and even identify with the "focus of inquiry" (Moustakas, 1990, p. 5). I realized that my own journey is a requirement for this research because only "through the exploratory open-ended inquiry, self-directed search, and immersion in active experience, one is able to get inside the question, become one with it, and thus achieve an understanding of it" (Moustakas, 1990, p. 5). Thus, the heuristic research became the research method of choice.

Furthermore, the intention of the research was to identify the typical characteristics of the transformational experience from not only the *interior* perspective of the business leader, but also from the *exterior* to notice the structural impact with respect to behavior, culture, society, and environment. In order to provide a comprehensive representation of this phenomenological research in consciousness, Wilber's (2000a) map of consciousness (AQAL) with its lines, stages, quadrants, states, and structures was chosen.

Wilber's (2000a) AQAL has been selected because it is dynamic and thus indicates that the evolution of consciousness has a direction, tends to occur generally towards "greater depth and less span," and takes place within "nested spheres, with each higher level transcending and including its predecessor. It is an actualization holarchy, each stage of which unfolds and then enfolds its predecessor in a nested fashion" (p. 128). Within this "actualization holarchy," it is important to differentiate between the "ladder, climber, and view" (p. 128). Wilber used the ladder as a metaphor to represent the "basic rungs of awareness," which once developed, remain in existence as "basic building blocks or holons of consciousness" (p. 132), at various developmental stages of the leader. Wilber argued that these components of consciousness "emerge in fairly discrete stages," development "enfolds" within certain spheres, and "each higher stage does not actually sit on top of the lower stage" (p. 129).

The current study addressed the climber of the ladder, the leader, who according to the above model evolves from the (small) egoic *self* to a higher *Self* (capital S) as the "timeless, eternal, unborn, unwavering, undying, ever and always present" (Wilber, 2000, p. 315). This "nuclear self" as Kohut (1985, pp. 10-11) calls it, grows along various lines of development including "self-identity, self-need, [as well as] moral sense" (Wilber, 2000a, p. 132). Furthermore, at each step of the scale, the climber faces a fulcrum or a three-step process of personal growth that contains "(1) fusion/identification; (2) differentiation/transcendence; (3) integration/inclusion" (p. 132). Exploring the growth of these lines of development is significant because it could help construct the missing link between the interiority, subjective aspects that address the making of the leader, and his or her exterior aspects such as behavior, as well as culture and the social environment.

As individual leaders grow internally along lines, stages, and structures of development they do tend to reach higher levels of consciousness especially the growth can be accelerated by altered states of consciousness discussed earlier. This assumption is supported by studies performed by various researchers including Alexander et al. (1990), Commons et al. (1990), Cook-Greuter (2008), Fowler (1995), Gilligan (1982/1993), Kegan et al. (1990), and Kohlberg and Ryncarz (1990). Thus, as we grow internally, our levels of consciousness seems to grow and our behavior is affected. In other words, the external transformation appears to be a function of the internal transformation, and the present research indicates which lines of development of the leader have been impacted most significantly.

During the analysis phase, certain *structural* patterns that connected the studied phenomena related by the research participants became obvious. In Wilber's (2006) words, "Phenomenology looks for the *direct experiences and phenomena*, structuralism looks for *the patterns that connect the phenomena*. These patterns or structures actually govern the phenomena, but without the phenomena ever knowing it" (p. 55).

Thus, the term *heuristic structuralism* was born and with it, the multiple methodological dimensions of this research also became apparent. These are: (a) the consciousness leaders evolved along the same paths described by Campbell (1949/1968) in his book *The Hero with a Thousand Faces* and which is represented in this study using the name *Hero's Journey*; (b) During each phase of the *Hero's Journey*, various *lines* of development (cognitive, emotional, physical, ethical, spiritual, and egoic) became obvious as the transpersonal phenomena along with their impact were described; and (c) The *structural* changes that occurred over the course of transformation became evident. *Heuristic structuralism* supports the development of a rich and deep characterization of significant life occurrences and essential meanings along all of these dimensions.

In summary, *heuristic structuralism* is a method of inquiry that goes between, across, and beyond both heuristic and structuralism. It could be described as a method of transdisciplinarity because it allows for the study of the research participants from the core of their humanity. Nicolescu (Nicolescu & Volckmann, 2007) explained the term transdisciplinarity, which was originally invented by Piaget (as cited in Nicolescu & Volckmann, 2007, p. 78), as a method that goes beyond "the Subject [which] cannot be captured through formalism. When you want to capture it, it's an ontological catastrophe, because the Subject is transformed [into an] Object" (p. 78).

The Role of the Researcher

After growing up in poverty under Ceausescu's dictatorship in communist Romania, I was blessed to emigrate to Germany at age 16. Following my graduation in computer science and artificial intelligence, I embarked on a successful high-tech career that eventually led to the active participation in the dot-com boom of the 1990s. However, the resulting material success seemed irrelevant compared with the transformative spiritual, emotional, and mental growth experienced along the way. My worldview evolved from an egocentric to a world-centric perspective (Beck & Cowan, 1996) and I realized that I was here to serve.

Therefore, having lived through a personal transformative experience that included several major shifts in consciousness, I am personally deeply vested in the proposed research. In the words of Moustakas (1990), "an unshakable connection exists between what is out there, in its appearance and reality, and what is within me in reflective thought, feeling and awareness" (p. 12). It is "the art of empathy, of communion with the object of inquiry . . . of talking to the object of inquiry, of penetrating from within, of indwelling in the other" (Braud & Anderson, 1998, p. 269) that enabled the personal connection with the research participants at a deep level.

As stated earlier, my own transpersonal experiences over the past 29 years have profoundly influenced and affected my relationship and interaction with the research participants. It manifested through feelings of deep compassion and empathy with their personal journeys, through tacit knowing, intuition, retrieval of my bodily knowledge, and my ability to immerse myself in all phases of the research.

Because the main instrument in qualitative research is the researcher (Mertens, 2005, p. 247), my personal assumptions, beliefs, and biases that could negatively affect the study have been consciously explored, declared, and exposed through journaling and other creative means.

Selection Criteria and Research Preparation

The 16 research participants have been chosen by me personally out of a pool of 389 top business leaders. In order to achieve maximum variation for the sample in the current study, the following selection criteria have been used:

1. They are all public figures and renowned business leaders or social entrepreneurs with the following statistics: 2 of the participants were former presidents of internationally known multibillion dollar companies, 1 was a former VP of Marketing of a multibillion dollar firm, 7 were current presidents of companies, and 11 participants were serial entrepreneurs.
2. They represent different types of businesses such as beverage, high-tech, low-tech, clean-tech, Venture Capital, Social Entrepreneurship, Wall Street financiers, law, health care, as well as music and entertainment.
3. They are all highly educated individuals most of whom have been trained at prestigious universities including Stanford University, MIT, and Harvard. Five of the participants have a doctorate degree, 6 have an MBA or other Master's degrees.
4. They are philanthropists or active with philanthropic organizations.
5. They have an openly declared transformational practice.
6. The following religions and/or spiritual practices were represented: 3 Jews, 7 Buddhists, 5 Christians, and 1 Hindu.
7. The age bracket is between 35 and 65 years.
8. They have a 10-year minimum of publicly visible social engagement.
9. They are not only financially successful but lead a life of balance in most areas of life including the physical, emotional, and mental.
10. They have close relationships with family and friends.
11. Men and women are equally represented (8 men and 8 women).

Given their public status and achievements, the interviewees are very well known and high-merit people who lead busy lives and have full agendas. All interviewees are people I knew personally prior to the research. They were without exception very supportive of this research and thus gave their written approval (Appendix A) prior to the actual interview. The confidentiality is assured by using aliases instead of real names and by preserving their identity as described in Appendixes A and B.

All interviews took place in an atmosphere of emotional opening. Each interview began with a small meditation and continued with the intention to stay open, aware, and mindful throughout the interview process.

During the interview, various techniques, including ever-present awareness and mindfulness, as well as Neuro-Linguistic Programming (NLP), were employed to connect with the interviewee at all times. O'Connor and Seymour (1990) defined NLP as "the art and science of personal excellence" (p. 1). The art component in the definition has to do with the fact that each individual is unique and his or her nature is therefore difficult to capture. The science part refers to the method and process of identifying and capturing the leadership patterns employed by "outstanding individuals in any field to achieve outstanding results" (p. 1). Applying NLP techniques includes building rapport with the conversation partner by mirroring and matching his or her breathing patterns, gestures, tone of voice, and other means of communication including audio, visual, and kinesthetic.

The intention was to encourage the participants not only to answer my open-ended questions but to (a) reveal not only their conscious but more important their unconscious minds; (b) share their most significant emotional, mental, physical, and spiritual experiences that triggered their own transformation; and (c) help them shift their own perception, meaning, process of learning, and attitudes as they gained new insights.

Data Collection

The data collection occurred in the following ways:

1. *Pre-Interview Profiling*: Due to the public presence of the interviewed leaders, there is an ample amount of information available about them and by them. This information includes

articles, papers, books, audio and video information, Internet presence, and so on. Much of this information has been studied in preparation for the interview. Wilber's (2000a) Upper Right, Lower Right, and Lower Left quadrants described in chapter 2 of this paper, has served as a guiding framework for the creation of a comprehensible, external portrait prior to the live interview. This process is considered as the pre-interview.

2. *Live Interview*: Each participant has been interviewed for approximately 60 minutes on average. The semistructured interview has been performed in the manner of exploratory inquiry with the intention to address the interiority of each individual, to identify his or her transpersonal experiences, and the structural changes that occurred over time. The interviews were semistructured, conversational, and contained open-ended questions in order to facilitate a deep emotional opening of the participant. Furthermore, the research approach and the interview methods applied in the current study have been influenced and informed by Kegan and Lahey (2001) through their work on "novel language forms" (p. 7) for "transformative learning and leadership" (p. 229) as well as his subject-object interview guide (Kegan, 1994, pp. 28-36) that is a formal method for assessing the level of consciousness in individuals that goes beyond the cognitive aspects of development, the structure of thinking (Kegan, 1982). Given the qualitative nature of this research, the main goal of the interview was to encourage the participant to share his or her most treasured transformational experiences and meaning making. Thus, I used "intention and attention" (Kegan & Lahey, 2001, p. 7) to (a) remain open and listen within and without; (b) stay flexible and adapt easily to the course of the interview; and (c) compassionately hold the space for the participant so he or she could open up, feel understood, and share their meaning making

and experience "accurately, comprehensively, and honestly" (Moustakas, 1990, p. 48). It is important to note that significant phrases and words that describe the essential transformational experiences had to be identified already during the interviews, and confirmed along with their meaning, by the participants themselves. The interviews were audio recorded and subsequently professionally transcribed. Finally, both data sources were compared to ensure accuracy. A transcriber confidentiality agreement is attached in Appendix B, and Appendix C contains a list of the interview questions.

3. *Auxiliary Data*: Further data has been collected through narratives, study of artwork of participants, personal objects, pictures, and journals, as well as books and other published and unpublished material that have been made available by the participants themselves during or after the interview.

4. *Researcher Insight*: Additional data has been collected from my own internal transformational process during the research period. This data acquisition has occurred as journaling, writing poetry, painting, study of revealed meanings, uncovering of possible biases, insights, and intuitions.

The 16 interviews occurred between May 27th and August 29th, 2008, with the intention to allow incubation time between the interviews and to honor the unique contributions of each individual participant. The need for fine-tuning was an intrinsic requirement of the research protocol.

Data Analysis

The data analysis in this research underwent the following steps, which have been applied between June 4th, 2008 and January 15th, 2009:

1. *Data Sequencing*: Through a process of total immersion, each transcribed interview, including all additional data (observa-

tions, narratives, journals, and unpublished material) have been brought together one by one "into a sequence that tells the story of each research participant" (Moustakas, 1990, p. 49).

2. *Researcher Immersion*: I have immersed myself in all existing material for each participant over several months until I had a comprehensive understanding of each individual experience, process, and structural impact. Each transcribed file was entered into MAXQDA, an automated coding system, after which it was coded and analyzed separately. In addition, the transcribed data was represented using mind maps and matrices to reveal patterns and enable both visual and contextual correlations between transformational categories and participants.

3. *Reduction and Elimination*: After a period of quiet incubation that enabled a fresh perspective on each individual participant, the data was analyzed, further distilled, reduced, and eliminated.

4. *Individual Portrait Creation*: An individual depiction of each participant in his or her own "voice" was created using units of meaning, common topics, and significant statements. This structural and textural depiction was represented using mind maps (Buzan & Buzan, 1996). These mind maps have two arms and were contextualized to match Wilber's (2000a) AQAL. The left arm represents the triggers and context of transformation (the before aspects) and the right arm reflects and describes the structural changes of each participant (the after aspects). The individual descriptions have been shared with each participant for approval, accuracy test, and additional input. However, due to the high profile and celebrity status of the participants, they have extremely busy calendars and some have not given their feedback yet

5. *Composite and Synthesis Depiction:* The main themes and meanings of the phenomenon from each participant have been gath-

ered together and a composite description representing the common qualities and descriptions of all participants as a group has been created using embodied writing in its synthesis.

Methods of Verification

All participants have been given the opportunity to review the findings in order to validate them. Their feedback and input as far as available has been included in the final description. However, it is important to note that due to their high social profile and busy schedules, some of the participants have been difficult to reach a second time and have not responded in a timely fashion. Therefore, in order to establish more credibility, member check (Mertens, 2005, p. 255) has been applied during the interview. Member check is the process during which the researcher makes sure that at the end of each interview what has been said is summarized and the participant has the opportunity to verify the notes and accurately reflect his or her position.

Furthermore, triangulation has been employed to support the validation process. It included the in-depth study of additional data sources such as narratives, artwork, journals, as well as published and unpublished material by and about the respective participant. Where possible, people close to the participants have been offered the opportunity to review and comment on the individual depiction.

The current study has also acquired additional validity through so-called "experiential adequacy" (Braud, 1998, p. 220) because every aspect of the essential transformation has been checked both through its truthfulness aspect in the experience of both the researcher and participants, and by "looking for an internal feeling of certainty, a noetic, intuitive, and persistent feeling that one's knowledge is true" (p. 221). Through the inclusion of physical, emotional, aesthetic, and intuitive indicators, the experiential adequacy has also been increased. Transferability was addressed through both the random selections of participants from various cultural and religious backgrounds as well as through the thick representation of their accounts (Mertens, 2005, p. 256). Additional pragmatic indicators have been selected to support the validity by asking what would be, for instance, additional social, cultural, and other individual implications that would support the consciousness leadership characteristics identified over the course of this research (Braud, 1998, p. 230).

Additionally, throughout the research process, the revealed insights, experiences, interpretations, tacit knowing, sympathetic resonance and understanding, as well as intuitions of the researcher herself have also been collected, recorded, analyzed, synthesized, and reflected upon within the context of each interview and research study (Braud, 1998).

Chapter Summary

This chapter has introduced, presented, and explained the heuristic structuralism research method applied in this dissertation. It explicated the selection criteria and the research preparation as well as the data collection process, the data analysis, and the methods of verification utilized in this research. The next chapter contains the detailed data analysis.

CHAPTER 4

DATA ANALYSIS

The previous chapter prepared the ground for the data analysis presented in this chapter by introducing the research method, the selection criteria, the research preparation, the data collection process, as well as the methods of verification utilized in this research. The data analysis represents the largest chapter in this dissertation and began with data sequencing, which was the process of total immersion with the collected data. Each transcribed interview and all additional data (observations, narratives, journals, and unpublished material) have been brought together into one sequential story line with which I have immersed myself over several months until I had a comprehensive understanding of each individual experience, process, and structural impact.

Each transcribed interviewed was entered into MAXQDA, an automated coding system, where it was coded and analyzed separately. After a period of quiet incubation that enabled a fresh perspective on each individual participant, the data was further distilled, reduced, and eliminated. An individual depiction of each participant in his or her own "voice" was created using units of meaning, common topics, and significant statements. This structural and textural depiction of each participant was first represented on paper using the dynamic mind maps technique developed by Buzan and Buzan (1996) and entered into the software based on the same technique called Mind-Manager. The structural—the top level structure of the mind maps—can be seen for each participant in their entirety in Appendix D. Each individual interview analysis is represented using one single mind map that is the foundation of the analytical representation that follows. Each mind map has two major arms and was contextualized to match Wilber's (2000a) AQAL. The left arm represents the triggers and context of transformation—the *before* transformation aspects—and the right arm reflects and describes the structural changes of each participant—the structural aspects after the transformation. Furthermore, each individual analysis will be introduced by a common topic.

To demonstrate the depth and breath of the analysis process employed in this dissertation, the first 4 individual representations are shown in more detail. Furthermore, it is important to point out that the first representation—that of Jade—also contains meta-data that provides additional information regarding the analysis process that has been applied in all cases. Therefore, in order to understand the depth of the entire analysis in this dissertation, it is important to understand Jade's analysis in detail. The interview analyses of the other 12 participants are shown here in a shorter representation. They focus mainly on the tipping points that led to the significant transformation as well as the structural aspects *after* the transformation of each participant. Appendix D contains the top-level mind map representations of all participants.

Actualization Holarchy

Common topic: Consciousness leaders seem to have evolved to higher levels
of egoic mastery by using their outstanding cognitive capacities to transcend
rational thought. Through that they began to become more present, see through
the thought-constructed world, give up resistance to and accept the ironies in-
herent in the world, and realize the pointlessness of materialistic attachment.

According to Wilber (2000), the evolution of consciousness has a direction, tends to occur generally towards "greater depth and less span,"
and takes place within "nested spheres" (p. 128). Each higher level transcends and includes its predecessor, very much like a holon, which is a term
coined by Arthur Koestler (Wilber, 1995). A holon is a whole that is at the
same time a part of another whole. Such a holon would be a molecule that
is a whole in itself while being at the same time part of a cell, which is in
turn, part of a larger organism, and so on.

As discussed in previous chapters, consciousness evolves in "an actualization holarchy, each stage of which unfolds and then enfolds its predecessor in a nested fashion" (Wilber, 2000a, p. 128). Within this
"actualization holarchy," it is important to differentiate between the "ladder, climber, and view" (p. 128). Wilber used the ladder as a metaphor to
represent the "basic rungs of awareness," which once developed, remain in
existence as "basic building blocks or holons of consciousness" (p. 132).
Wilber argued that these components of consciousness "emerge in fairly
discrete stages," that development takes place within certain spheres, and
"each higher stage does not actually sit on top of the lower stage" (p. 129).

Within the context of this research, the climber of the ladder is the
leader. According to the various developmental models highlighted before
and that include Commons et al. (1990), Cook-Greuter (2008), Fowler
(1995), Gilligan (1982/1993), Kegan et al. (1990), Kohlberg and Ryncarz
(1990), and Loevinger (1977), the leader's egoic self grows along various
lines of development including "self-identity, self-need, [and] moral sense"
(Wilber, 2000a, p. 132). At each step of the scale, the climber faces a fulcrum or a "1-2-3 process of ego/self growth that contains the following

steps: (1) fusion/identification; (2) differentiation/transcendence; (3) integration/inclusion" (Wilber, 2000a, p. 132). Wilber (2001) argued

> *At each point in psychological growth, we find: (1) a higher-order structure emerges in consciousness; (2) the self identifies its being with that higher structure; (3) the next-higher-order structure eventually emerges; (4) the self dis-identifies with the lower structure and shifts its essential identity to the higher structure; (5) consciousness thereby transcends the lower structure; and (6) becomes capable of operating on that lower structure from the higher-order level; so that (7) all preceding levels can be integrated in consciousness. (p. 92)*

Ego or *self-identity* is a very important line of development for the consciousness paradigm discussed here. Further tests and research would have to be performed to be able to have a firm assessment; however, the current phenomenological research could lead to the conclusion that the consciousness leaders studied here have reached mature levels of ego development and even transcendence. They have become "servant leaders" (Greenleaf, 1977) because they are now "working more from [their] souls rather than [their] egos" (Secretan, 2006, p. 188). The assumption made here is that as consciousness leaders grow within the Upper Left quadrant along the lines, stages, and structures of development, they move to higher levels of self-understanding and thus beyond Piaget's formal operations (Koplowitz, 1984, pp. 272-296) and reach later stages of postconventional human development (Alexander et al., 1990; Commons et al., 1984, 1990; Cook-Greuter, 2004; Loevinger, 1977; Torbert et al., 2004, 2008). As we grow internally, our own levels of consciousness grow and affect not only our behavior but also indirectly the consciousness of the people we touch, including the cultural and the social environment in which we live.

Jade's Individual Consciousness Leadership Profile with Transformational Characteristics

Jade is a well-known public figure and one of the most admired and sought after business executives in the world. He was trained at some of the most renowned universities in the world. In addition to his current business functions, Jade is deeply involved with several not-for-profit organizations and is redefining the rules for "conscious capitalism," the transformation of "consumerism," and "sustainable businesses" worldwide. Appendix D contains the mind map representing the key core topics and transformational profile that resulted from the interview performed with Jade.

Triggers, Context, and Process of Jade's Overall Transformation

Jade views his transformation as "a process" of "literally trial and error" that began in his "middle 30s" and took place along several major lines of development including the physical, spiritual, emotional, egoic, and cognitive.

Figure 5 shows the mind map mapping the triggers, context, and process of Jade's overall transformation into a consciousness leader with Wilber's (2000) AQAL. The four arms of the mind map represent the four quadrants of Wilber's AQAL and include the Upper Left, the Internal (I); the Upper Right, the External I also called the Behavioral (IT); the Lower Left, the inter-objective, also called the Cultural (WE); and the Lower Right, the inter-subjective, also called the Social and the Environment (ITS).

Behind each arm of the graph shown in each of the figures that follow there are the structural representations of the analysis in each quadrant with each circled plus sign indicating that there is more information behind it, including the actual quotes of the research participant. The analysis that follows expands the figures to explain their content and the core of the transformation in each of the quadrants with a special focus on the Internal (I) transformation.

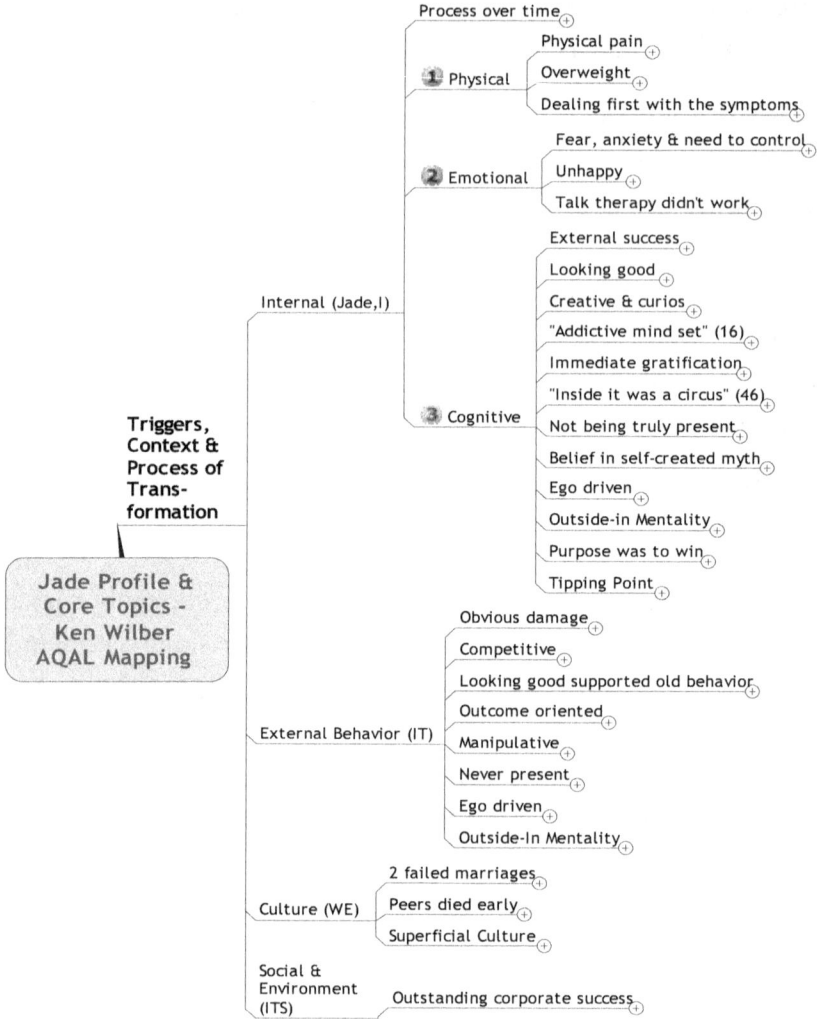

Figure 5. Triggers, context, and process of Jade's overall transformation.

Triggers, Context, and Process of Jade's Internal Transformation (I)

Being an "athlete" and a "kinesthetic person," Jade is physically well in tune with his body. Within the context of his transformation, pain was his greatest teacher because he "felt" it "more than" he "could articulate it at first" (see Figure 6).

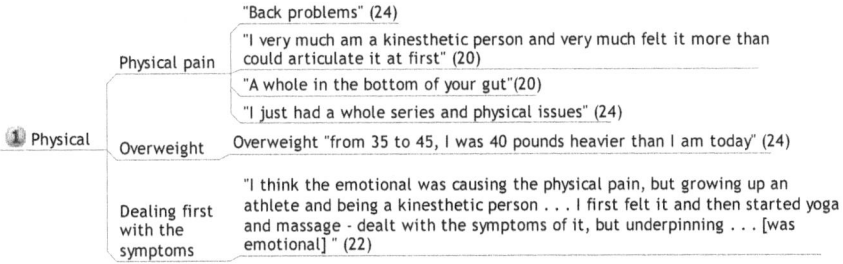

Figure 6. Components of Jade's physical transformation.

At the time, he "had a whole series and physical issues" including being "overweight" and perceived his pain as "a whole in the bottom" of his "gut."

Emotionally, Jade had "a high degree of anxiety" and heard "all of the fears screaming" in his "head" (see Figure 7).

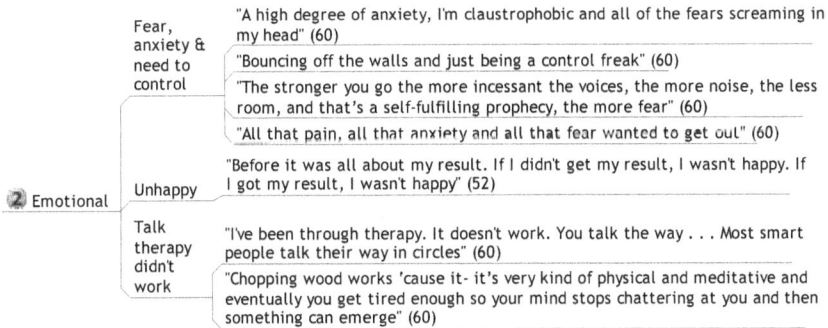

Figure 7. Triggers and context of Jade's emotional transformation.

His tendency to be "a control freak," exacerbated his pain because in his view, "the stronger you go the more incessant the voices, the more noise, the less room, and that's a self-fulfilling prophecy, the more fear." Thus, he knew that "all that pain, all that anxiety and all that fear wanted to get out."

Jade realized over time that his strategy, which "was all about" his "result," did not bring him the happiness he expected and he ended up in a double bind. He said: "If I didn't get my result, I wasn't happy. If I got my result, I wasn't happy." At first, he sought support in therapy, but he concluded, "it doesn't work" because "most smart people talk their way in circles."

Cognitively, Jade is aware of the fact that the keys to his external success included his education, his upbringing, his "creative side," as well as "tenacity and belief" in himself as well as "having some basic level of intelligence and drive" (see Figure 8).

To his own account, "everything" before his transformation was "craving," and about "immediate gratification." In his opinion, the cause of it was his "addictive kind of mind-set about just taking on the next thing."

Furthermore, he cognized that he was "ego-driven," "very intense," and "not open for feedback beyond what" he thought was "right." Jade has a deep understanding about his self-created "myth" and the "outside-in mentality" with its external traps that contributed to increasing his pain. He realized that he was driven by the "outside" world and "was perfectly engineered towards running down gold rings":

Basically living from an outside-in mentality, which was very productive when it came to getting promoted in a big corporate environment because as long as somebody defined a goal and said to you, "If you reach that—If you do these things, you'll reach that goal and if you get that goal we'll give you a prize," that I was perfectly engineered towards running down gold rings and the more I ran them down the more it reinforced that I was good at it. And so I convinced myself, I built the myth of myself, that I was better at it than anyone else. Then when people asked me how I got to be president of a large company and [at] age 40 it was because I convinced myself and totally believed that I was better at running down gold rings than anybody else, and that myth became a reality simply because of tenacity and belief in yourself and having some basic level of intelligence and drive.

External success
- "Basic level of intelligence" (16)
- "Belief in yourself" (16)
- "Successful enough . . . where everybody said everything was great" (46)
- "I had already had a lot of success" (16)

Looking good
- "I was . . . good looking enough" (46)

Creative & curios
- "I was always creative and explored a lot of different domains" (54)
- "I had trained myself because I had this creative side that was always crying to emerge and I just stuffed it down" (38)

"Addictive mind set" (16)
- "Addictive kind of mind set about just taking on the next thing" (16)
- "Everything before was craving" (50)

Immediate gratification
- "Before it was all about immediate gratification " (50)

"Inside it was a circus" (46)
- "There was always a tape" (46)
- "There was always noise in my head, a thousand monkeys, whatever" 46)
- **Lack of happiness** "Before it was all about my result. If I didn't get my result, I wasn't happy. If I got my result, I wasn't happy" (52)

Not being truly present
- "Never present in any conversation maybe I was ever in for 35 years" (46)
- "There was always noise in my head, a thousand monkeys, whatever" (46)
- "I don't ever recognize being present in a conversation" (46)

Belief in self-created myth
- "I convinced myself and totally believed that I was BETTER running down gold rings than anyone else and that MYTH became a reality simply because of tenacity, belief in yourself, basic level of intelligence and drive" (16)
- "Myth became a reality simply because of tenacity and belief in yourself and having some basic level of intelligence and drive " (16)
- "I convinced myself, I built the myth of myself, that I was better at it than anyone else" (16)

Cognitive

Ego driven
- "Was ego driven" (46)   Very intense, very driven" (46)
- **Resistance** "Everything before was resistance " (50)
- "Tenacity"
- "Before it was all about my result. If I didn't get my result, I wasn't happy. If I got my result, I wasn't happy" (52)
- "Not open for feedback beyond what I thought" (46)

Outside-in Mentality
- " Living from an outside-in mentality" (16)
- "It's bad strategy" (52)
- "I was . . . successful enough . . . where everybody said everything was great" (46)
- "The outside in [model], when they get what they want they're not happy and when they don't get what they want they're not happy. It's bad strategy" (52)

Purpose was to win
- "Before it was all about my result. If I didn't get my result, I wasn't happy. If I got my result, I wasn't happy" (52)
- "My purpose before was to win, whatever- or to not lose maybe is a more accurate description." (62)
- **Fulfill craving** "Everything before was craving" (50)

Tipping Point

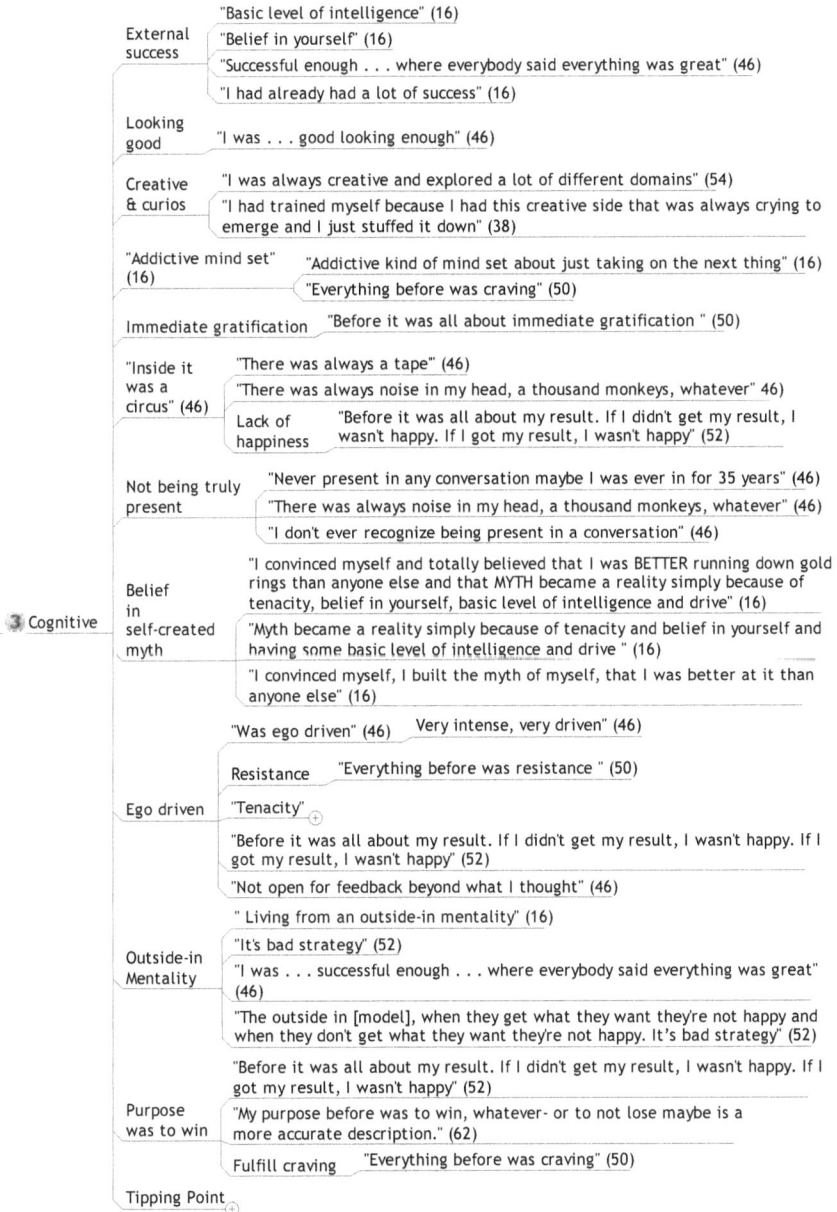

Figure 8. Triggers and context of Jade's cognitive transformation.

Being "ego-driven," he understood that his life's "purpose" before his transformation was "to win, whatever—or to not lose maybe is a more accurate description."

> *I was ego-driven, totally externally oriented, manipulative in dealing with human beings, not open to feedback beyond what I thought internalization and action on would help manipulate the outcome, totally outcome driven almost in everything. The process was irrelevant to me. All that mattered was outcomes, very intense, very driven, never present in any conversation maybe I was ever in for 35 years. I was always—If I was in a conversation, there was always a tape, something else running in the back of my [head].*

Looking from the outside "everybody said [that] everything was great," yet before age 35, he recognized to have "never" been "present in a conversation. There was always noise in my head, a thousand monkeys, whatever. I think very Dr. Jekyll and Mr. Hyde to most people."

As a result, "inside it was a circus" and the source of major pain.

Jade characterized his behavior before his transformation as (a) "acting out," (b) "competitive, (c) "outcome driven," (d) "perfectly engineered towards running down gold rings," (e) "manipulative in dealing with human beings," (f) "never present," (g) "ego-driven," and (h) "totally externally oriented." He viewed is conduct toward "most people" as behaving like "Dr, Jekyll and Mr. Hyde" (see Figure 9).

Culturally (WE) and *socially* (ITS), Jade lived in an environment of great stress in which his peers "died in their 40s at their desks" (see Figure 10).

Jade enjoyed outstanding corporate success and became the head of one of the largest companies worldwide. Yet, personally he was also confronted with two failed marriages.

Obvious damage — "Collateral damage associated with all those acting-out behaviors was becoming more and more evident to me" (16)

Competitive — "I convinced myself, I built the myth of myself, that I was better at it than anyone else" (16)

Looking good supported old behavior — "I was . . . good looking enough" (46)

Outcome oriented —
"Totally outcome driven almost in everything. The process was irrelevant to me. All that mattered was outcomes" (46)
"I was perfectly engineered towards running down gold rings and the more I ran them down the more it reinforced that I was good at it" (16)

Manipulative —
"Would help manipulate the outcome (46)
"Manipulative in dealing with human beings" (46)

External Behavior (IT)

Never present —
"Never present in any conversation maybe I was ever in for 35 years" (46)
"There was always noise in my head, a thousand monkeys, whatever" 46)
"Before the time I was 35, I don't ever recognize being present in a conversation" (46)

Ego driven —
"Was ego driven" (46)
"Before it was all about my result. If I didn't get my result, I wasn't happy. If I got my result, I wasn't happy" (52)
Very intense, very driven" (46)
"Not open for feedback beyond what I thought" (46)

Outside-In Mentality —
"Totally externally oriented" (46)
"If looking from the outside in it was very much everything was fine" (46)
"I think I was very Dr Jekyll and Mr. Hyde to most people because I was good enough with people and successful enough and good looking enough and all those things where everybody said everything was great" (46)

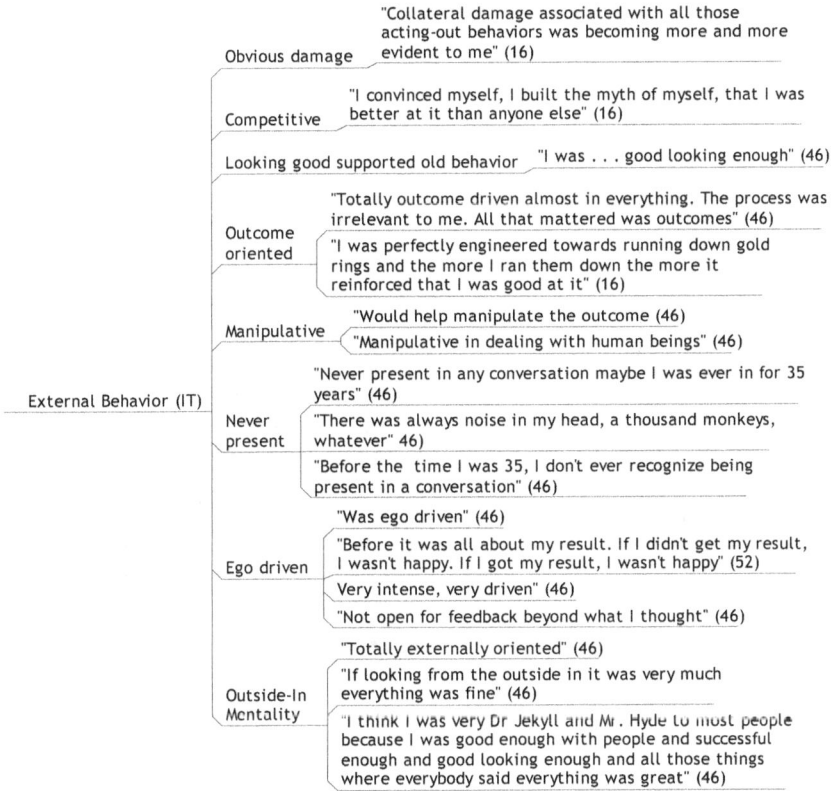

Figure 9. Jade external behavior (IT) before his transformation.

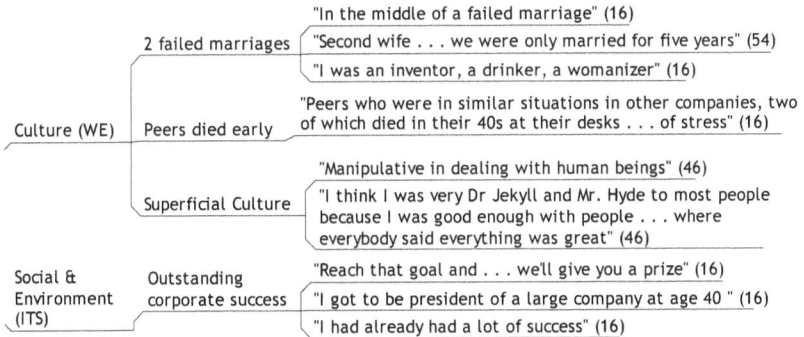

2 failed marriages —
"In the middle of a failed marriage" (16)
"Second wife . . . we were only married for five years" (54)
"I was an inventor, a drinker, a womanizer" (16)

Culture (WE)

Peers died early — "Peers who were in similar situations in other companies, two of which died in their 40s at their desks . . . of stress" (16)

Superficial Culture —
"Manipulative in dealing with human beings" (46)
"I think I was very Dr Jekyll and Mr. Hyde to most people because I was good enough with people . . . where everybody said everything was great" (46)

Social & Environment (ITS)

Outstanding corporate success —
"Reach that goal and . . . we'll give you a prize" (16)
"I got to be president of a large company at age 40 " (16)
"I had already had a lot of success" (16)

Figure 10. Culture (WE) and social environment (ITS) of Jade's transformation.

The Awakening Process and Significant Tipping Points

Jade's awakening process included the following tipping points repre-sented in Figure 11. At the peak of his brilliant career, Jade became aware of not only the physical and emotional challenges outlined earlier, but also

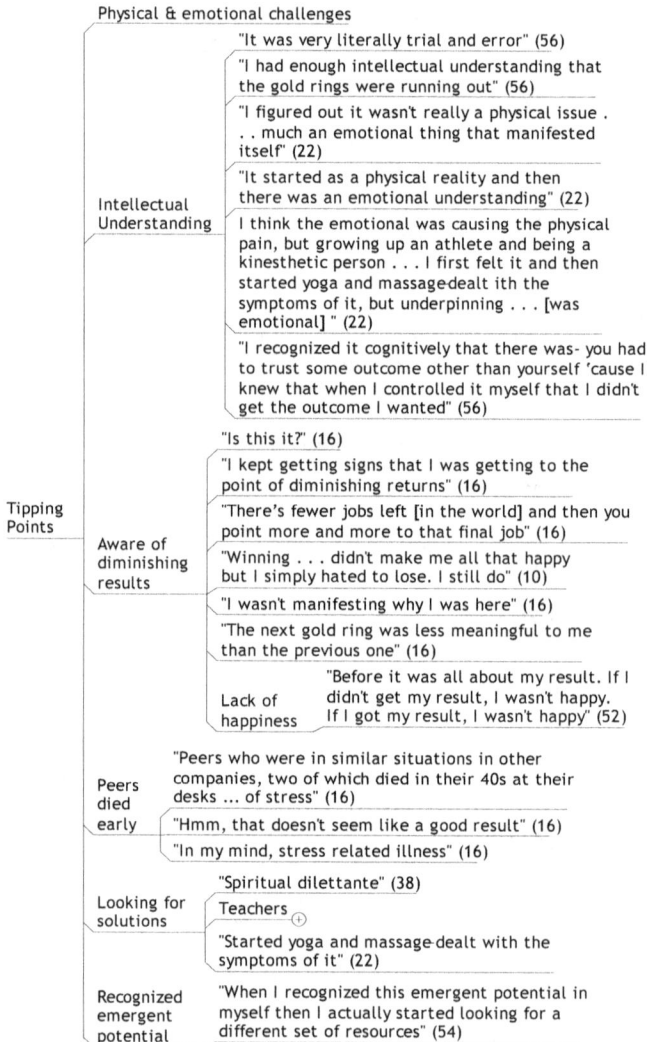

Figure 11. Tipping points of Jade's inner transformation.

of the futility of climbing up the corporate ladder. He understood that there were "fewer jobs left" for him in the world that could potentially give him the satisfaction he sought. He woke up to the fact that he "was getting to the point of diminishing returns," and missed authentic happiness. He said, "if I didn't get my result, I wasn't happy. If I got my result, I wasn't happy." Furthermore, he lost the significance of external success because "the next gold ring was less meaningful . . . than the previous one." When "a number of peers who were in similar positions in other companies . . . died [of stress] in their 40s at their desks," Jade realized that he "wasn't manifesting" why he "was here" and asked himself the key question "Is this it?"

In seeking "a different set of resources" Jade moved beyond the massage and yoga exercises that had previously helped him deal with the "symptoms" of his pain, and immersed himself into a process that he calls a "spiritual Ph.D." He began to work with world-renowned transformational experts, various shamans, and Native American teachers, who became not only "tremendous accelerators in this journey" but some of whom "ripped" his "head open."

In the beginning, one of his teachers recognized Jade's need to control and told him "You just chop wood until I tell you to stop chopping wood."

> *I chopped wood for 5 hours and . . . then we went through the [spirit lodge] process and it was a very powerful experience to go through. . . . I got a migraine and ended up throwing up for about 6 hours afterwards. It wasn't pleasant. . . . It took me weeks afterwards to figure out what was going on [with] all that pain, all that anxiety and all that fear [that] wanted to get out. . . . It was a classic purging kind of experience and the only way I could get quiet enough to even let the process work was to chop wood.*

Along with meditation, yoga, spirit lodges, and ballroom dancing, chopping wood has now become part of his integral life practice because it is "not cognitive." Being a "physical person," chopping wood helps him get out of his head. "Chopping wood works because it—it's very physical and meditative and eventually you get tired enough so your mind stops chattering at you and then something can emerge." What emerged for Jade over time is the experience of his "divine" nature and the visceral understanding that "we are all connected." In his understanding "we simply are God trying to emerge through one of the things that was created." Jade experienced a "massive shift" in consciousness and now knows that "at the heart of it is awareness of yourself outside yourself." He believes that "there is no stasis. You are either moving toward the light or away from the light." The universe is "constantly positively" surprising him "with its potential" if he "will simply get out of the way."

Structural Changes and Impact of Jade's Transformation

Jade's transformation has impacted all areas of his life (see Figure 12), including the Internal aspects of his own personality (I), the inter-objective domains of his Culture (WE), but also the External aspects of his life, his Behavior (IT) and the inter-subjective or Social Environment (ITS), which will be highlighted later.

Jade's overall priorities have significantly shifted due to his change in consciousness that led him to understand that "the greater purpose" is "not necessarily the shorter term end state" toward which we move "but the greater good, the greater end state, that we all, whether we know it or not, are either working for or against." Following his awakening to this new dimension of consciousness, Jade became "serious" about his spiritual quest (see Figure 13) and began working intensely with world-renowned teachers although he is "not a big believer in guruitis." By undergoing a "spiritual Ph.D." type of program, Jade was able to "recognize this emergent potential in" himself, to stop being "a spiritual dilettante," and to develop a "set of strategies, a way, a taxonomy of the resources that are available" for later reference.

In addition to yoga and meditation, Jade continues to attend spirit lodges and "chop wood" so that his "mind stops chattering" and "some-

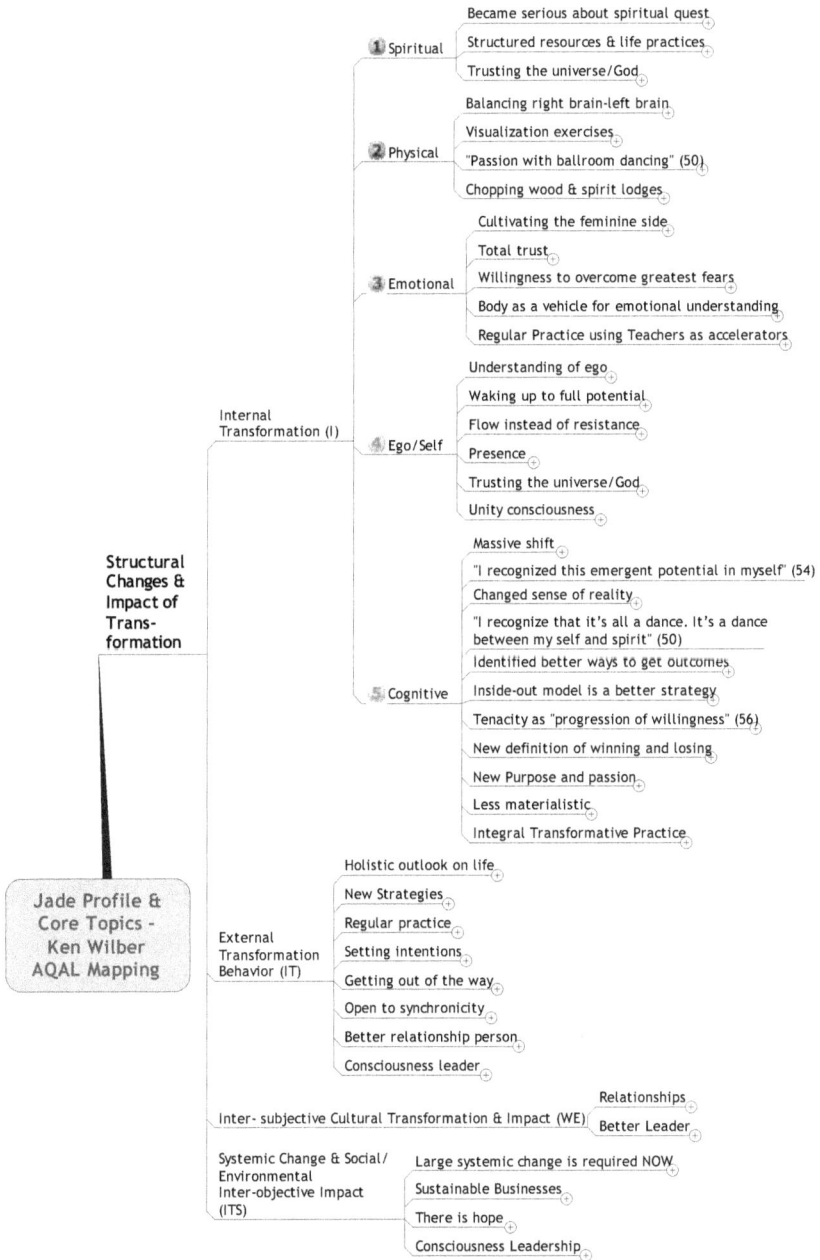

Figure 12. Structural changes and impact of Jade's overall transformation.

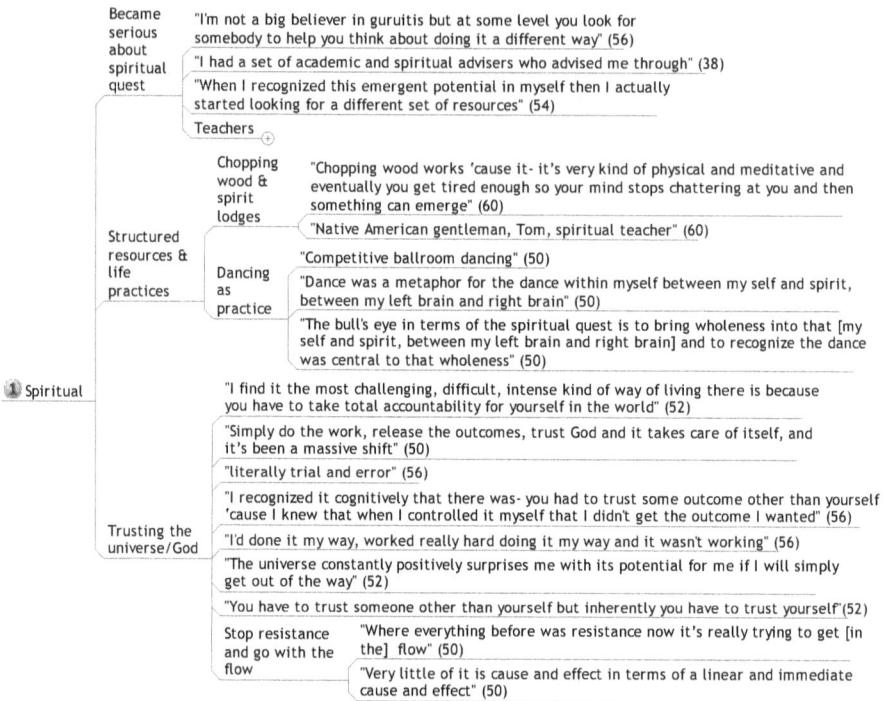

Figure 13. Structural changes and impact of Jade's spiritual transformation.

thing can emerge." Guided by the same intention to connect with "self and spirit," Jade developed a passion for "competitive ballroom dancing," which he considers to be "a metaphor for the dance within myself between my self and spirit, between my left brain and right brain."

Subsequently, Jade experienced a "massive shift" not only in his consciousness but also in all other areas of his life because he began to "simply do the work, release the outcomes, [and] trust God." Letting go of control and learning to trust "God" and the "universe" was significant:

> *I recognized it cognitively that there was—you had to trust some out-come other than yourself 'cause I knew that when I controlled it my-self that I didn't get the outcome I wanted. There was enough data*

*that said I'm doing it my way. It wasn't working 'cause I'd done it
my way, worked really hard doing it my way and it wasn't working,
so it was well, if not my way then whose other way?*

Through a tedious process of spiritual "trial and error" on his own and later under the guidance of his teachers, Jade was able to "experience" a new way to getting his outcome. He stated, "the universe constantly positively surprises me with its potential for me if I will simply get out of the way . . . where everything before was resistance now it's really trying to get [in the] flow." He considers his new path to be "the most challenging, difficult, intense kind of way of living there is because you have to take total accountability for yourself in the world." Yet, through the discovery of the deeper aspects of his interiority, Jade is tremendously hopeful regarding the future of us all and "the planet" no matter how big the challenges are that we collectively face: it's

*What's interesting to me in this process is that when I go inside
and I actually allow whatever is there to emerge in the way—in
whatever way it wants to emerge that I am constantly surprised
by the possibilities and that's what gives me hope.*

Physically, Jade continues to be well connected with his body. In addition to his "passion with ballroom dancing," and "chopping wood," he has also added a series of "visualization exercises" of "anthropological" nature to help him better understand his emotions: "I can now tap in and understand my emotions through where I hold them in my body, actually identify my emotions much better physically than I do cognitively."

Emotionally, Jade has been able to gradually let go of "being a control freak," of the "fears screaming in [his] head," and his "high degree of anxiety." In his view, his inherent "tenacity," "drive," and "willingness" to evolve has served him well throughout the process of transformation. A significant aspect of his emotional evolution is "wholeness" and the unification between the masculine and feminine aspects of his being. Jade grew up as "the youngest of five brothers" in a "highly patriarchal male, competitive, athletic culture" in which he has been "the most successful" career wise. As a result, he "was trying to access the feminine side of life through relationships and then they never worked because [he] could never access it" in himself. In his view, "ballroom dancing" allows Jade to access more of his own feminine side because it helps him "access" his "right brain" more effectively. This has also a positive impact on his intimate relationships with "women" but also with his "broader family," his "brothers," his "father and others."

Furthermore, Jade was able to free his "creative side that was always crying to emerge" and which he previously has "stuffed" down. He "trained" himself and cultivated his "very driven, very left brained" side to be able to survive both in his family environment and later in the business world. Through his transformation and the ongoing "spiritual" practice of ballroom dancing, he began living a more integral and fulfilled life:

> *Dance was a metaphor for the dance within myself between my self and spirit, between my left-brain and right brain, and so that really was the center point, the bull's-eye in terms of the spiritual quest is to bring wholeness into that and to recognize the dance was central to that wholeness.*

With respect to his *ego development* (see Figure 14), Jade realized that through his transformation he has been able to move beyond his former "ego-driven," "manipulative," and "outcome oriented" way of being toward unity consciousness:

> *I recognize that it's all a dance. It's a dance between my self and spirit. It's a dance between me and my ego. You can't subjugate it. What you resist persists. You can't resist your ego. It exists. It's just part of who you are. You have to dance with it and you have to understand that and so where everything before was resistance now it's really trying to get flow.*

He sees "the world in whole terms today" because "we are all connected" and "whether we know it or not, [we] are either working for or against" the greater good. Moreover, he views his egoic evolution as waking up from "being asleep" that means "simply about staying on a predeter-

Ego/Self

Understanding of ego

Ego driven in the past
- "Was ego driven" (46)
- "Before it was all about my result. If I didn't get my result, I wasn't happy. If I got my result, I wasn't happy" (52)
- Very intense, very driven" (46)
- "Not open for feedback beyond what I thought" (46)

- "A dance between me and my ego. You can't subjugate it. What you resist persists. You can't resist your ego. It exists. It's just part of who you are" (50)
- "My ego's part of myself and it's a dance" (46)
- "You have to dance with it" (50)
- "If I just get up and do my thing there's tremendous power. In fact, that's really ultimately the only power that exists really too. The rest of it's just the myth of control and ego and you just get up and do your thing"(83)

Waking up to full potential
- "Being asleep is simply about staying on a predetermined path that you've convinced yourself you're on and that you're anesthetizing yourself to anything other than that path" (12)

Flow instead of resistance
- "Where everything before was resistance now it's really trying to get flow" (50)
- "Very little of it is cause and effect in terms of a linear and immediate cause and effect" (50)

Presence
- "Never present in any conversation maybe I was ever in for 35 years" (46)
- "There was always noise in my head, a thousand monkeys, whatever" 46)
- "Before the time I was 35, I don't ever recognize being present in a conversation" (46)

Trusting the universe/God
- "Simply do the work, release the outcomes, trust God and it takes care of itself, and it's been a massive shift" (50)
- "Literally trial and error" (56)
- "I recognized it cognitively that there was- you had to trust some outcome other than yourself 'cause I knew that when I controlled it myself that I didn't get the outcome I wanted" (56)
- "I'd done it my way, worked really hard doing it my way and it wasn't working" (56)
- "The universe constantly positively surprises me with its potential for me if I will simply get out of the way" (52)
- "You have to trust someone other than yourself but inherently you have to trust yourself"(52)
- "I find it the most challenging, difficult, intense kind of way of living there is because you have to take total accountability for yourself in the world" (52)

Unity consciousness
- "We are all connected" (10)
- "Whether we know it or not, are either working for or against" (12) the greater good
- "When we create a compelling state in the future that compelling state is part of a greater state of future that we all have a stake in" (10)
- "I see the world in whole terms today. The world to me became integrated" (74)
- "I started thinking and making much more real time connections between people, places, things, events and saw the patterns much more in things" (74)

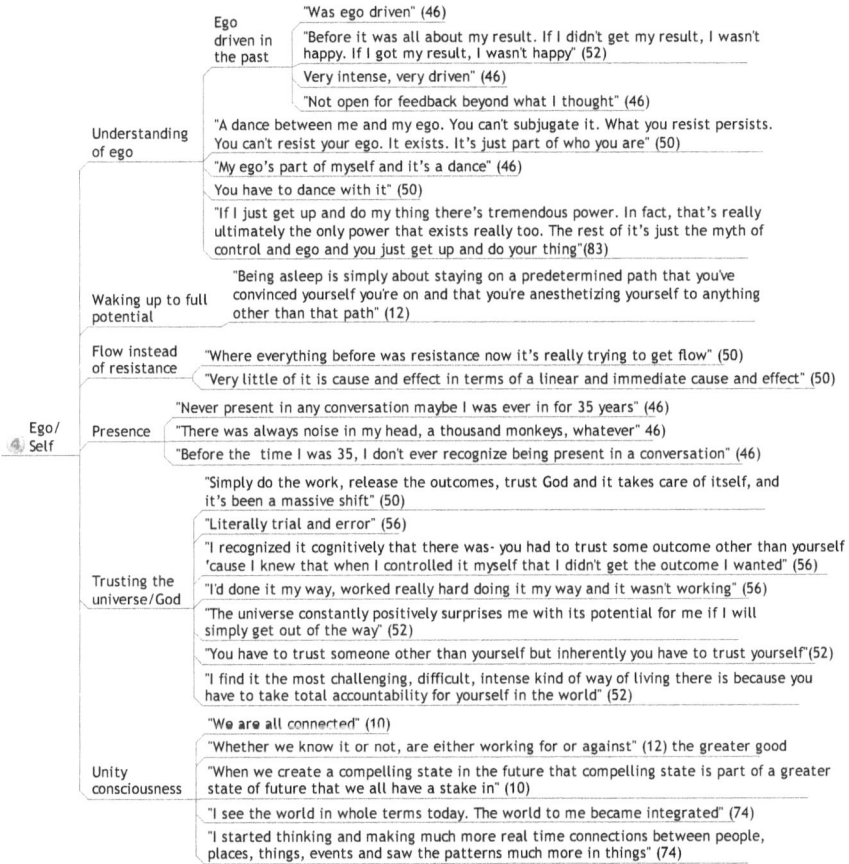

Figure 14. Structural changes and impact of Jade's egoic evolution.

mined path that you've convinced yourself you're on and that you're anesthetizing yourself to."

By cultivating new qualities such as "presence," "trust," and living in "flow," Jade recognized not only his full "potential," but more important, he has learned how he can achieve more with less effort:

> *If I just get up and do my thing there's tremendous power. In fact, that's really ultimately the only power that exists really too. The rest of it's just the myth of control and ego and you just get up and do your thing.*

Yet, giving up "resistance," letting go of the need to "control the out-come," and taking full responsibility for himself in the world is for Jade not only the most rewarding but also "the most challenging, difficult," and "intense" kind of "living." Whereas he is grateful for having "done the big scope stuff" Jade's path has become "much more personal" be-cause he loves "humanity" and cares deeply about "people's live" and his "real connection" with them at the human level.

Structural Changes and Impact of Jade's Cognitive Evolution

Through his "major shift" in consciousness, Jade re-cognized that the "authentic self is ever lasting," that we are "part of a greater whole . . . that is all energy," that "body, mind, and spirit" are "connected," and that "at the heart" of evolution there "is awareness of yourself outside yourself."

As previously discussed, Jade has reached a deep level of awareness and cognitive *understanding* regarding his *physical, emotional, egoic,* and *spiritual evolution.* In addition, he "recognized this emergent potential in" himself and the world at large. As a result, his entire life changed. A cognitive reflection of this transformation including verbatim quotes is shown in Figure 15. First and foremost, his sense of reality changed: "There's an amazing reality, I've experienced myself. . . . If you experience it yourself, it's no longer theoretical." As a result, he began trusting "God" and the "universe" and was able to release his old "control" and "fear" driven methods of achieving the "results" he wanted. More im-portant, he was able to identify better ways to get his outcomes by learn-ing how to set his "intentions," doing the "practices," as well as "being consistent" and "caring":

> *I've learned and internalized that setting your intentions the right way, doing the practices, being consistent with yourself, caring about yourself enough to do the right things for yourself and recognize that that's an everyday kind of thing, that the outcomes are always very good.*

Massive shift
- "Simply do the work, release the outcomes, trust God and it takes care of itself, and it's been a massive shift" (50)
- "The universe constantly positively surprises me with its potential for me if I will simply get out of the way" (52)

"I recognized this emergent potential in myself" (54)

Changed sense of reality
- "There's an amazing reality I've experienced myself, which is that change. If you experience it yourself, it's no longer theoretical" (82)
- "I've observed it myself. I've observed what it's meant to my relationships, to my family, and it also changes how I view things." (82)

"I recognize that it's all a dance between my self and spirit" (50)

Identified better ways to get outcomes
- **Releasing old outcome orientation**
  - "Before it was all about immediate gratification and now it's very little about immediate gratification. It's simply do the work, release the outcomes, trust God and it takes care of itself, and it's been a massive shift" (50)
  - "There was enough data that said I'm doing it my way. It wasn't working 'cause I'd done it my way, worked really hard doing it my way and it wasn't working" (56)
- "I've learned and internalized that setting your intentions the right way, doing the practices, being consistent with yourself, caring about yourself enough to do the right things for yourself and recognize that that's an everyday kind of thing, that the outcomes are always very good" (52)
- "Trust God and it takes care of itself" (52)
- Getting out of the way

Inside-out model is a better strategy
- "it works" (54)
- **Transition is tough**
  - "Very difficult to do it without really good teachers, tools, support" (50)
  - "Learning that there is a different way" (55)
  - "It's not the change that is tough. It's the transition" (54)
- **Absolute trust**
  - "You have to trust someone other than yourself but inherently you have to trust yourself"(52)
- **Most challenging way of living**
  - "I find it the most challenging, difficult, intense kind of way of living there is because you have to take total accountability for yourself in the world"(52)

Tenacity as "progression of willingness" (56)
- "Willingness is a huge thing here. It's like the tenacity in me . . . Once I had decided there was a different way that drives a lot of willingness in me because I just want to get better" (56)

New definition of winning and losing
- "Defining the parameters of winning and losing became more and more important to me over time and I was more discriminating because it used to be I didn't lose at anything" (4)

New Purpose and passion
- "I have one [a purpose] now, which is a good thing to have" (62)
- "My purpose before was to win, whatever- or to not lose maybe is a more accurate description, how- whatever the context of that was at the moment and it was very situational. It was very dull moves" (62)
- "My purpose today is to bring consciousness into the domain of business in a way that creates sustainable change relative to the human beings on the planet and ultimately bringing spirit into manifestation" (62)
- "That's why we are all here ultimately" (62)
- "I happen to operate in the business domain and I do believe that business if the people on this planet, the human beings and the planet itself, is to survive and more importantly thrive, that business is the vehicle by which large scale systemic change is going to be realized"(62)

Calling versus craving
- "I recognize the difference between craving and calling. Everything before was craving but now" it is about calling (50)

Less materialistic

Integral Transformative Practice

🔲 Cognitive

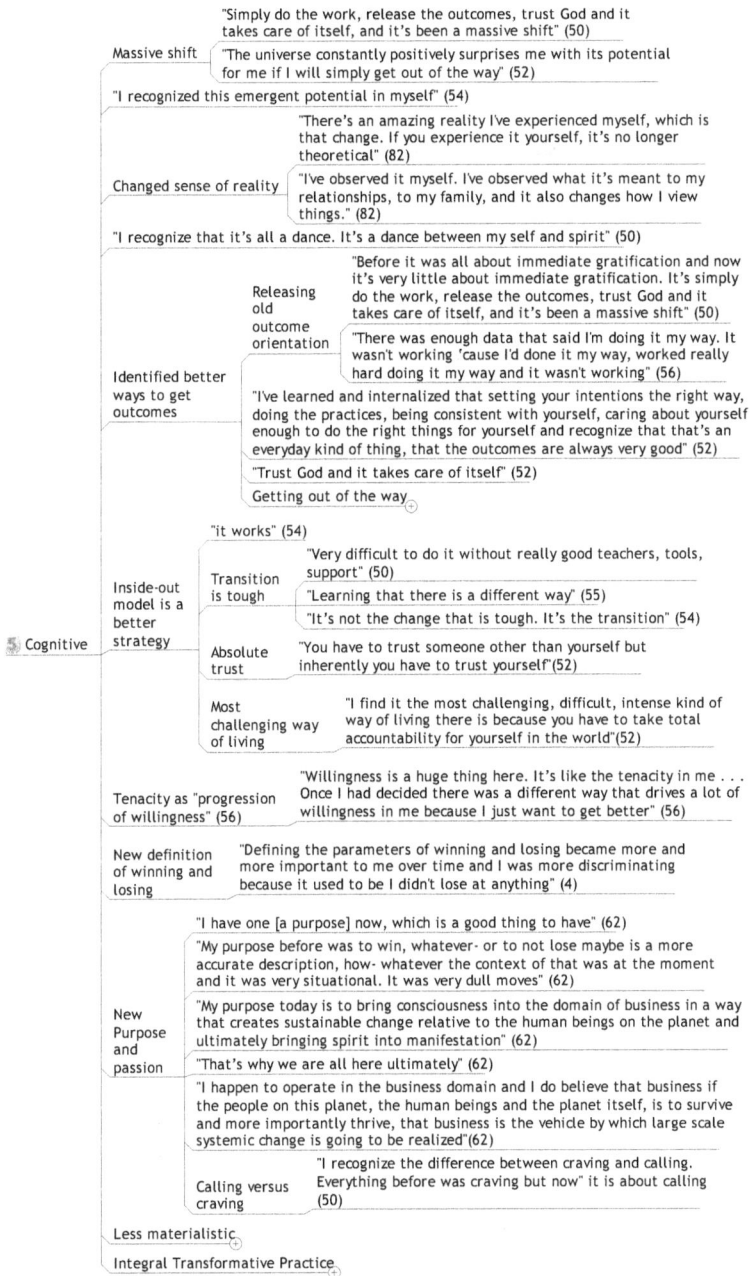

Figure 15. Structural changes and impact of Jade's cognitive evolution.

Whereas before, Jade had an "outside-in mentality," focused on "results" and "outcomes," he realized that "the inside-out model is a better strategy" because "it works" better if you "trust someone other than yourself but inherently you have to trust yourself." However, he finds this "the most challenging, difficult, intense kind of way of living there is because you have to take total accountability for yourself in the world." In his opinion, "it's not the change that is tough. It's the transition." He thinks that making the transition is "very difficult to do it without really good teachers, tools, [and] support." Furthermore, one has to be open to "learning that there is a different way" of achieving "more" by doing "less."

During his transformational process, Jade developed a new definition of winning and losing: "Defining the parameters of winning and losing became more and more important to me over time and I was more discriminating because it used to be I didn't lose at anything." He "still hate[s] to lose," but now he understands that within the larger context, "the outcomes are always very good. They are rarely what you think they're going to be though."

In addition to developing an ongoing integral transformative practice such as meditation, visualization, dancing, and yoga, Jade became less materialistic:

> *I don't need as many things as I used to need. In fact, things sometimes get in the way of what I'm trying to do . . . there is a certain level of quality of life you want but then I have too many friends who have a lot more things than I do . . . and who are deathly unhappy.*

One of the most significant realizations by Jade was the recognition of his new life's purpose within the context of his new "inside-out model." Whereas his "purpose before was to win, whatever—or to not lose," his "purpose today is to bring consciousness into the domain of business in a way that creates sustainable change relative to the human beings on the planet and ultimately bringing spirit into manifestation." He characterized the difference between his previous purpose and today's purpose as "craving" versus "calling":

I think my purpose before was to win, whatever—or to not lose maybe is a more accurate description . . . whatever the context of that was at the moment and it was very situational. . . . My purpose today is to bring consciousness into the domain of business in a way that creates sustainable change relative to the human beings on the planet and ultimately bringing spirit into manifestation.

Structural Changes and Impact of Jade's External/ Behavioral (IT) Transformation

Through his transformation, Jade began seeing "the world in whole terms" and he "no longer overly segmented things." He "started thinking and making much more real time connections between people, places, things, events and saw the [holistic] patterns" in his life (see Figure 16).

Jade adapted his behavior to accommodate an integral life by setting his "intentions the right way, doing the practices, being consistent with" himself, "caring about" himself, and by being open to "synchronicity." His new behavior made him also a "better relationship" person and a better leader, both of which are described in more detail below.

Jade's Inter-subjective Cultural Transformation and Impact (WE)

Jade's inner transformation affected his cultural environment beginning with his "nuclear family." He initiated "the first family reunion in the history of the family" and his family members see now the importance of a "networked model of resourcing each other." Furthermore, Jade has deepened the relationship with his sons, whom he "loves dearly" and who perceive their dad as "getting weirder and weirder" because they "don't quite understand what's happened." He has "had very deep discussions with them about this journey" because he wants "them to hopefully learn from it and not have to go through the same gates" he "went through." To get his sons to feel what it means to be awakened, Jade is creating "experiences for [them] to chop wood and to carry water" because he thinks

Holistic outlook on life
- "I see the world in whole terms today. The world to me became . . . I integrated and the world became integrated and no longer overly segmented things" (74)
- "I started thinking and making much more real time connections between people, places, things, events and saw the patterns much more in things" (74)

New Strategies
- "Set of strategies, a way, a taxonomy of the resources that are available to me emerged" (40)
- "Losing is not what I do" (10)
- Actionable projects on "the wheel of live" (40)

Regular practice
- "Passion with ballroom dancing and so competitive ballroom dancing" (50)
- Physical practice to get me inside myself (50)

Setting intentions
- "Setting your intentions the right way, doing the practices, being consistent with yourself, caring about yourself" (52)
- "That's an everyday kind of thing" (50)

Getting out of the way
- "The universe constantly positively surprises me with its potential for me if I will simply get out of the way" (52)
- "When I go inside and I actually allow whatever is there to emerge in the way- in whatever way it wants to emerge that I am constantly surprised by the possibilities" (82)

Open to synchronicity
- "That was really helpful to me in understanding everything happens if you allow it in a very wonderful way" (66)
- Received the book *Plan B* before major change in career

External Transformation Behavior (IT)

Better relationship person
- Family
- Full collaboration with others

Consciousness leadership

Total trust
- "There's a different way but in the different way you have to trust someone other than yourself but inherently you have to trust yourself" (52)
- "You have to take total accountability for yourself in the world" (52)

Openness & creativity
- "There is a different way and I think it's not impossible but very difficult to do it without really good teachers, tools, support" (54)
- "Be open enough to recognize that in that [old] model, the outside in, when they get what they want they're not happy and when they don't get what they want they're not happy. It's bad strategy" (51)

Became less materialistic
- "I don't need as many things as I used to need. In fact, things sometimes get in the way of what I'm trying to do" (82)
- "I have too many friends who have a lot more things than I do or- and who are deathly unhappy" (82)
- "If that's true for me, then maybe that's true for everyone at some level, that things, which we tend to focus on, is not the answer"(82)

Helping people

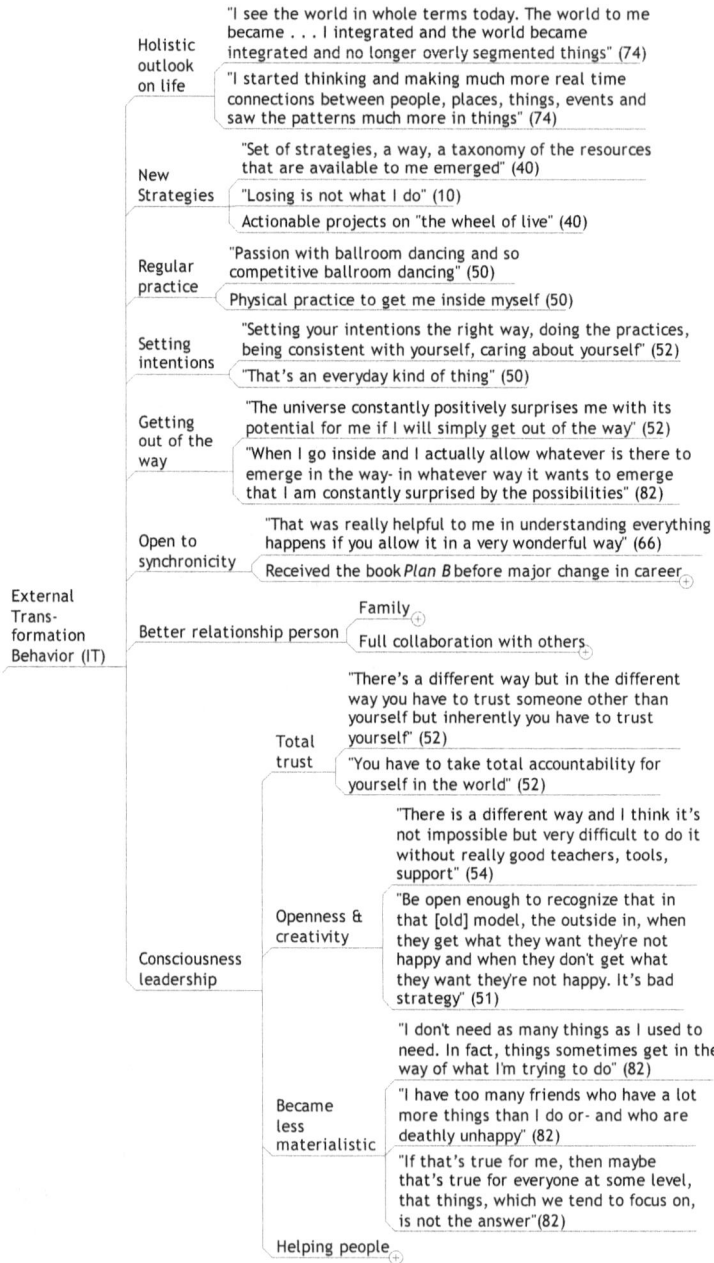

Figure 16. Structural changes and impact of Jade's external transformation (IT).

"that unless you bring it all the way back to that [experience] it becomes a large intellectual masturbation."

Outside his immediate cultural environment, Jade is empowering people to wake-up, stop "thinking in self-diminishing things about themselves," to "activate their own consciousness and ultimately collective consciousness," to acknowledge "their potential [that] is much greater than they give themselves credit for," and to connect with "their greatest manifestation."

I start this conversation with many people both [in] personal and professional life and I start with "Let's talk about your destination. Where do you want to end up? And I don't mean when you retire. I mean what's your greatest manifestation as you see yourself? What's possible?" And that leads into the whole question about how people see themselves and what's possible and the whole idea of human potential and potentiality. Their potential is many times much greater than they've even given themselves credit for because they've been processed into thinking the whole set of self-diminishing things about themselves and you have to unravel all that processing to get them to the point to even believe that there is potential there beyond some very limited set of options.

Systemic Change and Social/Environmental/ Inter-objective (ITS) Impact of Jade

Through the transformation of his interiority, Jade's impact in the world has a much more holistic nature and is primarily reflected in his understanding of Consciousness Leadership as shown in Figure 17.

Understanding "yourself" precedes understanding "those that are within your influence" said Jade. Furthermore, understanding the "context" of leadership is crucial because "we are all connected" and "whether we know it or not, [we] are either working for or against" the greater good.

The trick in consciousness leadership is to understanding the context of this thing you're leading, first yourself 'cause the first thing

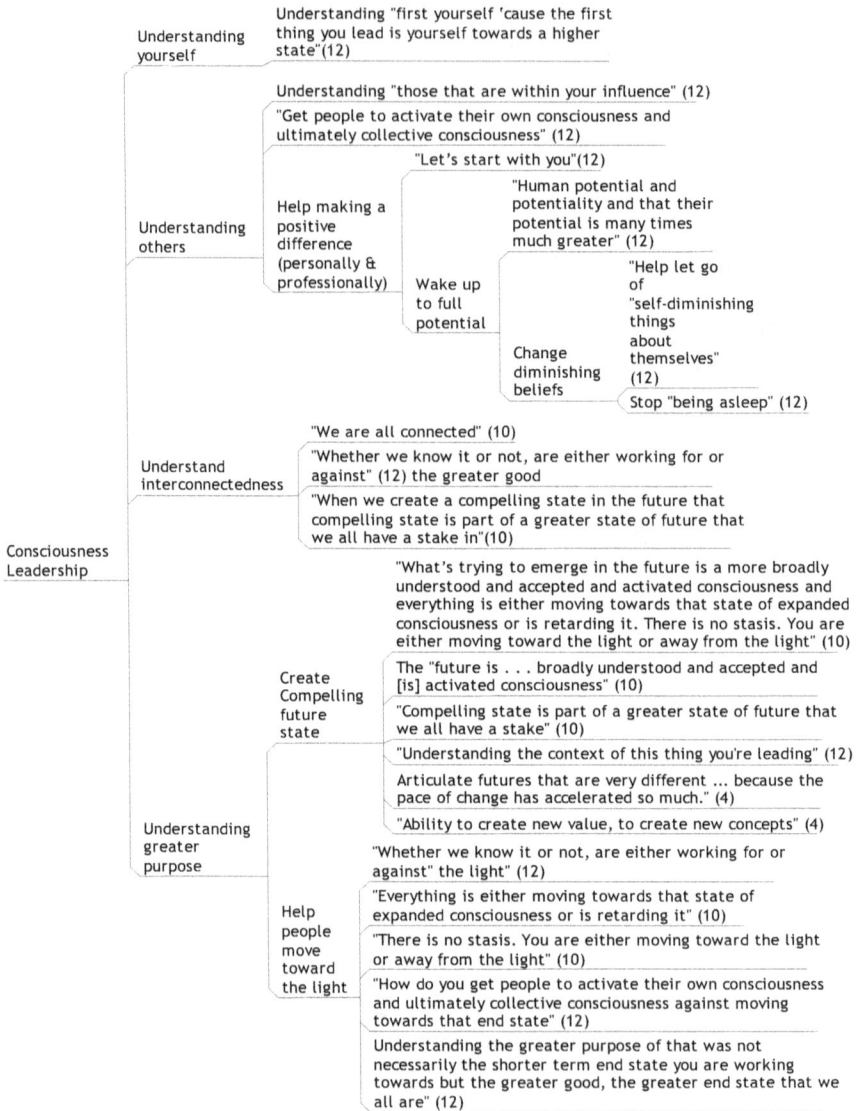

Figure 17. Jade's understanding of Consciousness Leadership.

you lead is yourself towards a higher state, and then those that are within your influence is how do you get people to activate their own consciousness and ultimately collective consciousness against moving towards that end state? And I think the trick for me at

*least is understanding the greater purpose of that was not neces-
sarily the shorter term end state you are working towards but the
greater good, the greater end state, that we all, whether we know
it or not, are either working for or against.*

In Jade's newly gained holistic view of the world, "when we create a
compelling state in the future that compelling state is part of a greater state
of future that we all have a stake in." Within his model, "everything is either
moving towards that state of expanded consciousness or is retarding it. There
is no stasis. You are either moving toward the light or away from the light."

Thus, change must happen systemically (see Figure 18) because it is a
matter of survival and "fortunately or unfortunately for us, it has to happen now." In his opinion, change must begin by reducing the "rampant
consumerism which has grown out" of a mostly "Western culture." The reality is "that the planet cannot sustain that level of growth," nor "the basic
underpinning structures that support that." In order to succeed, we must
change our "belief systems that suggest that only happiness can be achieved
through that consumerism; these are very deeply held, difficult to break."

Jade perceives the current global challenges as "the fundamental test
of humanity and it's our generation" that must change it now:

*I believe one of the major, major flaws in our political leadership
in the last 8 years is the whole abdication of global leadership on
these issues and the fact that it's allowed the dark in all these countries to say, "If the U.S. isn't going to provide leadership why
should we?"*

In his opinion, Jade considers businesses next to politics to be *the*
key players. He believes that "if the people on this planet, the human
beings and the planet itself, is to survive and more importantly thrive,"
businesses are "the vehicle by which large scale systemic change is going
to be realized." Jade considers that leaders are changing because they
find themselves pressured by "the short-term market-driven economic
realities of running one of these large companies" and by the "need to

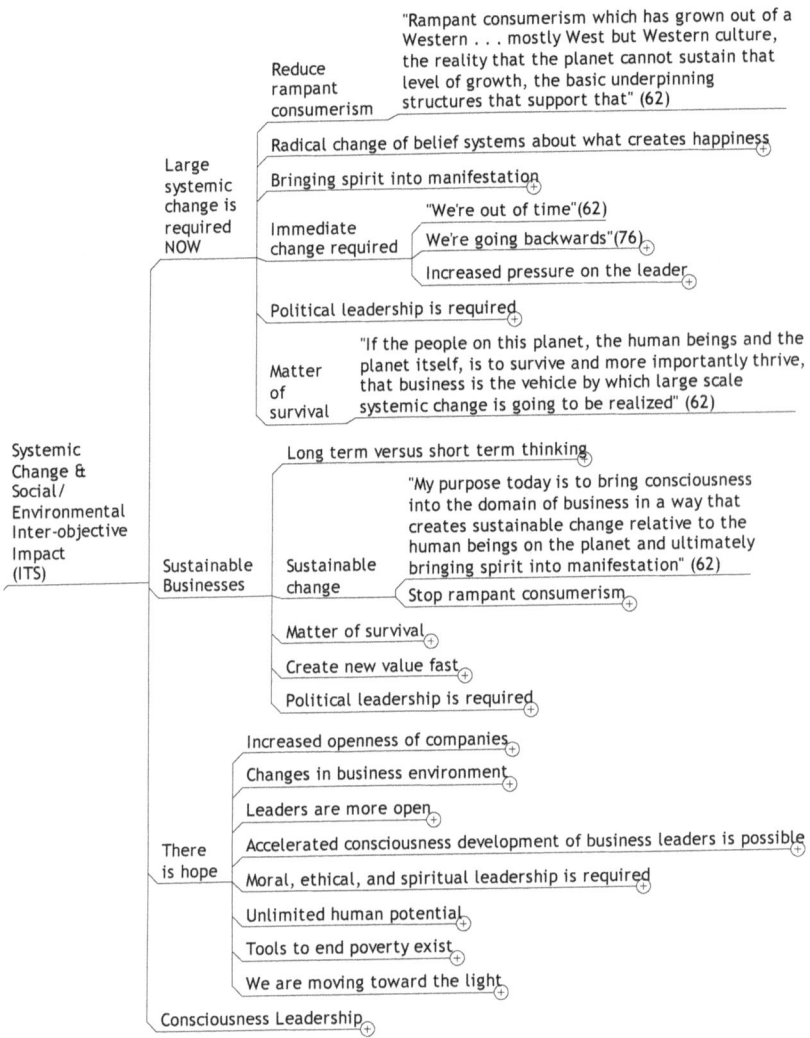

Figure 18. Systemic changes and inter-objective (ITS) impact of Jade.

balance that with the stake holder goods." Furthermore "the younger generations are pushing much harder for the social responsibility aspects of the business" and the leaders "have to go inside" and grow as human beings in order to respond appropriately. Jade sees his role in helping these leaders "build a set of tools" in order "to make that transition" fast because "they're not going to have the 10 years I had to go through it. They're going to have to go through an accelerated process of consciousness development."

Jade considers that the "totality of business" is not "making progress in this area of creating sustainable life" and "we're going backwards" with respect to the level of consumerism." However, he thinks that because "the vast majority of global corporations are still headquartered in Western Europe and the United States" they have the moral, ethical, [and] spiritual" obligation to provide "leadership." In his opinion, "the tools exist today to deal with these issues and the question is" whether or not we will "deal with them."

In summary, Jade's interior transformation into a consciousness leader can be characterized by five lines of development including the *spiritual, emotional, physical, cognitive,* and *egoic* line. Once he experienced a "massive shift" in consciousness and awakened to his "emergent potential" and "potentiality," Jade identified not only his new life purpose but became "serious" about his spiritual quest. To do that, he developed a set of integral life practices that include yoga, meditation, ballroom dancing, visualization exercises, and spirit lodges (Walsh & Vaughan, 1993; Wilber, 2006). By cultivating new qualities such as "presence," "trust," and living in "flow," Jade has realized that he can achieve more with less effort (Alexander et al., 1990). *Physically,* he continues to be deeply connected with his body whose messages he has learned to understand and leverage in a more efficient way (Leonard & Murphy, 1995; Murphy, 1993).

Emotionally, Jade has been able to gradually let go of his need to control and as a result, his formerly "high degree of anxiety" vanished. A significant aspect of his emotional evolution is the newly-found sense of "wholeness" demonstrated by the growing harmony between the masculine and feminine aspects of his being. His passion for ballroom dancing supports him in that growth because it helps him better "access" his "right brain" (Beauregard & O'Leary, 2007; Damasio, 2006; Saron & Davidson, 1997).

Regarding his *ego development* (Cook-Greuter, 2008; Loevinger, 1977), Jade realized that through his transformation he has been able to move beyond his former "ego driven," "manipulative," and "outcome oriented" way of being toward unified "consciousness" as a "greater whole." Furthermore, Jade is more present, has learned to go with the flow, has given up "resistance," let go of the need to "control the outcome," and is now willing and able to take full responsibility for everything in his life (Csikszentmihalyi, 1990; Csikszentmihalyi & Nakamura, 2002; Senge et al., 2005). As a result, he perceives his new way of living not only the most "rewarding" but also "the most challenging, difficult, [and] intense." He sees "the world in whole terms today" because "we are all connected" and "whether we know it or not, [we] are either working for or against" the greater good. Moreover, he views his egoic evolution as waking up from "being asleep."

Cognitively, his sense of reality changed because of his transpersonal experiences (Commons et al., 1984). As a result, Jade began trusting "God" as the "universe" of all being, and was able to release his "fear" and his need to "control." More important, he identified better ways to get his outcomes by learning how to set his "intentions," do "the practices," and be more "consistent" and "caring." Where as before, Jade had an "outside-in mentality," focused on "results" and "outcomes," he realized that "the inside-out model is a better strategy." In his assessment, "it works" better but "you have to trust someone other than yourself but inherently you have to trust yourself." He redefined the parameters for winning and losing and has become less materialistic.

The exterior impact is remarkable in that his relationships improved not only with his "nuclear family" but overall because he stopped being "Dr. Jekyll and Mr. Hyde." He is now empowering people to wake-up, stop "thinking self-diminishing things about themselves," "activate their own consciousness," acknowledge "their potential," and connect with "their greatest manifestation." Because he is already a force for good in the business world at large, Jade's global involvement has become much more "personal." Therefore, while keeping a systemic approach in mind, Jade is focusing on the inner transformation of top leaders who will have to go through an accelerated process of consciousness transformation in order to address the burning problems we are currently facing on earth today (Adams, 2005; Beck & Cowan, 1996; Boyatzis & McKee, 2005; Capra, 1993; Goleman et al., 2002; Renesch, 2002; Senge et al., 2005; Torbert et al., 2008).

Jade's overall ability to (a) take total "accountability" for his life; (b) to be at peace and live with a view of reality that is extremely complex and seems paradoxical; (c) his capacity to meet people at their own level of consciousness and adjust his supporting style according to their needs; (d) his aptitude to be an agent for systemic change with love and understanding instead of despair, and his humility, honesty, and willingness to make his impact in the world personal rather than organizational; (e) his vivid, authentic, playful, and direct language regardless of possible negative consequences ("intellectual masturbation," "inside it was a circus," being a former "drinker, a womanizer"); (f) his ability to balance out his feminine and masculine sides in an embrace between Eros and Agape (Wilber, 2000); and (g) his ability to transcend and include his ego as part of the "dance" of life, are strong indicators that Jade has reached the postconventional level of egoic development (Alexander et al, 1990; Commons et al., 1984, 1990; Cook-Greuter, 2005, 2008; Torbert et al., 2004). However, more research and quantitative tests (Cook-Greuter, 2008; Torbert et al., 2004) would have to be performed to reach a more informed conclusion.

Looking Beyond the Veil of Samsara

Common topic: Consciousness leaders appear to have developed to higher levels of consciousness through an evolutionary process that included peak experiences, significant transformational experiences, or exceptional human experiences.

All research participants confirmed without exception that their internal transformation took place over many decades. The personal growth was perceived as a process that affected several lines of development. These lines include cognitive development, ego-development, moral development, emotional development, spiritual development, and physical transformation. In all cases, the development process was accelerated by transformative experiences known as *transcendent* or *peak experience* (Maslow et al., 1998), *flow* (Csikszentmihalyi, 1990; Kjaer et al., 2002), *state* or *unity consciousness* (Cook-Greuter, 2004; Wilber, 2000a), *exceptional human experience* (White, 1998), *transpersonal experience* (Grof, 2006), and *spiritual emergency* (Vaughan, 2000).

These extraordinary human experiences occur in many ways but seem to be accelerated through sudden *peak experiences* (Maslow, 1968/1999), *meditation* (Alexander et al., 1990), *contemplation* (Beauregard & O'Leary, 2007), *near-death experiences* (NDE), *out of body experiences* (OBE; Alvarado, 2000), *exceptional human experiences* (EHE; White, 1998), and other states of *unity consciousness* and *awe* (Vaughan, 2000). Research (Alexander et al., 1990; Beauregard & O'Leary, 2007; Commons et al., 1984, 1990; Cook-Greuter, 2004, 2005, 2008; Pauchant, 2002; Torbert et al., 2004, 2008) indicated that such exceptional human experiences can move humans beyond duality, the good and the bad, the beautiful and the ugly.

The research participants in the current study reported experiencing such extraordinary states during meditation (unity experience), being in nature (feelings of oneness), through physical or emotional pain (shadow work), induced by spiritual teachers, or in the late 1960s through drugs. Although, these transformational and consciousness altering experiences play a significant role in the lives of the consciousness leaders researched, most participants found it difficult to explain the ineffable using our current vocabulary.

Further research that goes beyond the phenomenological aspects addressed here would have to be performed to assess to what degree the reported altered *states* of consciousness have contributed to the individual transformation toward higher *stages* of consciousness.

Star's Individual Consciousness Leadership Profile with Transformational Characteristics

Star, who grew up in her "early years in a trailer," is a highly educated individual who has earned several academic degrees from some of the most prestigious universities in the world. She is a serial entrepreneur, a high-tech and a clean-tech investor, and a self-made millionaire. Prestigious magazines such as *Business Week, Forbes Magazine, Harvard Business Review,* the *Women's Magazine,* and *The Financial Times* featured Star in their publications. For the past decade, her work has included worldwide academic teaching and speaking engagements on conscious business and integral life practice. Philosophically, she is combining sustainable business practices with various mystical and wisdom traditions. Appendix D contains the mind map representing the key core topics and transformational profile that resulted from the interview conducted with Star.

Triggers and Context of Star's Transformation

The triggers and context of Star's transformation into a consciousness leader are characterized by several major lines of development including the *cognitive, emotional, physical, egoic,* and *spiritual* (see Figure 19).

Cognitively, Star always had "a natural desire to continue to evolve" and leveraged her "very high intellect, rational, linear, logical" cognitive ability, creativity, curiosity, and academic education to arrive at "a pretty high echelon" of external success.

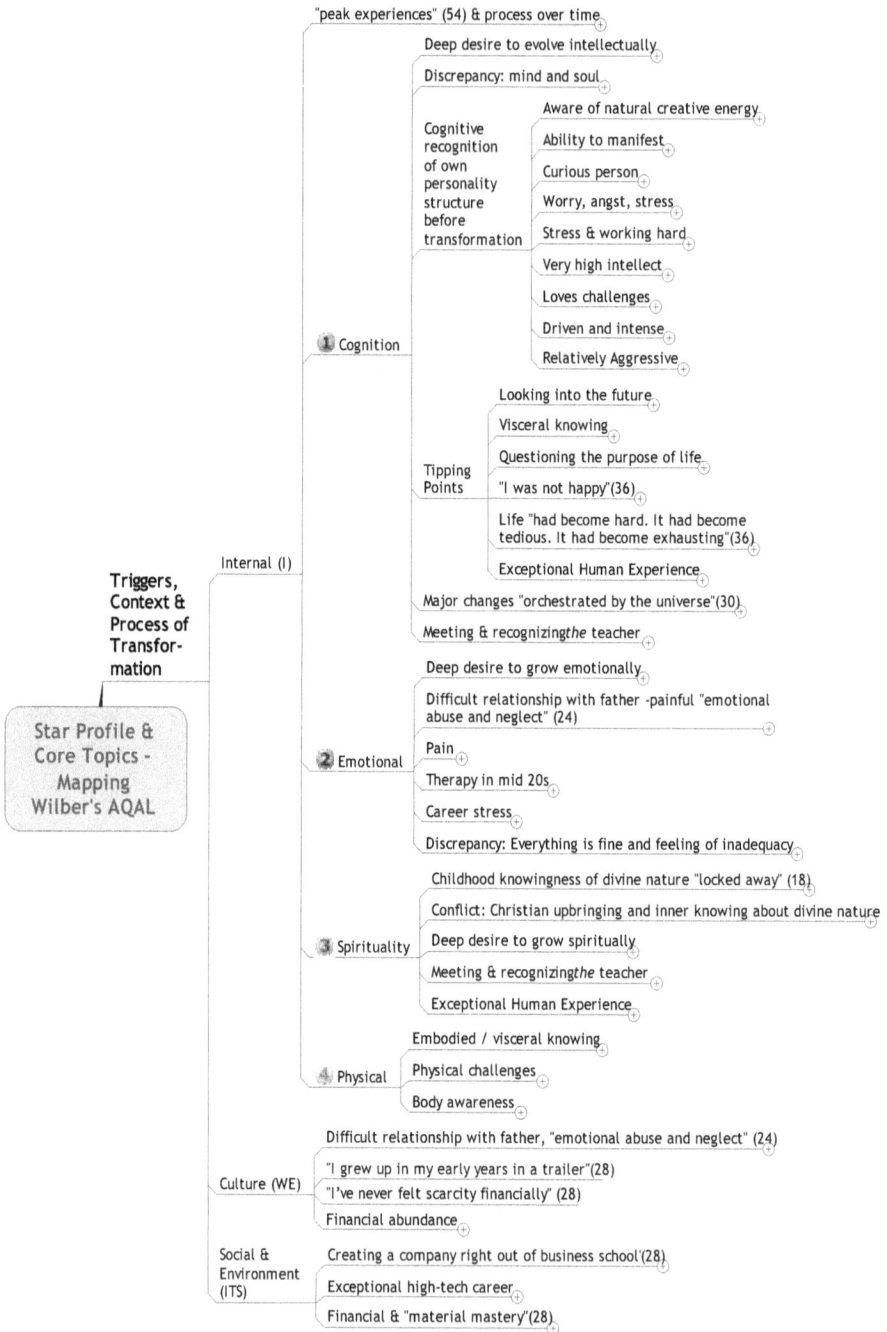

Figure 19. Context and triggers of Star's transformation.

Before her transformation, Star perceived herself as "really hard" working, sometimes stressed and concerned, "relatively aggressive," and "driven" (see Figure 20).

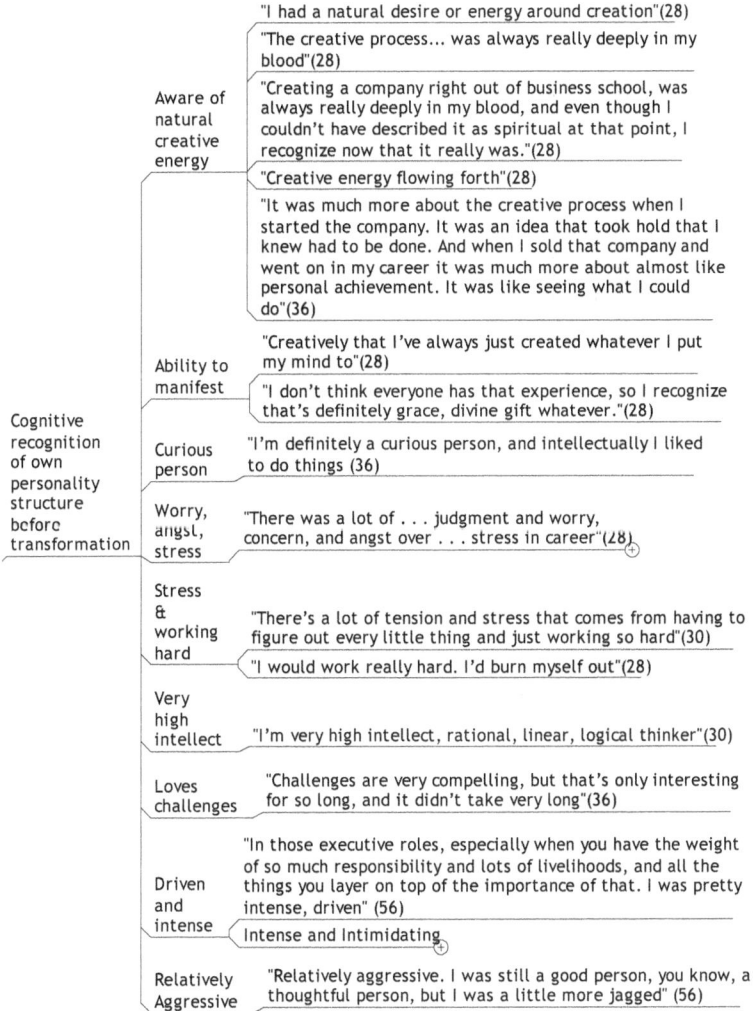

Figure 20. Star's own cognitive recognition of personality structure before transformation.

Physically, she "wasn't taking care" of her body and "would get sick often: colds and sore throats" which she "couldn't quite beat it because" she was often "so exhausted and worn out."

Emotionally, at "age 12 or 13" Star decided that she "wouldn't need anyone, and kind of closed down" her heart to be able to cope with "a very difficult relationship with" her "father." As a result, the high-school years and beyond "were much more about emotional evolution" but also included "reading spiritual books, and Eastern and Western philosophy." In intimate relationships, she "was never available" because she "was always in control." Yet she knew deep inside that she "didn't want to be that way in relationships," which led her to "therapy" in her 20s. She "wanted to be more open and available and vulnerable."

Spiritually, from an early age on, Star "knew" that she was "God" and "divine" like "everyone else" but stopped talking about it due to negative feedback from her environment":

> *As early as I can remember, like 5, 6, 8, I knew I was God. So, through a child's eyes, and I mean that with the most reverence to the divine oneness, it wasn't like this was a thought construct. I had no basis. I just knew that I was divine. Everyone else was too. It wasn't like I was special or anything, it was just "Don't you know? We're all God. We're all God." But I didn't have any teachers or role models. My parents weren't particularly, I mean they weren't religious. They certainly weren't spiritual. I did go to Sunday school with my grandmother so I got a little of that sort of inculcation in the Christian church, but I remember [telling] my Sunday school teacher at one point that "I'm God and so are you." And they did not like that at all. I kind of locked that away in the closet I realized that wasn't sort of kosher. Even though I knew it on some level, that wasn't a way that I could express it that seemed appropriate to people, or they didn't buy it, or it was actually offensive in some way.*

Maybe because she grew up "in a trailer," Star never believed in scarcity but in abundance. As a result, her professional success is characterized by creativity and curiosity and not by the need to make money:

I had a natural desire or energy around creation or the creative process. That took the shape of creating a company right out of business school, was always really deeply in my blood, and even though I couldn't have described it as spiritual at that point, I recognize now that it really was. It was sort of that creative energy flowing forth. I was lucky and I'm blessed in this lifetime that even though I grew up in my early years in a trailer, so we didn't have a lot of means. I've never felt scarcity financially. I just knew in my body there would always be enough. There would always be enough. It would always come at the right time. And creatively that I've always just created whatever I put my mind to, and I don't think everyone has that experience, so I recognize that's definitely grace, divine gift whatever. I'm humbly grateful for that.

The Tipping Point—Breaking Through the Wheel of Samsara

Cognitively (see Figure 21), Star stated that she "was self-actualized, but not self-realized" and began looking deeper.

Very soon, she recognized the "natural yearning of the soul" that "was sitting there waiting" for her to "clue in." "Even though I was sort of at a pretty high echelon, it also didn't feel like I'd arrived at any sense, so it was the hamster wheel of being in the Samsara." At the peak of external success, Star "woke up"

I had this moment where I looked into the future and all I saw was this endless stream of closing quarters. . . . And while there were fun things like building new markets and I really enjoy business, there was this sort of almost mind numbingly impossible monotony

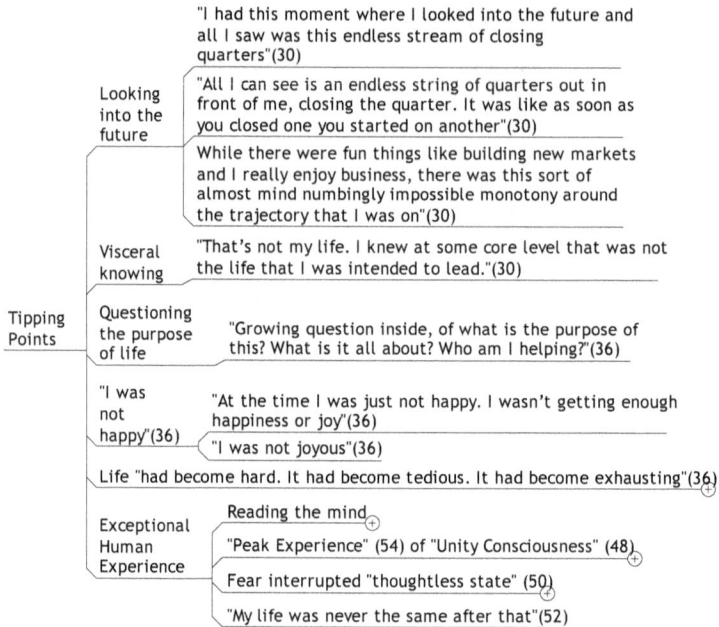

Figure 21. Star's significant awakening moments.

around the trajectory that I was on. Oh my God, that's not my life. I knew at some core level that was not the life that I was intended to lead. And so, I decided to take a year sabbatical. . . . For whatever reason I was drawn to India even though I didn't know why and I'd never been drawn there before.

A series of synchronicities, inner knowing, and visceral body reactions lead Star to meet and recognize her future spiritual teacher first in California and then in India (see Figure 22).

Based on her body reaction, Star knew from the very first time when she saw her teacher that they had a very deep connection with each other:

When I walked into the room . . . all of my intuitive senses went on alert. Every way my body could tell me to pay attention happened. I got goose bumps. My hair stood on end. I went kind of into an altered state. Just the whole world started spinning. It was almost like I kind of walked through a tear in the universe and my body-mind

Meeting & recognizing *the* teacher

in California

1. Synchronicity

"For whatever reason I was drawn to India even though I didn't know why and I'd never been drawn there before"(36)

"The week before I left I received an invitation to an event at the Palace of Fine Arts in San Francisco to come see this Indian swami who was speaking"(36)

Body awareness

"It was like all of my intuitive senses went on alert"(36)

"My hair stood on end"(36)

"I went kind of into an altered state. Just the whole world started spinning"(36)

"It was almost like I kind of walked through a tear in the universe and my body-mind was saying "This is an important moment. Pay attention.""(36)

"I felt this deep resonance with this man"(36)

2. Synchronicity

"At the end of the program they announced that he was having his birthday celebration in India in the exact city, the exact week that I had open on my calendar"(36)

In India

3. Synchronicity

"In the swirl of people I mean there were hundreds of people, he called me over from across the room, and asked me to go for a walk with him, and he didn't know who I was, where I had come from"(38)

"There was no humanly possible way for him to know anything about me, and we went for a walk on the beach"(38)

4. Synchronicity

"You're a successful business woman." And I thought ...how does he know that? I said "I suppose so, by external measures. I don't feel so successful because I'm not really happy right now." He says "Yes, that's because you've got the model all wrong."(44)

"He said "You think that you create through your effort and your will." He said "You will learn to create many, many, many things with ease and joy, but you won't do it through your willpower.""(44)

Deep Recognition

"I said 'Will you teach me?' And he looked at me like I was the most remedial student he'd ever had. I had just shown up in India. I was blown away, I didn't know who he was or anything. And he said 'Why do you think you're here? I've been waiting for you. This is what you came to learn.""(44)

"It was sort of like that recognition. I mean I had recognized him in the Palace of Fine Arts, and then throughout the course of the week, he'd been teaching on more esoteric and more spiritually-oriented things that blew me away. And then when he said this I realized it was true. I had come there at a time when I was ready to learn what we're really doing here" (36)

Exceptional Human Experience

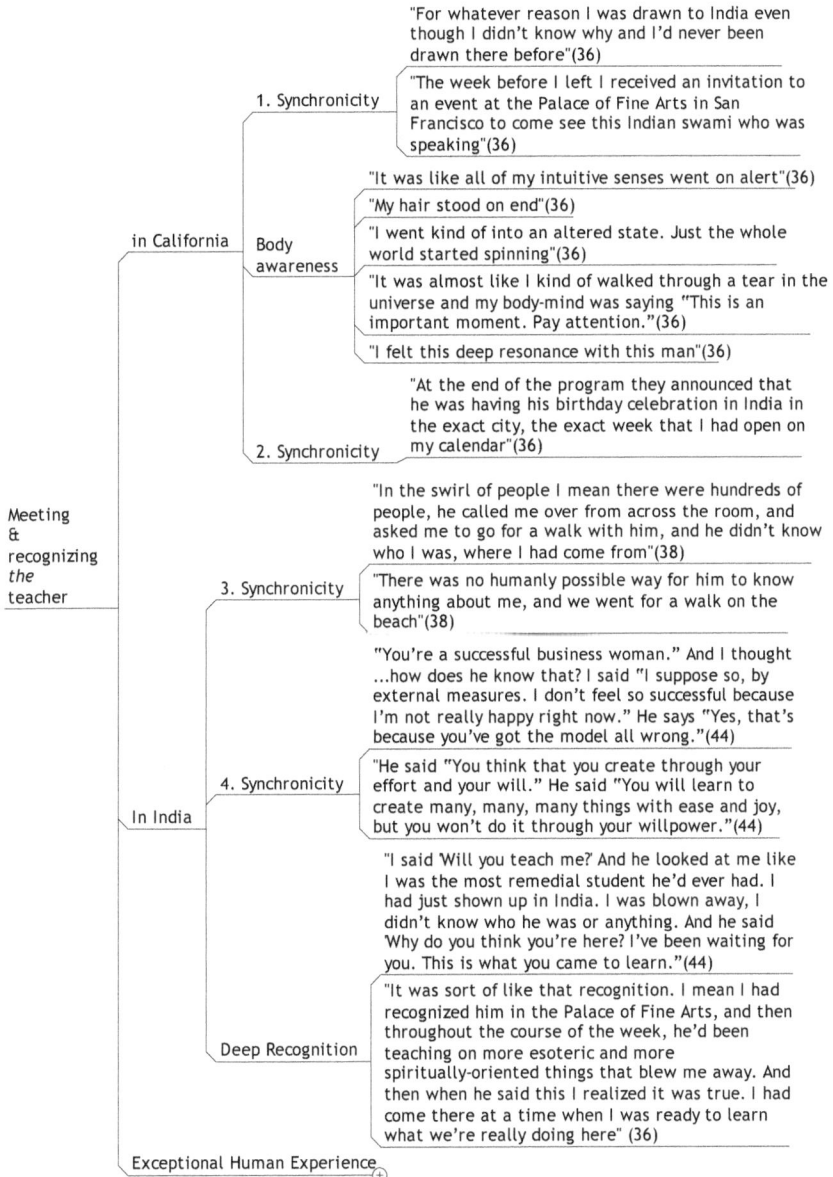

Figure 22. Star is meeting and recognizing her teacher.

was saying "This is an important moment. Pay attention." I felt this deep resonance with this man, this being.

Exceptional Human Experience: Mind Reading and Unity Consciousness

Toward the end of her India vacation, Star visited her future teacher at his ashram and joined thousands of other pilgrims who celebrated his birthday. Out of hundreds of non-Asian ashram visitors, he singled her out, asked her for a walk on the beach, and pointed out her predicament. Without having met her before he told her that she was "a successful business woman" who in his view "got the model all wrong," because she believed that we create through "effort" and "will." He told her that she could "learn to create many, many, many things with ease and joy," but she will not "do it through" her "willpower."

Her first lesson was on mind reading:

> *We proceeded to have a conversation where he read my mind and responded so I never opened my mouth. And we had a whole dialogue. He would say something, I would think the response before I could actually physically respond, he would answer and respond. It was a very much a full conversation. He was speaking but I wasn't. So he would read my mind and respond...I never actually had the chance to verbalize the responses. As soon as the thought-form arose, he would respond to it. So we were very much in a full dialogue. And I just remember thinking, oh my gosh, I didn't realize there were beings on this planet who could do this.*

Figure 23 shows the mind map of Star's exceptional human experience in with her own words. After communicating with Star in a non-verbal fashion, her teacher touched her "third eye" and sent her into the meditation room where she had a "unity consciousness" experience:

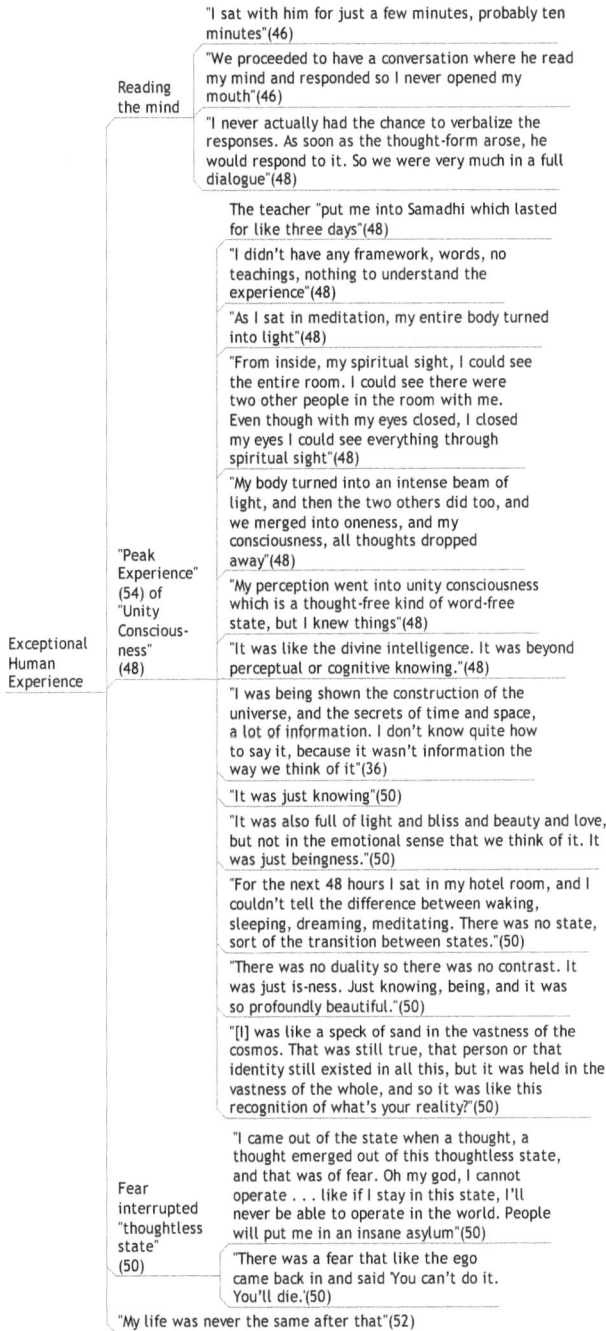

Figure 23. Star's exceptional human experience.

When I went into meditation, he put me into Samadhi which lasted for like 3 days. And I didn't know what Samadhi was. I didn't have any framework, words, no teachings, nothing to understand the experience. But as I sat in meditation, my entire body turned into light. I had from inside, my spiritual sight, I could see the entire room. I could see there were two other people in the room with me. Even though with my eyes closed, I closed my eyes I could see everything through spiritual sight. My body turned into an intense beam of light, and then the two others [with whom I meditated] did too, and we merged into oneness, and my consciousness, all thoughts dropped away. My perception went into unity consciousness, which is a thought-free kind of word-free state, but I knew things. It was like the divine intelligence. It was beyond perceptual or cognitive knowing. I was being shown the construction of the universe, and the secrets of time and space, a lot of information. I don't know quite how to say it, because it wasn't information the way we think of it.

In addition to learning the secrets of the universe, as well as time and space, Star experienced also inner knowing, bliss, beauty, love, just being, and non-duality:

It was just knowing. And it was also full of light and bliss and beauty and love, but not in the emotional sense that we think of it. It was just beingness. It's an experience that's really hard to put into words, because there wasn't any words there and to sort of transcribe it back into words here doesn't really work, but somehow I managed to get from the ashram back to my hotel, and pretty much for the next 48 hours I sat in my hotel room, and I couldn't tell the difference between waking, sleeping, dreaming, meditating. There was no state, sort of the transition between states. There was no duality so there was no contrast. It was just IS-ness. Just knowing, being, and it was so profoundly beautiful. The individual Star, it's like there was like a speck of sand in the vastness of the cosmos. That was still true, that person or that identity still existed in all this, but it was held in the vastness of the whole, and so it was like this recognition of what's your reality? That that's the truth of my being and your being and everyone's being. And yes, we do have an aspect which is the individual personality embodied in time and space right now in this lifetime, but there's many other dimensions that we're also playing at the same time and all that.

She "came out of the state when a thought, a thought emerged out of this thoughtless state, and that was of fear." She was afraid and she thought to herself: "I cannot operate [and] if I stay in this state, I'll never be able to operate in the world. People will put me in an insane asylum."

Structural Changes and Impact of Star's Transformation

The impact of her unity consciousness experience was significant because it represented a "major transition" point and affected all major aspects of her life: the Internal (I), the External I (IT), the Inter-objective/cultural (WE), and the Inter-subjective, the Social/Envi ronmental (ITS) (see Figure 24).

The interior transformation (I) is characterized primarily by a changed order of priorities: It was a gift that he [my teacher] gave. It was a momentary or a few days worth of being able to see beyond the veil of this individual perception that we have, and it was such a gift because . . . once you know, you can't un-know. My life was never the same after that. . . . That was a major transition for me, and then from that time it's sort of been a deepening process of getting more and more in tune, or integrating that experience and the experiences that have come since into my daily experience of life.

Before her shift in consciousness, Star's life was mostly driven by the outside world ("outside-in"). Yet, through the experience, the *spiritual* and *emotional* lines of development have gained top priority in her life with regular spiritual practice being now its foundation ("inside-out").

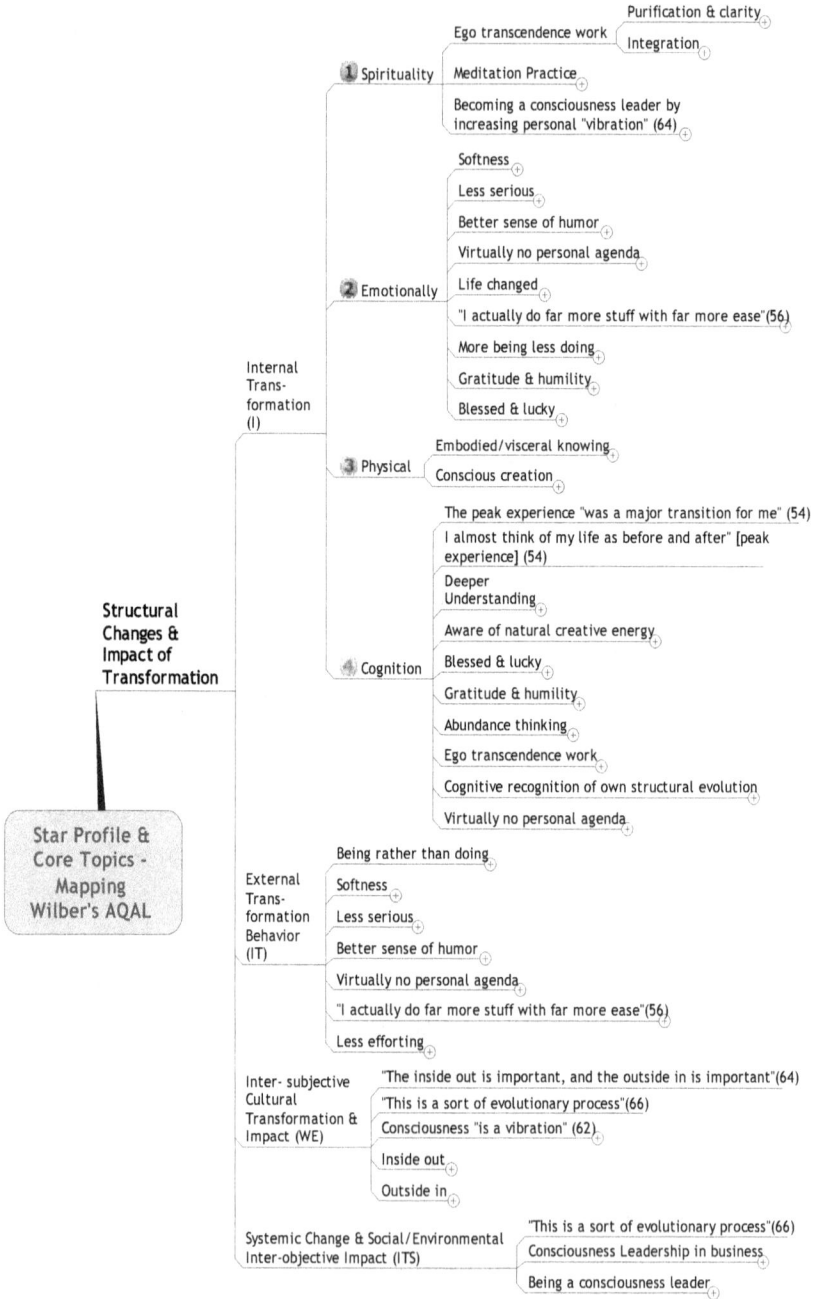

Figure 24. Structural changes and impact of Star's transformation.

In keeping with her newly gained "non-dual" perspective of the world, Star honors both dimensions equally and avoids moving "into any paradigm that has a duality inherent in it, so the inside-out is important, and the outside-in is important."

Spiritually, Star has intensified her meditation practice because it helps her (a) watch "the illusion" of reality "unfold," (b) cultivate her creative force to "create and or de-create," (c) be "more present," (d) "recognize the practical nature of this physical world," and (e) develop her awareness "of the truth." In her new understanding, that truth is "the unity state from which that duality arises," and which one is "able to collapse" or "expand it at will." Cultivating her sense of presence has become instrumental to her life because it is "the deepening practice of being alert to the arising" of her creative "energies" and vibrations within her "physical form." She is now "learning to more consciously create and or de-create [reality]." In addition, her spiritual practice helps her release "the grip of ego" and integrate her exceptional human experience into her "daily experience of life."

Physically, Star has developed a new understanding about the physical body and how our consciousness creates reality through "sound and energy." In her opinion, as "we go deeper in understanding" the energy "vibrations inside our own physical body," we let go of "the misperception of being separate, individual entities," and gain "an actual recognition and/or experience of ourselves as vibration" of the "fundamental building blocks" that "emanate forth from unity." As a result, Star continues to listen to her body, exercises regularly, and watches her diet to evolve and to be able to sustain for longer periods of time the high frequency vibration of her body.

Emotionally, she became "softer," "a little less serious," has a "better sense of humor," and is comfortable with not having "any sort of personal" agenda. Whereas she continues to feel deeply "grateful," "blessed," and "lucky" for the abundance in her life, she has the visceral knowing that everything she needs "would always come at the right time." In addition, she continues to focus on cultivating her "creative energy" and her "desire to have any sort of personal career is virtually gone."

Cognitively, Star has gained an irrevocable deep understanding about human nature and its role in the universe ("once you know, you can't un-know" (see Figure 25).

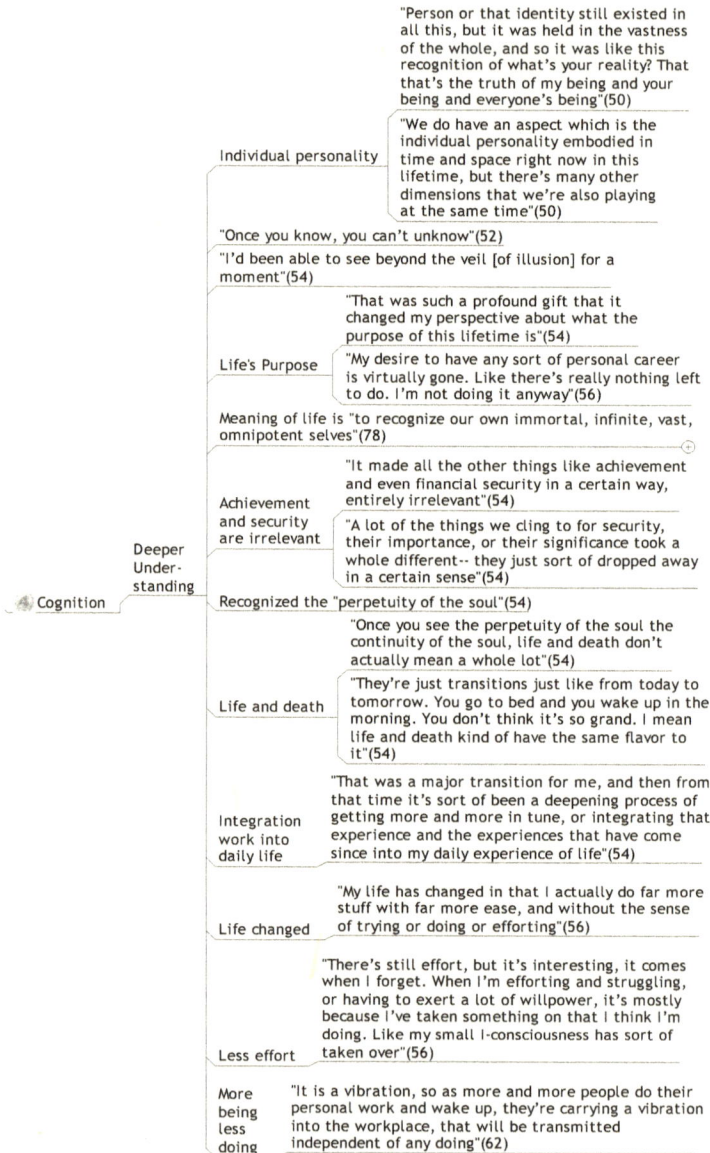

Figure 25. Star's deeper understanding of life.

In Star's view, "we do have an aspect which is the individual personality embodied in time and space right now" but there are "many other dimensions that we're also playing at the same time. With respect to her understanding of own *ego* and *self-identity*, Star has arrived to the conclusion that we are all interconnected and therefore the meaning of life is "to recognize our own immortal, infinite, vast, omnipotent selves." Once she was able "to see beyond the veil" of illusion, her life's purpose changed. She has now the "true sense" that "the divine is acting through this vessel" that is her entire being and "whatever personal agendas or motivations" she had before are now "largely irrelevant." In her view, "there's really nothing left to do. I'm not doing it anyway."

Thus, she is now doing less and by "doing less," Star is now able to achieve "far more" with "far more ease, and without the sense of trying or doing or efforting." She realizes that when she is "efforting and struggling, or having to exert a lot of willpower, it's mostly because" she has "taken something on that" she thinks she is "*doing.*" If effort comes in, she now knows that her "small I-consciousness" has "taken over."

Furthermore, she gained a deeper understanding about the meaning of life and death:

> *Once you see the perpetuity of the soul, the continuity of the soul, life and death don't actually mean a whole lot. They're just transitions just like from today to tomorrow. You go to bed and you wake up in the morning. You don't think it's so grand. I mean life and death . . . have the same flavor to it.*

By gaining a deeper knowing about the universe and consciousness in general, "all the other things like achievement and even financial security" became "in a certain way, entirely irrelevant."

Star's External Transformation: Behavior (IT)

Star's external behavior has changed along with the inner transformation outlined above. As shown in Figure 26, Star has become more open, more available, and more willing to live with uncertainty because life "often

"I only know how to be that in the moment. So you walk in the door and then you be in the moment. You're in presence and you sort of somehow know. The divine operates and you sort of know what to do next" (82)

Being present

"When we get too far into our heads and thinking we know the model, it actually stifles the true freedom which is to be in the presence. So it's almost like we need to go in and teach the presence" (82)

Being rather than doing

"That often doesn't necessarily include a full-scale knowing" (82)

Being open

"We're sort of planting seeds or flipping switches within those that were around, that might actually result in a spontaneous awakening or step change, or sort of a spontaneous opening of a new center within" (82)

Being a vessel for the divine

"I think as we each do that as teachers, we carry more and more and more light ourselves, that we will without any sort of conscious knowing of how we did it, because it's not really us, it's not that we're doing anything; but the divine will actually activate" (82)

External Transformation Behavior (IT)

Softness — "My friends say I've become a lot softer" (56)

Less serious

"I'm a little less serious now" (56)

"I still get gripped all the time, but I don't take things as seriously, so a little bit more spaciousness" (56)

Better sense of humor — "I have a little better sense of humor" (56)

Virtually no personal agenda

"My desire to have any sort of personal career is virtually gone. Like there's really nothing left to do. I'm not doing it anyway" (56)

"There's a true sense of like the divine is acting through this vessel so whatever personal agendas or motivations I had are sort of largely irrelevant." (56)

"They're kind of goofy. The more I try to do something based on my agenda, the more it becomes constricted and small" (56)

"I actually do far more stuff with far more ease"(56)

Less efforting

"There's still effort, but it's interesting, it comes when I forget. When I'm efforting and struggling, or having to exert a lot of willpower, it's mostly because I've taken something on that I think I'm doing. Like my small I-consciousness has sort of taken over" (56)

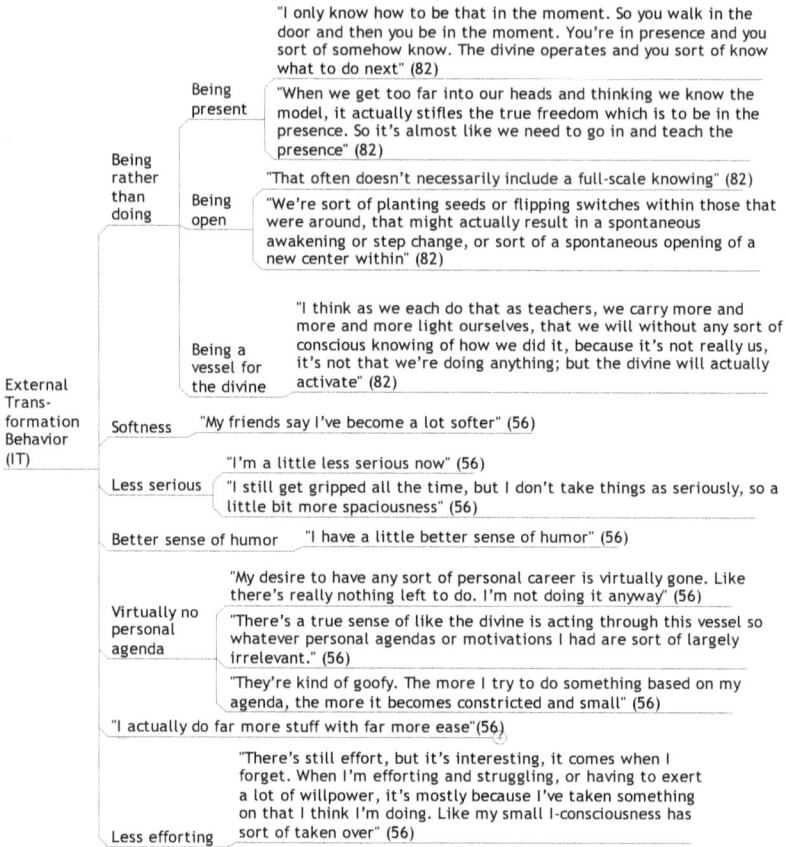

Figure 26. Star's external transformation: Behavior (IT).

doesn't necessarily include a full-scale knowing." Her external behavior is now a reflection of "a continual process of just opening into more presence, and to more awareness, and to more moment-by-moment attentiveness."

Through her changed behavior, Star is now able to achieve

Far more stuff with far more ease, and without the sense of try-ing or doing or efforting. I mean there's still effort, but it's in-teresting, it comes when I forget When I'm efforting and struggling, or having to exert a lot of willpower, it's mostly be-cause I've taken something on that I think I'm doing. Like my small I-consciousness has sort of taken over.

Star's Inter-Subjective Cultural Transformation and Impact (WE)

The cultural impact of Star's inner transformation can be recognized in many dimensions, some of which are represented in Figure 27.

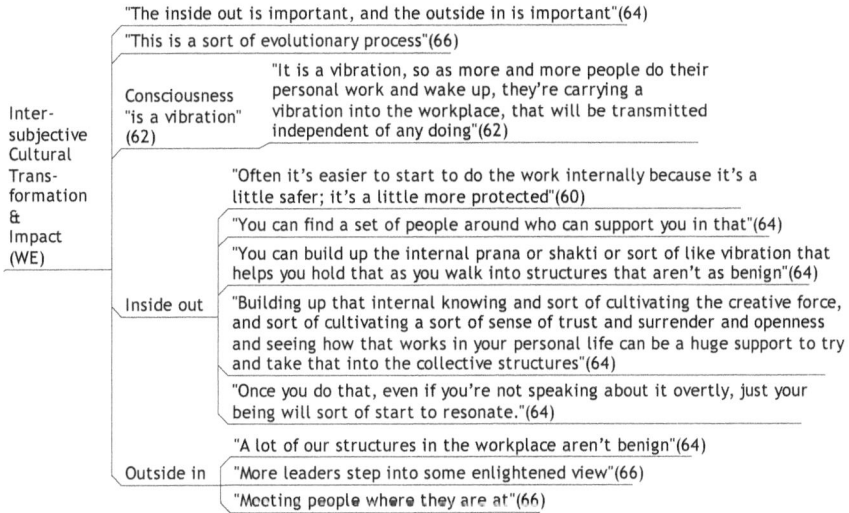

Figure 27. Inter-subjective and cultural impact of Star's inner transformation.

Her non-dual understanding of reality leads Star to encourage and honor both directions of transformation, the inside-out as well as outside-in, without preferring one over the other. However, based on her personal experience that confirms "a lot of our structures in the workplace aren't benign" when it comes to supporting people on their spiritual path, she would encourage individuals to begin doing "the work internally because it's a little safer; it's a little more protected." Once we have built up "that internal knowing" and cultivate "the creative force," we have a "sense of trust and surrender and openness" to higher levels of consciousness and see "how that works" in our "personal life" as well. Thus, we seem to be much better equipped to take our newly gained sense of self "into the collective structure."

As a consciousness leader, Star maintains that it is important to meet "people where they are" when in comes to supporting their development to higher levels of consciousness. Yet, as "more leaders step into some enlightened view" and "as more and more people do their personal work and wake-up, they're carrying a vibration into the workplace, that will be transmitted independent of any doing." In other words, she is convinced that transformation will eventually occur naturally because it is an "evolutionary process."

Systemic Change and Social/Environmental Inter-objective Impact (ITS) of Star

As she continues both her entrepreneurial and philanthropic work in the world, Star applies her newly gained consciousness leadership abilities as shown in Figure 28.

Being an integral thinker, Star is currently involved with building sustainable structures to bridge both the for-profit and not-for-profit organizations that are currently conflicted in their goals and missions. In using the chakra system to explain the differences between the two types of organizations, Star considers it difficult to "bring a new" consciousness model into "the old paradigm" because there are many components involved that are interrelated. There is "the goodness of the community, the planet, the ecosystem, [and] the environment" which must be balanced while maximizing "the value and the gain of [each] individual entity." In her assessment, one of the reasons for these difficulties comes from the fact that these organizations operate at different energetic levels. In her view, the old business model operates at "lower chakra structures" that work through a "top-down command and control, do as I say" model. This structure conflicts "with the relationship-oriented, heart-oriented human aspects of the higher chakras."

Star is still developing her integral strategy, however, in her opinion some of the new structures in the for-profit business could include the integration of the "good parts" of the old paradigm such as the "right use of power," "the right use of controls and measures and metrics," and the "discipline or structures or financial sustainability" with the energy of higher chakras. Yet, she knows from experience that "it's hard to take a first chakra company and jump into a fifth chakra company" and "quite

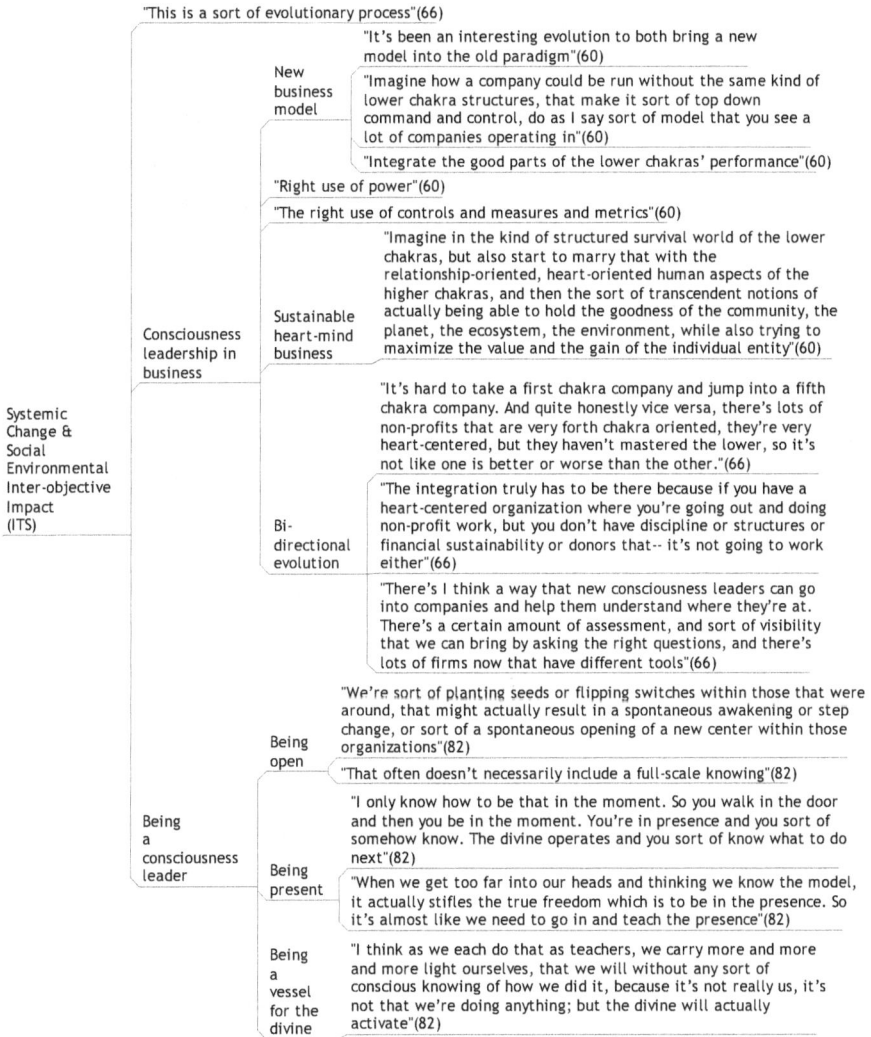

Figure 28. Systemic change and social/environmental inter-objective impact (ITS).

honestly vice versa." She knows that there are "lots of non-profits that are very forth-chakra oriented" and "very heart-centered," but that "haven't mastered the lower" chakras. She knows one is not "better or worse than the other," but a better structure must be developed:

I tried to take the old model into the new paradigm and that was like a double disaster. It's been an interesting evolution to both bring a new model into the old paradigm, and to try and imagine how a company could be run without the same kind of lower chakra structures, that make it sort of top-down command and control, do as I say sort of model that you see a lot of companies operating in.

Yet, consciousness leaders can play a major role in this systemic transformation because they "can go into companies and help them understand where they're at. There's a certain amount of assessment, and sort of visibility that we can bring by asking the right questions." In her opinion, consciousness leaders are "planting seeds or flipping switches" that might actually result in a "spontaneous awakening or step change, or sort of a spontaneous opening" to a new level of consciousness. However, it is important that we stay "open" and learn to live with the uncertainty that there is not always a "full-scale knowing" of what to do. Thus, the way of the consciousness leader is to be always present and recognize that "we carry more and more and more light ourselves," that we do the right thing without "conscious knowing of how we did it." In her view, "it's not really us, it's not that we're doing anything; but the divine" that "will actually activate" through our awakened consciousness.

In summary, the tipping point of Star's lasting transformation into a consciousness leader was her "peak experience" in India. Every line of development that characterized her prior evolution seems to have prepared her for experiencing "unity consciousness" as described by Grof (2006, pp. 34-39) and Yogananda (2002, pp. 142-148). Further research would have to be performed to find out how these particular states of unity consciousness have been transformed into permanent stages of consciousness. However, the fact that Star has apparently (a) embraced non-duality; (b) can live with paradoxes and be joyous, fulfilled, and serene; (c) accepts reality as is; (d) has transcended her rational mind to include ineffable dimensions; (e) cultivates her capacity for compassion, empathy, and unconditional love; (f) can live in the present and day by day; (g) she has stopped trying to solve, explain, and fix inner and outer conflicts; (h) has no fear of death; (i) is aware of language limitations and constructs; (j) lives a simple life of global service; and (h) is implementing the unification between the masculine and the feminine sides both in herself and her environment are strong indicators of postconventional stages of development as described by Alexander et al. (1990), Commons et al. (1984, 1990) Cook-Greuter (2004, 2005, 2008), and Torbert et al. (2004, 2008).

Pain is Part of Life—Suffering is a Choice

Common topic: Based on the premise that pain is part of life, but suffering is a choice, consciousness leaders have been able to use emotional, physical, spiritual, or other kinds of pain as an agent for awakening and deeper transformation.

Throughout history of humanity, people have been motivated by the need to avoid pain and the desire to gain pleasure (Aristotle, 2002; von Bertalanffy, 1969/2006; Capra, 2002; Eisler, 1995; Plato, 1938/1961). Individual pain can manifest itself physically, emotionally, mentally, or spiritually. Whether we are able to consciously choose our reaction to pain or not depends on various factors including the level of (a) *emotional* development (Goleman, 1995; Goleman et al., 2002; McCarthy, 2003a), (b) *physical* development (Leonard & Murphy, 1995; Murphy, 1993; Saron & Davidson, 1997), (c) *cognitive* development (Capra, 2002, Commons et al., 1984, 1990), (d) *ego* development (Cook-Greuter, 2005; Kegan, et al., 1990; Loevinger, 1977; Wilber, 2000c), (e) *spiritual* development (Alexander et al., 1990; Walsh, 1999; Wilber, 1999, 2000a, 2006), (f) *moral* development (Gilligan, 1982/1993; Kohlberg & Ryncarz, 1990), and the correlation between all of these lines of development (Alexander et al., 1990; Kegan et al., 1990; Koplowitz, 1990; Wilber, 2000c, 2006).

Whereas not everybody has equal access to the necessary resources that would enable an empowering action in response to pain, all research participants in the current study have used pain to transform and transcend the challenges posed by their lives.

Paloma's Individual Consciousness Leadership Profile with Transformational Characteristics

Paloma, who "was adopted at 3 days old," is a public figure, a very successful top business executive, a philanthropist, and a global activist who was educated at some of the most prestigious universities. Appendix D contains the mind map representing the key core topics and transformational profile that resulted from the interview conducted with Paloma.

Triggers and Context of Paloma's Transformation

Paloma's inner transformation was triggered by and evolved within the context of four major lines of development, the *physical, emotional, cognitive,* and *spiritual* (see Figure 29).

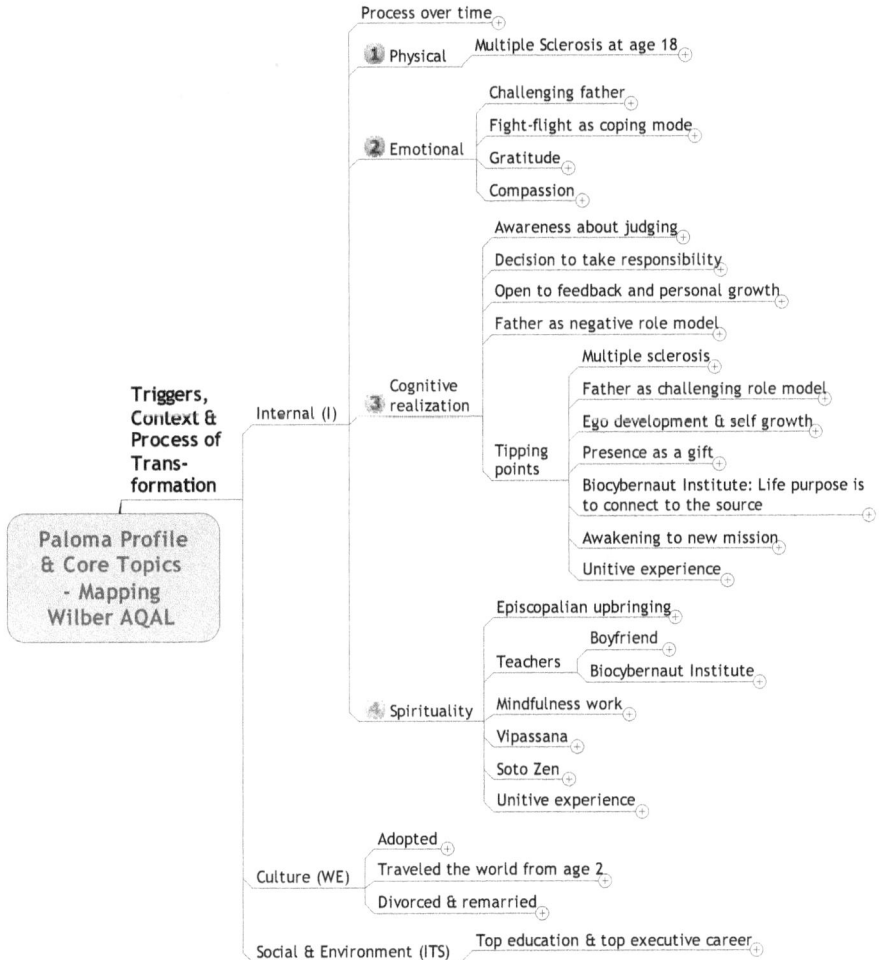

Figure 29. Triggers and context of Paloma's transformation.

Physically, she was diagnosed with MS at age 18 and because none of her family members knew how to deal with this disease "it was frightening, of course." She was "paralyzed and numb from the neck down and it stayed that way for the summer." When a family friend asked her "What is this disease here to teach you?" Paloma learned about "accountability" and "the greater metaphysical nature of the universe." Luckily, she "started getting gradually better" and today she is "very thankful for this disease" because it became her life-long "platform for self-health."

Emotionally, Paloma lives her life from a perspective of gratitude:

> *Gratitude that I feel to my parents who wanted a baby really badly and couldn't have one. To be wanted that much and then to have the opportunity to have the life I was given, to be brought into this family . . . to know that I was loved very deeply.*

Yet, she "didn't want to be like" her "father, who was fairly narcissistic" as well as "an "extraordinarily judgmental and critical human being." She said, "It was really, really difficult, enormously difficult to feel criticized and judged all the time." In her father's eyes, Paloma could not do many things to his liking including cutting "a tomato correctly" or driving "a car correctly." To be able to cope, she "would go into fight/flight with" her father and as a result, she "became, the defender of justice in what was right." She was "willing to stand up to him" and this helped her develop "a lot of leadership capacity or capabilities" from the earliest "age" because she "wasn't willing to take anything from anybody."

Spiritually, "the whole area of mindfulness and consciousness has been an evolution" for her beginning with the early 1990s. After "having grown up Episcopalian," she made her "own way" to figure out what she "believed from a spirituality perspective":

> *I discovered this whole area of mindfulness [through Soto Zen] and then Vipassana, which was even more powerful in terms of watching your thoughts without judging. I became very con-*

scious of how judgmental I was about myself and other people and I decided, I didn't want to be like that. I certainly didn't want to do that to myself and I didn't want to bring that into the work place.

In her view, this was her "first taste of really being accountable" for her "behavior."

The Tipping Point—The Awakening

Paloma's transformation was accelerated through several additional turning points and factors shown in Figure 30. The diagnosis of multiple sclerosis at age 18 was the

greatest gift to waken me to the sense of abundance and grati-tude for that which appears on the surface as something to be angry about rather than grateful for. And then deepening that, coupled with my relationship with my father, I've just found that these contrasting events in my life, if that's what you call them, a difficult father, a challenging health problem, and a willing-ness to be completely open and direct and not shove anything under the rug, that you really want to explore this. How can I control any of this? What can I do to make positive change in my life, not only for myself and the course of the disease, but then ultimately for other people and how I bring myself to relationships into the work-place, into my relationships, my intimate relationships and I would say that those are all the reasons why I got involved with the consciousness studies.

The love and gratitude that connected Paloma with her adoptive parents was overshadowed by a "narcissistic" father who "criticized and judged [her] all the time." As a result, she became "very conscious of not want-ing to be like that" and made her become "the defender of justice in what was right." Yet, her "fight/flight mode" of coping did not work for her and she searched for better solutions. That led her toward Buddhism that she

Multiple sclerosis

Father as challenging role model

"I was very clear I didn't want to be like, and that was my father, who was an extraordinarily judgmental and critical human being(18)

"It was really, really difficult, enormously difficult to feel criticized and judged all the time. I couldn't cut a tomato correctly. I couldn't drive a car correctly . . . 'Honey, here's how you do this properly'(36)

Ego development & self growth

"The sales manager or the coach that I was working with, was commenting sometimes that I came across really strong in certain meetings, or that I was using language that . . . made people feel like they were being condescended to or judged in some way"(16)

"I really wasn't aware that I was either being short with people or coming across the way that she was giving me feedback that I was coming across, so I think it took an individual that was working with me, who had the courage to share direct feedback with me and the willingness"(16)

"As I started to decide that I was responsible for how I am in this world and how I come across, that those two married together became the work for me was to be more mindful of how I am with other people, how I can come across"(16)

Presence as a gift

"It was around Christmas time and it was kind of a wish list of things that he could give his friends and family for Christmas on a, not a necessarily material level and he wished that he could give me the gift of presence"(32)

Biocybernaut Institute: Life purpose is to connect to the source

Awakening to new mission

"In the past, I was an individual contributor and it was about what I could do to go up the corporate ladder to succeed. And I realized in 1999 that that's not what I wanted at all and that wasn't my mission in life was to get the brass ring at some corporation"(104)

"I was much more entrepreneurial and I didn't want to go and do the corporate thing any longer and that was my decision to take a sabbatical and I then never went back"(104)

Unitive experience

"I had this image during one meditation that when we sit on our cushion, the technological equivalent is like having our i-pod or our cell phone in a docking station, that we are being plugged in to receive an energy that's greater than we are"(94)

"When we can stop the chatter in the monkey-mind of our brain long enough to allow the spirit and the life force that is who we are to shine through, then we are our most authentic self"(94)

"That's when we shine through"(94)

"There is this greater source that we're all connected to, that no one is apart from that, that my place, or part of my reason for being here is to stay connected to that source myself so that I can become a light for others to help them find their lights"(94)

"It was just a recognition that this is grace"(94)

Tipping points

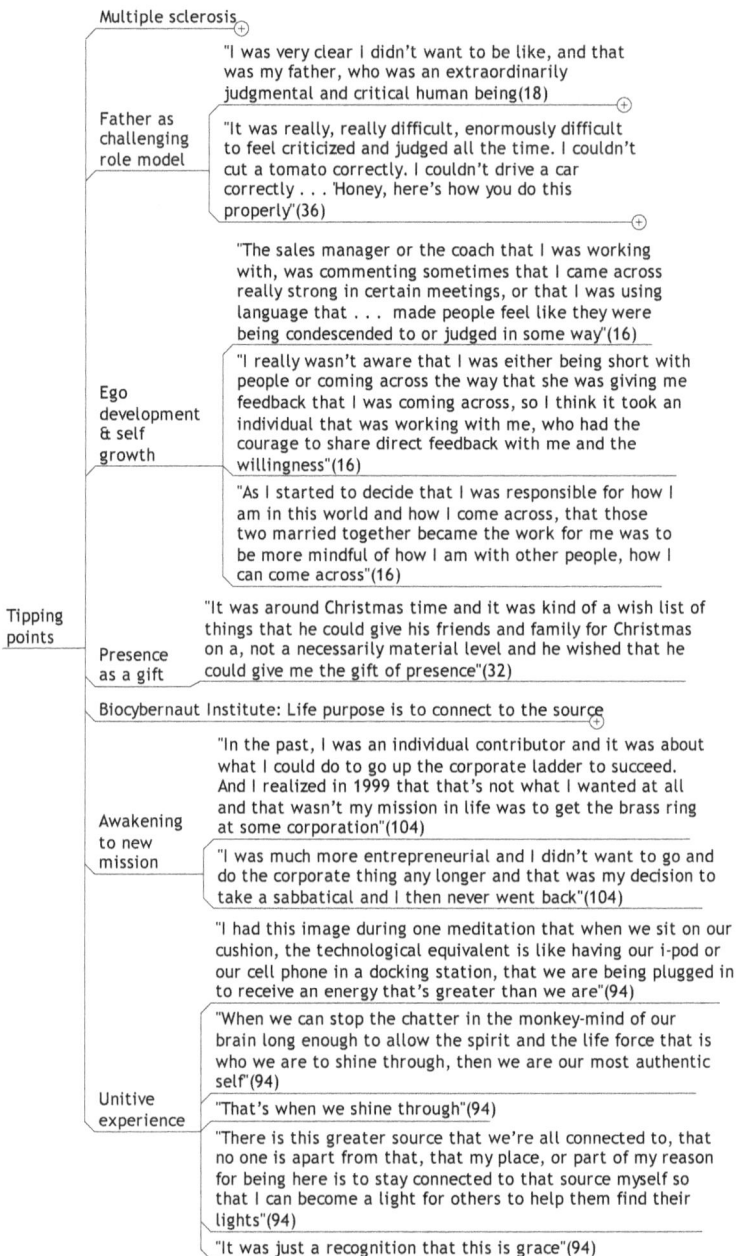

Figure 30. Paloma's transformational tipping points.

regards as "a philosophy more than a religion of living life in a way that you're responsible for your actions, [where] there is a cause and effect for how you are in the world. So a deep desire to be the best human being that I can be [arose] and I decided that it was all about love."

At the peak of her career, Paloma realized that it was not her "mission in life to get the brass ring at some corporation." It was then that she "discovered" her "truth," which was that she "was much more entrepreneurial" and she "didn't want to go and do the corporate thing any longer." Thus, she decided "to take a sabbatical" and she "never went back" to Corporate America.

Through neuro feedback work and meditation practice, Paloma identified her life's mission and realized her new purpose, which was to "be connected to the source"

> *So that I could help others connect to theirs as well, to their source and that's what I'm here to do. . . . I had this image during one meditation that when we sit on our cushion, the technological equivalent is like having our ipod or our cell phone in a docking station, that we are being plugged in to receive an energy that's greater than we are. And when we can stop the chatter in the monkey-mind of our brain long enough to allow the spirit and the life force that is who we are to shine through, then we are our most authentic self. That's when we shine through. And I'm not doing this. I'm being done and it was just a recognition that this is grace. It's a perfect word, that I'm just a conduit or vehicle for whatever I'm supposed to do. . . . This knowledge, which is deeper than just cognitive knowledge, that there is this greater source that we're all connected to, that no one is apart from that, that my place, or part of my reason for being here is to stay connected to that source myself so that I can become a light for others to help them find their lights.*

Structural Changes and Impact of Paloma's Transformation

Paloma's transformation affected all the components of her life internally (I), externally (IT), inter-objectively/culturally (WE), and socially/environmentally (ITS).

The interior transformation (I) represented in Figure 31 is characterized by six major lines of development: *spiritual, self/ego line, cognitive, moral, physical,* and the *emotional* line of development.

Spiritually, Paloma continues to evolve supported by her daily meditation and yoga practice. Furthermore, she uses "Holosynch" and "HeartMath" as additional tools to help her stay present, mindful, open, and detached. She finds "that the mindfulness work" supports her to stay "centered in the present moment, and to realize the higher order of what's most important, which is to maintain the peace, sometimes at all costs." Her regular spiritual practice has helped her "not being so attached to the outcome and living life with open hands as opposed to grasping at things."

Through her spiritual evolution, Paloma has reached a level of *egoic mastery* and *self-identity* that is characterized by several components including higher self-confidence. She said, "I feel in my bones that I'm more comfortable with who I am." She has a" higher sense of "accountability," greater "courage," feels more "kind" and "compassionate," has an increased ability to "let go of outcome," as well as a "deeper understanding that life is a journey." She knows that life is "about service," and that "there's nothing short-term about it, that we're in this for the long-term." In addition, she lives in a mindset of abundance and does not come "from a place of either desperation or lack, and so it's helped not only me, but this is who I am and I bring this to my sales team and this is how they see me with clients and interacting with prospects and so fort" (see Figure 31).

Cognitively, Paloma continues to evolve through her integral life practice, focuses on being "present," "authentic," and "open." She has gained

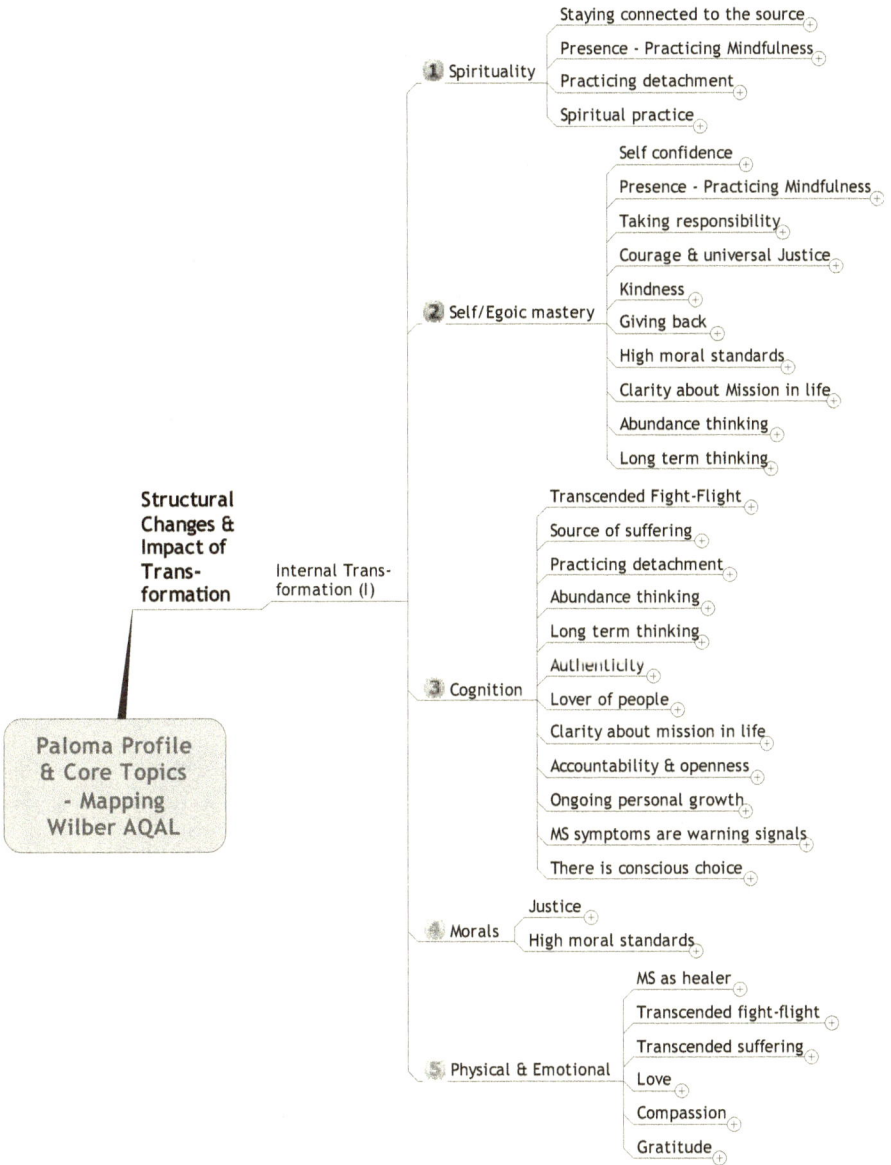

Figure 31. Paloma's structural changes and interior (I) impact.

a deeper understanding about the source of suffering because in her view "there are no tragedies; it's how you look at it." Furthermore, she realized that the "apparent suffering on the surface" can "turn out to be the greatest gifts." She believes that "it's our challenge and sometimes our choice on how we view" suffering. Her purpose in life is "about service" and about "connecting with the source so that" she "can help others connect as well."

Emotionally, Paloma, who lives in deep "gratitude," "joy," and appreciation for the gift of life, has been able to transcend to a large degree her "fight and flight" behavior and the pain associated with her father. She said, "I'm not always perfect with it but it certainly helped in minimizing or really curtailing the fight/flight mode that I was set up for from age 3."

Moreover, Paloma took advantage of her father's challenge to develop a *high standard on moral and justice* that helps her "stand up for what's right," take "a stand for what" she believes in, as well as put her "neck out and do the right thing whether it's popular or not" (see Figure 31).

Physically, Paloma, who is an athlete, is using her multiple sclerosis as a "platform for self-health" because MS has become her "early warning signal" for stress.

As could be expected, Paloma's internal transformation has had a significant impact on her external behavior (IT) and in her cultural and social environment (see Figure 32). In her view, she has become a better leader because "what used to be about [business] numbers is now" about "being centered, and meditating, and letting things go, and breathing, and values." As a result, she is convinced that "everybody individually as well as collectively" has become "much more successful."

In summary, there are several lines of development that characterize Paloma's interior evolution as a consciousness leader. *Physically*, she was able to use her body as a vehicle for awakening (Murphy, 1993) and to transcend the life-threatening aspects of multiple sclerosis (Kolb & Whishaw, 2003). As a result, she is not only leading a normal life today but also has become a role model and a consciousness leader. Paloma was able to overcome her greatest challenges by going beyond traditional med-

Internal Trans- formation (I)

Self confidence

Presence - Practicing mindfulness

Courage & universal justice

External
Transformation
Behavior
(IT)

Kindness

Giving back

High moral standards

Awakening to new mission

Attitude of abundance

Accountability & openness

Practicing detachment

Abundance thinking

Better leader

Long term thinking

Structural
Changes &
Impact of
Trans-
formation

Consciousness
leadership

Meditation and number
crunching

Greater success

Paloma Profile
& Core Topics
- Mapping
Wilber AQAL

Inter-
subjective
Cultural
Transformation
& Impact
(WE)

Being of service

Bringing the best in others

Courage

Better relationships

Father figure

Lover of people

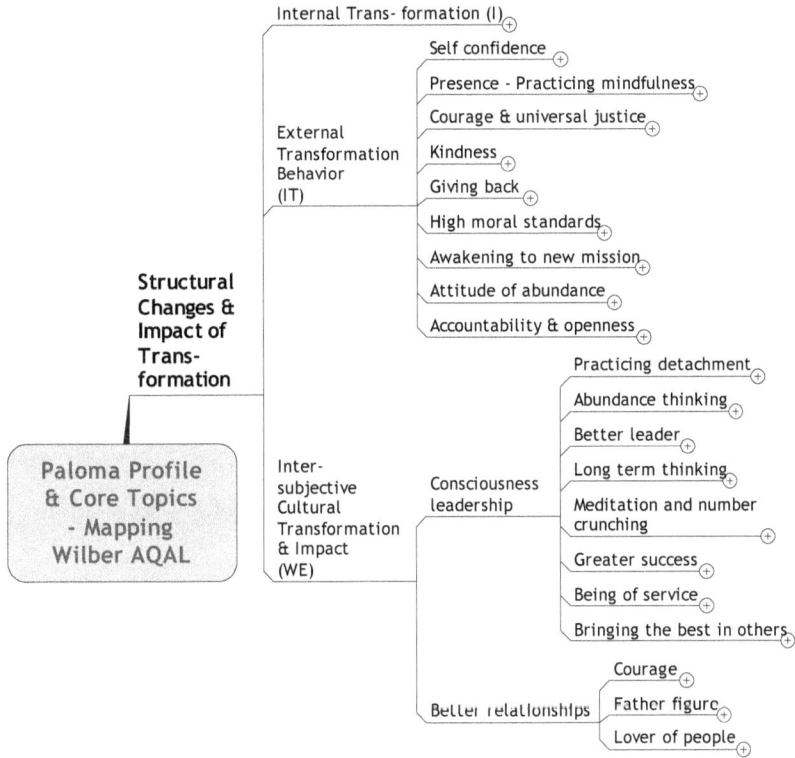

Figure 32. Paloma's cultural (WE) and behavioral impact (IT).

ical approaches, understanding the hidden messages MS carried for her, and by beginning to live her life from an integral perspective (Wilber, 1997). She continued her journey by addressing the emotional issues related to her narcissistic father (Barlow & Durand, 2005) and by developing a strong sense for morals and justice (Gilligan, 1982/1993; Kegan et al., 1990). Her intelligence, curiosity, openness, sense of accountability, willingness to be present and grow in all areas of life (Beck, 1976; Gardner, 1993; Wilber, 1997), guided Paloma early on toward meditation and mindfulness work (Walsh & Vaughan, 1993). Through her own integral life practice (Wilber, 2006, pp. 202-205), her self-confidence increased along with her sense of purpose, which is to be of service to humanity (Beck & Cowan, 1996; Rooke & Torbert, 2005, 2008).

Further research will have to be performed for a more accurate assessment. However, based on the phenomenological observations made through the current research, Paloma's (a) genuine joy, gratefulness, and life affirming attitude; (b) her willingness to live "life with open hands"; (c) the simplicity of her unassuming presence; (d) her enthusiasm for turning inside when looking for answers; (e) her ability to live life in the moment; (f) her sense of detachment from the outcome; (g) her abundant being; (h) her feeling of connectedness with the source of creation; and (i) her ability to transcend and turn her multiple sclerosis into an opportunity for self-growth and service to humanity are strong indicators for a later stage of ego and self-development; one that goes beyond the postconventional stage (Alexander et al., 1990; Commons et al., 1990; Commons et al., 1984; Cook-Greuter, 2005, 2008; Torbert et al., 2004, 2008).

Shadows, Traps, and Golden Chains

Common topic: Living in the spotlight of public lives, consciousness leaders face the challenge of having to live up to the demands of external success at the expense of their interiorities. Therefore, facing their shadows has become a decisive component not only of their interior transformation but also of their ongoing consciousness leadership ability.

In analytical psychology, the term "shadow" (Vaughan, 2000, pp. 49-52) refers to unconscious, often archetypal (Jacobi, 1959; Stein, 2004), aspects of the personality that have been neglected, rejected, and repressed (Fadiman & Frager, 2002, pp. 98-100) because they do not seem to comply with our persona and social standards (Vaughan, 2005). Therefore, not developing the capacity to face the shadow and reclaim what has been denied, repressed, or disintegrated from our personality, leads to vulnerability. We risk to become trapped by not only the psychopathologies of our own mind, but also those of the collective shadows (Vaughan, 2005).

Thus, the willingness to confront the various manifestations of the shadow such as fear, anxiety, inflated egos, self-doubts, and judgmental attitudes present an opportunity for ego transcendence and self-growth (Cook-Greuter, 2008; Dacey & Travers, 2006; Erikson, 1980; Loevinger, 1977).

All consciousness leaders researched in the current study have evolved and been transformed by facing their shadow sides. This process was triggered either by exaggerated social conditioning, exceptional human experiences, pain, disease, or simply through personal decision. The willingness to face the shadow paid off in terms of higher levels of joy, happiness, fulfillment, and ultimately greater success that occurred with less effort. These leaders have understood that in confronting their greatest fears they have the opportunity to free themselves and grow toward higher meaning in life.

Further research would have to be performed to find out to what degree the shadow work and altered states of consciousness experienced by the research participants lead to the permanent structural changes (Wilber,

2001, p. 92). However, based on observation, it would be fair to assume that these people have been transformed at a structural level because once we have a glimpse of our true identity unencumbered by our personal or public projections, we cannot turn back and must continue on the path to awakening (Progoff, 1973; Vaughan, 2000; Watts, 1989).

Stan's Individual Consciousness Leadership Profile with Transformational Characteristics

Stan is a well-known public figure, a published author, a serial entrepreneur, a philanthropist, an award winning financial expert, and a self-made millionaire who grew up in a predominantly Jewish and Italian community on Long Island, New York. He received an outstanding education from elite universities and spent 20 years on Wall Street where he "was able to enjoy the game of it." Appendix D contains the mind map representing the key core topics and transformational profile that resulted from the interview performed with Stan.

Triggers and Context of Stan's Transformation

The context of Stan's transformation is characterized by several major lines of development including the *cognitive, egoic, emotional,* and *spiritual* (see Figure 33). *Cognitively,* he was very aware of the context and triggers of his social conditioning that lead to his egoic transformation:

> *I was getting enough of an ego stroke. . . and we've been conditioned to allow it to rule our lives. That's what we've been conditioned, to just do the superficial, can't be too rich or too thin model of life. I was in a good profession, I was being respected, I was buying a house in one of the highest-priced neighborhoods in the world, blah blah blah blah. So it was very easy to settle for that especially . . . when we are so encouraged to do so [because] we get so much*

"Defining moments" (22) & process over time

Old Belief System
- Money makes you happy
- "You're good" (36) because you made money

"Ego stroke" (36) prevented earlier transformation

"Good profession" (36)

Influenced by "mob psychology" (26)

Comfort prevented change

Superficial social conditioning

Cognitive Realization (1)
- Social recognition & reinforcement
- Noticed collective insanity
- Noticed absurdity of the money game
- Missing true fulfillment
- Tipping Point

Enjoyed the financial game

"Slow start" (24)

Fear & anxiety

Happiness depended upon stock market behavior

Emotional (2)
- Group Healing
- Not allowing feelings
- Worried about finances
- Feeling comfortable prevented change
- Courage & permission to face all pain

Exceptional Human Experience

Spiritual (3)
- Shadow Work
- New level of consciousness

Internal (I)

Triggers, Context & Process of Transformation

Stan Profile & Core Topics - Mapping Wilber AQAL

External Behavior (IT)

"I was very financially driven"(22) on Wall Street
- Enjoyed the financial game
- Purchased expensive real estate
- Worried about finances
- Wearing coat of armor
- Slaying financial dragons
- Asking essential questions
- Facing dark night of the soul
- Open for group healing
- Not allowing feelings
- Courage & permission to face all pain

Culture (WE)
- Jewish upbringing in New York
- Outstanding education
- Wife diagnosed with cancer

Social & Environment (ITS)
- Financial recognition and success on Wall Street
- 1 failed marriage & death of 2. wife
- Purchased expensive real estate
- Social recognition & reinforcement

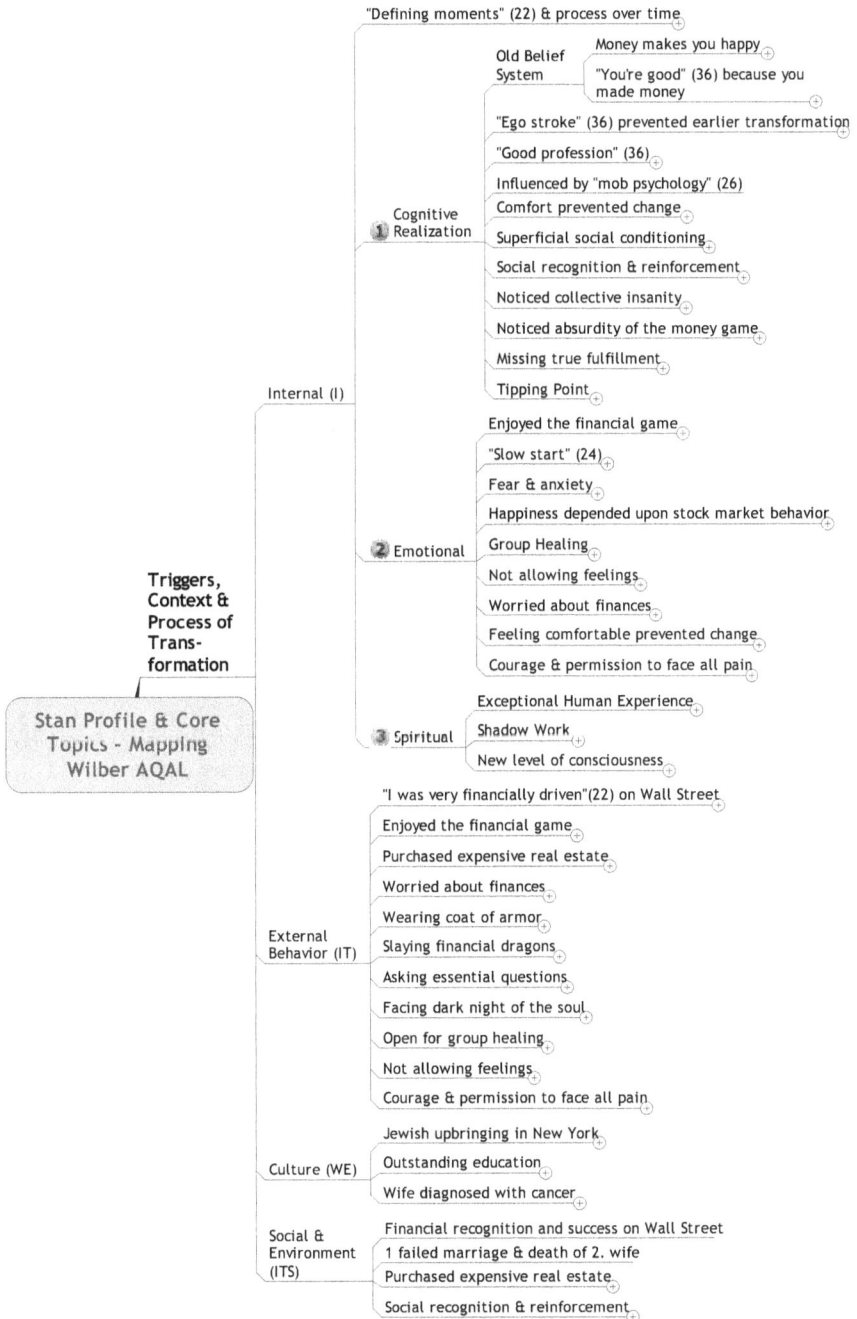

Figure 33. Triggers and context of Stan's internal transformation.

socialized reinforcement and approval that because you've made money you're good on some level.

Before his transformation, Stan subscribed to the belief system in which

You make your money, you live happily ever after, you buy a few toys, you have some good times, people respect you, you have your what-ever, American dream thing, and . . . you just fade off into the sun-set on your yacht somewhere.

In addition to social acknowledgment and external success, Stan as-sumes that his transformation was accelerated by (a) the fact that he "was too comfortable" and "had to have a very dramatic circumstance" in his life to "wake" him; (b) "the mob psychology" of Wall Street telling him whether he was "having a good day or not," which on a profound level he knew "was completely absurd and no way" to live his life; (c) the environ-ment because he "wasn't alone" because "the smartest people in the world [were] doing the same thing. It seemed to be standard operating procedure for this thing called human being, at least a successful one"; (d) his old be-lief system and "ego strokes" with respect to money as the key measure-ment for being "good" and living "happily ever after because you made your money"; and (e) the attachment "to being in the [financial] busi-ness." At the same time,

I noticed that my relationships were not as fulfilling as they could be, I knew there was more to life and I could certainly observe people who had hundreds of millions of dollars to their name or more not really seeming to be any happier, and in many cases noticing how the money and the possessions were owning them.

Emotionally, Stan "stayed up nights worrying" about his "financial con-dition" and could not help but allow "the market" to make him "crazy . . . . anxious and filled with worry" no matter how much wealth he had accu-mulated. What kept him on Wall Street was his ability to "embrace the un-known" and the fact that he "was able to enjoy" his work because "it was like the ultimate video game, picking stocks and watching the screens and seeing the moves and buy, sell or whatever it was." His capacity to live with "the unknown" enabled him "to navigate and enjoy the stock market business" for a long time because in his view "if you're not comfortable with the unknown in the stock market go somewhere else. It's the great unknown. It's one of the great mysteries."

Spiritually, Stan grew up in a Jewish environment, yet he questioned traditional definitions and used the word consciousness to describe the "defining moments" of his own awakening and transformation (see Figure 34). He "saw the hollowness" of the money game and his "consciousness started to shift" as he "began to ask" questions. Eventually, he "made quantum leaps in consciousness" and in his view it all comes "down to faith and it's really faith in my consciousness ultimately."

The Tipping Point—Facing the Shadow

Figure 34 summarizes Stan's "decisive moments" that represent the tipping points of his transformation beginning with his wife's terminal disease.

When his "wife got diagnosed with cancer at the peak" of his "financial success" it "threw" his "life upside down in terms" of what he "thought the script" of his "life was supposed to be." The decision to join his wife in a group healing session with a shaman lead to a "holotropic breathing exercise" during which Stan was willing to address the most important question for him at the time, namely "Why do I allow the [financial] market going against me to make me so crazy, to make me so anxious and filled with worry?"

Knowing that at the root of his anxiety was "self-doubt," Stan allowed the holotropic breathing exercise to move him even deeper and he found himself invoking the spirit of his "father who had passed a couple years earlier." Stan requested more help:

> *After some period of time of this deep breathing and the tribal drums and being completely shifted, all of a sudden I was a 4-year-old boy sitting in my father's lap feeling so safe, so loved and so nurtured*

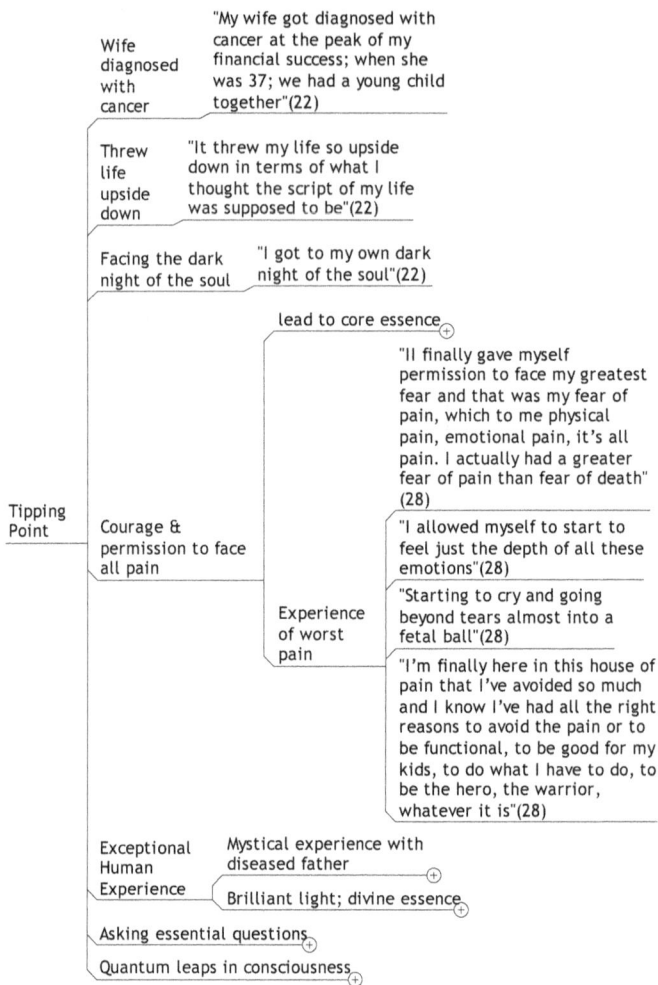

Figure 34. Stan's tipping point of transformation.

. . . and I just started literally crying tears of joy to have this re-connection and have it feel so physical as well as so just emotion-ally vulnerable and beautiful. I asked him, "Where do I get my self-doubt from?" and he said back to me, "It's not yours. It's mine." So I was ready for the follow-up question: "Well, would you take it back?" At first nothing happened and . . . all of a sud-den I felt a lightning bolt moved through my body and I observed

that my body was shaking literally uncontrollably like being elec-
trocuted . . . Something dislodged from my system.

This exceptional human experience that he called "mystical," had a significant impact on Stan. Although he "had plenty of moments of self-doubt
or questioning self-confidence [after that]. . . . [but] it has never been as
severe or as long lasting as a result of that one leap in consciousness."

In addition, Stan cognized that his experience must have involved an
"outside [divine] guidance of some kind." The same "guidance" that
seemed to have been present again a couple of years later when he "was in
the throes of grief about" his wife who was dying of cancer.

The Dark Night of the Soul

While his wife was dying of cancer, Stan was "literally slaying financial
dragons" every day, "wearing that coat of armor to be functional for everybody." Furthermore, he had to take care of his infant child at night and
could not allow himself "to feel the sadness, the grief . . . the disappointment . . . anger, and perilousness" of his situation. This went on until "one
weekend" when he was at home alone and could finally give himself "permission" to face his "greatest fear," namely the "fear of pain," which was
greater than his "fear of death":

> *I allowed myself to start to feel just the depth of all these emotions*
> *and I remember starting to cry and going beyond tears almost*
> *into a fetal ball, just really tight and wound up saying, "Okay.*
> *I'm finally here in this house of pain that I've avoided so much*
> *and I know I've had all the right reasons to avoid the pain or to*
> *be functional, to be good for my kids, to do what I have to do, to*
> *be the hero, the warrior, whatever it is," and said, "Okay. I'm fi-*
> *nally here. Bring it on." And I don't know how long I was in that*
> *position. It could have been hours. I think it was hours and at*
> *some point as I asked, "And what else is there? What else do you*
> *have?"*

The courage to face his greatest nightmare turned into a "major leap in consciousness" in which he experienced his true "essence" as "warm, brilliant light."

> *After a while that which looked—with my eyes absolutely clenched shut looked so black and dark after a while I started seeing—literally seeing pinholes of light and the whole fabric of that darkness started to shred until it shredded completely and there was just nothing literally but a feeling, and actually I could see it with my eyes closed, of warm, brilliant light. And I knew without question that that is in fact my essence . . . that nobody can take from me what I am . . . and knowing the only reason I was able to experience so deep, intense pain is 'cause I loved so deeply. That was such a source of relief to me to have that knowing that that experience was a major leap in consciousness for me and I very much know the truth of that. It's present in all moments.*

Structural Change and Impact of Stan's Transformation

Stan's "mystic" experiences were major turning points that exacerbated his already active internal (I) transformation at the *cognitive, emotional,* and *egoic* levels (see Figure 35).

Cognitively, Stan arrived at a deeper understanding about his own essence that is independent from external reality. At a very "profound" level he knows that "nobody can take from me what I am." He is now able to embrace "the unknown," even deeper than before, live in the "present" moment, and give up "resistance" to change because he recognized that the "level" of resistance determines "our degree of pain." Through his transformational experiences, Stan arrived at a "profound knowing" that his "needs will always be met," and that "fear of failure" is not "sustainable." He has now "less self-doubt," and can remain "truthful and undefended in the process" of interacting with other people and life in general. Although he recognized and is grateful for the

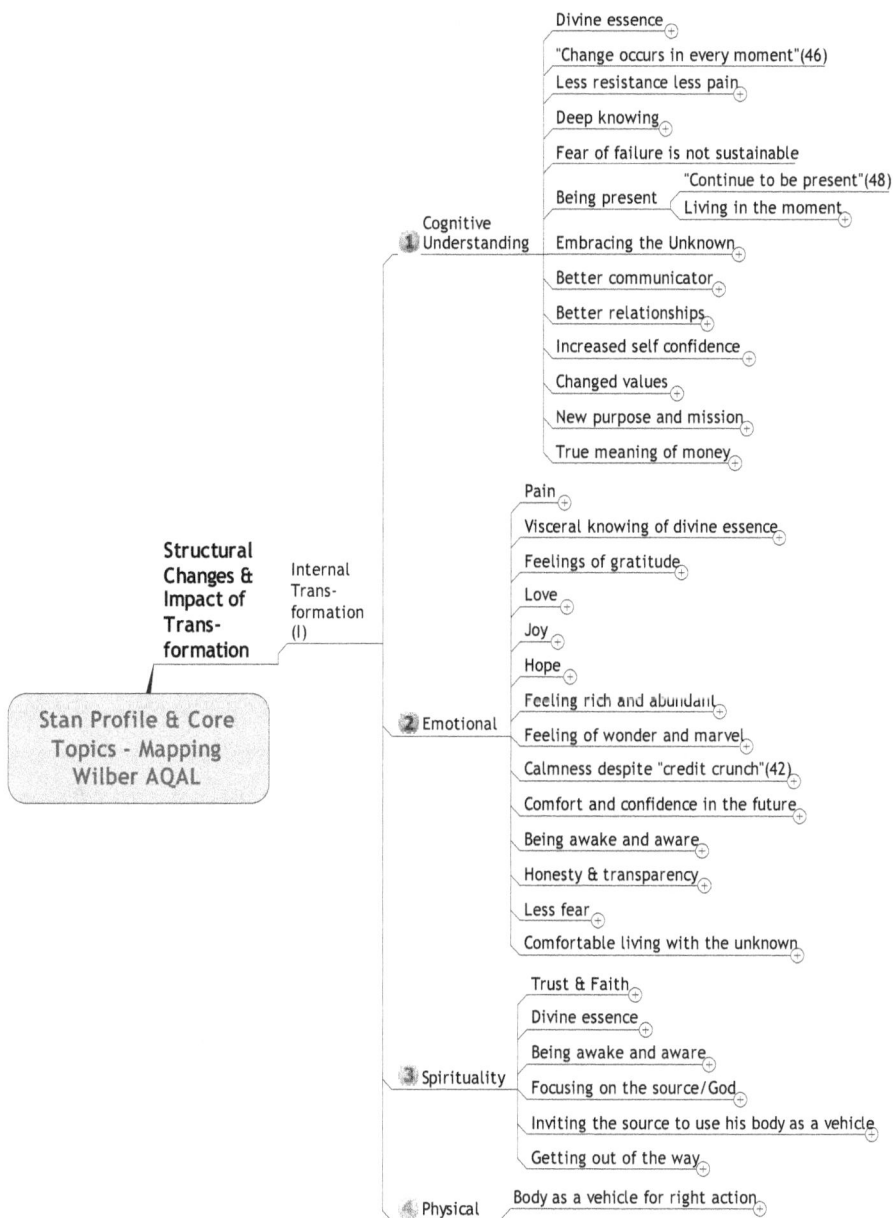

Figure 35. Structural changes and impact of Stan's internal transformation.

fact that the money he made "helped to finance and allow for" his personal growth, his entire attitude toward money changed because he "saw the hollowness of it." He realized that money "wasn't buying" him what he "really wanted."

Emotionally, Stan experienced a major "shift in consciousness" that enabled him to transcend his original "fear of pain," let go of self-doubt, and "feel absolutely grateful and joyful to be alive in this moment." His newly gained "energy of joy and hope . . . feels very rich and abundant." His transformation was so profound that it keeps him balanced despite the current "credit crunch." Although he can "certainly see the opportunity to go to a place of intense fear" he chooses not go there and is surprised by his tranquility. Not only that, but through his newly gained ability to stay "awake and aware," he is in a much better position to focus his "attention and intention" on what he needs to do to solve his problems with "complete honesty and transparency."

Spiritually, Stan has grown to have "absolute trust and faith" in "consciousness" and to focus his "attention on [the] source" that he calls "God for lack of a better word." He views his physical body as a vehicle for God and in his worldview the "source [is] literally breathing through me as me, using my body [as a] vehicle for its pleasure and its experience of this material plane, of this 3-D plane." He now sees that all he needs to do to fulfill his life's mission is to "get out if the way":

> *It feels wonderful to be of ultimate service to that which is all that is ultimately unembodied . . . I'm its own dream in a way and I'm just inviting it in to play with this vehicle as much as possible and to the extent I invite in others who can respond on some level, even if it's not putting their finger on exactly what it is but being attracted to the energy.*

At the *Behavioral* (IT) level, represented in Figure 36, Stan ended up "leaving the money management field because it became clear to" him that he was "here to do something other than to help extremely wealthy people become wealthier." Instead, he recognized his true mission in life,

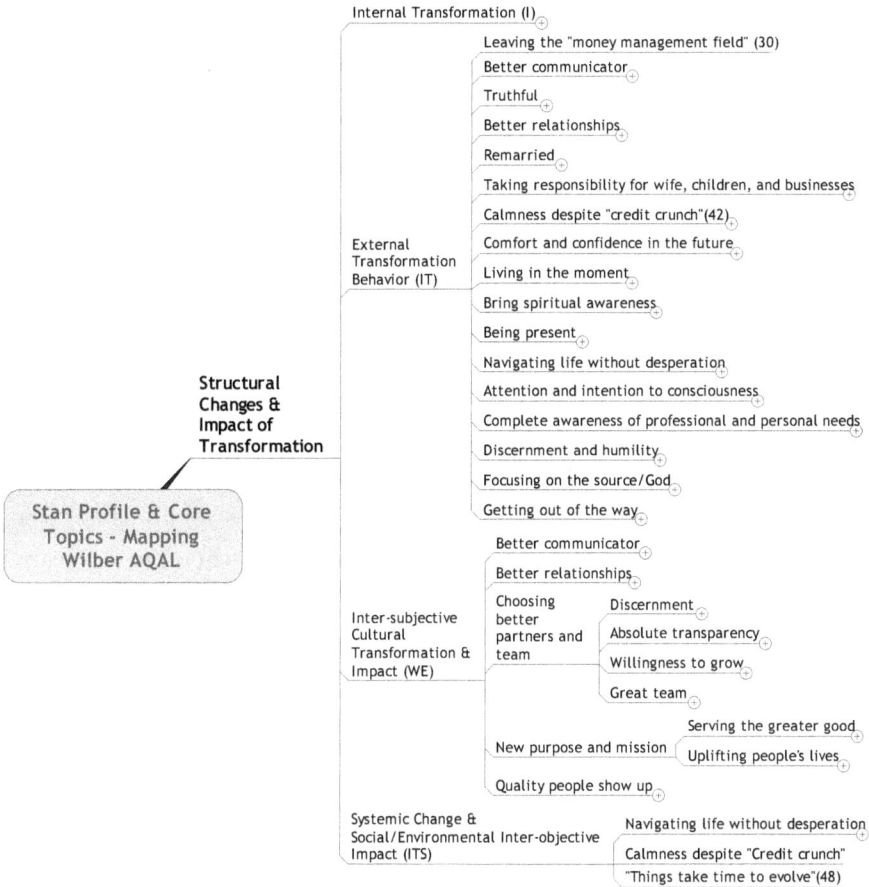

Figure 36. Behavior (IT), cultural (WE) and social impact (ITS) of Stan's transformation.

which is "to be of greater service to a greater good," uplift "people's lives," and help them connect with their "profound joy . . . as a possibility for their own existence."

Culturally (WE), Stan, who remarried, became "more truthful in all" his communications. His relationships improved "as a result of being truthful and undefended in the process" and "amazing people show up" in his life. Furthermore, his leadership teams and businesses have improved as well.

Socially (ITS), Stan is committed to "help raise consciousness on the planet" and realizes that "things take time to evolve." Therefore, after his major transformation, he is more calm and able to "navigate life without desperation" because he knows that "it's a game of consciousness." All he does now is his "best" and trying to "stay out of the way" (see Figure 36).

In summary, Stan's internal transformation into a consciousness leader is characterized by several lines of development including the *cognitive* (Commons et al., 1984; Commons et al., 1990; Koplowitz, 1984), *egoic* (Cook-Greuter, 2005, 2008; Loevinger, 1977), *emotional* (Goleman, 1995; Kegan et al., 1990; Wilber, 2000a), and *spiritual* (Fowler, 1995; White, 1998).

When faced with his wife's terminal disease, Stan had the courage to challenge his own belief systems and the prevailing "mob psychology" about money along with its traps and golden chains. His enthusiasm for personal growth, his courage and ability to live with uncertainty, and his willingness to "embrace the unknown," all of which served him so well on Wall Street, turned out to be also his greatest strengths when the time came to face his worst fears and his shadow self (Vaughan, 2005).

Through his extraordinary human experiences (Cardena, Lynn, & Krippner, 2000; Grof, 2006), Stan had a "quantum leap in consciousness," was able to transcend his traditional Jewish upbringing along with his self-doubt and fear, experience his authentic Self as "divine essence," and become more aware of his true nature. He discovered that "on a deep, profound level we are energy; we are energetic beings." By questioning his old values he found not only unshakable joy and happiness, but a new mission and meaning in his life (Cook-Greuter, 2005; Fowler, 1995; Kegan et al., 1990; Wilber, 2000a).

Today, Stan sees himself of "ultimate service" to and as a "vehicle" for the "divine" energy. In all humility, he regards himself as a catalyst for change and his mission in life is to "be of greater service to a greater good." He feels "profound joy" in being "truly dedicated to communicate even nonverbally this energy of joy and hope [that] in many ways feels very rich and abundant" and which "money can't buy."

Stan's transformation becomes obvious also from his use of language (Cook-Greuter, 2008). He seems aware of his constructs and projections, as well as the limitations of language to express himself. For example, instead of saying human being, he said, "this thing called human being." Another indication of his transformed language habit is his new definition and questioning of our definition of poverty. He said:

> *If you feel, you could live on one fish a day out by a beach some-where, well, then maybe that's not being poor. Maybe it's just not having money. It has to do with the self-judgment around failure and the self-judgment around not achieving goals.*

Further research and quantitative tests (Cook-Greuter, 2004; Torbert et al., 2004) would have to be performed to reach more clarity, however, all of the above qualities paired with Stan's deep-seated sense of security that goes well beyond his old identity, his new non-demanding way of relating to people and businesses, his language habit, and his unassuming presence and humility are all indicative of postconventional levels of development (Alexander et al., 1990; Commons et al., 1990; Cook-Greuter, 2008; Koplowitz, 1984; Wilber, 2000c).

The Coming Out Party

Common topic: Eventually, all consciousness leaders have arrived at a point in their lives when their interiority had to be reconciled with their exteriority. Not living in line with their interiorities was no longer tolerable and they felt morally and ethically obliged to come out, speak up, and live with the consequences.

Research indicates that ethics, morals, and spirituality are increasingly more important in business environments as people decide to reconcile the dilemma between what they feel inside and what's expected of them in a business setting (Klein & Izzo, 1999; Kofman, 2006; Marques et al., 2007; Mitroff & Denton, 1999; Pauchant, 2002; Secretan, 2006; Toms, 1997; Wilber, 2006). The present phenomenological research performed with consciousness leaders validates existing research. Although further testing and analysis would have to be performed to arrive at a more concrete assessment, the current study shows how consciousness leaders have grown through the pain of separation and eventually were able to become more integrated. It confirms that deeply fulfilled and self-actualizing individuals lead from the heart because they recognized and transcended the need for self-care as a premise for caring for others as one of the primary tasks in their lives (Maslow et al., 1998).

Moreover, even if their original motivation to grow was driven by *selfish/preconventional* motives (Dacey & Travers, 2006), these people have over time outgrown and transcended the *conventional* stages of care (Kohlberg & Ryncarz, 1990), and arrived at the *postconventional* level of *universal* care as a later stage of moral development (Commons et al., 1990; Gilligan, 1982/1993; Kegan et al., 1990; Kohlberg & Ryncarz, 1990; Wilber, 2000c). Unfortunately, narcissism, low morals, and greed have been and still are the predominant components in the current business paradigm (Harman & Hormann, 1993; Mitroff & Denton, 1999; Pauchant, 2002; Paulson, 2002; Secretan, 2006; Toms, 1997).

Therefore, business people in general and top executives in particular have much to lose if they decide to live in line with their moral and ethical beliefs. Yet, the consciousness leaders researched in the current study show what it took, how they did it, and what were the consequences of their integration.

Topaz's Individual Consciousness Leadership Profile with Transformational Characteristics

Topaz is not only one of the most respected top executives, but also a well-known book author, a public figure, an academic teacher, and a philanthropist. He has been trained at prestigious universities from which he also holds a doctorate degree. Appendix D contains the mind map representing the AQAL structure and the core topics of Topaz's transformation into a consciousness leader.

Triggers, Context, and Process of Topaz' Overall Transformation

Topaz regards his transformation into a consciousness leader as "a messy" and "never ending process" with "jagged edges" because in his view we "always smack up against our own limitations" (see Figure 37).

He had his first encounter with authentic *spirituality* as a child when he "loved" serving the "6:00 a.m. Mass" because "there was something very special about being in a quiet church in the early morning." He was "drawn" to the "feeling of peace" and the "feeling of there being something more . . . to life" than the obvious reality. This "profound" feeling of "knowing something without having any other way of knowing it" never left him and guided him throughout his life. Topaz had a "chaotic" upbringing and grew up having "a lot of responsibility for other people" since he "was a very small child." His cultural and social conditioning, paired with an outstanding intelligence and his love of people helped him build a brilliant career and become one of the most successful executives in the world.

"Slow and difficult " (13) "messy process" (19) of
consciousness expansion over time & individual moments

Difficult integration between "spiritual yearnings [and]
corporate life"(23)

Paths to integration

20 years of deep Spiritual practice

Understanding economy is part of "deep spiritual practice" (47)

1 Spirituality

"Spirituality is everything"(51)

Engaged spirituality"(31)

"Altar boy" experience (53)

Deep knowing

Feeling of emptiness inside

Deep emotional decision

Physical decision

Emotional/Physical Pain

2 Mental decision

"Deep sadness and almost shame" (27)

"Intolerable" (27) split between corporate and personal values

"I felt like I was a totally un-integrated person"(33)

"Chaotic ...upbringing" (47)

"Lot of responsibility for other people"(57)

Evolution of self

"Inability to ever really understand my own passion, my own desires"(57)

"Following a script that wasn't authored by me"(57)

"Increasing emergence of dissatisfaction"(57)

Identified own passion

Internal (I)

Teachers

3 Cognitive

Tipping Point

Personal Context

Business Pressure /Context

"20 years of self-work, therapy . . . intellectual work"(47)

Understanding economy is part of "deep spiritual practice" (47)

Connecting intellectual work with spiritual work and social transformation work"(47)

Hard work

Triggers, Context & Process of Transformation

Topaz Profile & Core Topics - Mapping Wilber AQAL

Significant Personal Change in future management style

External Behavior (IT)

Inner Courage

Decision to lead from the heart

Giving people choice between taking responsibility and pointing fingers

"Chaotic . . . upbringing" (47)

Culture (WE)

Married & children

Corporate Culture

Social & Environment (ITS)

Graduate education

Top education

"PhD in psychology"(23)

"Several years of training to be an Episcopal deacon"(57)

President of international company

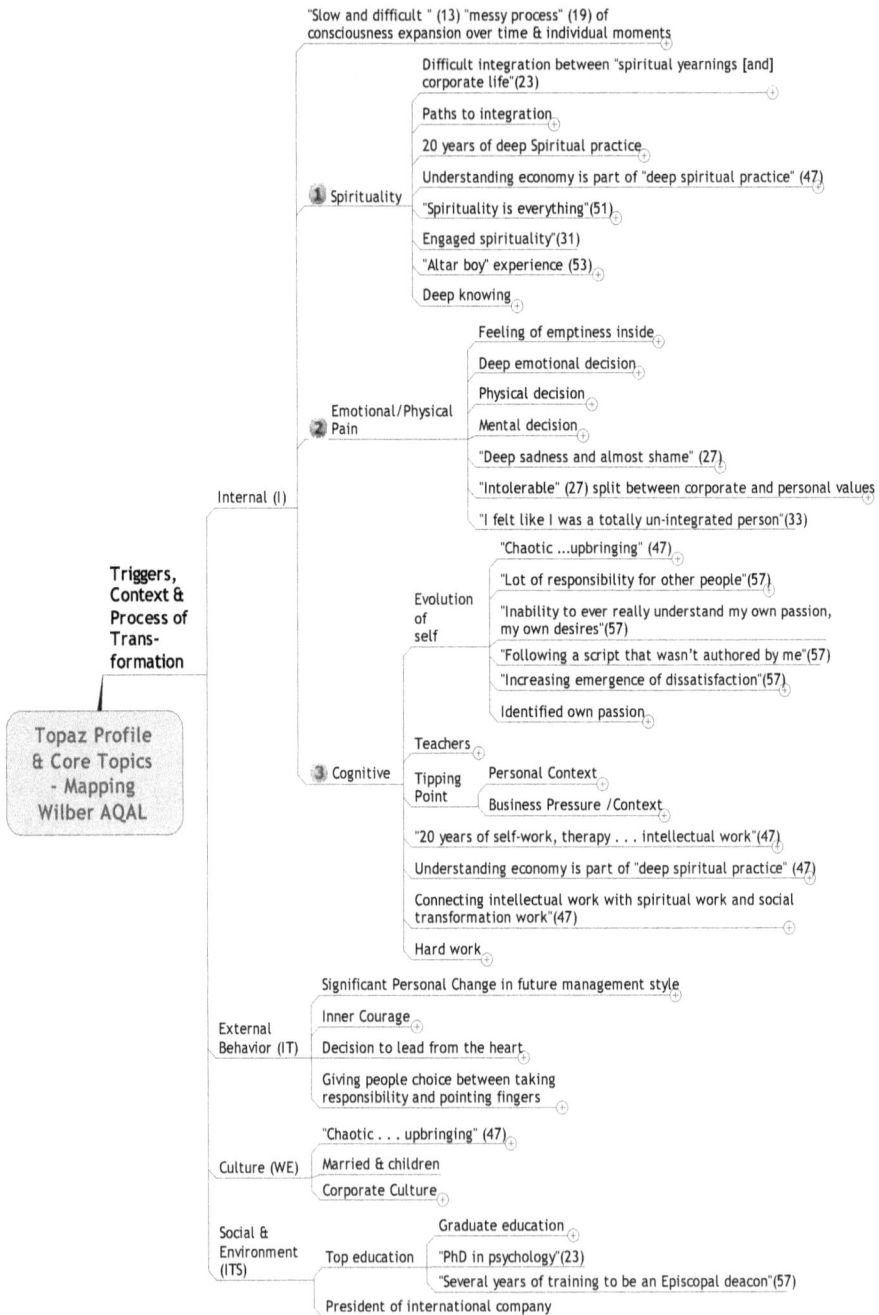

Figure 37. Triggers, context, and process of Topaz's overall transformation.

While working on his career, Topaz had "complete lack of awareness" of his "own self" and what he "actually liked or wanted in life." For a long time he was not aware of his "inability to ever really understand" his "own passion" and his "own desires." Yet, he remained connected with his spiritual roots and "came very close to becoming an Episcopal priest." During his training, Topaz did "a lot of deep personal reflective writing that was often tied to scriptural passages," which he "interpreted" in "a very personal, very contemporary way." This process "unearthed a lot" within his interiority and Topaz realized that he was "following a script that wasn't authored" by him. He was able to acknowledge the "emptiness" inside and it was "only through the gradual but ever increasing emergence of dissatisfaction" in his life that he started to explore his own *self* more deeply.

Having climbed up the career ladder to the highest ranks of the corporate world, Topaz *felt* "a deep sadness and almost shame of not being true to" his "values and being somewhat of a hypocrite." Therefore, living "in a traditional corporate setting" and "operating against traditional corporate values became intolerable" because he "felt" like "a totally un-integrated person." He experienced much "internal angst around the integration" between his "spiritual life," his "ethical belief system," and the requirements of his "corporate role." In trying to reconcile his dilemma, he enrolled for and eventually received a "Ph.D. in psychology." With one of his mentors, Topaz had the opportunity to study "a lot of engaged spirituality and a lot of social theory and philosophy," all of which had a tremendous impact.

After a "20 years" long process "of self-work, therapy, a lot of spiritual work, and a lot of intellectual work," Topaz "started to change" because "there was no energy left to keep going unless a shift happened." In the beginning, he thought that he "really needed to get out of corporate life and do something else," because he "found for many years that it was extraordinarily difficult" to integrate his "spiritual life" and his "spiritual yearnings with corporate life." This is "not an easy thing to do," yet one day, Topaz, had the courage to do it.

The Tipping Point—The Coming Out Party

Following "3 or 4 years of very, very strong performance" as a top executive in an international corporation, the "business was very soft," the "sales were down," the "squeeze was on," and everybody was wondering what Topaz "was going to do" about it. This crisis turned out to be one of the finest moments in Topaz's career. In preparing his strategy to address the crisis, Topaz decided to break through his own "angst" and limitations, and practice the long yearned need to integrate his "spiritual life" with his "ethical belief system" in business.

Because of his integral view of the world, he understood that the overall "economy" is "part of a deep spiritual practice." Therefore, he decided to move beyond the old business paradigm and "lead from the heart." For the first time in his career, he "didn't really care how anybody was going to evaluate" how he "handled this crisis." He decided to trust himself unconditionally and do what he "really thought was best."

Topaz prepared "the usual sort of presentation," numbers, charts, plans, and strategies, and went to bed. In the morning, he woke up with "great clarity" and came up with one single slide that represented the core of his message to his employees. It contained the following question: "What kind of people will we choose to be?" By asking this question, Topaz encouraged the personal growth of his employees and persuaded them to reach within themselves for solutions rather than "pointing fingers at one another." He guaranteed them his full support in the process, encouraged them to "recognize" their own "complicity" in the "misery," and "look within first" for solutions. The impact was tremendous and affected all areas of his life including becoming the president of his company several years later (see Figure 38).

Structural Changes and Impact of Topaz's Transformation

The decision to be totally "authentic" and "lead from the heart" made Topaz *feel* "like a million bucks." For the "first" time in his life, he knew "very clearly" that he was "not a hypocrite." By taking the courage to jump into the unknown, by "stepping out," and by "declaring" himself, he had

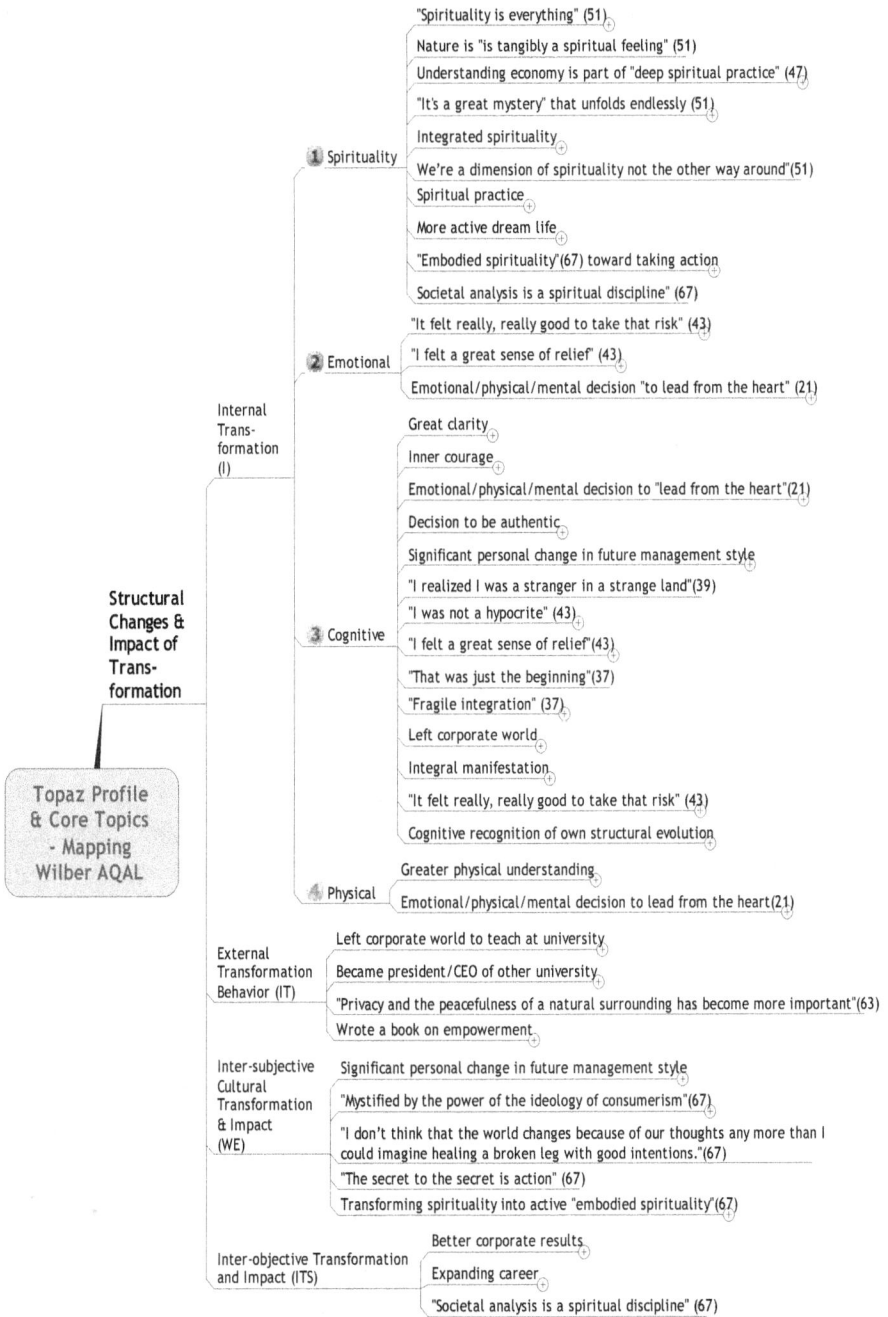

Figure 38. Structural changes and impact of Topaz's transformation.

"a great sense of relief" that *felt* "almost like a coming out party." It "felt really good" to take the "risk" that "people would think" that he "was crazy." A "huge weight was lifted" off his shoulders and his "management style from that day forward" became total authenticity.

Topaz believes that "taking" the "risk to declare more fully who you are" is "one of the greatest things that a person can do." He has become "much truer" to himself in "all aspects" of his life. He is "overtly aware and conscious of really expressing and behaving toward others in a way that" he considers to be "genuinely loving" and of "service." Another positive outcome was that his "career just kept expanding and growing in leaps and bounds" after this particular event.

The integration of his interior and exterior success, led Topaz, who has been a "meditator for over 30 years," toward an integral philosophy of reality. Today, he views *spirituality* as "everything" not just "as a dimension of human life." He sees "everything as a dimension of spirituality rather than spirituality as a dimension of life." In his integrated worldview, "the doctor who can set your leg even though he may be a Western puricist is part of spirituality."

Topaz thinks, "Physical incarnation is not a mistake, that we're here to create and to co-create together and that doing so requires our bringing a spiritual intention to all of the so-called material tools that are at our disposal." As an empowering force for systemic change in the world, Topaz who is "mystified by the power of the ideology of consumerism," believes in a "hands in the dirt spirituality." We must take "action" and become agents of transformation. He does not "think that the world changes because of our thoughts any more than" he "could imagine healing a broken leg with good intentions."

In conclusion, Topaz's transformation that began more than 30 years ago is characterized by several lines of development including the *spiritual* (Fowler, 1995), *cognitive* (Alexander et al., 1990), *moral* (Kohlberg & Ryncarz, 1990), *emotional* (Goleman, 2000; Saron & Davidson, 1997), and *egoic/self* (Cook-Greuter, 2008). While rising up to the greatest ranks of corporate America, Topaz continued to develop his spirituality up to the point where the discrepancy between traditional corporate values and his own was no longer tolerable. Eventually, he committed himself to integrate his inner with his outer life by "coming out." He asked his people to take charge and address collectively existing business problems instead of blaming others. He encouraged them to become more response-able by looking within first for the necessary solutions and then become part of the solution rather than part of the problem. By reconciling his "ethical" dilemma, Topaz felt not only a "great sense of relief," but also the business that he conducted with his new management style became more success-ful than ever. He had proof that he was not a "hypocrite" and he was able to move on as a more fully "integrated" person.

Based on this phenomenological research, the following major factors are strong indicators that Topaz has reached postconventional stages of human development (Alexander et al., 1990; Commons et al., 1990, 1984; Cook-Greuter, 2005, 2008; Koplowitz, 1984, 1990; Torbert et al., 2004; Wilber, 2000c):

1. Topaz' "language habit" (Cook-Greuter, 2005, p. 29) testifies to his ability to live in unity with all there is. It can be seen for instance in the ways he understands consciousness "as an ever blooming flower of awareness," in his own success. I "never really feel or think of myself as being particularly successful in any way." Topaz sees leadership "as an inverted pyramid" within which "people have both the opportunity and the desire to make their own maximum contribution." He has a highly developed sense of belongingness to other people and the world and sees himself create the "playground for the working out of all sorts of issues that we all drag with us to work" and which "we can't separate it out."

2. He subscribes to "peak values" (Kohut, 1985, p. 262) and has a strong need to live up to the highest possible standard of truth, morals and ethics (Gilligan, 1982/1993; Kegan, & Lahey, & Souvaine, 1990): "I had been going through a lot of internal angst around the integration of my spiritual life and my ethical belief system and what was being asked of me in a corporate

role . . . I found for many years that it was extraordinarily difficult for me to integrate my spiritual life and my spiritual yearnings with corporate life and it's not an easy thing to do . . . I felt
like I was a totally un-integrated person." Topaz mentioned the
word "integrated" 11 times during the interview compared with
the other participants who used it twice on average.

3. He views the work environment "as a mechanism for bringing
things into consciousness and working them through once and
for all so that we don't repeat the same patterns over and over
again . . . the real gifts of any sort of human collaboration including corporate based human collaboration" (Mitroff &
Denton, 1999; Pauchant, 2002; Senge et al., 2005).

4. His unassuming and empathic presence paired with his outstanding inter-personal skills is an additional sign of ego-transcendence and later stage of development (Cook-Greuter, 2005;
Rooke & Torbert, 1998; Torbert et al., 2004, 2008). These are
indicated by statements such as "I think also I'm more overtly
aware and conscious of really expressing and behaving toward
others in a way that I consider to be genuinely loving and sometimes being genuinely loving is being confrontational" or "I
think I'm much more conscious of the ways in which I might either facilitate or inhibit another person's spiritual growth and I
try to really be aware and conscious of that so that I'm not
doing anything that isn't of service."

5. He operates within a time-space continuum in which everything
is "a part of spirituality rather than spirituality being a part of
us." In his view, "the societal analyses that we might use to really try to understand how the economy is working and how
ideologies are limiting our freedom of choice is a spiritual discipline" (Rooke & Torbert, 1998; Torbert et al., 2004).

Further research and quantitative tests (Cook-Greuter, 2004; Torbert
et al., 2004) would have to be performed to be able to make a more-in-
formed assessment of Topaz's overall stage of development.

The Soul of Wealth

Common topic: Material abundance and outstanding external success in the business world characterizes all consciousness leaders in the current study. Yet, all of them without exception seem to have arrived at the conclusion that more money and material gain will not enhance how they feel and relate to other human beings and their environment. As a result, they have transcended the importance of money and material gain in their lives.

In the light of the current financial crisis and because of the nature of this research, this study intends to also reflect upon our understanding of capitalism and its most significant driving forces including capital, money, and financial systems in general. Over time, having money and material gain have become some of the most treasured values in human life, the world economy, and global politics (Lietaer, 2001; Twist, 2003). Collectively, we seem to have forgotten that money was invented to serve us and instead we are serving it. Often at all cost, we sacrifice our most sacred values (Zweig, 2007). Money has become the symbol of power and authority to the point of self-destruction, individually as well as collectively (Lietaer, 2001; Paulson, 2002; Senge et al., 2005; Twist, 2003). It has become the measure for "our competence and worth as people" (Twist, 2003, p. 6) and is rarely a "place of genuine freedom, joy, or clarity" (p. 9). To make money, we seem to be ready to sacrifice our planet (Gore, 1992), poison our bodies, the environment, and our food (Sachs, 2008), send our own children to war, and are even ready to kill for it (Secretan, 2006, p. 22)

We live in a time that requires a redefinition of our financial and monetary systems, a redefinition that must come from higher levels of consciousness. In other words, trying to address the current financial challenges by using the tools of a system that has obviously failed will most probably not bring the desired results and end the crisis (Lietaer, 2001, pp. 285-298). Through the Internet revolution, humanity has entered the era of accelerated globalization and that of a new value system. This is an era, in which we have free access to information, human resources, telephony, virtual businesses, and most important, free communication. Through cyberspace, the world has truly become a global village in which new rules must be created that transcend our old view about finances and monetary systems. For the first time in human history, Internet users have access to free virtual human capital, virtual real estate, and virtual currency. As a result, we have now not only access to an open society, resources and information, but more important can access an infrastructure that is bypassing old and inflexible monetary structures (Lietaer, 2001). It has become obvious that the newly born and unofficial currency is increasingly that of the Internet Globally, the call for a new financial system is immanent.

This collective external transformation seems concurrent with the transformation that is taking place on the interiority of people that have evolved beyond postconventional levels of consciousness (Alexander et al., 1990; Cook-Greuter, 2008; Torbert et al., 2004). The researched participants in the current study indicate that in its highest manifestation, human consciousness has evolved beyond the information age. They are pointing out that the current breakdown of existing financial structures is a clear indication that our societies and cultures must adapt to the requirements of the modern world. Money transcendence is just one component in this process.

Harbin's Individual Consciousness Leadership Profile with Transformational Characteristics

Harbin achieved world fame by becoming a serial entrepreneur and one of the most respected and well-known female venture capitalists in Silicon Valley. In addition to being an award-winning philanthropist, she is a lyricist, a book author, an inspiring role model for women, a celebrated public speaker, and a media darling. Harbin holds several academic degrees from an elite university. Appendix D contains the mind map representing the key core topics and transformational profile that resulted from the interview performed with Harbin.

Triggers, Context, and Process of Harbin's Transformation

Harbin's transformation into a consciousness leader was a process that took place over many decades. It began when she "was 20" years old and her "fiancé was killed in a plane crash." Her entire life changed in "1 day" and "allowed for a very harsh view" of her existence. She decided that she was "never going to base" her "happiness" and "her success in life" on what somebody else was going to "deliver" to her. Instead, she chose to learn a "very painful but very important lesson" which meant taking "responsibility" for her own life by referring to her interiority rather then her exteriority. She was "going to live or die" by what she did for herself including "enjoying" herself every day, having fun every day," and surrounding herself with wonderful people. Furthermore, she learned that most of our "possessions are ultimately meaningless." Not that she does not enjoy "these things" but "if tomorrow they were all swept away," and she still had her "husband and her children," her "health," and her "relationships," she "could survive." Even if she "lost one of those" such as the "spouse equivalent," her fiancé, she knows that she can "move on" and "still find joy in life" because she doesn't believe in defining her life by her "loss."

Harbin was able to validate and implement these early life lessons through her brilliant career in the high-tech world both as an entrepreneur and later as a venture capitalist. Her next decisive turning point came during the dot-com bust, when "a number of things came to a head at the same time" (see Figure 39).

Harbin did not "have big, cataclysmic changes, same house, same marriage" but having "a career change," being "forty-five pounds" overweight, and "turning 50 allowed for more introspection." She realized that she was in a "vicious cycle" that resulted "in physical degradation and weight gain," because she was "using food to assuage what then turns out to be the very thing the food is causing." Then "you're sad or just you're unhappy in your body, and you keep doing the same things that make it even worse and worse, because they provide temporary relief."

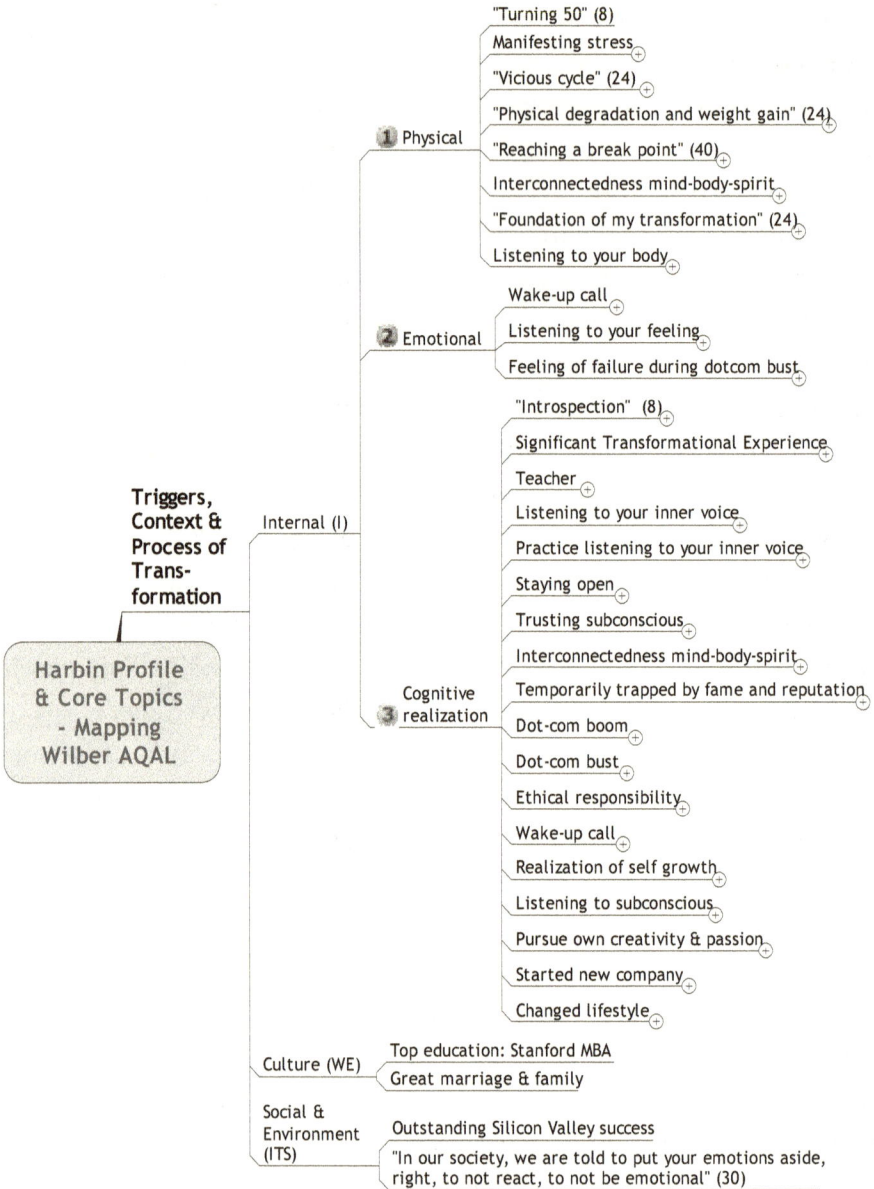

Figure 39. Triggers, context, and process of Harbin's internal transformation.

Eventually, Harbin was able to break the vicious circle not only with respect to her physical challenges but also she became a role model for integral living and consciousness leadership. She is convinced that "a big foundation" of what her "transformation has been, is the difference between finding temporary relief and making permanent incremental lifestyle changes."

The Tipping Point—The Wake-up Call

During the dot-com bust, when her company decided "not [to] stay in business as a venture firm" and "not to raise another fund," she continued to identify herself with being a "venture capitalist." As a result, she found a company that she "aligned with, with a partner" whom she "really liked." When "one day he cancelled an interview," she "felt relief." She recognized it as a "wake-up call" from her "subconscious" mind.

> *That was a wake-up call to me. I thought my emotions are trying to tell me something, which is I'm interviewing for a job that I must not want, because if you feel relief at the prospect of having an interview cancelled, this must not be what you want. So I thought to myself, okay, I'm going to have to let this go. Instead of thinking, defining myself by my role and by my paycheck and by my title, I need to define myself by what I get up and enjoy doing everyday.*

Staying true to her old mantra to enjoy every day of her life, Harbin was able to let go of her former identity and asked the following questions "What is my body telling me? What do I feel?" By answering these and many other questions, Harbin was able to change her entire life. Figure 40 shows various components of the structural impact of her transformation.

Structural Changes and Impact of Harbin's Transformation

Harbin "changed" not only on the inside. She lost her extra pounds, brought her body back in shape, and installed a regular integral life prac-

Figure 40. Structural changes and impact of Harbin's transformation.

tice to maintain her health and vitality. Moreover, she even started a company to share her wisdom with the world and to empower people in similar situations.

However, the main key to her external transformation is her capability for "introspection" and her willingness to "peel the layers away and think more about" what is "really important" in life. In her integral worldview, she sees the "big connection" between the "physical manifestation" and the "mental, spiritual, what's going on on the outside and what's going on on in the inside." She is able to live integrally by "incorporating the joys of life" every day and by "asking" herself: "Am I happy in what I'm doing?" She knows that "if you're not getting up and looking forward to your day everyday, you probably need to rethink how you're spending your days." She said, "You need to think of the interplay that each aspect of your life has on other aspects of your life, your physical, your spiritual, your mental, your emotional, your relational. You have to think about that stuff."

From personal experience, she knows that there is a "real battle for achievers between living in the moment and planning and achieving an accomplishment." She believes in "living in the moment" and balancing living in the now with planning for the future. She believes that we have the opportunity to choose

> *How you want to live your life, and how you want to feel, and what things you want to bring into your life, and what things you want to consciously let go of, whether that's food, drink, exercise, friends, family, lovers, whatever it is, and giving yourself the license.*

In addition to practicing the power of presence, Harbin is a believer in giving up resistance and "accepting" the things that cannot be changed, in "learning" how to listen to the "inner voice," in "the freedom to listen to what" the "emotions are saying," and using the internal reference as a means to let go of other people's opinion about one's self.

In summary, Harbin's transformation is characterized by several major lines of development including the *ego/self* identity line (Erikson, 1980; Rooke & Torbert, 1998), the *emotional* line (Goleman, 2000), the *moral* line (Gilligan, 1982/1993), the *cognitive* line (Koplowitz, 1984), and the *physical* line of development (Leonard & Murphy, 1995).

Further research and more quantitative tests (Cook-Greuter, 2004; Rooke & Torbert, 2005; Torbert et al., 2004) would have to be performed to arrive at a more concrete assessment. However, there are strong indications that Harbin's center of gravity is at the postconventional level of development (Cook-Greuter, 2008; Rooke & Torbert, 2005; Torbert et al., 2008). Some of these indicators include: (a) becoming a catalyst of mass transformation; (b) "language habit" (Cook-Greuter, 2008) with vivid, complex, authentic, insightful, and wise responses; (c) her honesty, innate joy, and directness ("getting [life] blows," "fits my ego," "life has this nasty habit of changing)"; (d) having very high moral standards (she apologized to investors in high-risk businesses although the dot-com bust was not her fault); (e) living an integral life; and (f) money transcendence.

Primal Leadership—The Power of Emotional Maturity

Common topic: All consciousness leaders researched in the current study have potentially reached higher levels of emotional mastery with gratitude, love, compassion, joy, and appreciation as their dominating emotions.

Since the ancient Greeks (Aristotle, 2002; Brennan, 2003; Plato, 1938/1961), the Western world has predominantly operated under the assumption that thought or cognition and emotions perform separately (Capra, 2000). Like Plato before him, Descartes (2003) accepted the divine authority of God, which should "be preferred to our perception" (p. 144). With respect to emotions, however, Descartes argued, "it is very inappropriate for a philosopher to accept anything as true that they never perceived as true; and it is even more inappropriate to trust in the senses" (p. 144).

With his famous sentence, "I think, therefore I am" (p. 18), Descartes (1998) thought that "the whole essence of nature . . . is simply to think" (p. 19). Subsequently, he was able to lead humanity out of the dark ages into modernity by emphasizing the logical thinking abilities, the brain, and that which could be verified objectively. This was the birth of the "Cartesian dualism" (Schwartz, 2000, p. 198) that separated the cognitive processes of the mind from the body and the physical world. Through it, Westerners have equated "their identity with their mind, instead with their whole organism" (Capra, 2000, p. 23) including emotion. It seems that the emphasis on the mind as our intellectual capacity to control the visible world has distracted us from focusing on what has heart and meaning including joy, happiness, and true fulfillment, in short the way we feel, our emotions.

Like Harvard professor Daniel Brown (Saron & Davidson, 1997), psychologist Welwood (1985) also supported the idea that emotion is a complex concept and attributes the difficulties of modern Western psychology in dealing with emotions to our perception of emotions as "the most confusing and frightening phenomena of every day life" (p. 79). However, the brain imaging technologies of the past 2 decades have allowed deeper insights into the seat and origin of both thoughts and emotions (Barlow & Durand, 2005, p. 83). These insights support the view that emotional input influences cognitive functioning and the other way around (Schwartz, 2000, p. 489). This includes learning, problem-solving abilities, stress-processing capabilities, the ability to judge, and extraordinary sports performances (Andreas & Faulkner, 1996). It seems now beyond question that an emotionally heightened state creates indeed not only physical but also mental health (McCraty, 2001; Saron & Davidson, 1997).

Regardless of the state of the art in scientific research regarding the definition, source, and seat of emotions, the consciousness leaders researched in the current study have been able to experience the nature of emotion as an integral part of their being that is deeply connected with the mind. As a result, they have been able to corroborate that the heart has a *mind* of its own and "every change in the mental emotional state, conscious or unconscious, is accompanied by an appropriate change in the physiological state" (McCraty, 2003, p. 8).

All of the research participants without exception have focused on their emotional development and therefore seem to have reached high levels of emotional mastery (Cook-Greuter, 2008; Goleman et al., 2002; Maslow et al., 1998) and live their lives mostly in gratitude, love, joy, and contribution to humankind (Greenleaf, 1977; Maslow, 1968/1999; Senge et al., 2005).

Hahm's Individual Consciousness Leadership Profile with Transformational Characteristics

Hahm is a highly accomplished human being who has been involved with the human potential movement for almost 4 decades. He is a world-renowned public speaker, the author of several books and papers, and a successful entrepreneur with high academic degrees. Appendix D contains the mind map representing the key core topics and transformational profile that resulted from the interview performed with Hahm.

Triggers, Context, and Process of Hahm's Transformation

The context of Hahm's transformation is represented in Figure 41.

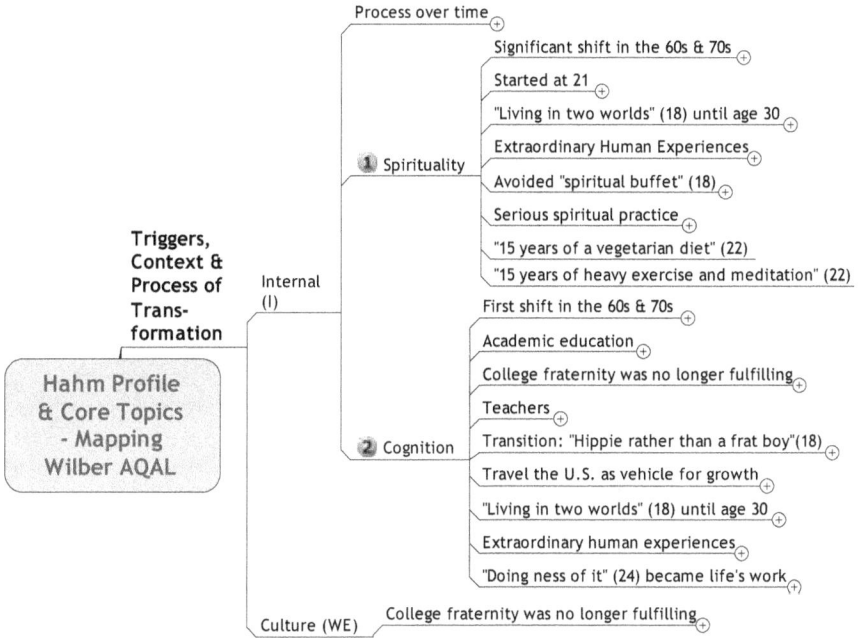

Figure 41. Triggers, context, and process of Hahm's transformation.

His evolution to a consciousness leader "was a process" and there "have been many events along the way" that served as "validation benchmarks" and confirmed that he was on the growth path. His transformation started at age "21." It was "at a relatively young age" when he "became interested in something more than the normal." It was in the "late '60s, early '70s" when the lives of "millions of people" changed collectively. At that time, there was a "dimensional opening of sorts for the planet, where people were getting a taste of what it would be like to be" awake. However, Hahm lived in "two worlds" until his "early 30s." On one hand he was in the "music business," on the other hand he was "pursuing spiritual things." He pursued a "serious personal discipline" and spiritual practice, and "read a lot of books" by Yogananda, Alice Bailey, and Gurdjieff.

The Tipping Point—Experiencing Grace

Hahm's life shifted significantly through several extraordinary and unitive experiences that he calls Grace because "sometimes those things find you, more than you finding them":

> *Grace is when you get something that goes beyond what you deserve and it's sort of payoff in a certain way of the cumulative effort over time; that sort of downloads at the right time in the right place to give you the most fulfilling experience you can have.*

His experiences "became so tangible and so real" that he felt his "heart was exploding with love. It was past any kind of physical orgasm you could possibly imagine." His state of "awareness" increased and he felt not only "connected to the world but so much more beyond it." At times this "feeling would be so powerfully strong that it was almost to the point where you couldn't walk." After "15 years of a vegetarian diet" and "heavy exercise and meditation," Hahm met his latest teacher who became a "very important influence" in his life. His teacher "was very helpful" in that he cautioned him "not to get caught up" in a "spiritual buffet where you run from one thing to the next."

Instead, his teacher encouraged him to live his spirituality rather than study it.

> *I really didn't study too much past that in terms of spiritual or esoteric teachings. It's just I felt like, at that point, it was about us sort of pioneering our own way of approaching it and it was all about the heart.*

Following his encounter with his teacher, Hahm decided to dedicate his life to help humanity awaken to higher levels of consciousness through emotional and spiritual maturity. Almost 2 decades ago, he co-founded a very successful company whose mission is to do exactly that.

Structural Changes and Impact of Hahm's Transformation

Hahm has been on a dedicated path to transformation into a consciousness leader (see Figure 42) for almost 4 decades. He and his team are living examples on how consciousness development can happen through emotional and spiritual development. In his view, *emotional maturity* is "the next frontier in human revolution." Based on the scientific research performed over the past 2 decades, Hahm has arrived at a rather deep un-

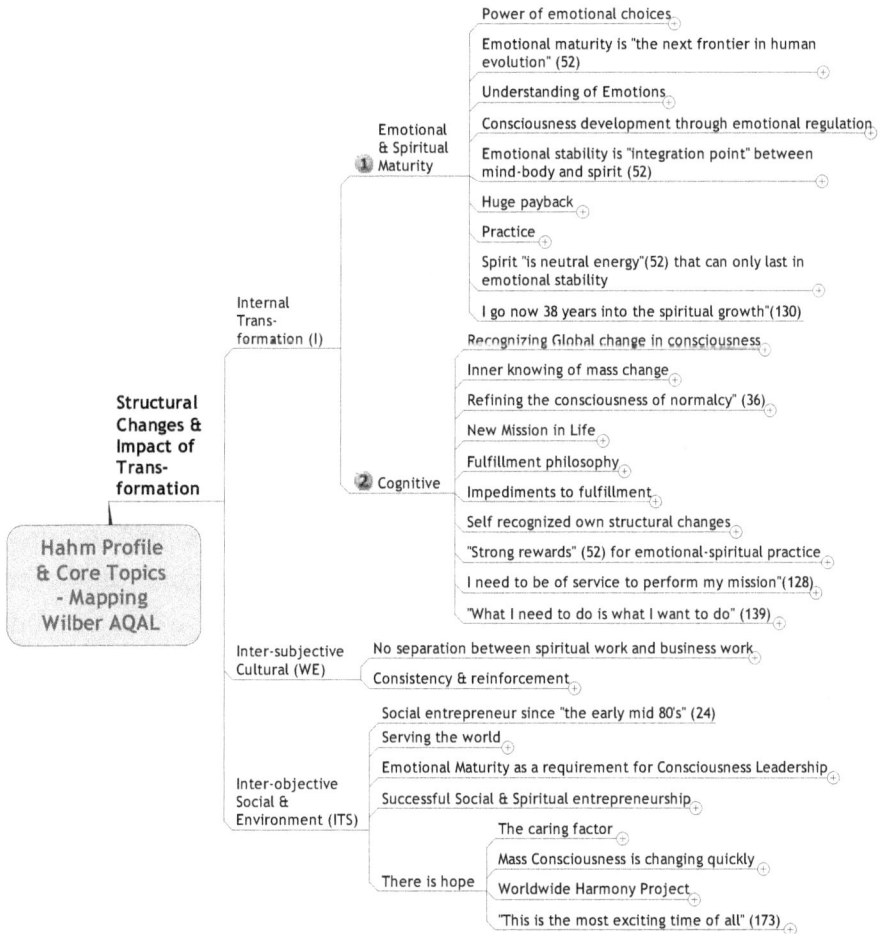

Figure 42. Structural changes and impact of Hahm's transformation.

derstanding about the nature of emotions and the conclusion that "people can choose an emotion more than they can think." He has dedicated his life to helping people learn how to choose an emotional response by leveraging the intelligence of the heart that represents "one of the most important inputs into the brain":

> *If you try to live life through the heart and approach it with more of a positive emotional state in the first place, you begin to change the way the brain functions, the circuitry in the brain itself can change. And so, you'll still have the emotional triggers, you can still feel hurt, you can still feel jealous, you can still feel angry, but those things become less attractive and less the norm. That's regulating emotion.*

This "regulation" however, does not happen by thinking "your way through it" because "thought against thought" or "thought against emotions" is "a pretty slow process and has a random effect." Instead, his company developed products to teach people how to "live life through the heart and approach it with more of a positive emotional state in the first place." By doing that, people "begin to change the way the brain functions [and] the circuitry in the brain itself can change" over time.

As expected, Hahm's high level of emotional stability is achieved through daily practices such as meditation, "heart lock ins," and moment to moment awareness of "mind, feelings, and emotions." The "payback" of his practice is so rewarding that "it's way worth the time and energy to do it." He does not "believe that we can get to the things that we really want unless we take another level of emotional maturity as an approach."

Spiritually, Hahm has been "now 38 years into the spiritual growth." In his view, spiritual evolution occurs via emotional maturity. Yet, that is "usually the missing step, especially in spiritual practice." Hahm knows that "everybody wants to be having these wonderful [spiritual] experiences, but they still don't put the emphasis on what gets in the way of having them," which is emotional maturity. In Hahm's model of the world "we have a physical body, a mental body, an emotional body," and so on all of which vibrate at "different frequencies." However,

> *Spirit itself, is a very powerful neutral energy that can come into our lives and it's a very caring energy. If it tries to come into our lives through a distorted emotional field, that neutral power that comes in simply just makes the field of our emotions more unstable. The spirit doesn't work that way, it's not going to destabilize us, so it withdraws. So if people really want more of this higher dimensional access and all of these things that people aspire to have, they can't skip the step of learning how to stabilize the emotional nature because that's the integration point within the human system.*

In other words, Hahm is convinced that emotional evolution is the prerequisite to spiritual evolution. Through the past 4 decades of practicing lived spirituality and emotional maturity both personally and professionally, Hahm moved beyond the desire to have more exceptional human and spiritual experiences. He does not "care about them that much" anymore because authentic spirituality is his life now. Hahm found his true life's mission and "a strong heart's desire to want to see other people be fulfilled." His life's purpose is "not so blatantly devoid" of his "personal own interests" but he thinks that he has "become much more decentralized" in his thinking to where it's much easier" for him "to have other people have certain things and not worry about" himself. In "the last 10 or 15 years" his life has "been much more about really refining the consciousness of normalcy," about "what's really going on in a normal day and a normal moment" and not about "the cosmic experience." His life is now more about doing the work and putting his "nose to the grindstone" to serve humanity.

His mission is about service because he sees "so many people that just aren't happy and most are not happy, and [their] life seems to still be such a struggle." He believes that "every person" is born into life "with a fulfillment package: it's like a present," and "the mission is to unwrap the package," yet "most people never get past the bow." He wants to help people let go of "so much regret . . . judgment . . . and self-judgment" and realize that they must take action and "have to do something" to unwrap their fulfillment package.

In summary, Hahm realizes that without his emotional mastery he would have never reached his full potential and would have "never been an author," or become an "executive," or a "business man." He attributes his personal growth to his emotional and spiritual dedication and practice that helped put him in a position to be "out there as willing to do, willing to go forth, willing to change, willing to grow, willing to take on and learn new things." Today, he perceives himself as a man "that loves more and judges less than the one" he "would have been" without his evolution. Through the development of his interiority, Hahm has access to an "inner knowingness" and "awareness" that help him see that humanity is "headed towards extraordinary times of mass change" which he perceives to be "the most exciting time of all." More evaluation, testing, and research would have to be performed to be more accurate, however, the following aspects provide a strong indication that Hahm has reached later stages of post-conventional development (Alexander et al., 1990; Cook-Greuter, 2008; Goleman, 2000; Torbert et al., 2004, 2008): He (a) has embraced non-duality; (b) can live with paradoxes and be joyous, fulfilled, and serene; (c) accepts reality as "is"; (d) no separation between spirituality and life (personal and professional); (e) cultivates his capacity for compassion, empathy, and unconditional love a couple of times daily; (f) can live in the present and day by day; (g) is humble and has an unassuming presence; (h) moved beyond emotional and spiritual mastery; (i) is detached from the outcome; (j) lives a simple life of global service; (k) displays genuine joy, gratefulness, and has a life-affirming attitude; and (l) his ability be present and connected with the source of life.

Achieving More with Less Effort

Common topic: All consciousness leaders researched in the current study confirm that as they evolved to higher levels of understanding and consciousness, they were able to access a different kind of information and wisdom that is helping them achieve more with far less effort.

Maslow (1968/1999) confirmed that self-actualizing individuals are people who have peak experiences more frequently than regular people do (pp. 106-107). Through these experiences, they come closer to the core of their true identity. They begin to achieve far more in life with much less effort because they can now actualize more of their potentials. This is due in part to the fact that they are able to access additional resources that they were not aware of before (Csikszentmihalyi, 1990; Ram Dass, 1989, CD 1).

Moreover, what characterizes consciousness leaders is their ability to *act* upon their new recognitions and realizations.

Once people experience different dimensions of their being, they become more aware of and open up to synchronicities, which simplify their individual lives but also impact their cultural and social contexts (Progoff, 1973). Research (Pauchant, 2002) on ethics and spirituality in business indicated that those companies who were able to integrate ethics with spirituality could do it not only "without compromising the efficiency of their organization" (p. 212) but they were able to increase their productivity.

Within this context, it is important to note that all participants in the current study refer to spirituality from an internal point of reference that appears to be independent from those of traditional religions.

Cassandra's Individual Consciousness Leadership Profile with Transformational Characteristics

Cassandra is a highly educated woman, a venture capitalist, serial entrepreneur, a self-made millionaire, a philanthropist, a force for good focusing on empowering businesswomen worldwide, an international speaker, and a well-known public figure. Appendix D contains the mind map representing the key core topics and transformational profile that resulted from the interview performed with Cassandra.

Triggers, Context, and Process of Cassandra's Transformation

Cassandra's evolution to a consciousness leader was a process as well as a series of emotional and spiritual events (see Figure 43). She regards herself as a "lucky person, to have been born into a family that is just so full of love and support." The high standards were set by her parents who "have had one of the most amazing love stories," who "achieved great success," who "have made the world a significantly better place." Cassandra married in her 20s who she thought to be her "lifetime soul mate." After 8 years of marriage, her ex-husband "made a momentary lapse in judgment," betrayed her, and wanted a divorce. Given her high family value system, Cassandra was "fully prepared to forgive him" but he divorced her against her will.

Because of her tendency "to be a bit of a control freak," this divorce "significantly shook" her. It "wasn't something" that she "was in control of," which she "really hated." She had high family values and "core principles." She believed in forgiveness and in working through problems to address and to heal them. However, she was not given that chance and was deeply hurt.

Cassandra's divorce became "probably one of the worst things that ever happened to" her, yet she is "very clear" that she "wouldn't be where" she is "today had that not happened." For the following 27 years, Cassandra focused on what she could control namely her career, her humanitarian work, and her relationship with family and friends. She concentrated mostly on the outside and built an extraordinary company with an outstanding reputation. "For a long time" she "decided that no one would ever get close" to her so that she "wouldn't hurt like that again." Consequently, she "successfully set up such high barriers" around her "that no one got close," which, "by the way, means that no one loves you."

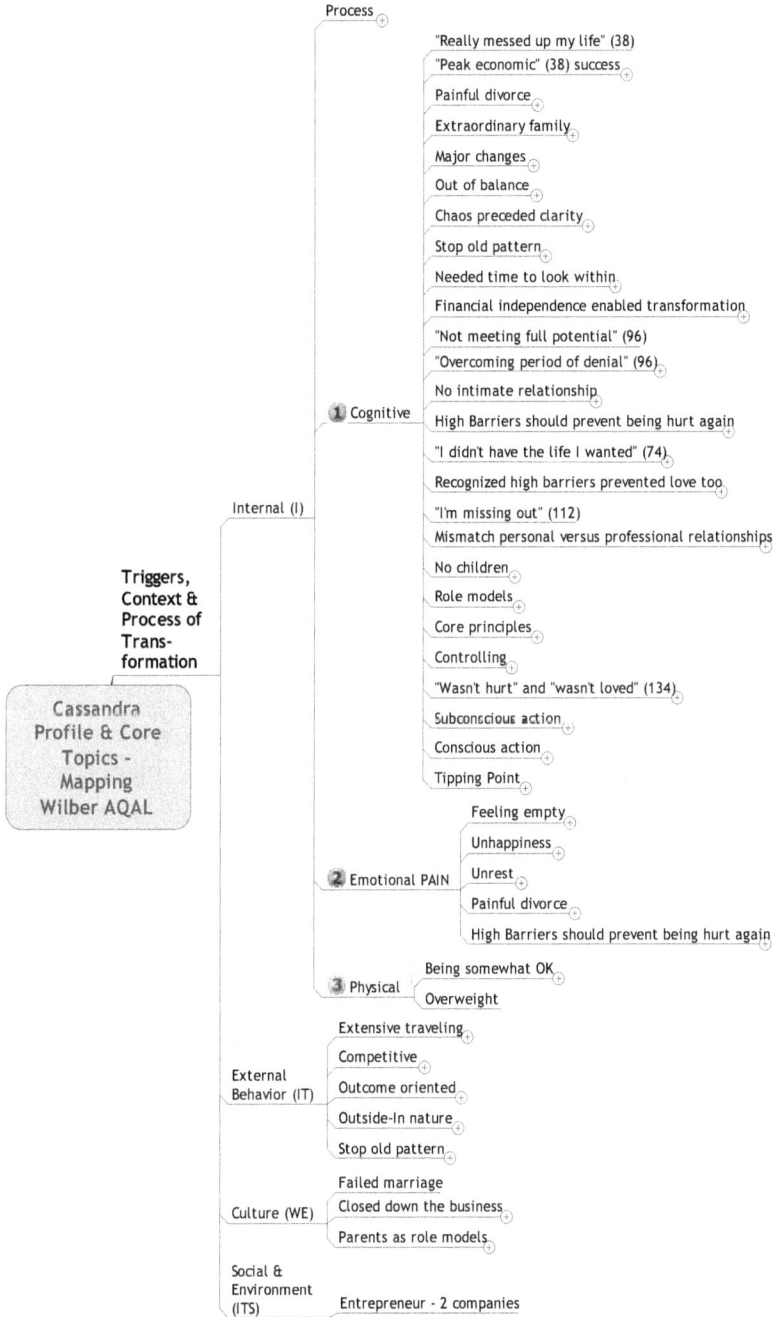

Figure 43. Triggers, context, and process of Cassandra's transformation.

The Tipping Point—The Wake-up Call

At the "peak" of her "economic" and professional success up to that point, Cassandra received a "really big box" from "United Airlines. It could have been American or Delta." At that moment in her life, she "was living on a plane," was "always flying from one place to another," and "racked up a huge amount of miles." "Receiving the gift" from the airline was "the ah ha moment" where "all came together, but it had definitely been percolating before that." She realized, "this is probably the nicest gift I'm going to get this holiday season and it's from a corporation, not from somebody that I love."

She "started thinking" about "how much time and attention" she had "been placing" on her "friends" and "family" compared to work. "In that moment" she "knew that" she "had crossed over a line." She realized "that business and tasks and to dos had become more important than the people" she "loved and cared about," that she "was seriously out of balance," and that she had "really messed up" her life. Although, it is her "nature to be "more focused on others" than on herself, she noticed that she was spending around "98, 99 %" on the exterior of her life. She realized that she was "unhappy" and "knew" that she was not "meeting" her "full potential" because the lack of balance started "showing up everywhere" in her life. Luckily, Cassandra had her "extraordinary family, which has always been" her "rock." Thus, with the emotional support of her family and friends, she was able to overcome the "period of denial" and changed radically.

Because she "had accumulated enough wealth" to sustain herself, Cassandra "shut down" her business "in a responsible way" over 18 months after which she took "3 months of serious me time." After "another year to 18 months of very actively, very consciously trying to explore and look at and think about and research," something significant happened. She had an extraordinary experience, a "spiritual-type moment." Her entire plan for the future came through:

> *I got the full book. It came to me, you know, in this incredible,*
> *complete with cover, table of contents, and detailed chapters. And*

I was talking with somebody and the book arrived in my head, just whrooom. I was downloading. And it just like totally came to me. So then I got home and I, you know, got on my computer and I started refining the idea. And literally within a week I had a finished document.

Her "document" came with total "clarity" and included all aspects of her life including health, career, finances, and the exact "list of what" she was "looking for in" her "life partner." As a result, she "ended up making a lot of very, very major changes," which caused her "to shift and to become who" she is "now" (see Figure 44).

Structural Change and Impact of Cassandra's Overall Transformation

Cassandra began implementing the new life plan by "acting" upon it and starting a new company. Everything worked effortlessly and perfectly. "The economics worked, the team worked" and the universe kept bringing her the right "business partners" and the "perfect" team.

Physically, Cassandra who was in her "40s before" she "figured out" that she had to start "taking care" of her "body if" she "was going to live a long life." She lost weight and began to exercise regularly.

Emotionally, Cassandra cognized that she had "set up all these really high barriers" and that "in fact" she "was not being hurt by anybody" but also "wasn't being loved by anybody." Her old "lifestyle . . . seriously prevented" her "from being able to be physically close to anyone for more than literally 2 days at a time." After her spiritual "downloading," she stopped feeling "real empty" and "unhappy." Being now in touch with her interiority, Cassandra had an inner knowing and another "ah ha moment" in the form of clairaudience, when she met her current soul mate "for the first time" at a restaurant:

I got there a little early, probably the only time in our relationship that I got there early, but I did. And so I'm standing there at the

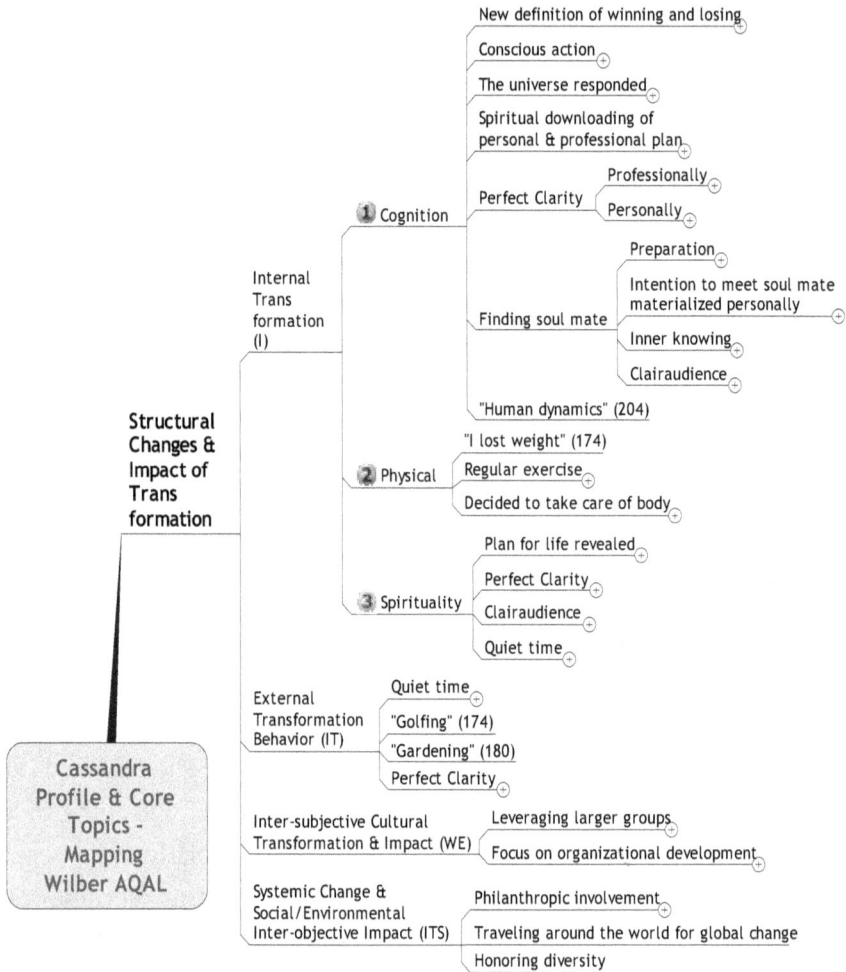

Figure 44. Structural change and impact of Cassandra's transformation.

door of the restaurant looking out onto the parking lot, and I'd seen his picture online so when he got out of the car and he started approaching the restaurant, I knew that it was physically him. And then I heard this loud voice in my head that said, "Cassandra, pay attention. This is the one." And I remember thinking, because it was such a loud voice. And remember, I'm in a large restaurant and there's a lot of noise going on in the background. I remember turning around and saying, "Who said that?" And then I realized that, you know, that nobody had said that to me, that it was coming from inside. And, you know, he walked through the door and we did kind of that peripheral, you know, social kiss that everybody did. But there was a visible spark that passed between our lips, and I just, I knew he was the one.

Through her new integral life practice, Cassandra was able not only to let go of control, live more in the present moment, but she redefined her notion of winning and losing to include the "collaborative" aspects in which "everybody wins." Thus, she has become a force for good in the world through her philanthropic activities, by focusing on integral "organizational development," and by helping "business women globally."

In summary, Cassandra's transformation into a consciousness leader is characterized by several lines of development. These lines include the *emotional* (Goleman et al., 2002; Ricard, 2003), *physical* (Leonard & Murphy, 1995), *cognitive* (Commons et al., 1990; Beck, 1976), *value* (Beck & Cowan, 1996), *egoic* (Erikson, 1980; Loevinger, 1977), and *spiritual* (Mitroff & Denton, 1999). Further research needs to be performed to reach a clearer understanding, but Cassandra's humility, her willingness to let go of control and face her worst nightmares, her ability to tap into deep sources of wisdom and listen to it, her access to intuition, the capacity to observe herself, her selflessness, and her dedication to serving humanity, are clear signs of postconventional levels of development (Cook-Greuter, 2008; Commons et al., 1984; Rooke & Torbert, 2005).

Drinking Out of the Fire Hose

Common topic: All consciousness leaders in the current study have reached a stage in their personal development in which the opening to the spiritual or the transpersonal realm has become a necessity in order to feel whole and integrated.

Most leadership styles have traditionally avoided the spiritual, or the transpersonal realms (Boyatzis & McKee, 2005; Collins, 2005; Porras et al., 2007; Ray & Myers, 1989). However, research (Adams, 2005; Goleman et al., 2002; Marques et al., 2007; Mitroff & Denton, 1999; Pauchant, 2002; Paulson, 2002; Renesch, 2002; Senge et al., 2005; Taylor, 2005) indicates that at this stage of human evolution, a consciousness leadership paradigm must include the transpersonal aspects such as spirituality.

Pauchant (2002), for example, referred to a forum of studies on international management, ethics, and spirituality, which was the first of its kind that was held at an internationally recognized business school. It contained the views of 6 CEOs and 6 scholars of ethics and spirituality from Australia, Canada, the United States, and Switzerland. These case studies from five organizations such as finance, nutrition, health, education, and politics strongly suggested that people are indeed seeking more meaning at work. Such studies indicate that the quest for meaning leads inevitably to a deeper search for higher ethics, morals, and spirituality. They have also clearly revealed both the benefits and dangers associated with it.

The research presented in the present confirms the need for lived spirituality within the context of the consciousness leader. As consciousness leaders begin to integrate their interiority with their exteriority, they also feel the need to expand their leadership platforms to include the transpersonal domain (Ram Dass, 1989, CD 1; Walsh, 1999). Furthermore, no participant in this research believed in a personified God.

LaCroix's Individual Consciousness Leadership Profile with Transformational Characteristics

LaCroix is a highly accomplished, highly educated entrepreneur, and a successful venture capitalist focusing on "multiple energy sources." Appendix D contains the mind map representing the key core topics and transformational profile that resulted from the interview performed with LaCroix.

Triggers, Context, and Process of LaCroix' Transformation

LaCroix's transformation occurred as a process that began several decades ago and was driven by his "upbringing," "curiosity," and "intelligence." Figure 45 shows the main triggers.

LaCroix's father was a "professor." As a result LaCroix grew up in an academic environment and became aware of his "mental powers from age 6" on. His "strong qualitative capability," his "strong ability to focus for many hours a day, days on end," and his "curiosity and openness" earned him several degrees from two outstanding American universities. He remembers "from an early age, just thinking about business and making money." As a result, his willingness to "work hard," his natural curiosity, his willingness to learn, his "high energy," and "creativity" guided him toward achieving extraordinary "financial success" and "a wonderful family." LaCroix has no "religious background" but "more of a spiritual focus" and thinks that "spirituality" is "something innate" to him.

The Tipping Point—Drinking Out of a Fire Hose

At "age 35," for no apparent reason, he followed the advice of "a group of friends" who were "a little different" and whom he "enjoyed." He signed up for and eventually graduated with a "Master's degree in Spiritual Psychology." LaCroix

> *Took one month at a time. It was a process of learning that touched me, especially over time, not necessarily grabbed me at*

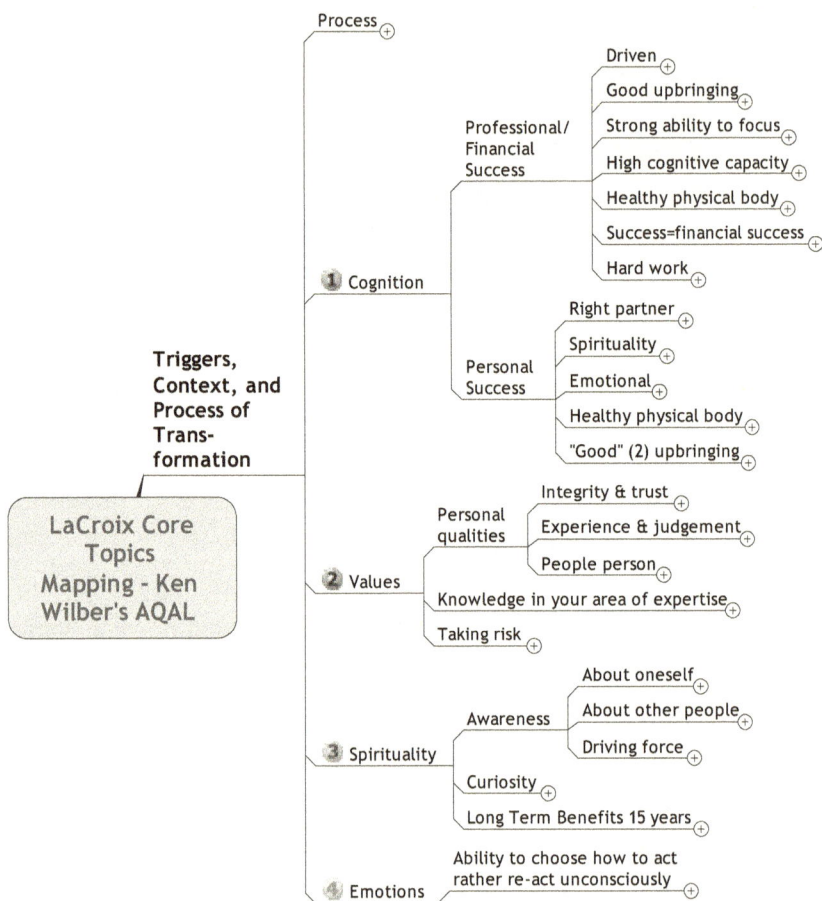

Figure 45. Triggers, context, and process of LaCroix's transformation.

once. It was one that was, *"Okay, that's interesting."* You couldn't step out. You had to keep going through the whole program because it was all built on it but you could quit anytime. You paid month by month tuition. There's no commitment for the period so you could always leave. So, every month was, *"That was interesting. I don't know."* Then the next month was, *"That was interesting. I don't know. Okay, I have time. I'll do it again."* I kept doing it. And even after the first year I was like, *"Do I want to do the second year? I don't know. I'll go the first month."*

It was not until he finished "the end of the second year" of the program that LaCroix "really appreciated the journey" that had a "huge impact" and changed his life forever. The program took "the spirituality" and the "emotional" sides of him, areas that were "way under built" and gave him "a lot of learning and a lot of experience and exposure and depth." It was "an extremely valuable use" of his time that provided him with wonderful "training and experience with some brilliant teachers and a program that is set up in a brilliant way." LaCroix is "sure" that without this program he "would not have had . . . the same capabilities" he now possesses in "this area." He has now "the strength and the core and the awareness to take a different view on a much more enriched—a greater view of multiple issues." More important, he discovered his "deep core essence" by just "going in deeper and deeper and peeling the onion and keep peeling layers away and deeper and deeper and deeper; you get a sense of who I am as a core essence." This training was "an epiphany" that "had a major impact" on his "life." In his view,

> *MIT and Stanford and Stanford Business School were like drinking out of a fire hose for academic and business issues. This was like drinking out of a fire hose for emotional, spiritual and consciousness issues. I was blessed to have all these wonderful programs that would develop me in these ways.*

Structural Changes and Impact of LaCroix's Transformation

In LaCroix's model of the world we live "on these four levels: mental, physical, emotional, spiritual" (see Figure 46). The Master's program "rounded" him, "balanced" and gave him "structure and specific knowledge" as well as the "experiential process of learnings in the *emotional/spiritual* side that" were "under built" and to which he had "very little exposure" before. He considers this experiential program a "blessing" because he feels now "much more comfortable and capable" as a human being.

He has become "fairly well-rounded" in all areas of life and considers himself "a much better person."

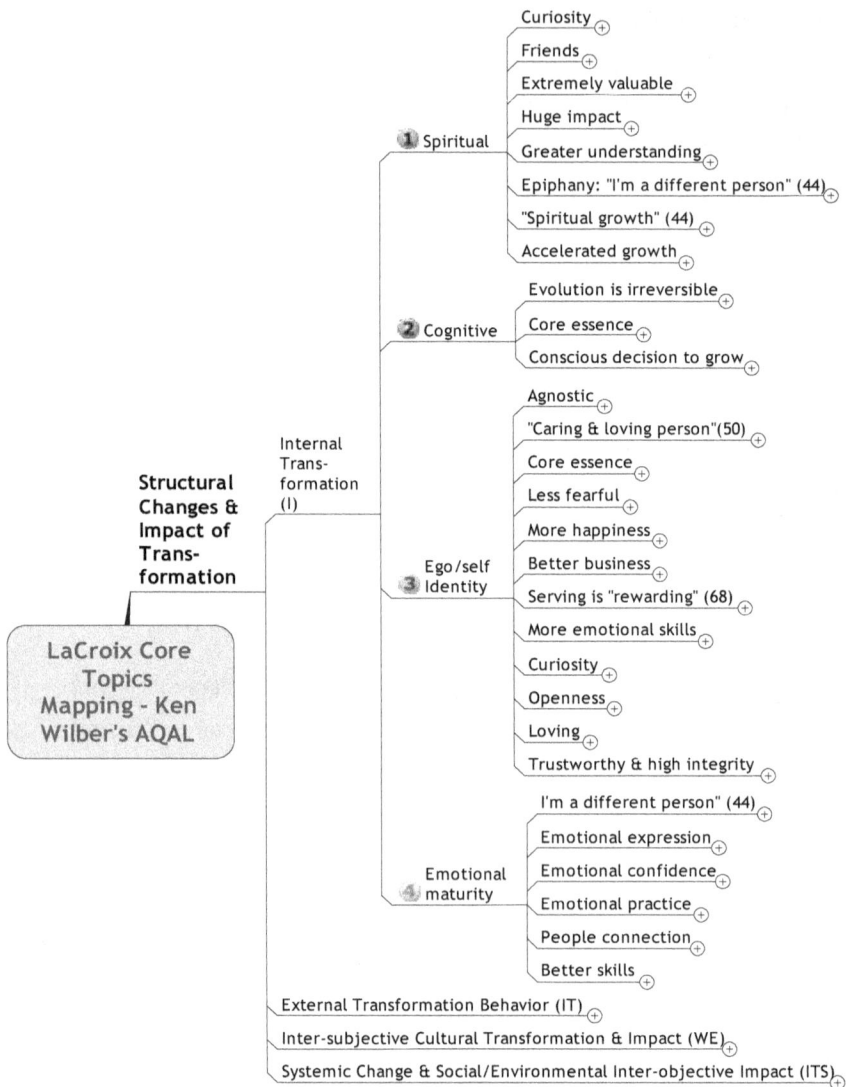

Figure 46. Structural changes and impact of LaCroix's transformation.

I had great experience on two levels and weak experience on two levels. This specific program gave me great exposure on the other two levels. It balanced me and I think made me a much better person because of it. That was a very specific catalyst, great program that just does a brilliant job at helping people on those two levels, all levels but

I didn't need the help on the first two. They really catered to the second two. I was fortunate to have that. I think while I'm still probably stronger in the mental/physical I am much stronger than I was in the emotional/spiritual. I'm much more comfortable and capable. I think I'm fairly well-rounded on all of those levels, which is wonderful. It's a blessing to have that and feel comfortable on those levels.

LaCroix views himself as a "caring, loving person" all throughout his life but before this program he "was careful with expressing" his "emotions and letting" them out. Today, he is "happy to go there" and is "not afraid" of emotions anymore because he has "more skills in that area." He "got more maturity in the sense of being able to express" his "emotions with confidence and by doing that" he gained more "confidence" and became more "strong." He characterizes his transformation "like going from black and white to full color. It's a maturity and growth of yourself that you can look back and say, 'Wow. I'm a different person.' That's the epiphany."

Over the past 15 years since his spiritual training, LaCroix has continued to grow and is in a much better position to deal with stress of any kind. His "consciousness about it" has increased because he is "more mature" and feels "more comfortable" although "the magnitude of the issues are [*sic*] dramatically higher now because" he is "dealing with businesses that are much bigger" than "before." He is now able to "laugh" about it. He thinks, "it's just fun" to deal with the ongoing issues in a much more "conscious way."

LaCroix perceives his training "like drinking out of a fire hose for emotional, spiritual and consciousness issues." He "progressed more rapidly and took a shift" in all areas of his life. He considers himself still an "agnostic" and believes in "spirituality, not a God-ness per se." Thus, he stays open and honors the "inner core spirit and sense" of people and life.

Furthermore, through this training, he became a better people person and developed "the ability to watch other people go deep and see their core essence." He learned to look beyond the façade and ask

Why are they saying this? This isn't about me. It's about what are they saying and how are we doing this? Because I have the strength

and the core and the awareness to take a different view on a much
more enriched – a greater view of multiple issues that I would not
have been aware of prior to going through this program and then
having the experience over the years on that.

LaCroix perceives it to be "very rewarding to try to help people to share" his "learnings with other people, and help them move through" their issues with ease. LaCroix is now able to connect "with people at a deeper, emotional level," which "has been very satisfying." Whereas beforehand he "might have been afraid to connect at an emotional level, after the program, he feels it is "very rewarding to connect at an emotional level." Moreover, LaCroix has "a definite interest" in "conquering world problems" and contributes to them on a very large scale.

In summary, LaCroix's transformation into a consciousness leader is characterized by several major lines of development, including the *emotional* (Goleman, 1995, 2000; Goleman et al., 2002; Ricard, 2003) and the *spiritual* (Wilber, 1999, 2000c). Being "blessed" with a good "cognitive capacity," a very "high intelligence," and "good health," LaCroix was able to not only earn two Master's degrees from two top American universities, but also became extraordinarily successful financially early on in his life. Yet, he became a more integrated human being only after attending a 2-year Master's program in Spiritual Psychology and cultivating his emotional and spiritual lines of development. Further research and quantitative tests (Cook-Greuter, 2004; Torbert et al., 2004) would have to be performed to be able to make a better informed assessment. However, based on the observations drawn from the current research, the following aspects are strong indicators that LaCroix has reached a postconventional stage of development: (a) his commitment to self-growth; (b) his awareness of cultural conditioning and willingness to move beyond it; (c) his multifaceted understanding of human beings; (d) his love of people and ability to connect with them at a deeper, emotional level; (e) his willingness to help and make the world a better place; and (f) his commitment to emotional and spiritual growth.

Entering the Market with Helping Hands

Common topic: All consciousness leaders in the current study have achieved high levels of consciousness through various kinds of Integral Life Practice (Wilber, 2006). The practice includes daily emotional, physical, mental, and/or spiritual practice that supports the interior evolution as a vehicle for service to humanity.

As we evolve as human beings, we seem to develop the ability to live at several levels of consciousness concomitantly (Aurobindo, 1993; Ram Dass, 1989; Walsh, 1999). That means that an awakened being is aware of the *physical, mental, emotional, soul*, and *spiritual* realms at the same time (Wilber 2000a). This seems to be a transpersonal characteristic of an integral human being (Vaughan, 2000, 2005; Walsh, 1999; Walsh & Vaughan, 1993; Watts, 1989, 2003; Wilber, 2000a). Within this context, it is important to note that consciousness leaders have experienced that an extraordinary *state* of feeling awake is not sufficient to become a permanent trait or a *structure* of being (Wilber, 2001). Thus, they have all installed various practices to support them because their paths are no longer about them but about service to humankind.

Wilber's (2006) Integrative Life Practice (pp. 201-205) provides an integrative collection of ancient and modern wisdom traditions that has been shown to further human evolution toward more permanent structures (Alexander et al., 1990; Leonard, 1991; Leonard & Murphy, 1995; Murphy, 1993; Walsh, 1999).

Within the context of the current study, it is also important to realize that all participants have seemingly evolved to become systems thinkers in service of humanity. To use the *Ox Herding Pictures*, a Zen Buddhist model of evolution, consciousness leaders appear to have reached later stages in which they enter "the market with helping hands" (Vaughan, 2000, p. 123).

Darlene's Individual Consciousness Leadership Profile with Transformational Characteristics

Darlene is not only a highly educated human being who holds a Ph.D. in psychology, but is also the author of multiple books, a serial entrepreneur, a well-known public speaker, a top executive, and a philanthropist. Appendix D contains the mind map representing the key core topics and transformational profile that resulted from the interview performed with Darlene.

Triggers, Context, and Process of Darlene's Transformation

The main triggers and context of Darlene's transformation into a consciousness leader are represented in Figure 47. Her spiritual evolution began early and she remembers at "age 5," when she "knew" that she was there "to serve" and at age 9, when "Jesus came to her" although she was Jewish. She evolved in a process of "gradual growth" with "slipping and sliding" and which included various exceptional human experiences and "grand [spiritual] openings." Darlene has been on the consciousness "path for years and years and years as a meditator, practicing very, very diligently" because she "wanted to get enlightened" and "would do anything to do that." Eventually, she moved to California and became deeply involved with the New Age movement in the 1960s.

As she was earning her Ph.D. in consciousness studies and psychology, Darlene began practicing yoga and started having even deeper "experiences" and "direct insights." These awakenings included "pure white light at the center" of her "heart burning right to the pure core essence" as well as "new ways of perceiving, chakras opening up" and "visual experiences":

> *All of a sudden, I would be seeing like an internal television camera. My eyes were [like] a TV camera looking through that and I knew something had opened up or also my heart opened and I*

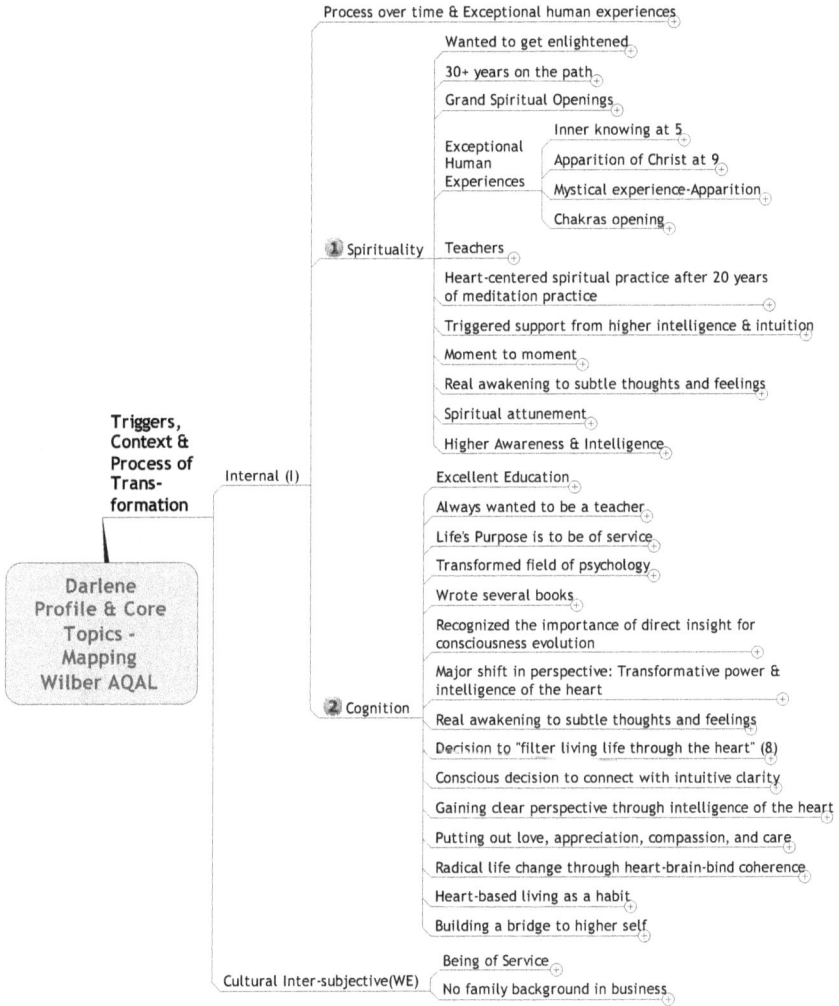

Figure 47. Triggers, context, and process of Darlene's transformation.

could feel every bird and insect as part of me, every being. It's the feeling of expansion.

Although she did not come from a family background rooted in business, did not "care about money," thought "business was about the head, self-serving, and making money," Darlene started her own company soon after her doctorate. She followed her calling to be of service and considered business as a spiritual path and as "an incredible laboratory for consciousness research because it involves how people treat themselves, treat each other, handle energies":

> *It was really interesting to apply what we do at night in our study groups, in our meditations and [be] all sweet and loving and caring with each other. . . . It was like a family business and from there that's when we started several other businesses. All the businesses had products that were services to the planet.*

Darlene began already in the early 1970s to develop consciousness businesses with her "friends." They were already "exploring consciousness" business practices and studied "processes like creative conflict and creative conflict resolution." She laid the foundation for consciousness leadership in business and integral living where "all came together, psychology, business, consciousness enfoldment, [and] serving the planet with products and services that were beneficial."

The Tipping Point—Awakening the Wisdom of the Heart

Darlene's real "shift in perspective" happened after 20 years of being a "meditator" when she met her teacher who "Talked so casually and from such a seasoned wisdom place about the heart and the intelligence of the heart and learning to filter one's perceptions, thoughts, attitudes, feelings through the heart like it was a sieve."

She began practicing the "wisdom of the heart" and "within 3 days" she "got really awakened to a lot of subtler thoughts and feelings" she "didn't know" she had. She knew that "there was nothing more important to do than to keep filtering living life through the heart and from the heart." She started to "perceive more" and her "higher intelligence or intuition would come in" to "help make adjustments" and create "spiritual attunement" that she "had not experienced" yet The "heart-based living" changed her entire life and took it to the next level of evolution.

Structural Changes and Impact of Darlene's Transformation

The main structural changes and impact of Darlene's continued transformation into a consciousness leader are remarkable and are shown in Figure 48.

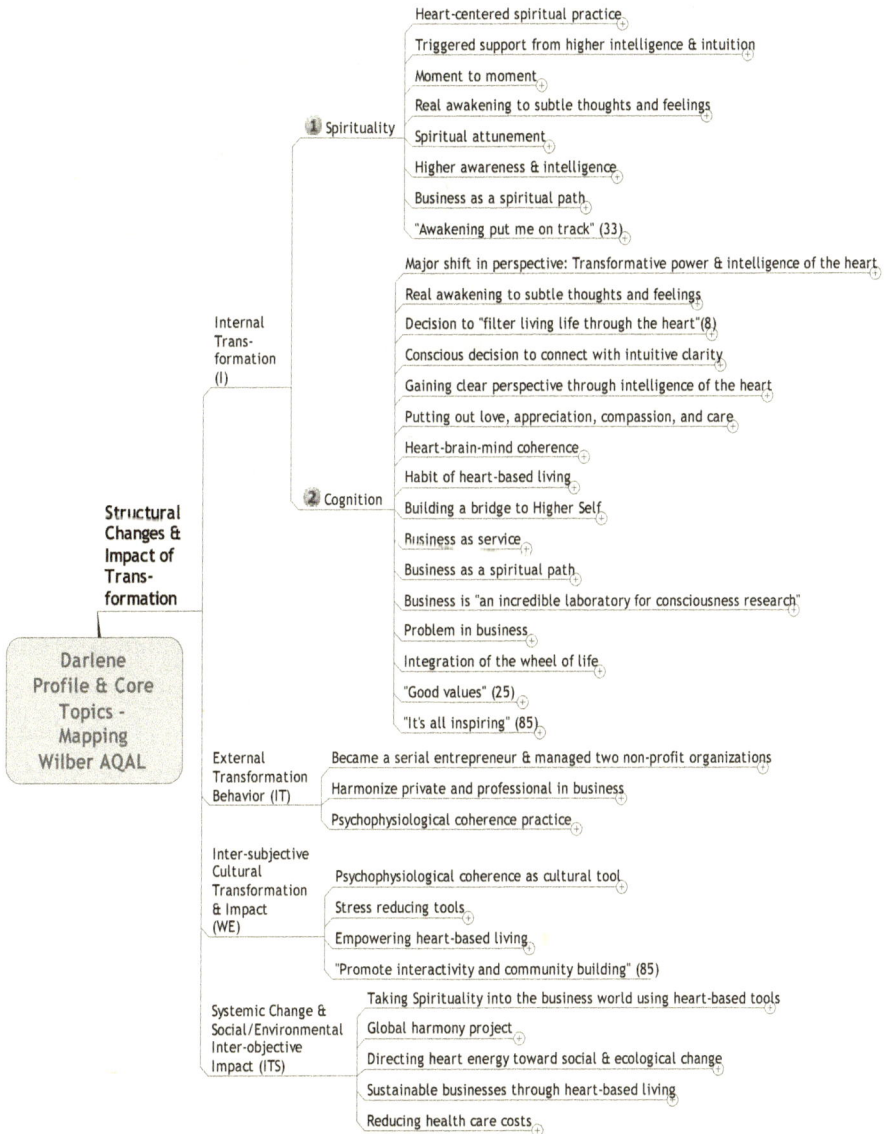

Figure 48. Structural changes and impact of Darlene's transformation.

Darlene continued on her spiritual-based, consciousness-driven, business path, and as she began practicing "heart-based living," her "life changed" significantly. She "could see" how the "intelligence of the heart" aligns "the brain [and the] mind with it in a higher dimensional state" that allowed more "intuitive clarity," wisdom, and true emotional mastery:

> *As I filtered feelings and thoughts and ideas through the heart and then just stepped back, it's like an adjustment wheel happened inside. My perspective would clear and I would see oh, I don't want to do, say that, or think that.*

Her spiritual and emotional practice today includes setting her "frequencies in the morning through the heart," putting out "love and care and appreciation, non-judgment and forgiveness, if needed, as well as compassion." She repeats this process several times per day and it helps her stay present and in attunement with her higher self.

She continues to view business as a spiritual path and as a "a way of helping people support themselves, as a way of getting good products and services out" to other people. She finds unfortunate that "most people in business don't have spiritual awakenings." She believes that "heart-based living" is necessary for people to "improve" their "internal coherence and then the team coherence and then the business coherence" because "you have to have an emotional alignment to really be effective and fulfilled." Darlene believes in "psychophysiological coherence" as a desirable state in which heart, brain, mind, emotions, and nervous system are in harmony with one another. She thinks that there should be no separation between people's interior and exterior lives. She thinks that "the types of conflicts that most companies have and just shove under the carpet" have to do with the idea that people are expected to "just get [their] job done, go home and deal with" all other problems at home.

In her view, "psychophysiological coherence" helps address all major conflicts because "when your heart, brain, and nervous system; the heart, mind and spirit, are all well aligned" more "intelligence can come in, more joy, more positive emotions of appreciation, joy, [and] care." Research

(McCraty, 2003) shows that "psychophysiological coherence" resolves "stress" and makes people more fulfilled and as a result "more productive." She is convinced that people, businesses, and organizations need "more global coherence" so that "the energetic shift" toward more emotional and spiritual harmony can occur because "this planet needs" the "spirit, heart, mind," and emotions to be in "alignment." From her personal experience over the past 4 decades of practicing consciousness business, Darlene knows that it is possible to "improve the quality of life while we improve the business outcomes at the same time" because "the two go together." In her view, it all "goes back to listening to your heart and what does that mean? It means listening to what feels right, what feels good, what feels right, what feels best for the whole."

In summary, Darlene who began her spiritual quest almost 4 decades ago, has apparently achieved a high degree of *emotional* (Goleman, 1995, 2000; McCraty, 2001, 2003), *spiritual* (Alexander et al., 1990; Wilber, 1999) and *egoic* mastery (Cook-Greuter, 2005; Kegan et al., 1990). Further quantitative tests (Cook-Greuter, 2004; Torbert et al., 2004) would have to be performed in order to be able to make a more informed assessment, however there is strong indication for later stages of development including the following: (a) her unassuming and humble presence; (b) her total dedication to service to humanity; (c) her sense of inner security resulting from emotional, egoic, and spiritual maturity; (d) through her books and speeches she has become a catalyst for change; (e) her unconditional love; (f) her ability to meet people at their own level of consciousness; (g) her sense of belongingness and connectedness with all there is; and (h) her extraordinary achievements are not seen as anything special but as a part of normal evolution.

Pioneers of Change

Common topic: All consciousness leaders in the current study have become pioneers of and catalysts for change. As they evolved on the inside, they wanted to have an impact on the outside to the benefit of all. However, because they had evolved beyond the center of gravity of their present environments, consciousness leaders encountered various difficulties. They felt estranged and no longer fully understood by the people they lead. For a while, they tried to influence and change their old environments but eventually they gave up and left. Eventually, they became systems thinkers who are now able to meet people at their own levels of consciousness.

Koplowitz (1984) argued that experienced systems thinkers have to adapt their worldviews as they grow because they realize that the world is defined by its relationship to the context or the environment. In other words, what we understand to be goodness or what the standard is for right or wrong, changes with its context and the environment. Thus, the view of the individual with respect to their environment changes with the individual self.

Unfortunately, leaders cannot expect the people they lead to do the same and must make it very easy for others to follow them. This is often a dilemma because depending on their level of consciousness, people have different views of the world and thus different dilemmas (Wade, 1996). As they become more adept at the art and science of changing their own and other people's minds, consciousness leaders become systems thinkers (von Bertalanffy, 1969/2006) who are able to influence the various cultural and social dynamics of their environments (Beck, 2000). Thus, flexibility, coherence, and their ability to apply various types of leadership intelligences become some of their main characteristics (Gardner, 1993, 2004).

DeSiena's Individual Consciousness Leadership Profile with Transformational Characteristics

DeSiena is a highly educated woman and best-selling author, serial entrepreneur, well-known public speaker, top executive, and philanthropist. Appendix D contains the mind map representing the key core topics and transformational profile that resulted from the interview performed with DeSiena.

Triggers, Context, and Process of DeSiena's Transformation

DeSiena's transformation into a consciousness leader was triggered by several lines of development represented in Figure 49. These lines included the *emotional, spiritual, physical,* and *cognitive* line. She was very close to her mother who was this "incredible force of common sense spirituality" and who raised her in the Christian faith. Yet, DeSiena's "first awakening to consciousness and to real spirituality was when" she "started doing yoga at Integral Yoga Institute" in San Francisco at age 20. Her teacher helped her and through his "energy," she "started feeling peace" and awoke "to something that was not constructed by man."

Spirituality and spiritual practice became her life-long companions because she felt how well they served her:

> *I remember doing the yoga and I remember just feeling like a wind, like peace coming in like a wind and me feeling that I was going to be okay, that I was okay and that my spirit was whole.*

After several years of studying with her guru, DeSiena sensed that it was time for her to move on. The "closer" she "got to the guru," the more she "saw his manipulation" and the "suffering" of so many people around him. She began to "see the flaws" and "left" because she got regular "migraines." She realized that "we must always listen to our bodies; they are vehicles for truth and they are vehicles for our truth." In her view, her "soul was obviously doing it's own work and having it's own experience and then it became burdensome."

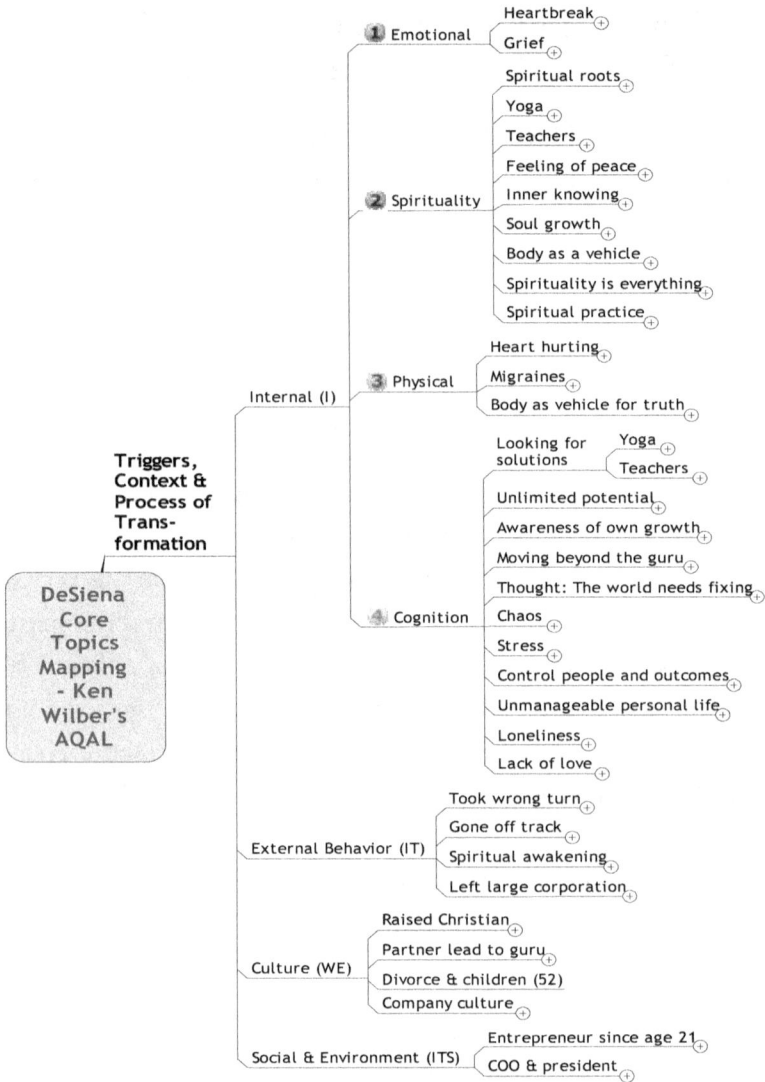

Figure 49. Triggers, context, and process of DeSiena's transformation.

Upon leaving her guru, DeSiena, who had her own company since age 21, began not only a family but eventually became the Chief Operating Officer of a world-renowned company. Through her spiritual and emotional mastery, she had reached a "certain level of consciousness" that was "open to light and truth and all the power that is." Thus, she was now ready to lead from that high level of consciousness. For the following 20 years, she tried to "influence the way [her employees] did business." She felt they "did have a responsibility to carry out" her "business in the way" she "wanted it." She "was trying to control outcomes" until she eventually learned that she "could not control those outcomes, nor could [she] control those people."

The Tipping Point—The Pie in the Sky

For many years, DeSiena was "trying" to lead with an "open heart and she "could not see that the other people did not hold" her "vision" or her "intention" to lead with "integrity." She thinks her leadership style "was ridiculed because" she "had this whole way of being that people really didn't even relate to. They kinda thought" she "was pie in the sky maybe." Eventually, she "was out of alignment" with her employees. Her life "was constantly in chaos" and became "unmanageable." She felt "really alone," and "very unloved."

Through her ongoing integral practice, she discovered soon that her "stress" came from "trying to live in the light in an environment that really didn't want" her "light." Her employees only did certain things because they wanted to "please" her because she "was signing the checks, but [they] didn't want to live that way." She noticed that her hardship came from "trying to pull people along" to her own level of consciousness about which they did not care.

Eventually, she understood, accepted, divorced her husband, left her old company, started a new business, and began a new life. Afterward, she felt "like" being on a "little cloud" because she "wasn't carrying [the] people" who did not want to or could not change anymore.

Structural Changes and Impact of DeSiena's Transformation

DeSiena's life transformed significantly (see Figure 50) over the past 4 decades since she embarked on a spiritual quest as the integration point between her interior and exterior lives. She is convinced that she "would not have survived anything without" her "spiritual life" and cannot "imagine living without" her daily "communing with spirit." Before, she "was

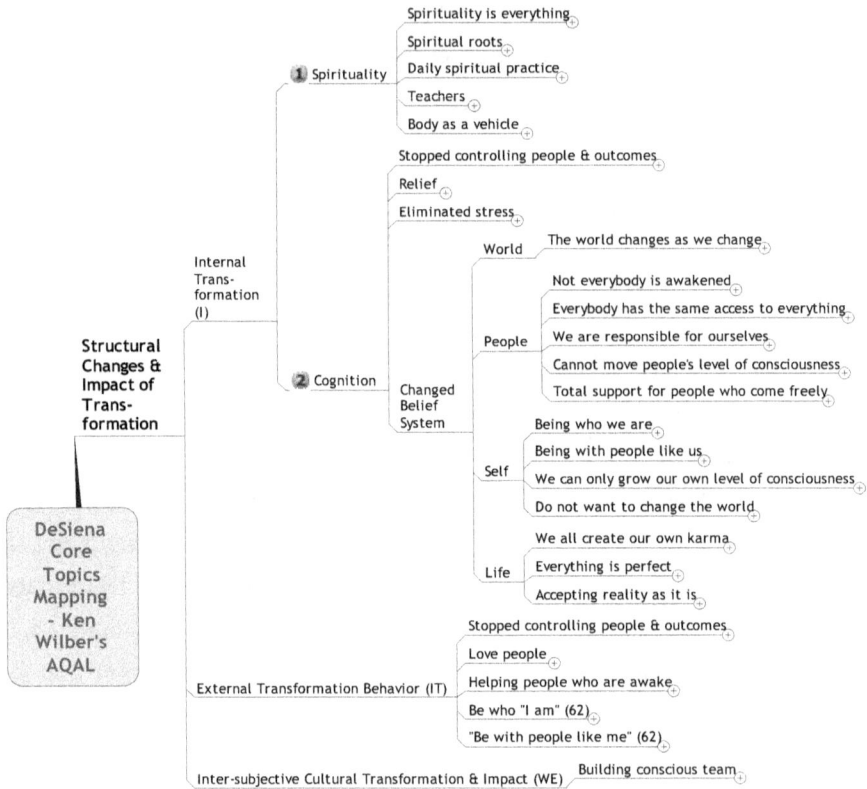

Figure 50. Structural changes and impact of DeSiena's transformation.

more asking for help and direction" whereas today, she is "being silent and opening" her "heart and feeling what's next."

Through her "painful" experience, she has become a much better leader because she is convinced that we "will help the world by being whole ourselves" first. She trusts that "by us carrying who we are and living who we are, we will raise the [global] consciousness by our very beings." In her view, we "can only raise our own level of consciousness." In her experience, we "can't move [other people's] level of consciousness" because "people are at the level of consciousness they are." She knows that "those who are drawn to us will come on," and today she chooses to be "with people" who are "in alignment" with her. She thinks that she is "actually diminishing" people's "life by trying to tell them the right way or even influence them in any way."

DeSiena continues to be of service to humanity, however, she "learned" that she does not want to "change the world" anymore. She no longer looks at today's challenges as "a problem" but as "reality." She is at peace with it because she knows "that everything is perfect" and presents "an opportunity to grow" both individually and collectively.

In summary, DeSiena's interior transformation into a consciousness leader is characterized by several lines of development including the *emotional* (Gardner, 1993; Goleman et al., 2002), *spiritual* (Alexander et al., 1990; Kegan et al., 1990; Kohlberg & Ryncarz, 1990), *egoic* (Cook-Greuter, 2005), and *value* line of development (Beck, 2000; Beck & Cowan, 1996). She has been on a consciousness path for more than 4 decades during which she evolved tremendously. Being a leader, pioneer, and agent for change, DeSiena tried very hard also to influence collective "outcomes" (Beck, 2000; Gardner, 2004). After 2 decades of tremendous effort within the corporate world, she eventually came to the realization that people are at different levels of consciousness than her own and they change when they are ready. As a result, she gave up the need to control, left her old environment, and is now compassionately meeting people at their own levels of consciousness with much better success (Beck & Cowan, 1996).

Further research and quantitative tests (Cook-Greuter, 2004; Torbert et al., 2004) would have to be performed to gain greater clarity, however, the following facts are a strong indication that DeSiena has reached later stages of human development (Alexander et al., 1990; Commons et al., 1990, 1984; Cook-Greuter, 2005, 2008; Koplowitz, 1984, 1990; Torbert et al., 2004; Wilber, 2000c). These facts include (a) her humility and unassuming presence regardless of her outstanding achievements (she is "really loving to work and not minding doing all of the jobs, whether it's taking out the trash or sweeping, serving someone tea, or coffee or signing the checks and depositing the money"); (b) her "integrity," her "pure heart" and determination to lead "people with light";(c) her appreciation of and acceptance for "what is" as being "perfect"; (d) her sense of "presence"; and (e) her willingness to let go of "control," and to go with the flow.

No Fear—No Death

Common topic: All consciousness leaders in this phenomenological study indicated that fear has been a tremendous teacher. By confronting their greatest fears, they reached higher levels of consciousness and transformed in all areas of their lives, internally and externally.

There are many theories about the root and nature of fear, but Williamson's (1996) words below have traveled cyberspace for many years because they ring true:

> *Our deepest fear is not that we are inadequate. Our deepest fear is that we are powerful beyond measure. It is our light, not our darkness that most frightens us. We ask ourselves, Who am I to be brilliant, gorgeous, talented, fabulous? Actually, who are you not to be? You are a child of God. Your playing small does not serve the world. There is nothing enlightened about shrinking so that other people won't feel insecure around you. We are all meant to shine, as children do. We were born to make manifest the glory of God that is within us. It's not just in some of us; it's in everyone. And as we let our own light shine, we unconsciously give other people permission to do the same. As we are liberated from our own fear, our presence automatically liberates others. (pp. 190-191)*

The main question is "How to liberate ourselves from fear?" It is virtually impossible to eliminate it because it is part of the Hero's Journey (Campbell, 1949/1968; Catford & Ray, 1991; Pert, 1997). However, there are various degrees of fear and all consciousness leaders researched in the current study confirm their struggles with fear. As they reached higher levels of consciousness (Cook-Greuter, 2008; Rooke & Torbert, 1998; Wade, 1996), they recognized the seat of happiness as the "here and now" (Nhat Hanh, 2002, p. 105), and were able to transcend various levels of fear by learning how to be present and go with the flow (Epstein, 1995; Watts, 2003).

Bianco's Individual Consciousness Leadership Profile with Transformational Characteristics

Bianco is a highly educated individual who received his degrees from a world famous university. He is a celebrated lawyer, a very successful serial entrepreneur, the author of multiple books, a poet, and an angel investor. He is deeply involved with "social entrepreneurial philanthropy" and with "creating different methods of distribution." Appendix D contains the mind map representing the key core topics and transformational profile that resulted from the interview performed with Bianco.

Triggers, Context, and Process of Bianco's Transformation

Bianco's transformation is an ongoing "creative process" that was triggered by several lines of development represented in Figure 51.

In his opinion, Bianco "was born into fear." He "got all the fear built into" him through his mother who was "absolutely fearful of everything." She was so "fearful" that in her mind his "dad died a thousand deaths . . . every time he didn't show up at 4:00 in the afternoon." Thus, addressing fear constituted a large component of Bianco's transformation over the past 4 decades.

Although he "didn't grow up wanting to be a lawyer," Bianco became an excellent one and built a prestigious law firm with hundreds of lawyers. He perceives himself not as a "natural lawyer" but he "loved" the creative, "counseling part of it." Although he "hated" the "documentation side" of it, he "forced" himself to do it. In order to be successful, he became a "workaholic" and worked "around the clock trying to document things" without enjoying it. This lifestyle created "tension" within. Eventually he "got tired of pushing and pushing and pushing and pushing that envelope." Nevertheless, he continued that stressful life style for several decades during which he built with his partners an exceptional law business that opened the door to "basically . . . anybody" he "wanted to see." That lifestyle enabled him to "do anything" he "wanted to do." However, he "didn't want to be thought of" as a lawyer but "do something totally different," which is what he is "doing right now." Yet, it took him many years to make it happen.

Figure 51. Triggers, context, and process of Bianco's transformation.

Bianco has always been deeply rooted in his "creative spark." He believes that life is about the "creative process" and the human ability "to express yourself in different ways." Therefore, he used his cognitive and creative abilities to "figure out" in his own "sort of egotistical way how things worked" and "just kept on digging."

For instance, he sought answers to key questions about money and resources and "tried to figure out why it was that economics was defined as the efficient allocation of scarce resources." In his view, "if you believe in a creative process or you believe in an evolutionary process then it's not about scarcity, it's about abundance." Therefore, he worked on redefining "economics as the efficient allocation of abundant resources" and eventually wrote an entire "textbook" on the topic.

During the many decades as a full-time lawyer, Bianco married twice, had five children, lost both wives to cancer, and ended up twice being "mother and father" to his children. He married a third time, yet his marriage did not withstand his ongoing transformation or the decision to move out of "his historical bias" or former environment by leaving his law firm.

The Tipping Point—Getting Fed up with Fear

Long before it became apparent to the outside world, Bianco used his "creativity" as a vehicle to grow further and break out of his social conditioning, which he calls "historical bias." In his model of the world, "if you believe in creativity, you should be able to move outside of that historical bias so that you're not just doing the same thing over and over again." Triggered by the Challenger disaster, Bianco wrote his first book as a means to release the tension he felt between "fear and desire." The book is "about a person who is creating himself; in other words, changing." Bianco took advantage of his "creative process" to break free and "move from one paradigm" to another. He believed that by being able to "project yourself outside yourself and seeing yourself as who you are, and then imagining moving into another space" one could create "another way of being."

His struggle between two extremes "fear/desire, fear/desire, fear/desire, fear/desire . . . overcoming fear of going to desire" went on for quite some time. By writing fiction, Bianco experimented with breaking out of his social conditioning that at times was so "flipping fearful." He knew that "if you could see yourself outside of yourself, observe yourself outside of yourself," he could free himself and unleash his unlimited "potential" to get where he actually wanted "to be."

In his view, the source of fear was a collection of elements with a common pattern out of which he wanted to escape: "I think a lot of that came about by my first wife passing and my second wife passing, and just some of the other elements. My mother being fearful and everything else. So there was a pattern there."

At the same time, his law practice grew and he realized that it became very difficult for him to oscillate between what he "liked" and what he "hated" within his profession. The paperwork became "suffocating":

> *Very, very difficult to be really a good lawyer because you're dealing with volumes and volumes of paper. When we started out you'd have one document that would be four pages long. A typical Deed of Trust today, if you're in the real estate world and you're trying to secure a note with a lien on a piece of property, you create a Deed of Trust. It can be 125 pages long. If you don't read every word of it every time, then you're not doing your job. You can't rely upon somebody else's redline or anything. You don't know what they're doing. So it becomes suffocating. So all these people are suffocating under enormous, enormous amounts of paper.*

Eventually, Bianco realized not only that he did not enjoy the documentation side of his profession but he got so "fed up" with fear that he decided to change his identity as a lawyer: "I didn't want to be thought of that way. I wanted to do something totally different and that was what I'm doing right now."

He awakened to the power of choice and realized that "within every moment called now you have a choice." He discovered a different dimension of consciousness:

> *All of a sudden really the light bulb goes on, and the light bulb is you're dealing in an abstract world. A cup is not a cup. The word is not the thing. So all of a sudden you're in an abstract world. You're looking at things with money and you're looking at dif-*

ferent kinds of things in a very abstract sense and what is under-
lying that is another reality that's rich and vibrant.

Eventually, Bianco left his law firm and moved to California where he "started a bank," got involved with several start-up companies, and continued to be a "social entrepreneurial" philanthropist.

Structural Change and Impact of Bianco's Internal Transformation

Bianco's transformation into a consciousness leader is characterized by several lines of development represented including the *cognitive, spiritual, egoic, emotional,* and *physical* lines (see Figure 52).

He was able to address his "fear" by "learning how to be present to a much larger entity," which meant that he had "to go and trust":

Trust has been the most difficult element. I trust myself within the context of things that I can see. I do not tend to trust myself outside of the context of what I can't see, when I don't know everything that's going on. So it's sort of like I needed to know everything that was going on. So the learning curve has been not to worry about that.

Moreover, he learned how to be present by "accepting" what is, "letting go of control," getting "out of the mental stuff and right down into just the basic feeling of it," and by "getting out of the abstract, mostly in getting down into the basic elements of life."

Bianco knows that there is "potential everywhere" and that is where he wants "to be. So that's why I'm attempting to be all the time, but to do that you have to be, like [Eckhard] Tolle says, present." Having been an exceptional athlete all his life, Bianco knows that "being in the zone" means "being present." Thus, he uses his regular exercise such as Pilates, yoga, balancing on a ball, or "pushing weights" as a vehicle for mindfulness work and for being present in the "vibrational field" of consciousness. Today Bianco's life is "not so much" about "trying to write" anymore as "much

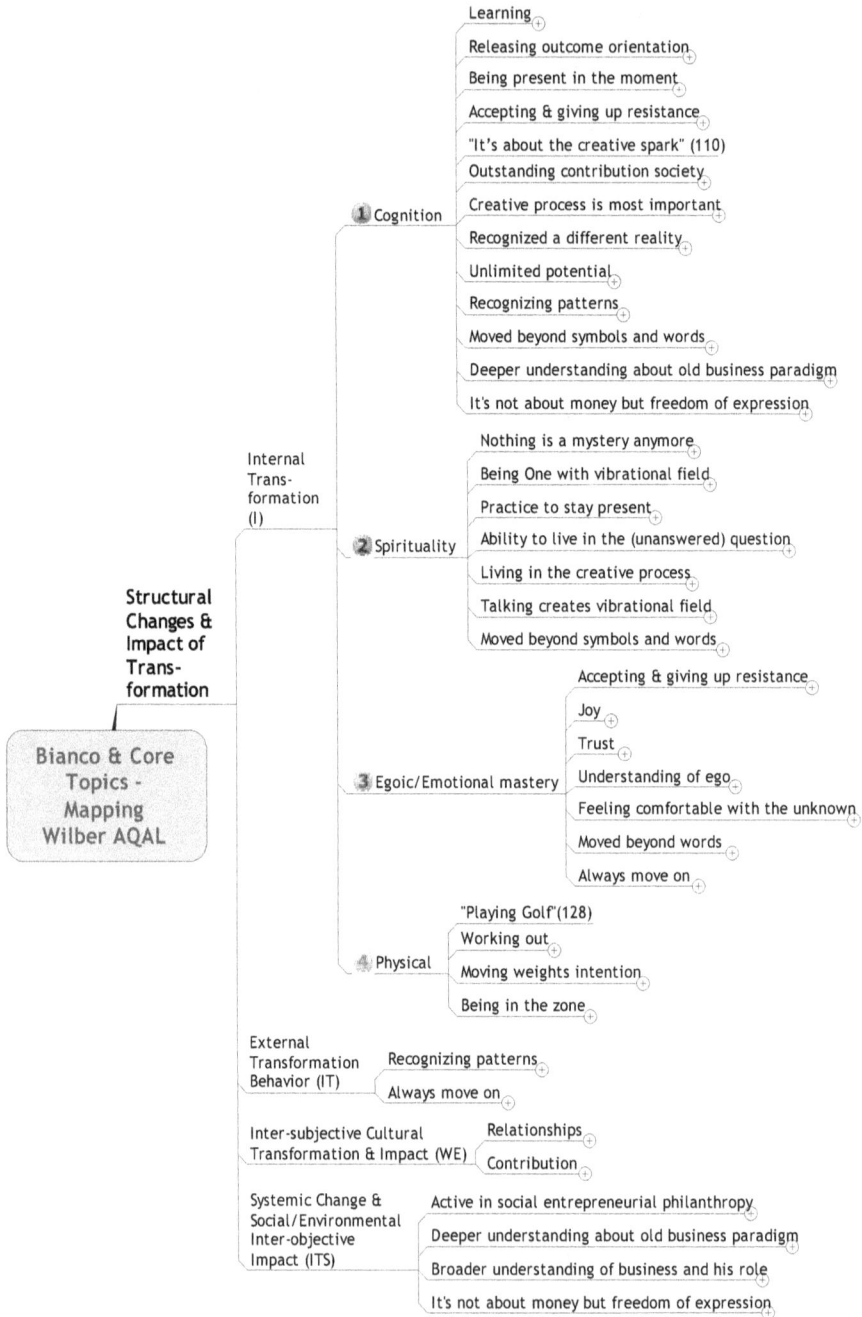

Figure 52. Structural change and impact of Bianco's internal transformation

as [it is about] experiencing it." He knows that "underlying" the obvious there "is another reality that's rich and vibrant." After many decades of evolution, Bianco has reached an "understanding of [the] spiritual or metaphysical" and knows that life is "about the creative spark" and "about getting beyond words." To be able to describe the ineffable, Bianco began taking photographs and writing poetry, which constitutes the content of another book he published. He lives his life by trying to be "present and in the moment and enjoying it" well knowing that

> *I'll always be moving on. So when my sense of my input or my value to whatever the resonant field is or whatever, interference patterns or whatever dissonant patterns are there, yeah I'll probably just move on to something else and it's a creative process. So a lot of things that I've created, and I've just sort of went on. It's just an evolutionary process.*

Further research and quantitative tests (Cook-Greuter, 2004; Torbert et al. 2004) would have to be performed to be able to have a quantitative assessment. However, based on the observations of this qualitative study, it appears that Bianco has reached postconventional levels of development (Commons et al., 1984; Cook-Greuter, 2008; Koplowitz, 1990) through his (a) humility and modest presence, (b) acceptance of reality as it is, (c) courage, (d) connection with and pursuit of creativity, (e) deep caring for all there is, (f) transpersonal understanding of leaders and leadership, (g) talent to make himself redundant as a leader, (h) ability to be in the zone and in the flow, (i) capability to move "beyond words," (j) capacity to become comfortable with uncertainty because there is "no mystery" left for him, and (k) trusting his "inner knowing."

From the Information Age to the Transformation Age

Common topic: All Consciousness Leaders are characterized by extraordinary cognitive abilities that were demonstrated not only through their high academic achievements but also through extraordinary successes in the business world. Yet, it is their integral transformational abilities that enable them to lead from the information age to the transformation age.

The cognitive ability in itself would however not be sufficient to contribute to the making of a consciousness leader as understood within the context of the current study. In the words of Kegan (Kegan & Lahey, 2001), our society suffers from the "maddening insufficiency of being well informed" (p. 230) because in his opinion "we are already the most overinformed, underreflective people in the history of civilization" (p. 234). The consciousness leaders researched in the current study seem to have recognized the truths expressed by Kegan. They realized that knowledge by itself is not power, but the ability to act upon it in an integral way could be empowering. These people became consciousness leaders not only through their cognitive capabilities but by combining their multiple intelligences (Gardner, 1993) with other transformational characteristics researched and discussed in this dissertation. Through these abilities, they can change their own and other people's minds with wisdom, compassion, love, and humor (Gardner, 2004, p. 184). As a result, the consciousness leader becomes the change agent needed to lead from the information age toward the transformation age. To indicate how the cognitive abilities played a key role in such a transformation, the structural and textural analysis of Lia, Chuck, Poet, and ElCore will be presented together by taking advantage of "referential adequacy" (Lincoln & Guba, 1985, p. 313). Referential adequacy is possible within the context of the present analysis, because the data are coherent with that of the other research participants and can "be shown to be representative" (p. 313).

Consciousness Leadership Profiles and Transformational Characteristics of Lia, Chuck, Poet, and ElCore

Lia, Chuck, Poet, and ElCore are highly educated individuals who have earned several academic degrees including doctoral degrees from prestigious school such as Stanford University. They are successful business people, social entrepreneurs, philanthropists, and renowned public figures. Appendix D contains the mind maps representing the individual key core topics and transformational profiles that resulted from the interviews performed with these research participants.

Triggers, Contexts, and Process of Transformation

All 4 participants confirm that their transformation occurred as a "process," a "journey," or a "continuum" that was accentuated by individual transformative events and "seminal points" (Lia) that were, at times, "incredibly painful" (Poet). The cognitive line of development was in all cases in the current study the main driving force. Furthermore, the "intellectual curiosity" (Lia), the willingness to "work hard" (ElCore), the drive toward personal "growth," the determination to contribute to a better world, the high value system such as "high integrity" (Chuck) and "equality and freedom" (Lia), catapulted them toward top executive positions, world fame, and financial abundance. As they became increasingly more successful career wise, they began missing the deeper dimensions in life. They began feeling out of line with traditional business values and had the desire to do "something that's much more aligned" with what they "would call the realization of what a purposeful life actually means" for them "as a soul" (Chuck); they noticed "a growing, gnawing, unfulfillment of maximizing shareholder value as an end goal" (Poet).

The stress associated with their former lifestyle manifested itself as (a) *physical* pain—"I was always in pain. Always bloated, always in pain. Couldn't eat anything. I always felt like I was 3 months pregnant" (ElCore); "physical things . . . like an appendectomy. I tore my ACL and just watching the different person that kind of shows up or the things that happen when you're not [present]" (Lia), and (b) as emotional/psychological pain—"I was really depressed and not feeling well, but mostly depressed" (ElCore); "obviously moments of pain [such as a] divorce, failures [to name] a couple of those" (Lia); "one of my blind spots, or I guess you could say growth development points was an insecurity that manifested itself in a need to be seen and a need to be taken seriously" (Poet); "I cannot really work with low-integrity people who stab me in the back" (Chuck).

In trying to cope with her challenges, Lia, like ElCore, continued to grow, began focusing more on what she could influence such her family, and sought support through "some wonderful coaches and friends, other people that have been there on the journey" (Lia). After realizing that traditional medicine could not help her, ElCore discovered the power of enzymes as a "lifesaver" and joined a spiritual cult whose guru taught her "laying on of hands," a process that transformed her "in many ways" and that represented "an important transformation as far as consciousness" is concerned (ElCore).

Poet describes his coping mechanism and the context of his transformation in the following way:

> *I was being fast-tracked at [my company] and all the trappings of success that I ever dreamed of had come to me. Yet a funny thing happened on the road to living happily ever after. I noticed that the pace I was keeping, which was very similar with anyone in business and in the world today, that I was just miserable. I was completely unhappy. There was this silent voice that became less and less silent. It just wouldn't go away. This voice just kept telling me over and over, reminding me that it was a little direct. It was that I did not like my life. I kept exhaling whenever I took a moment to slow down and even unconsciously, I wasn't allowing myself to even slow down. If I did slow down even for a moment, I started to realize how desperately unhappy and unfulfilled I was. Almost consciously by design or unconsciously I kept myself so busy.*

The Tipping Point—From Information to Transformation

The tipping point toward becoming a consciousness leader was represented through pain and triggered by different individual events. For Lia, it was the birth of her third child and the realization of her unconditional "love for another human being. It really is on top for everything. That's one of those real moments of truth" (Lia). She recognized that her external success and career was nothing compared with the love she felt for "this little baby and I wouldn't have traded anything in the world for him. That was like a real graphic moment, one of those moments when you really see oh my God, what have I been striving for? What is it all about?" (Lia).

Despite her Jewish background, ElCore felt attracted to Buddhism early on and spent "10 years" growing spiritually and studying with a world renowned guru who taught that "there's no way to heal this ego. The only way to heal is to transcend it, liberate from it" (ElCore). To "this day" she feels "that [this work caused] a significant change and it helped [her] see that healing . . . was about conscious energy on participation and love" (ElCore). However, when she became aware of the unethical conduct within her cult as well as the fact that "there was a lot of sexual abuse" hidden behind "the realm of spiritual practice," ElCore had the courage to leave the group, become a consciousness leader herself, and "serve people" through her own integral life practice.

Chuck's major tipping point occurred when he found out that his boss lied to him. At that time, Chuck had already become financially independent but continued to work in his old company to help it overcome the challenges it was facing. However, living with integrity has the highest priority on his value's scale and its violation "was so dramatic" to him that he went "out in the parking lot and cried" before he decided to quit because he could not work with "low-integrity people who stab [him] in the back" (Chuck).

Poet shifted to a higher level of consciousness at the peak of his professional career when "three things happened" around the same time: (a) he lost his mother, (b) he met his wife, and (c) he worked with his life coach and realized that he "was a complete hypocrite" because his lifestyle and his livelihood did not match up against his values.

Structural Changes and Impact of Transformation

The structural changes and impact of transformation were significant for all participants. Lia comprehended the importance of living an integral life in which the interior aspects must be balanced with the exterior because "you can't separate your life" (Lia). She realized "how much gender stereotypes hold us back," how important it is to have "a set of values that you've thought about and adopted so that it's your choice [and] that you're going to be those values", how family and relationships come before career, and how significant "the value of truth and honesty and integrity" (Lia) are for her. After leaving Corporate America, she embarked on her own leadership journey to help everybody but especially women fulfill their greatest potentials. She is now not only an active philanthropist, but she is teaching how to "self-select" and live through higher standards and "strong values" such as credibility, truth, honesty, authenticity, love, trust, and integrity. While doing that, Lia continues to stay open, be a good listener, practice a beginner's mind, and "keep reminding" herself "that there is no real truth or [that] very few things are the way we think they are" (Lia).

After her negative experience with her guru, ElCore found it "hard to even read a book, meditate, [or] talk about spiritual practice" for a while. Yet, today she meditates regularly and has a "spiritual practice" that enables her to be "more open," "less dogmatic," and "feel more mature". Furthermore, she "believe[s] in intentions" rather than "goals," her "self-confidence" and intuition have increased, and she is "less concerned with material things" than before. She feels that her "conscious [leadership] practice . . . made a difference" in her life and enabled her to become a better mother, a better healer due to her "compassion for people." In her view, she became a better "teacher" and a better "leader." Therefore, her new mission in life is teaching, healing, and "serving other people," a desire that also drove her toward earning two doctorate degrees. In her opinion, "service is really the key" in her life, but she does not see it as a conscious act as much as being a conduit or the "vehicle" and "energy" for its manifestation (ElCore).

Following his demission from his corporate America job, Chuck decided to pursue his spiritual quest and deepen his understanding regarding "the interconnectedness or the oneness or the holistic nature" because in his understanding, "once you really internalize that" then "there's no going back." Despite the financial abundance acquired through his entrepreneurial and investor activities, Chuck did not fall into the "wealth trap" because in his worldview material "wealth is actually a bad thing . . . for humans." In his assessment, money is "seductive on an ego base" and he thinks that it "takes an evolved consciousness not to fall into these traps." Chuck, who has a doctorate in computer science, believes that his opening to a higher level of consciousness was triggered by the "out-of-body experience early on" in his life. It expanded his understanding about life and showed him "very clearly that" he is "not [his] body" (Chuck). Further nonordinary state experiences made him want to know more about how the "universe actually works from a physical perspective." The result was his understanding that "time is an illusion of the mind" and that he has "absolutely no fear of death" (64). In fact, he believes in a "great opportunity upon death to move forward." He considers that "enlightenment is not a goal" and is "comfortable not knowing" what comes next in his life. Following his transformation, he replaced "goals" with "intentions," is open to "synchronicity," practices being the observer to "stay sane," and has a regular spiritual practice that entails yogic exercises, "nature walks," and meditation. Chuck's life purpose also changed toward an "impactful contribution to sustainability, holistic sustainability . . . to explore and lead and show different ways of creating social enterprises and different financing mechanisms that are behind that, so that we move capitalism beyond the pure maximizing of profits."

After losing his mother, Poet "was devastated." This experience changed him deeply and triggered a process during which he "was being rewired." In his view, everything he "used to think was important was no longer important." Before his transformation, everything "was me, me, me and my fabulous career and how do I help create more money for [the company], so I can create more money for me and more success for me and more power for me." After being "rewired" he realized that his old way of life "was just a small game, [but] it felt like a big game." Today he things that after his transformation, he noticed that his former career that he perceived like "the biggest game in town" now feels "like the smallest game in the universe":

> *When you really make that shift and you start playing for an idea bigger than yourself and you start sensing into what is that divine creative impulse that's seated within me that is my gift to the planet? Within that surrendering was recognizing that there's something unique within me that I was born to become and that by surrendering to that, by paying attention to that, by allowing that to emerge within myself, that I could play a much bigger game, a much more fulfilling game, a much more meaningful game in terms of being able to create from that space in service to a much deeper and broader concept.*

After turning his back away from the business world for "2 years," Poet returned to the business world and in all humility he perceives himself today as a "full-spectrum, conscious leader." Today he thinks that he is much better able to integrate all aspects of his life than before. His professional life is much more in line with his personal one and he is much better able to balance the relationship with his wife, his children, with his "self interest and concern for others and caring for others." Whereas in the beginning of his transformation, he was very critical of his past professional success and brilliant career, today he "started to recognize [that] it was such a blessing that" he "had these 15 years of training in the Fortune 100 world." He sees that he can now "fully embrace [his experience,] fully show up, and use business to help build a better world." In order to do that, he realized that "had to re-imagine the possibility of business. Recognizing that business has become the most powerful, the most creative, the most innovative, the most effective institution on the planet." Poet transcended his original "rejection" of the old business paradigm and considers living in "an extraordinary time" in which he finds himself "deeply grateful" to "be alive." With his newly acquired acceptance for what is, he is now able to "just go quietly out the door and just be with humility and perseverance" around people who disagree with him. He can now meet them where they are and "connect with their unfulfilled needs and help them get to the next point where they wanted to be, rather than getting them to where [he] wanted them to be." In his opinion, he is now "completely" able to embrace paradoxes and "acknowledge that all is necessary" (Poet) within the evolutionary process.

In summary, based on existing research on adult development (Alexander et al., 1990; Commons et al., 1990; Cook-Greuter, 2008; Goleman, 2000; Torbert et al., 2004, 2008) the consciousness leaders researched here appear to have moved to later/postconventional stages although more research would have to be performed to gain deeper insights. However, the following indicators signify postconventional levels of development: Lia, ElCore, Poet, and Chuck appear to (a) have awakened to and embraced non-duality; (b) be able to live with paradoxes and be creative, joyous, fulfilled, and serene most of the time; (c) live in the present moment and accept reality as "is"; (d) have their spirituality be an integral part of their personal and professional lives; (e) cultivate their capacity for compassion, empathy, and unconditional love through integral practices; (f) be able to live in the present and day by day; (g) be humble and display an unassuming presence; (h) have learned how to master their emotions; (i) be detached from their outcomes and set intentions instead; (j) have transcended money and the material world; (k) live simple lives of global service; (l) experience genuine joy, gratefulness, and have a life-affirming attitude; and (m) have a sense of interconnectedness with others and the source of life.

Chapter Summary

This chapter contained the analysis of the individual transformation of the research participants in the present research. Thirteen common topics have been identified that precede individual analysis. The intention of this chapter was to preserve each individual voice, to relate the meaning and interpretation of each participant, and to provide a thick interior description of the nature and process of transformation toward becoming a consciousness leader. The individual analyses attempted to represent as precisely as possible the phenomenological first-person account, the inside-out representation, as well as the structural transformation within his or her own cultural and social context. The next chapter contains the composite depiction of the 16 participants in this research.

CHAPTER 5

COMPOSITE AND SYNTHESIS

The previous chapter contained the analyses of the individual transformation of the research participants in this heuristic structuralism-based research. By being embedded in the concrete evolutionary structure represented by the Wilberian (2000a) AQAL map of con sciousness, each individual analysis was mostly characterized by verbatim accounts of every participant. The intention was to preserve each individual voice, allow for his or her meaning and interpretation, and provide a thick interior description of the nature and process of transformation toward becoming a consciousness leader. As accurately as possible, the individual analysis attempted to represent the phenomenological first-person account and the inside-out representation of the transformation from the perspective of the participants as they see themselves embedded in their own cultural and social context.

This chapter provides a composite depiction and synthesis of the research participants and contains the common topics, themes, and universal qualities of their experience and transformation as they have been identified in the previous chapter and emerged over many months of deep immersion with the research material. The *first dimension* of the composite representation is the dynamic story of becoming a consciousness leader. It is presented using the three major phases described in Joseph Campbell's (1949/1968) book *The Hero with a Thousand Faces*. The three phases are *Departure, Initiation*, and *Return*. The journey of becoming a consciousness leader is called the Hero's Journey and "includes exemplary narratives, descriptive accounts, conversations, illustrations, and verbatim excerpts that accentuate the flow, spirit, and life inherent in the experience" (Moustakas, 1990, p. 52).

In keeping with the consistency of the Wilberian (2000a) map of consciousness (AQAL) and the heuristic structuralism research method chosen for this research, the composite depiction of the present study includes a *second dimension*, which contains the lines of development involved at each of the three stages of the participants' transformation.

The essence of the transformation toward consciousness leadership will be extracted, illuminated, and explicated not only from the *inside-out* view of the participants themselves but also from my *outside-in* perspective. Thus, this section will mainly offer my own interpretation and show the "patterns or structures [that] actually govern the phenomena" (Wilber, 2006, p. 55). When representing the transformational characteristics of the consciousness leader especially as they relate to both nonordinary *states* as well as *stages* of consciousness of the participants, my own voice will no longer be muted, and I invite the reader to actively participate, critique, and validate my interpretations and the extracted meanings.

The Making of the Consciousness Leader

All research participants without exception confirm that their becoming a consciousness leader is a continuing process that has been going on between 1 and almost 4 decades. As shown in their own words displayed in the Figure 53 below, the leaders refer to a journey of "trial and error" that is "incredibly painful," "slow," and a "messy process."

In building the composite representation of a consciousness leader, it became obvious that each participant underwent the so called *Hero's Journey,*

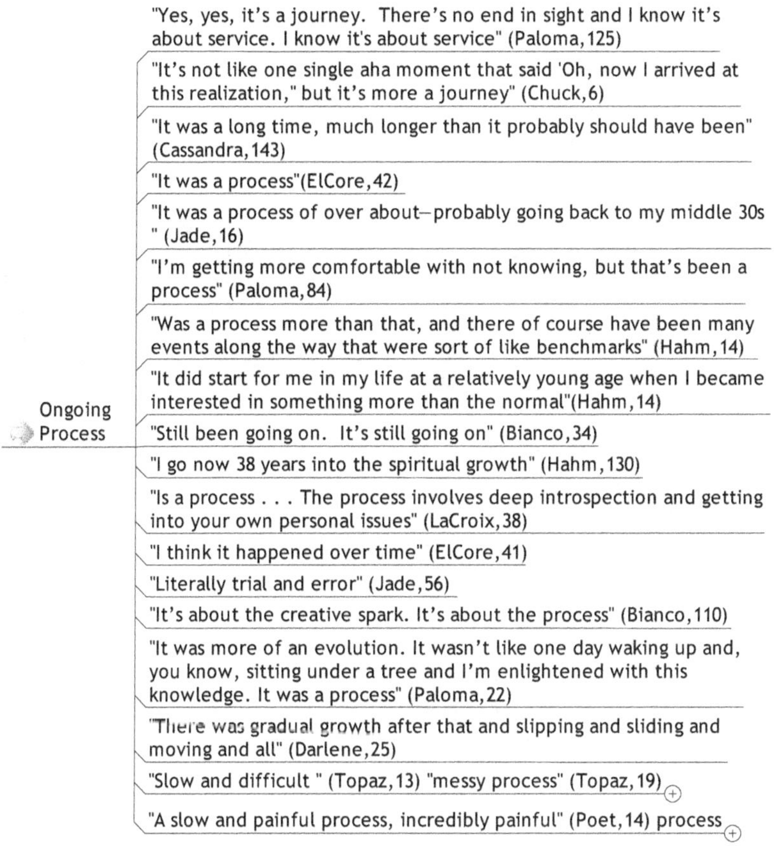

"Yes, yes, it's a journey. There's no end in sight and I know it's about service. I know it's about service" (Paloma, 125)

"It's not like one single aha moment that said 'Oh, now I arrived at this realization," but it's more a journey" (Chuck, 6)

"It was a long time, much longer than it probably should have been" (Cassandra, 143)

"It was a process"(ElCore, 42)

"It was a process of over about—probably going back to my middle 30s " (Jade, 16)

"I'm getting more comfortable with not knowing, but that's been a process" (Paloma, 84)

"Was a process more than that, and there of course have been many events along the way that were sort of like benchmarks" (Hahm, 14)

"It did start for me in my life at a relatively young age when I became interested in something more than the normal"(Hahm, 14)

Ongoing Process

"Still been going on. It's still going on" (Bianco, 34)

"I go now 38 years into the spiritual growth" (Hahm, 130)

"Is a process . . . The process involves deep introspection and getting into your own personal issues" (LaCroix, 38)

"I think it happened over time" (ElCore, 41)

"Literally trial and error" (Jade, 56)

"It's about the creative spark. It's about the process" (Bianco, 110)

"It was more of an evolution. It wasn't like one day waking up and, you know, sitting under a tree and I'm enlightened with this knowledge. It was a process" (Paloma, 22)

"There was gradual growth after that and slipping and sliding and moving and all" (Darlene, 25)

"Slow and difficult " (Topaz, 13) "messy process" (Topaz, 19)

"A slow and painful process, incredibly painful" (Poet, 14) process

Figure 53. Ongoing process of evolution.

which according to Campbell (1949/1968) has three major phases, namely *Departure, Initiation, and Return.* The Wilberian (2006) AQAL/IMP representation of the composite depiction and the three phases of the *Hero's Journey* as they apply to the consciousness leader in business are shown in Figure 54.

The three phases are: (a) The Awakening of the Consciousness Leader, (b) The Initiation of the Consciousness Leader, and (c) The Emergence of the Consciousness Leader.

The Making of the Consciousness Leader Composite Profile & Core Topics - Mapping Wilber AQAL (IMP)

CONTEXT, TRIGGERS, & INITIATION OF THE CONSCIOUSNESS LEADER (PHASE I & II)

EMERGENCE OF THE CONSCIOUSNESS LEADER & COMPONENTS OF STRUCTURAL CHANGES (PHASE III)

INTERNAL TRANSFORMATION & IMPACT (I)

1. COGNITIVE — What I am aware of?
- Unleashing unlimited potential
- New purpose and passion
- Courage & creativity
- Detachment—less efforting
- Intentions instead of outcomes
- Letting go of control
- Accepting what is
- Changed material orientation
- There is conscious choice
- Taking responsibility & openness
- Integral consciousness & living
- Great clarity

2. SPIRITUAL — What is of ultimate concern?
- Serious spiritual quest & practice
- Trusting the universe/God
- Ongoing unity consciousness experiences
- Deeper understanding
- Business as a spiritual path: Embodied spirituality

3. PHYSICAL — How should I physically do this?
- Regular physical practices
- Body as a vehicle for right action
- Visualization exercises
- Integration of the wheel of life

4. EMOTIONAL — How do I feel?
- Dominant positive emotions
- Willingness to face greatest fears & shadows
- Better skills to transcended suffering
- Fear transcendence (no fear of death)
- Higher emotional awareness

5. VALUES — What is significant to me?
- Being of service
- Integrity, truth, honesty
- Authenticity & credibility
- Truthfulness & humility
- Oneness & humanity

6. ETHICS & MORALS — What I should do?
- Social justice
- High moral standards
- Taking responsibility/accountability

7. EGO/SELF — Who am I?
- Actualization holarchy
- Flow instead of resistance
- Cultivating presence
- Openness & creativity
- Trusting the universe/God

- EXTERNAL BEHAVIOR TRANSFORMATION & IMPACT (IT) - How do I relate to others?
- INTERNAL CULTURE INTER-SUBJECTIVE TRANSFORMATION & IMPACT (WE) - How do we relate to each other (cultural center of gravity)?
- EXTERNAL INTER-OBJECTIVE SOCIAL & ENVIRONMENT TRANSFORMATION & IMPACT (ITS) - How should we interact socially?

INTERNAL (I) — Ongoing Process

COGNITIVE — What I am aware of?
- High intellect & desire to evolve
- Creativity & curiosity
- Working hard
- Outside-in Mentality
- Ego driven
- External success & financial abundance
- Resources: teachers, books, seminars, friends
- What Prevented Growth

PHYSICAL — How should I physically do this?
- Back problems
- Overweight
- Other physical issues

EMOTIONAL — How do I feel?
- Fear and anxiety
- Unhappiness, lack of fulfillment & emptiness
- Need to control & judgement
- Looking for help through therapy & counseling
- Eventually: Courage & permission to face all past

SPIRITUAL — What is of ultimate concern?
- Conflict: Religious upbringing and inner knowing about divine nature
- Yearning for postmodern spirituality

EGO/SELF — Who am I?
- Self understanding
- Emotions
- Working hard

TIPPING POINTS
- Physical & emotional pain & challenges
- Cognitive decision to face the dark night of the soul
- External events
- Exceptional human experiences
- Impact

- EXTERNAL BEHAVIOR (IT) - How I relate to others?
- INTERNAL CULTURE INTER-SUBJECTIVE (WE) - How do we relate to each other (cultural center of gravity)?
- EXTERNAL INTER-OBJECTIVE SOCIAL & ENVIRONMENT (ITS) - How should we interact socially?

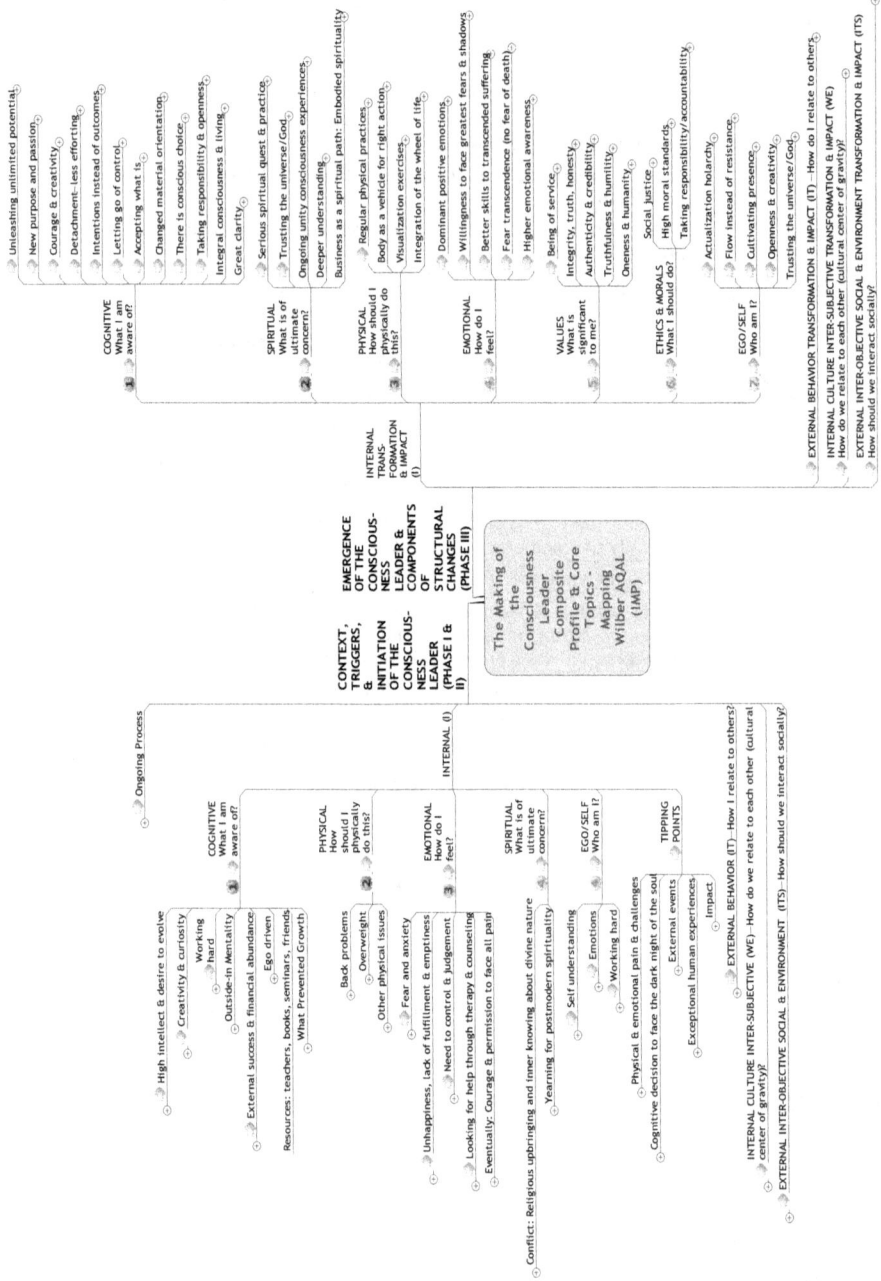

Figure 54. The making of consciousness leaders—
Composite profile and heroic phases.

The Awakening of the Consciousness Leader: Phase I

The analysis chapter made it easy to recognize that the cognitive line of development (Gardner, 1993) is the key driving force in the life of the consciousness leader (see Figure 55).

In other words, all consciousness leaders are blessed with and are aware of their high levels of intelligence that enabled them to take advantage of the social and cultural opportunities in which they developed. No matter

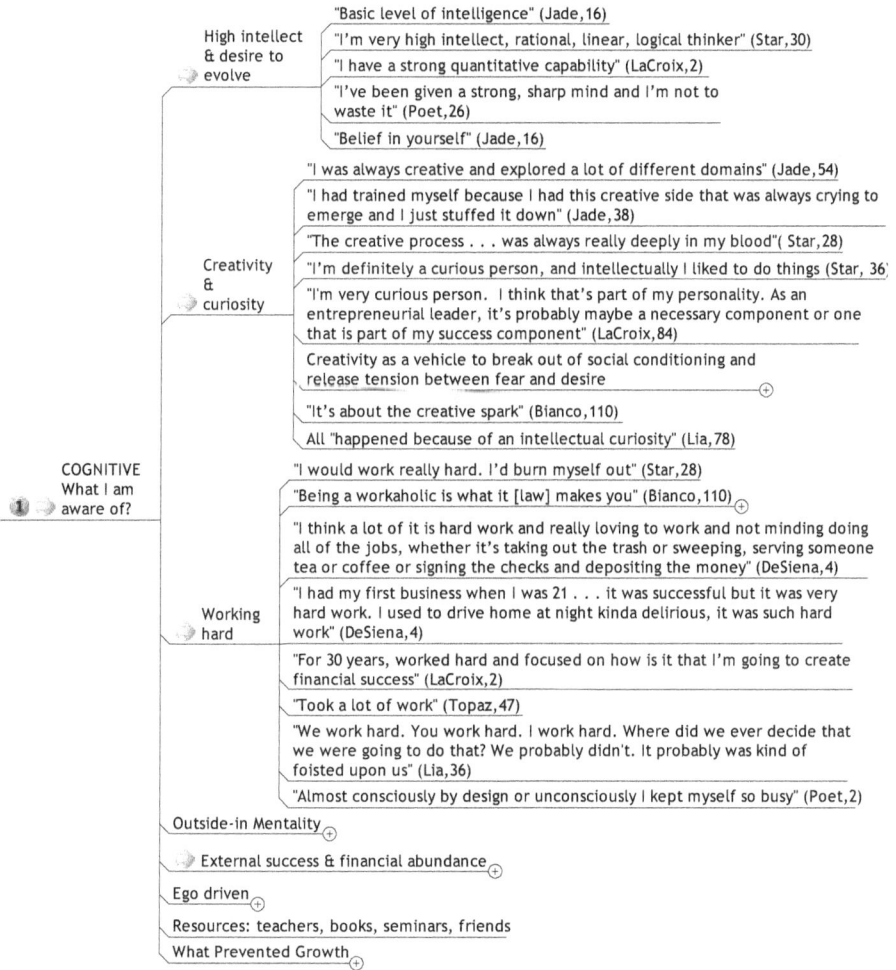

High intellect & desire to evolve
- "Basic level of intelligence" (Jade,16)
- "I'm very high intellect, rational, linear, logical thinker" (Star,30)
- "I have a strong quantitative capability" (LaCroix,2)
- "I've been given a strong, sharp mind and I'm not to waste it" (Poet,26)
- "Belief in yourself" (Jade,16)

Creativity & curiosity
- "I was always creative and explored a lot of different domains" (Jade,54)
- "I had trained myself because I had this creative side that was always crying to emerge and I just stuffed it down" (Jade,38)
- "The creative process . . . was always really deeply in my blood"(Star,28)
- "I'm definitely a curious person, and intellectually I liked to do things (Star, 36)
- "I'm very curious person. I think that's part of my personality. As an entrepreneurial leader, it's probably maybe a necessary component or one that is part of my success component" (LaCroix,84)
- Creativity as a vehicle to break out of social conditioning and release tension between fear and desire
- "It's about the creative spark" (Bianco,110)
- All "happened because of an intellectual curiosity" (Lia,78)

COGNITIVE
What I am aware of?

Working hard
- "I would work really hard. I'd burn myself out" (Star,28)
- "Being a workaholic is what it [law] makes you" (Bianco,110)
- "I think a lot of it is hard work and really loving to work and not minding doing all of the jobs, whether it's taking out the trash or sweeping, serving someone tea or coffee or signing the checks and depositing the money" (DeSiena,4)
- "I had my first business when I was 21 . . . it was successful but it was very hard work. I used to drive home at night kinda delirious, it was such hard work" (DeSiena,4)
- "For 30 years, worked hard and focused on how is it that I'm going to create financial success" (LaCroix,2)
- "Took a lot of work" (Topaz,47)
- "We work hard. You work hard. I work hard. Where did we ever decide that we were going to do that? We probably didn't. It probably was kind of foisted upon us" (Lia,36)
- "Almost consciously by design or unconsciously I kept myself so busy" (Poet,2)

- Outside-in Mentality
- External success & financial abundance
- Ego driven
- Resources: teachers, books, seminars, friends
- What Prevented Growth

Figure 55. The cognitive line of development at phase I and II.

how challenging the social and cultural environments were, they provided these leaders with the opportunity to receive an outstanding education as the basis for outer success and achievement. All leaders seized that educational opportunity, received academic degrees from prestigious universities, and became life-long learners. Because the cognitive line is the main driving force in the *Hero's Journey* of consciousness leaders, it has been marked with the number 1 in the above figures.

As can be seen through the verbatim accounts displayed in Figure 55, the leaders' desire to grow was fueled by their innate curiosity and creativity as well as the willingness to work very hard. Furthermore, their social conditioning led over time to belief systems and "self-created myths" about the leaders' unique abilities to manifest financial and material abundance. The self-reinforcing "outside-in mentality" was nourished by high-intelligence, great education, drive, tenacity, hard work, outcome-orientation, competitiveness, and the ability to be an achiever in a highly supportive environment. It helped build outstanding reputations, highly admired social statuses, extraordinary wealth, strong egos, and the belief that one is in control (see Figure 55).

The upward spiral of external success seemed secured until it was not. The *Hero's Call to Adventure* (Campbell, 1949/1968) occurred when the consciousness leader was made aware of the place beyond the familiar world. The *Call to Adventure* was triggered by pain.

The source of pain was often *physical*—market with the number 2 and shown in Figure 56. It showed up as simple dysfunctions such as "back problems," "heart hurting," "migraines," "colds and sore throats," weight gain, or more serious diseases such as multiple sclerosis or acute food allergies.

Some other times, the source of pain was of emotional nature (see Figure 57) and was caused by a "horrible divorce," the death of a loved one, a challenging relationship with a parent or significant other, and of course, business "pressure."

The emotional pain showed up as a "high-degree anxiety," "worry and fear," "heartbreak," tension between "fear and desire," "grief," the "need" to be accepted by the outside world, and frustration (see Figure 58).

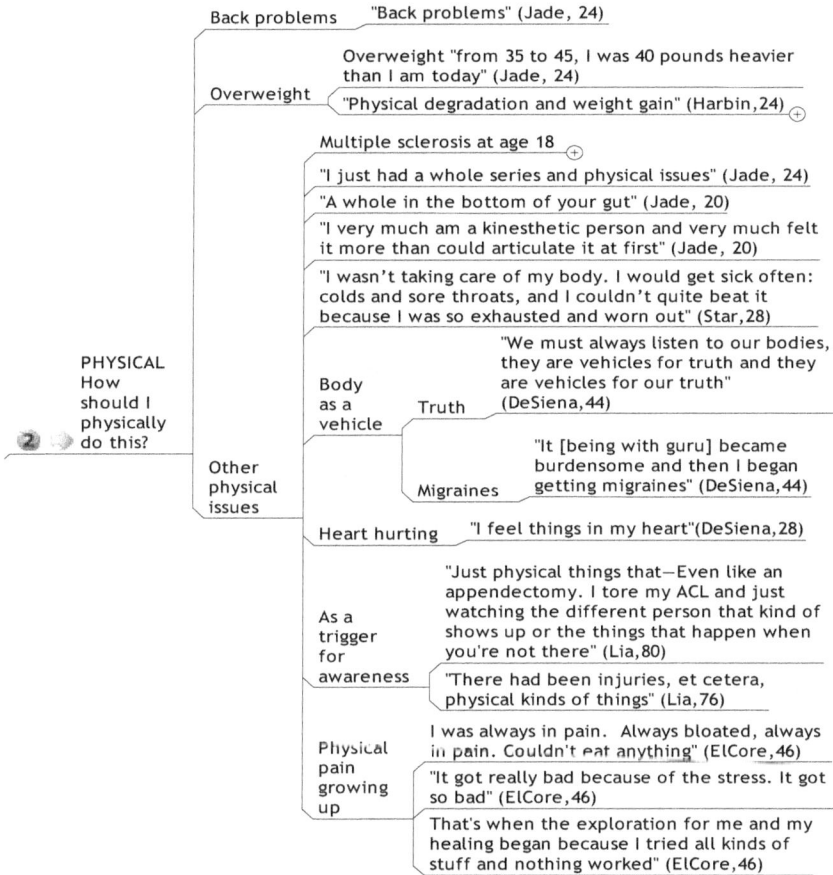

Figure 56. The Call for Adventure through physical pain.

The pain was fueled by "unhappiness," lack of fulfillment, "deep sadness and almost shame," lack of "love," "unrest," lack of trust, and lack of "joy" (see Figure 59).

At first, most leaders *Refused the Call* (Campbell, 1949/1968) to go beyond the known world. Instead, they tried to control the situation and its outcomes (see Figure 60).

They attempted to address their pain using their cognitive abilities and some of the same skills that helped them become outstanding achievers in the business world. One of these skills is their ability to be in control of people

EMOTIONAL
How do I
3 feel?
- Fear and anxiety ⊕
- Unhappiness, Lack of fulfillment & Emptiness ⊕
- Need to control & judgement ⊕
- Looking for help through therapy & counseling ⊕
- Eventually: Courage & permission to face all pain ⊕

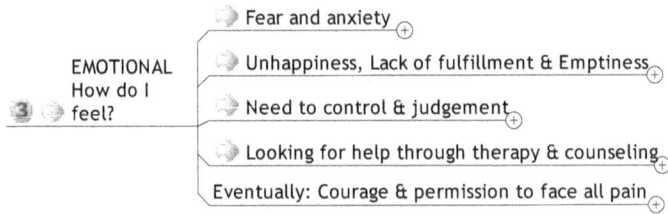

Figure 57. Emotional pain at phase I.

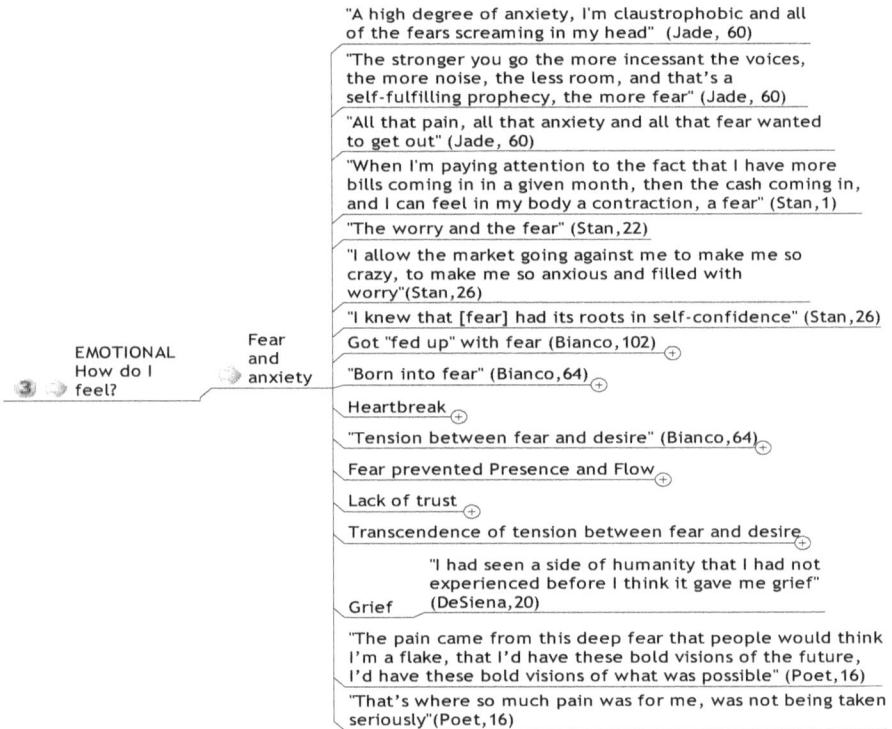

EMOTIONAL
How do I
3 feel?

Fear and anxiety

- "A high degree of anxiety, I'm claustrophobic and all of the fears screaming in my head" (Jade, 60)
- "The stronger you go the more incessant the voices, the more noise, the less room, and that's a self-fulfilling prophecy, the more fear" (Jade, 60)
- "All that pain, all that anxiety and all that fear wanted to get out" (Jade, 60)
- "When I'm paying attention to the fact that I have more bills coming in in a given month, then the cash coming in, and I can feel in my body a contraction, a fear" (Stan, 1)
- "The worry and the fear" (Stan, 22)
- "I allow the market going against me to make me so crazy, to make me so anxious and filled with worry" (Stan, 26)
- "I knew that [fear] had its roots in self-confidence" (Stan, 26)
- Got "fed up" with fear (Bianco, 102) ⊕
- "Born into fear" (Bianco, 64) ⊕
- Heartbreak ⊕
- "Tension between fear and desire" (Bianco, 64) ⊕
- Fear prevented Presence and Flow ⊕
- Lack of trust ⊕
- Transcendence of tension between fear and desire ⊕
- Grief: "I had seen a side of humanity that I had not experienced before I think it gave me grief" (DeSiena, 20)
- "The pain came from this deep fear that people would think I'm a flake, that I'd have these bold visions of the future, I'd have these bold visions of what was possible" (Poet, 16)
- "That's where so much pain was for me, was not being taken seriously" (Poet, 16)

Figure 58. Fear and anxiety at phase I.

and outcomes. This is another common characteristic of the consciousness leader. Some of them began "being a control freak," others tried to exercise control by "closing down" their hearts, "never" being emotionally available, "wearing a coat of armor," and raising "such high barriers" around them that "no one would ever get close" to "hurt" them again.

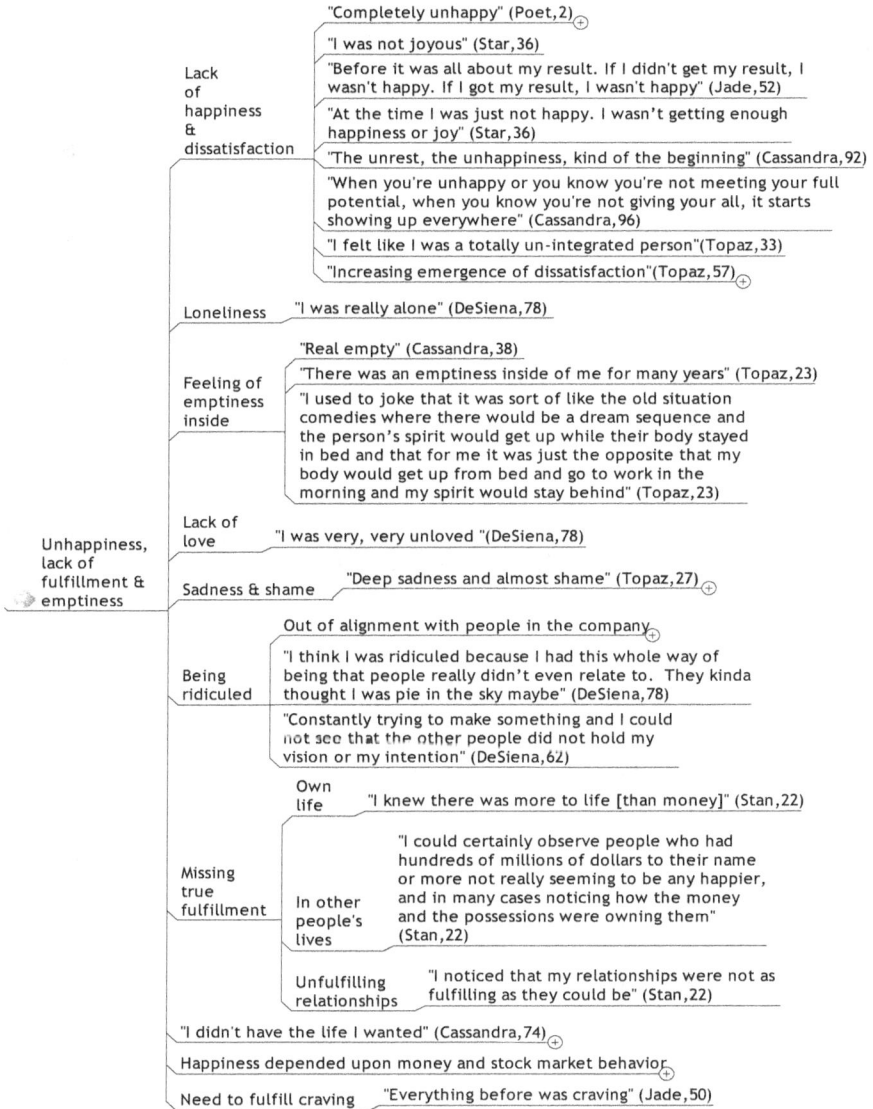

Figure 59. Unhappiness, lack of fulfillment, and emptiness at phase I.

Furthermore, they began "dealing with the symptoms" of their pain by studying books, consulting with experts, and taking better care of their bodies through yoga exercises, massages, and better nutrition. Often, as soon as the pain went away, they went back to the old behavior and known

Controlling people and outcomes

"I was trying to influence the way they did business because I felt they did have a responsibility to carry out my business in the way that I wanted it" (DeSiena, 70)

"Bouncing off the walls and just being a control freak" (Jade, 60)

"I was trying to control outcomes" (DeSiena, 78)

"I was never available. I was always in control" (Star, 24) in relationships

"I tend to be a bit of a control freak" (Cassandra, 132)

"The divorce for me was a really . . . it was a big shift moment for me, and it wasn't something that I was in control of, which I really hated" (Cassandra, 132)

Difficulties understanding other people

"People were just at a different point in their individual and collective interior journeys. That brought a tremendous amount of pain for me" (Poet, 18)

"I really had to let go of others' expectations and others' thoughts of acknowledgement or of seeing me as this highly successful business person who suddenly cared about all these different things that they didn't care about and was, at that point, deemed in their view not to be as highly successful as I was before" (Poet, 18)

Judgement about other people's levels of consciousness

There was a judgment that was living in my heart that I was at a higher place or that others needed to shift to meet me." (Poet, 24)

Need to control & judgement

Control should block feelings

Sadness & grief

"Not allowing myself to feel the sadness and the grief" (Stan, 28)

"Closed down my heart" (Star, 24)

Disappointment & anger

Disappointment and anger and perilousness and all those things" (Stan, 28)

"I'm particularly thick" (Stan, 30)

"Wearing coat of armor" (Stan, 30)

High Barriers should prevent being hurt again

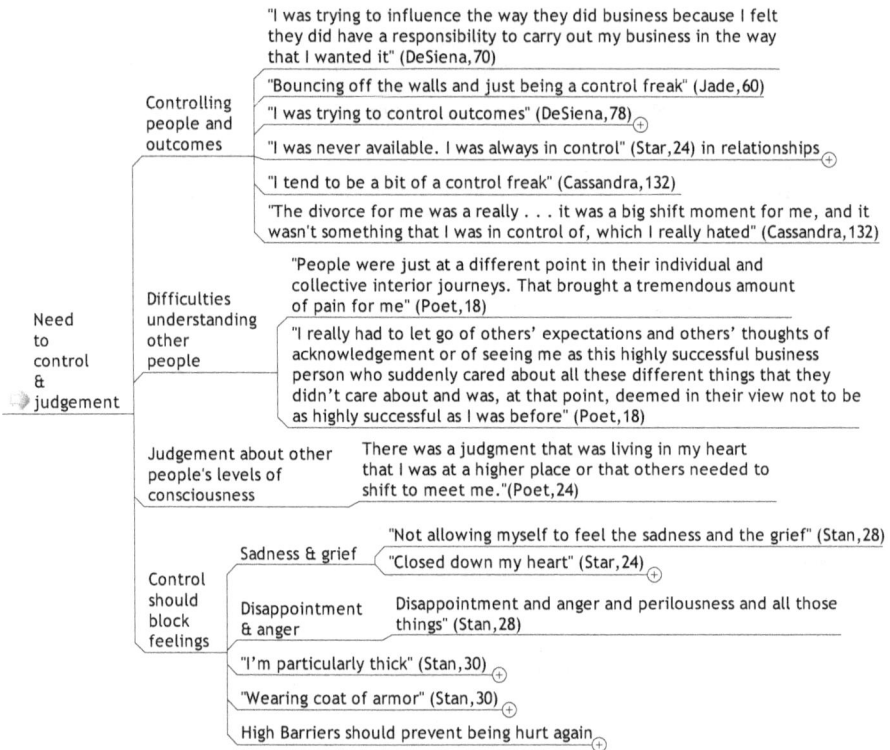

Figure 60. Controlling pain in phase I.

territory until the next painful challenge showed up. However, the pain increased over time and therefore, more resources were needed including better "teachers," transformational "seminars," "counseling," and "therapy," many of which provided a glimpse of a transpersonal reality and unfamiliar spiritual openings.

A further fact common to the researched consciousness leaders is their inner conflict regarding their religious environment or upbringing. The cause of this conflict may be rooted in the inner yearning for "a common sense spirituality" (Vaughan, 2000; Walsh & Vaughan, 1993) that possibly conflicted with the scientific and/or academic education and background (Capra, 2000; Damasio, 2006; Harman & Hormann, 1993). As can be deduced from their own words represented in Figure 61, consciousness

"I was brought up Catholic but really never gained any traction spiritually with the Catholic tradition, but it just really confirmed me not to really choose a religious path" (Chuck,64)

"My parents weren't particularly, I mean they weren't religious. They certainly weren't spiritual" (Star,18)

"No religious background in my upbringing so I don't have a deep religion focus. I have more of a spiritual focus and just an innate being and belief in spirituality and the beliefs of that" (LaCroix,2)

"I did go to Sunday school with my grandmother so I got a little of that sort of inculcation in the Christian church, but I remember to my Sunday school teacher at one point that 'I'm God and so are you.' And they did not like that at all" (Star,18)

"I don't necessarily believe in the things that some people believe in [a personal God] that call themselves spiritual and have a belief in God" (LaCroix,33)

"I kind of locked that away in the closet. I realized that wasn't sort of kosher" (Star,18)

"Even though I knew it on some level, that wasn't a way that I could express it that seemed appropriate to people, or they didn't buy it, or it was actually offensive in some way" (Star,18)

"Having grown up Episcopalian, then making my own way to figure out what I believed from a spirituality perspective" (Paloma,14)

"I grew up in a suburb of Long Island where it was all Jews and Italians and it seemed to be very much of a kind of normal American existence" (Stan,22)

"I place attention on source, whatever we call that. I typically use the word "god" for lack of a better word but source literally breathing through me as me, using my body vehicle for its pleasure and its experience of this material plane" (Stan,64)

Emotional pain through Jewish upbringing as a girl

Conflict: Religious upbringing and inner knowing about divine nature

SPIRITUAL
What is of ultimate concern?

"There seemed to be a natural desire to continue to evolve"(Star,18)

"That included reading spiritual books, and Eastern and Western philosophy" (Star,18)

"Natural yearning of the soul and my soul had already been on a path for many lifetimes" (Star,20)

"I have more of a spiritual focus and just an innate being and belief in spirituality and the beliefs of that" (LaCroix,2)

"Spirituality, I think is something innate to me" (LaCroix,2)

"I think that was sort of innate in me but I didn't know how to describe it or communicate until later in life" (LaCroix,2)

"My roots which were spiritual" (DeSiena,22)

"My mother "became this incredible force of common sense spirituality that I was raised on" (DeSiena,4)

Yearning for postmodern spirituality

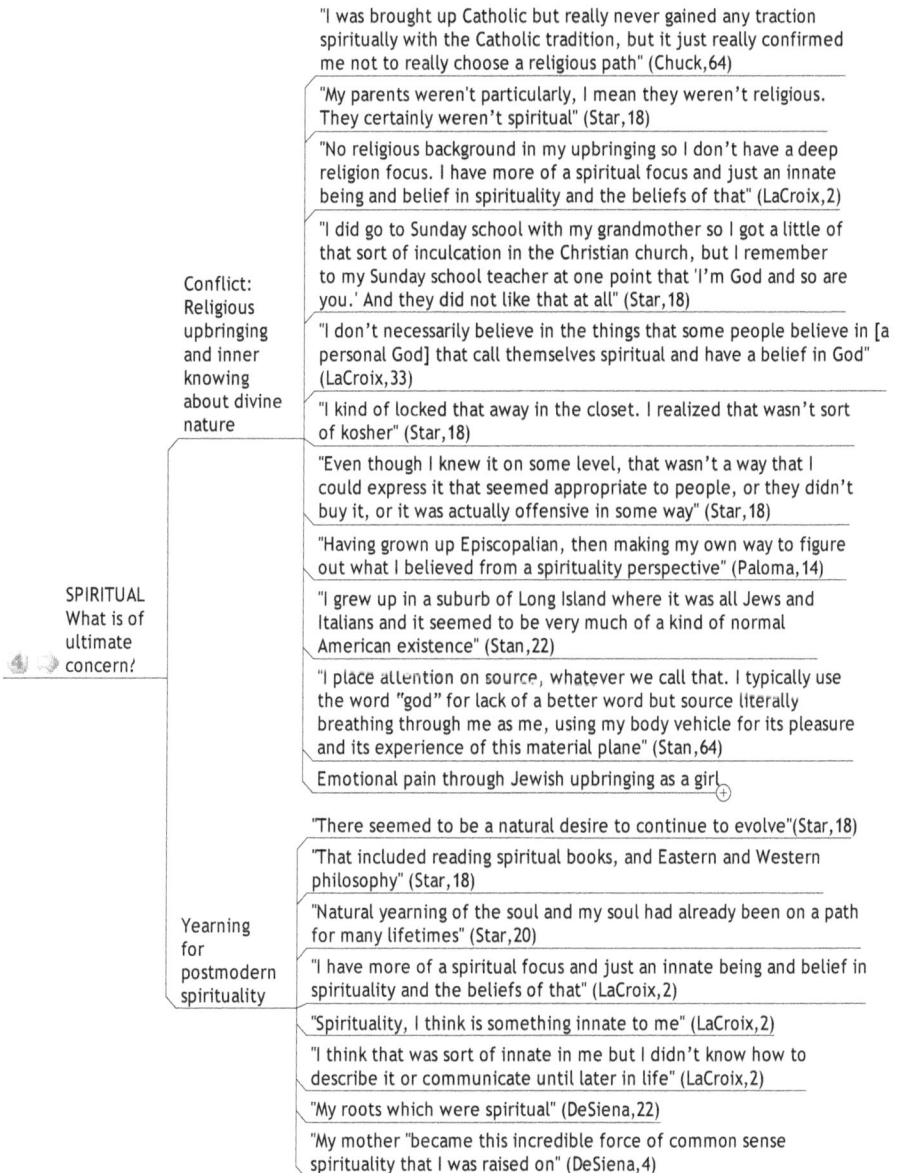

Figure 61. Spiritual context and triggers at phase I of the *Hero's Journey.*

leaders have deeply questioned or even rejected outdated religious values and dogmas. Yet, even if the family background was "not religious," all consciousness leaders confirmed that their "roots" were spiritual. They all seemed to yearn for a new and different language to express their "natural desire" for being connected to the "source" or the "light."

Because their spiritual foundation was not yet fully formed and their old emotional, physical, and cognitive adaptation abilities failed to show the desired results, the consciousness leaders were forced to *Cross the Threshold* (Campbell, 1949/1968). The pain had become unbearable and their courage helped them face the ultimate pain, namely their own shadows (Jacobi, 1959; Progoff, 1973; Stein, 2004; Vaughan, 2005).

The Tipping Point

The tipping point for *Crossing the Threshold* was different for each consciousness leader. However, it is important to note that it was mostly triggered by cognition, courage, and the conscious decision to face straight on the challenges at hand. Among these challenges were significant emotional events such as wife "diagnosed with cancer," loss of "second wife to cancer," death of "mother," the birth of a "baby," being "fired" from a prestigious position, or not being promoted to the desired job.

The process of facing the shadow was different for each individual research participant. It ranged from the decision to experience the "dark night of the soul" through holotropic breathwork, over the willingness to face the "worst [emotional] pain" after 5 hours of "chopping wood," to meditation, "vision quests," and asking essential questions regarding the true meaning of life. In any event, the sum results of the shadow work were significant experiences such as *transcendent* or *peak experiences* (Maslow et al., 1998; Maslow, 1968/1999), *meditative* or *contemplative experiences* (Alexander et al., 1990; Beauregard & O'Leary, 2007), *near-death experiences* (NDE), *out of body experiences* (OBE), (Alvarado, 2000), *flow* (Csikszentmihalyi, 1990; Kjaer et al., 2002), *state* or *unity consciousness experiences* (Cook-Greuter, 2004; Wilber, 2000), *exceptional human experiences* (White, 1998), *transpersonal experiences* (Grof, 2006), or other spiritual emergencies (Vaughan, 2000). These events were described as a "lightning bolt [that] moved through my body," a "feeling [that] would be so powerfully strong that it was almost to the point where you couldn't walk," a "mystical experience," "divine light," "divine intelligence," the "heart was exploding with love," "my body turned into an intense beam of light," "my heart opened and I could feel every bird and insect as part of me," receiving "an energy that's greater than we are," and as having other "grand [spiritual] openings" (see Figure 62).

When relating to the extraordinary human experiences described by the research participants, it is important to keep in mind that these people are non-religious people who had enjoyed high academic, scientific, and/or business educations. They were running extremely successful businesses and in some cases even multi-billion dollar concerns. At that time, many of them did not have any framework or the proper language to explain or make sense of the extraordinary experiences they were having. Moreover, the entire worldview of the consciousness leader was shattered as soon as he or she gave up control and surrendered to the shadow, the unknown, and to "unbearable fear" and pain. It caused a "major shift" and "quantum leap in consciousness." Life could never be the same again.

Scientific research (Alexander et al., 1990; Beauregard & O'Leary, 2007; Commons et al., 1984, 1990; Cook-Greuter, 2004, 2005, 2008; Pauchant, 2002; Torbert et al., 2004) indicated that such exceptional human experiences can move the participant to higher levels of ego development and even beyond duality, the good and the bad, the beautiful and the ugly (see Figure 63)

In addition, it is important to note that all research participants grew up and evolved in democratic Western societies. Based on the observations derived from this phenomenological research, it seems that the cultural and social centers of gravity of the participants before their transformation could be positioned within the framework of the Spiral Dynamics model (Beck & Cowan, 1996) between the blue and orange memes (pp. 229-

Physical & emotional pain & challenges

Cognitive decision to face the dark night of the soul
- "I got to my own dark night of the soul" (Stan, 22)
- Courage & permission to face all pain
- Got "fed-up" with fear (Bianco, 102)
- "Because it was so flipping fearful" (Bianco, 100)

Peers died early

"This is probably the nicest gift I'm going to get this holiday season and it's from a corporation, not from somebody that I love," and in that moment I started thinking about, you know, how much time and attention had I been placing on my friends and my family" (Cassandra, 36)

"Receiving of the gift from United was kind of the ah ha moment where it kind of all came together, but it had definitely been percolating before that" (Cassandra, 94)

"Saved by the love of a good woman" (Poet, 2)

Painful divorce

Being "mother and father" to several children (Bianco, 104)

External events

Mother being "fearful" (Bianco, 112)

Business pressure

Being lied to [by old boss] had dramatic impact

Moments of truth
- Third baby
- Experience with "women in seminar" (Lia, 10)
- "[Divorce] was a big shift moment for me" (Cassandra, 132)

"You eventually end up [in pain] and I don't know where it goes from here" (Lia, 10)

Ego transcendence work

Break with cult for ethical reasons

Death of important person

TIPPING POINTS

Spiritual evolution & emergency

Mind reading

Unitive experiences

Mystical experience with diseased father

Spiritual downloading

Quantum leaps in consciousness

Direct Insight for consciousness evolution

Exceptional human experiences

Brilliant light

Clairaudience

Grand spiritual openings

Mystical experience/apparition

Chakras opening

"Out of body experience" (Chuck, OBE) at age 22

Ancestors Encounters

Impact

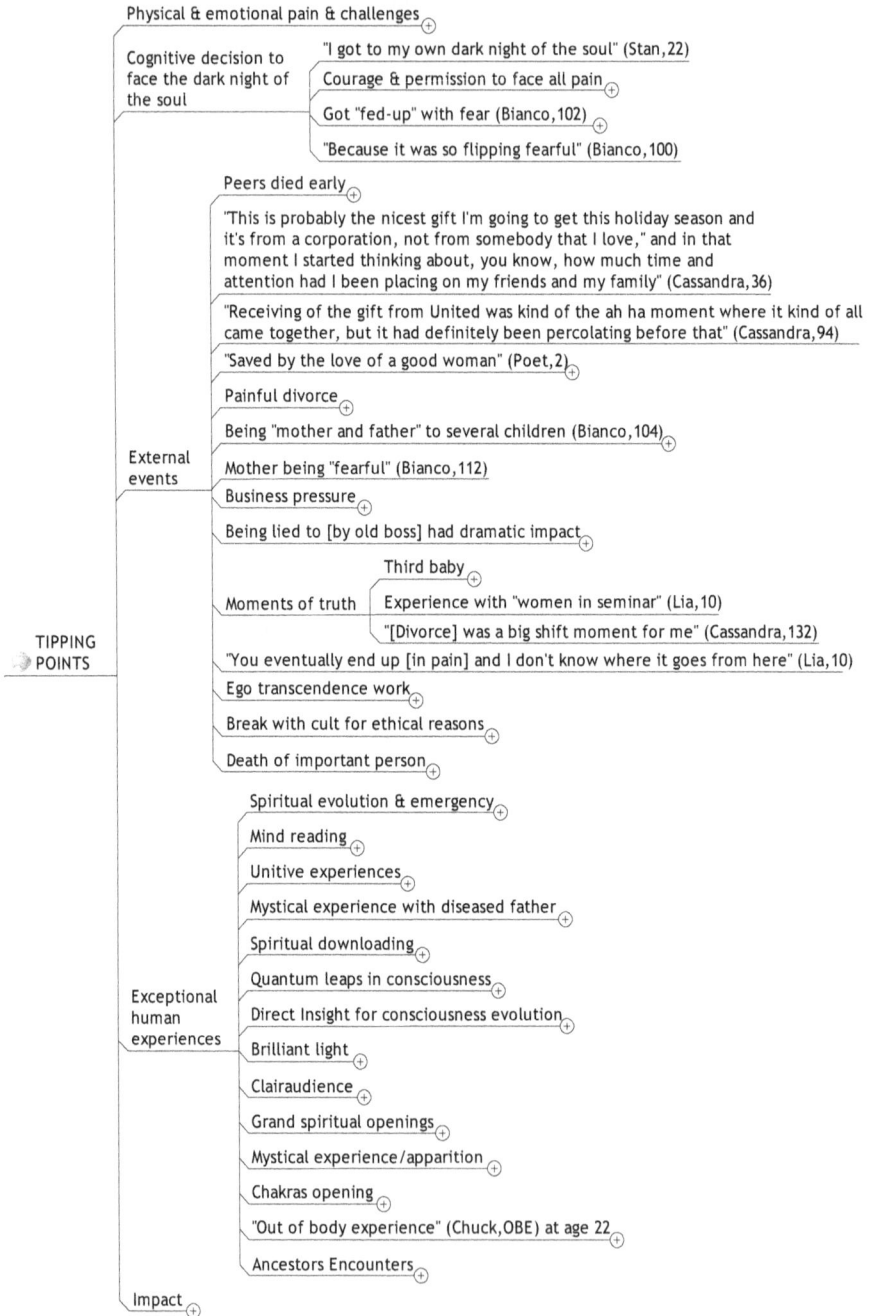

Figure 62. Challenges leading to *Crossing the Threshold* of *Hero's Journey.*

Spiritual evolution & emergency

"We proceeded to have a conversation where he read my mind and responded so I never opened my mouth" (Star, 46)

Mind reading

"I never actually had the chance to verbalize the responses. As soon as the thought-form arose, he would respond to it. So we were very much in a full dialogue"(Star, 48)

"Peak experience" (Star, 54) or "unity consciousness" (Star, 48)

"From inside, my spiritual sight, I could see the entire room. I could see there were two other people in the room with me. Even though with my eyes closed, I closed my eyes I could see everything through spiritual sight" (Star, 48)

"I had this image during one meditation that when we sit on our cushion, the technological equivalent is like having our i-pod or our cell phone in a docking station, that we are being plugged in to receive an energy that's greater than we are" (Paloma, 94)

"Experience itself became so tangible and so real to the point where . . . it would be like a feeling inside your heart like your heart was exploding with love. It was past any kind of physical orgasm you could possibly imagine" (Hahm, 32)

"Awareness state that was like connected to the world but so much more beyond it" (Hahm, 32)

"Feeling would be so powerfully strong that it was almost to the point where you couldn't walk" (Hahm, 32)

Unitive experiences

Out of body experience

"I was just resting on the bed and when I started getting outside of my body, and really looking down from the ceiling onto my body, yet feeling very, very strong connection with the cord that sort of connect us the spirit if you wish and the body . . . I got really scared actually, because I wanted to get back in my body. I didn't want to get too far out"(Chuck, 42)

Clairaudience

"I heard this loud voice in my head that said, 'Cassandra, pay attention. This is the one" (Cassandra, 170)

Clairvoyance

"All of a sudden I would be seeing like an internal television camera, like my eyes were a TV camera looking through that and I knew something had opened up or also my heart opened and I could feel every bird and insect as part of me, every being. It's the feeling expansion" (Darlene, 59)

Chakras opening

"New ways of perceiving, chakras opening up which are like awakenings inside, visual experiences back then" (Darlene, 57)

Exceptional human experiences

Mystical experience / apparition

Yogananda

Ancestors Encounters

Mystical experience with diseased father

Grand spiritual openings

"Your spirit gives you sometimes these grand openings" (Darlene, 14)

Spiritual downloading

Brilliant light

Quantum leaps in consciousness

"All of a sudden I felt like a lightning bolt moved through my body and I observed that my body was shaking literally uncontrollably like being electrocuted or something on the floor and something happened. Something dislodged from my system where I've had plenty of moments of self-doubt or questioning self-confidence, many, many moments, but it has never been as severe or as long lasting as a result of that one leap" (Stan, 26)

"Visceral, experiential . . . I could call it leap in consciousness" (Stan, 28)

Major shift in perspective: Transformative power & intelligence of the heart

Direct insight into consciousness evolution

"In the late '60s, early '70s, that there was a movement of consciousness, meaning awareness expansion, meaning understanding what life's about, what's really going on, not from just what you read but from direct insight" (Darlene, 14)

"I was having those awakenings" (Darlene, 14)

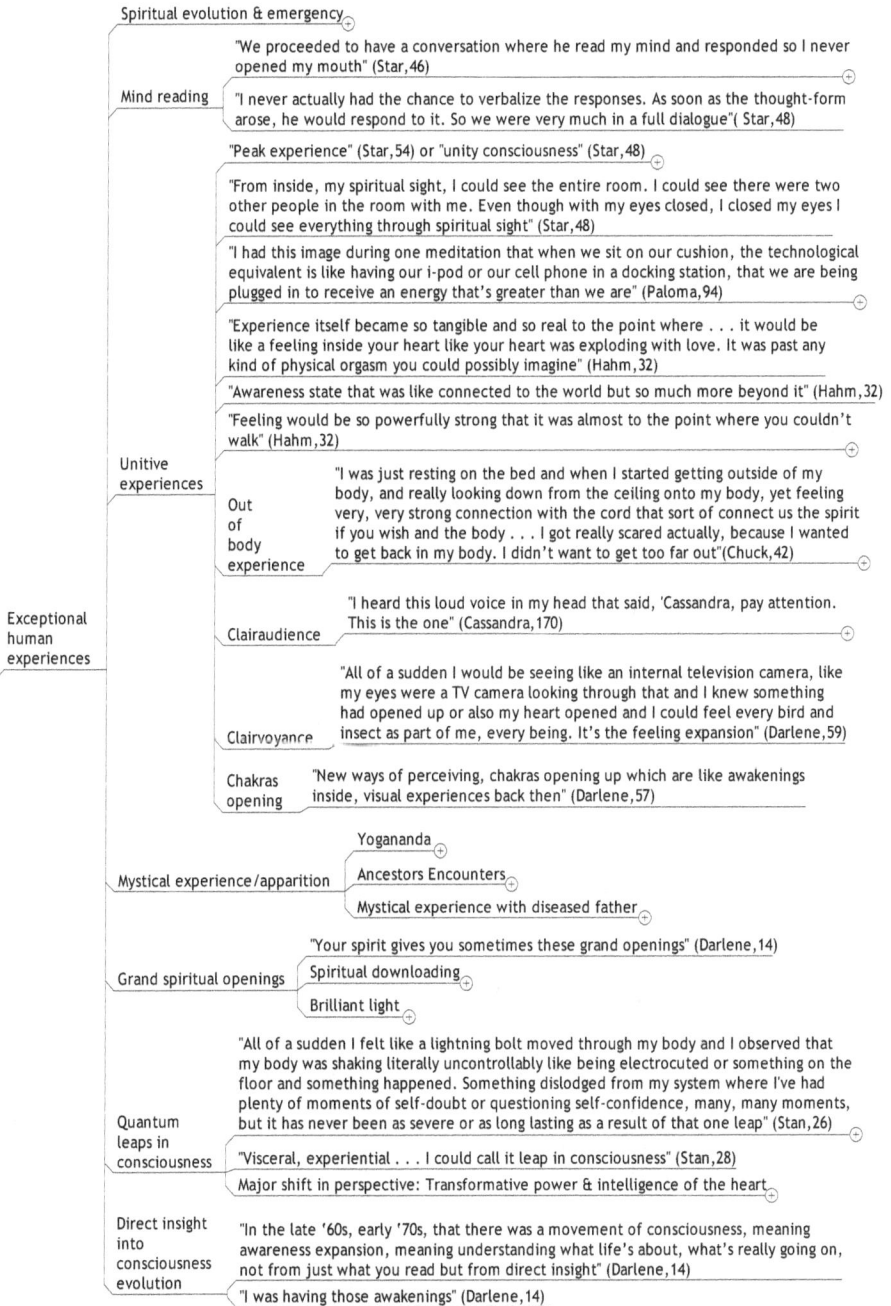

Figure 63. Composite of exceptional human experiences.

259) with a special emphasis on the orange meme with its orientation toward achievement and material success. Thus, the environment of the consciousness leader was mostly characterized by financial abundance, material orientation, and outer success all of which were achieved through sheer determination and "very hard work." As a result, it could also be assumed that the self-identity of the research participants at the beginning of phase I of the Hero's Journey may have also been centered around the orange meme (Beck & Cowan, 1996), also known for instance as the conscientious stage of ego development (Cook-Greuter, 2005, pp. 17-21). However, further research and quantitative tests (Cook-Greuter, 2004; Torbert et al, 2004) would have to be performed for more accuracy.

After facing their shadow, the lives of the participants were "never the same," and they were ready for phase II of the *Hero's Journey*, the Initiation phase (Campbell, 1949/1968).

The Initiation of the Consciousness Leader: Phase II

Once they have received a taste of the deeper interior dimensions of life, the consciousness leaders pursued their further growth with the same dedication with which they developed their careers. The initiation into exceptional states of consciousness and other extraordinary human experiences had a tremendous impact on them (see Figure 64).

One of the most significant impacts was related to fear transcendence. For instance, after having an out-of-body experience, the research participant Chuck, who has a Ph.D. in distributed computer systems and was a co-founder of a major Silicon Valley company, realized that he has "absolutely no fear of death." Hence, he sees death as a "great opportunity to move forward" on his path. To various degrees, all consciousness leaders have transcended their fear of death or failure because they realized that (a) "nobody can take" from them who they are, (b) "fear of failure is not sustainable," and (c) they are no longer "not afraid to go" into fear. Facing their worst fears taught them how to "listen to [their] inner voice" and connect with their "divine nature" to access better resources.

Asking essential questions

Noticed collective insanity — "I wasn't alone. We had the smartest people in the world doing the same thing. It seemed to be standard operating procedure for this thing called human being, at least a successful one" (Stan,22)

Recognizing own passion and unlimited potential
"When I recognized this emergent potential in myself then I actually started looking for a different set of resources" (Jade,54)
"One of the first areas of awareness for me to evolve was recognizing what really turned me on, what I really felt passionate about" (Topaz,57)

"I wasn't manifesting why I was here" (Jade,16)

"Following a script that wasn't authored by me" (Topaz,57)

Noticed absurdity of the money game — "I knew on a profound level was completely absurd and no way for me to live my life" (Stan,26)

"I had this moment where I looked into the future and all I saw was this endless stream of closing quarters" (Star,30)

"I kept getting signs that I was getting to the point of diminishing returns" (Jade,16)

Lack of meaning — "While there were fun things like building new markets and I really enjoy business, there was this sort of almost mind numbingly impossible monotony around the trajectory that I was on" (Star,30)

"There's fewer jobs left [in the world] and then you point more and more to that final job" (Jade,16)

"Increasing emergence of dissatisfaction"(Topaz,57)

Diminishing returns

Maximizing share holder value was not fulfilling — "There was a growing, gnawing, unfulfillment of maximizing shareholder value as an end goal and being in conversation with the top five, six, eight people that were actually running the organization worldwide" (Poet,14)

Lack of depth within business context

Feelings of Emptiness inside

Difficult integration between "spiritual yearnings [and] corporate life" (Topaz,23)

Deep emotional decision

Awareness of dilemmas & being a hypocrite
Physical decision
Mental decision
Emotional/physical/mental decision to lead from the heart
Decision to stop being "somewhat of a hypocrite" (Topaz,27)

"I remember looking at a white board and just popping and seeing that I was a complete hypocrite. I had these values, but those values weren't being lived out in my lifestyle when I was working 90 hours a week" (Poet,14)

"I had to find a way to be me" (Topaz,23)

Change became unavoidable: "no energy left" (Topaz,31)

Realization of irreversibility of own change

Looking for solutions

Needed to take time off

TIPPING POINTS — Impact

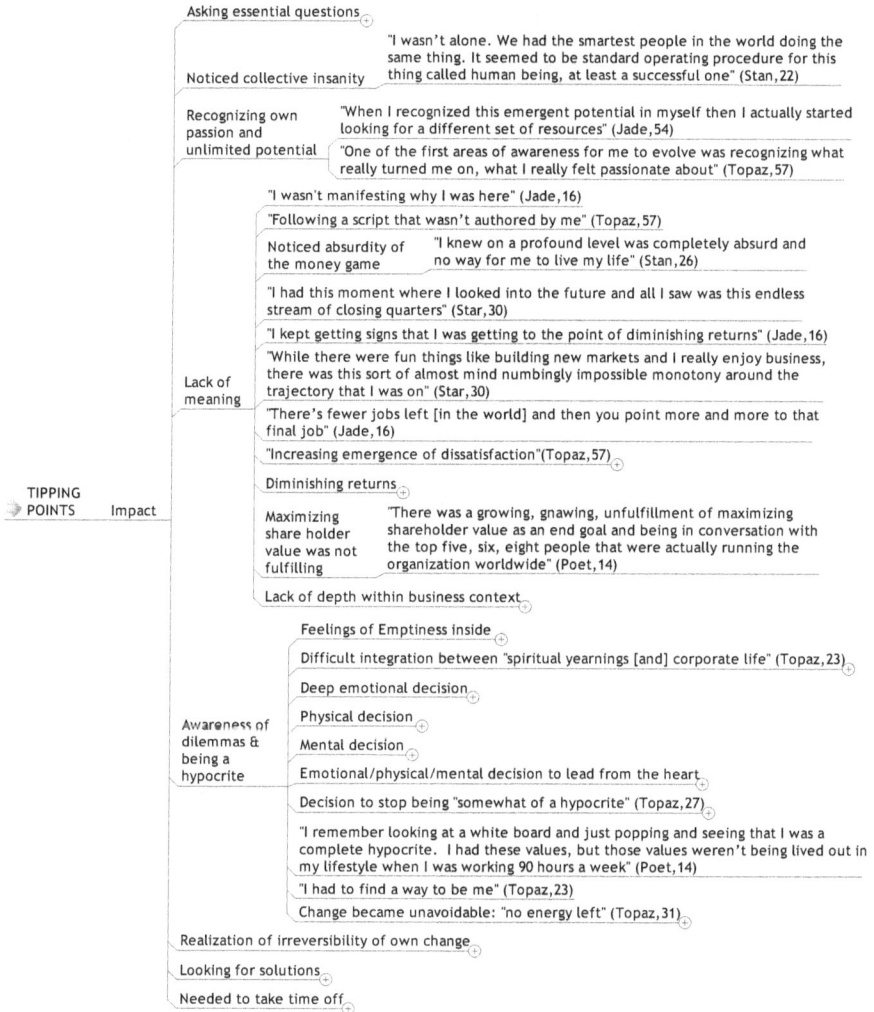

Figure 64. Impact of exceptional human experiences–phase II of *Hero's Journey.*

These transpersonal experiences lead the consciousness leader to ask essential questions such as "Who am I? "Why am I here?" "Is this it?" and "Why do I let the mob psychology tell me whether I was having a good day or not?" Their transpersonal experiences induced significant doubt regarding their current worldviews and encouraged them to question more deeply the status quo of their lives. They noticed the collective insanity of the "money game" and questioned whether the "standard operating procedure" for a "successful" person was still the game they wanted to play. Furthermore, they noticed that they were not "manifesting" their *raison d'être*, the values they "adopted" were not "self-selected," and they were "following a script that was not" authored by them. As they "looked into the future" and saw the "endless stream of closing quarters" that are the essential driving force in the business world, they detected the "almost mind numbingly impossible monotony around the trajectory" on which they were. They comprehended that the rewards "were running out," the next "gold ring" was no longer tempting, that there were "fewer [attractive] jobs left" for them in the world, and that "maximizing shareholder value" was no longer enticing.

Again, the cognitive drive guided them toward identifying and taking advantage of the best available resources such as teachers, books, therapy, counseling, and seminars. Having been significantly impacted by visceral experiences of the "divine," the consciousness leader focused on repeating the experience. This is why, for a while, they lived the life of a spiritual seeker or as Jade called it the life of a "spiritual dilettante." They learned and exposed themselves to a whole host of techniques, philosophies, and teachings. However, at some point, the leaders discovered one certain teacher and/or method with which they could identify and which they practiced for a longer period, sometimes for several decades.

Yet, using the mind to go beyond it and experience the ineffable is not easy for a person who is a master of the cognitive ability. The time to grow to higher "state stages" (Wilber, 2006; p. 87) of their interiority had arrived and only a good teacher seemed to be able to show the way. Among the personal teachers chosen by the research participants in the current study were Swami Satchidananda, Bubba Free John (also known as Adi Da), Donald Rothberg, Donna Markova, Doc Childre, Deepak Chopra, as well as various Native Americans, and other shamans. However, some consciousness leaders also chose nature, dancing, gardening, and other Integral Life Practices (Wilber, 2006, pp. 202-210) to help them on their paths.

When on the *Road of Trials* (Campbell, 1949/1968), the consciousness leaders evolved from "personal limitations" to realizing their "unlimited" potentials. The road of the transpersonal transformation was paved with trials and tribulations. They learned new disciplines such as meditation, yoga, and how much more pain had to be experienced as they "tried to take the old model into the new paradigm" and created "double disasters." More often than not, the pain originated also from the clash between the Eastern teachers and their Western disciples. The mostly Eastern philosophy-oriented and spiritually highly evolved teachers were often operating presumably from premodern cultural centers of gravity that were often patriarchic, sexist, or androcentric.

As novices, the consciousness leaders trusted them and followed their teachings that led to countless transpersonal and "unitive experiences" that transformed them even further and in significant ways. The promise of "enlightenment" kept them on the path for many years and gave them both a language and an infrastructure for the new territory. During their training, the consciousness leaders (a) learned how to "reconnect to that authentic self"; (b) realized that we are all "part of oneness, a greater whole"; (c) developed the ability to understand their "own consciousness," the "collective consciousness" and how we "are part of that greater human consciousness and then beyond"; (d) understood the dimensions and interconnectedness of body, mind, and spirit"; (e) became more "rounded [and] balanced"; and (f) received more "structure and specific knowledge" and more important underwent the "experiential process of learning" to deal with "the emotional/spiritual side" to which they had "very little exposure" before. In short, the conscious leaders became "much better," happier, and more "joyous" people.

Yet, in several cases, "the closer" they "got to the guru," the more they saw "his manipulation," "the suffering," the "sexual abuse," the "flaws," and the "hierarchy" in the "oneness." In the mind of the postmodern person, these were contradictions that their teachers should have been able to reconcile but they did not because they could not. Based on their Eastern training or upbringing, it would be fair to assume that these teachers lived at a different cultural stage and center of gravity than his extraordinary disciples; this assumption would have to be researched further. In any event, the consciousness leaders took the teachings and moved on.

Whether the personal teachers continued to be in their lives or not, the consciousness leaders learned how to unleash the unlimited potentials within their own interiors. With or without a personal teacher, the consciousness leaders realized that the Initiation phase into their *Hero's Journey* was significant. As LaCroix expressed it, it was

> *like going through a college program, which is a rapid introduction to something and exposure to something—Like turning on a fire hose. This was like drinking out of a fire hose. In this area, MIT and Stanford Business School were like drinking out of a fire hose for academic and business issues. This was like drinking out of a fire hose for emotional, spiritual and consciousness issues.*

Equipped with *The Ultimate Boon* (Campbell, 1949/1968) such as new tools, skills, and a deep understanding about their "unlimited potentials," the "interconnectedness, the oneness, and the holistic nature of things" the consciousness leaders were ready for the next step in their lives. There was "no going back" because "change became unavoidable," and the consciousness leaders had to take these changes into the real world to follow their higher calling. That calling was in all cases driven by "the realization of what a purposeful life actually means" for the individual as a "soul." That calling "evolved into something" significant such as leveraging their "talents to make a meaningful and impactful contribution to the sustainability of the planet" (Chuck).

In some cases, the consciousness leaders declared their new path publicly through an action or event that "felt" like a "coming out party." In other cases, they quit their jobs to leave the unsupportive old business environment to pursue solely the newly discovered spirituality for a while. However, in most cases, the consciousness leaders led for several years the existence of a closet mystic. During this phase, they led a double existence. While preserving their business façade, they pursued their spiritual paths. While being on this journey, their creativity and courage continued to help them integrate their double identities. For instance, Jade used his "creative side that was always crying to emerge" to create a movie of his life and its integration. Bianco used "the creative process" to write several books that helped him intellectually "move from one paradigm" to another and out of his "historical bias," which is his language for social conditioning.

However, all steps of the *Initiation* phase (II) prepared the consciousness leader for the *Apotheosis* (Campbell, 1949/1968), which consisted of the final departure from old business structures that were no longer acceptable. This act happened quietly or through a public declaration.

A common characteristic of consciousness leaders is their financial abundance. This financial abundance enabled the inner transformation to take place in a financially secure environment. More research would have to occur to know for sure, but financial abundance seems to be one key reason that enabled the consciousness leaders to leave their conservative business environments for a while. It helped them focus on their inner growth and integrate their interiorities with their exteriorities before coming out to "change the world" (see Figure 65).

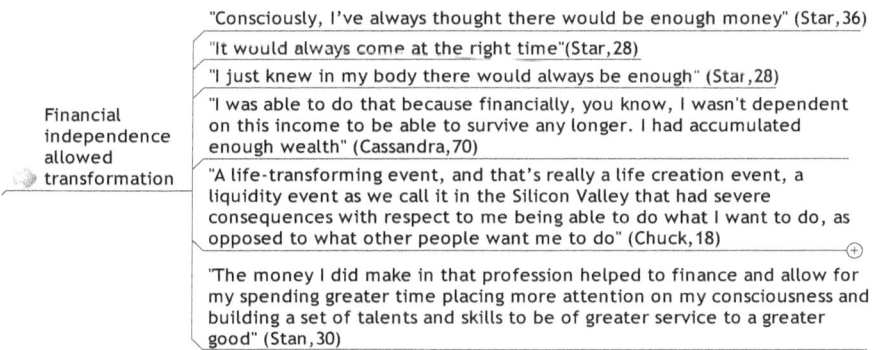

Financial independence allowed transformation	"Consciously, I've always thought there would be enough money" (Star, 36)
	"It would always come at the right time"(Star, 28)
	"I just knew in my body there would always be enough" (Star, 28)
	"I was able to do that because financially, you know, I wasn't dependent on this income to be able to survive any longer. I had accumulated enough wealth" (Cassandra, 70)
	"A life-transforming event, and that's really a life creation event, a liquidity event as we call it in the Silicon Valley that had severe consequences with respect to me being able to do what I want to do, as opposed to what other people want me to do" (Chuck, 18)
	"The money I did make in that profession helped to finance and allow for my spending greater time placing more attention on my consciousness and building a set of talents and skills to be of greater service to a greater good" (Stan, 30)

Figure 65. Financial independence as a common topic.

Further testing would have to be completed in order to make a more informed assessment, however, through the data in the present research the following observation becomes obvious: The inner-state changes, triggered by the extraordinary human experiences highlighted earlier, seem to have laid the foundation for a long process of purification and illumination of the self, and lead to various state stages within the interior dimensions of consciousness leader (Underhill, 1911/2002). In Wilber's (2000a) words, the consciousness leader evolved through a fulcrum or a three-steps process of personal growth that contains the following general components "(1) fusion/identification; (2) differentiation/transcendence; (3) integration/inclusion" (p. 132). It appears that these state stages led to further structural changes. Highlighting some of these structural changes along with their integration is the focus of phase III of the Hero's Journey also called *The Return* (Campbell, 1949/1968), which is discussed below.

The Emergence of the Consciousness Leader: Phase III

Having recognized their true meaning in life and having integrated their interiorities with the exteriority through the trials and tribulations of the *Initiation* phase of their journey, the consciousness leaders appear to have become the *Masters of the Two Worlds* (Campbell, 1949/1968), namely the interior and exterior, the heart and the mind, and the cognitive and the psychospiritual. They are now ready to *Return* to and share their gifts with the world.

For the scope of the composite depiction in this dissertation, it will be sufficient to focus on the structural discussion especially as it relates to the ego/self development. The theory of adult ego development addresses a psychological system that contains interrelated lines of development all of which have been referred to and highlighted in the current study (Cook-Greuter, 2005). These lines are the *behavioral* (operative), the *emotional* (affective), and the *cognitive*. In the words of Cook-Greuter (2005),

> *the operative component looks at what adults see as the purpose of life, what needs to act upon, and what ends they are moving towards. The affective component deals with emotions and the experience of being in the world. The cognitive component addresses the question of how a person thinks about him or herself and the world. It is important to understand that each stage emerges from a synthesis of doing being, and thinking despite the term logic, which might suggest an emphasis of cognition. (p. 3)*

The next mind map (see Figure 66) represents the emergent components of the consciousness leader within the framework of Wilber's (2000a) AQAL. In its expanded version, the mind map contains the verbatim accounts of the research participants. The impact for themselves and the world are highlighted subsequently.

Integrating Life's Purpose and Mission

With the identification of their unlimited potentials, the consciousness leaders were ready to implement their new life purpose and passion that consists in bringing "consciousness into the domain of business in a way that creates sustainable change relative to the human beings on the planet and ultimately bringing spirit into manifestation" (Jade). After having left the old business environment, after having been "rewired," after receiving new skills, and after having integrated their new interior structures with the outer ones, the consciousness leaders "are back to business," as the old adage has it.

They see their new lives' purpose as having an even "bigger impact" in the business world than before and in a much more integrated way because they now see business as an "incredible laboratory of consciousness." They (a) regard "societal analysis [as] a spiritual discipline", (b) see business and "understand the economy" as part of "deep spiritual practice", (c) want to "move capitalism beyond the pure maximizing of profits", (d) desire to "explore and lead and show different ways of creating social enterprises and different financing mechanisms that are behind that", (e) believe in "engaged spirituality", (f) want to work on "different governance models and different business models" to start integrating their social mission with their evolving "human condition", and (g) continue to be inspired and make sure they are "taking care" of themselves and their "community at the same time."

In short, they seek to lead a "purposeful life" in which they can use their talents and the process of "consciousness development, to make an impactful contribution to sustainability, holistic sustainability" (Chuck). It is important to note another important common characteristic regarding

COGNITIVE
What I am
① aware of?
- Unleashing unlimited potential
- New purpose and passion
- Courage & creativity
- Detachment—less efforting
- Intentions instead of outcomes
- Letting go of control
- Accepting what is
- Changed material orientation
- There is conscious choice
- Taking responsibility & openness
- Integral consciousness & living
- Great clarity

SPIRITUAL
What is of
ultimate
② concern?
- Serious spiritual quest & practice
- Trusting the universe/God
- Ongoing unity consciousness experiences
- Deeper understanding
- Business as a spiritual path: Embodied spirituality

INTERNAL
TRANS-
FORMATION
& IMPACT
(I)

PHYSICAL
How should I
physically do
③ this?
- Regular physical practices
- Body as a vehicle for right action
- Visualization exercises
- Integration of the wheel of life

EMOTIONAL
How do I
④ feel?
- Dominant positive emotions
- Willingness to face greatest fears & shadows
- Better skills to transcended suffering
- Fear transcendence (no fear of death)
- Higher emotional awareness

VALUES
What is
significant
⑤ to me?
- Being of service
- Integrity truth honesty
- Authenticity & credibility
- Truthfulness & humility
- Oneness & humanity

ETHICS & MORALS
⑥ What I should do?
- Social justice
- High moral standards
- Taking responsibility/accountability

EGO/SELF
⑦ Who am I?
- Actualization holarchy
- Flow instead of resistance
- Cultivating presence
- Openness & creativity
- Trusting the universe/God

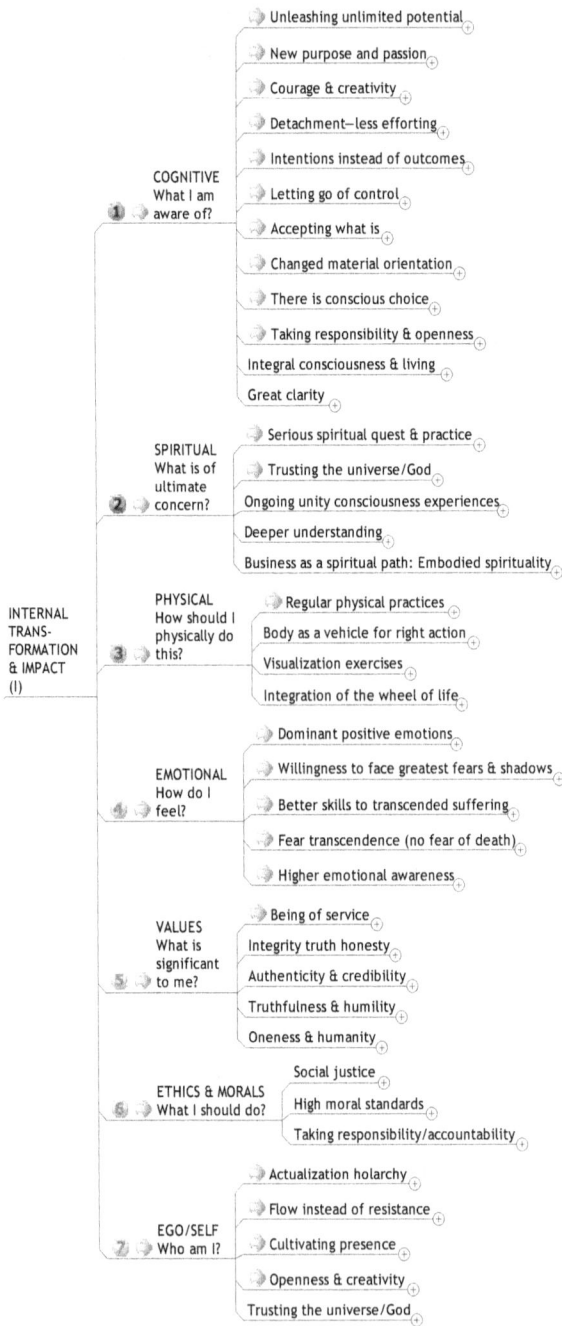

Figure 66. The components of structural changes of consciousness leaders.

the integration between their interiority with the exteriority. Hahm expressed it succinctly in the following way:

> *The new purpose is "not so blatantly devoid of my personal own interests. But I think I've become much more decentralized in my thinking to where it's much easier for me to have other people have certain things and not worry about myself . . . I'm about mission and I'm about helping.*

Moving Beyond Ego Boundaries

Having gone through *The Hero's Journey* (Campbell, 1949/1968), the consciousness leaders appear to have not only recognized their unlimited potentials, but they could see that they have been "rewired" toward a "unity consciousness" identity or service orientation that is generally characterized as having "shifted from a mentality" from "what's in it for me to what's in it for us." Poet, who ran the marketing division of a multibillion-dollar company before his transformation, described his process of awakening, surrendering, and becoming a consciousness leader in the following way:

> *At the time, I had no clue what was going on. Basically, I was being rewired. Everything I used to think was important was no longer important to me. It was me, me, me and my fabulous career and how do I help create more money for the company, so I can create more money for me and more success for me and more power for me? I was never a bad guy, but it was just a small game. It felt like a big game. I thought it was the biggest game in town. But suddenly when I was rewired, it felt like the smallest game in the universe. When you really make that shift and you start playing for an idea bigger than yourself and you start sensing into what is that divine creative impulse that's seated within me that is my gift to the planet? Within that surrendering was recognizing that there's something unique within me that I was born to become and that by surrendering to that, by paying attention to*

that, by allowing that to emerge within myself, that I could play a much bigger game, a much more fulfilling game, a much more meaningful game in terms of being able to create from that space in service to a much deeper and broader concept.

Values, ethics, and morals. The tremendous transformation of consciousness leaders resulted also in having new and consciously chosen, or "self-selected," values. The values that are at the foundation of being of service in the world are integrity, authenticity, truth, truthfulness, honesty, humility, and unity consciousness. Figure 67 contains the verbatim accounts of the research participants.

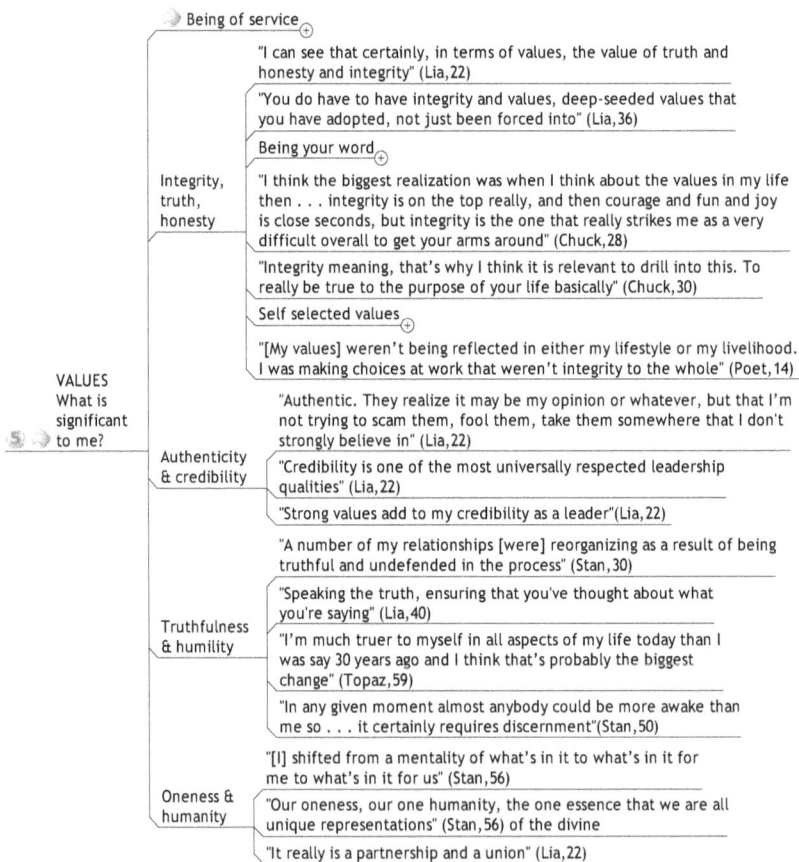

Figure 67. The values of consciousness leaders.

These values go hand in hand with high ethics and moral standards that help consciousness leaders "stick" their "neck" out, perform "social justice," and "do the right thing whether it's popular or not."

Self-confidence increased. Along with a new sense of identity, the self-confidence of the consciousness leaders studied increased. They grew beyond being "ego-driven" to feeling "more comfortable with whom" they are, to be able to "take the risk" of declaring "more fully" what they want, and to trust the messages from their increased sense of awareness and consciousness (see Figure 68).

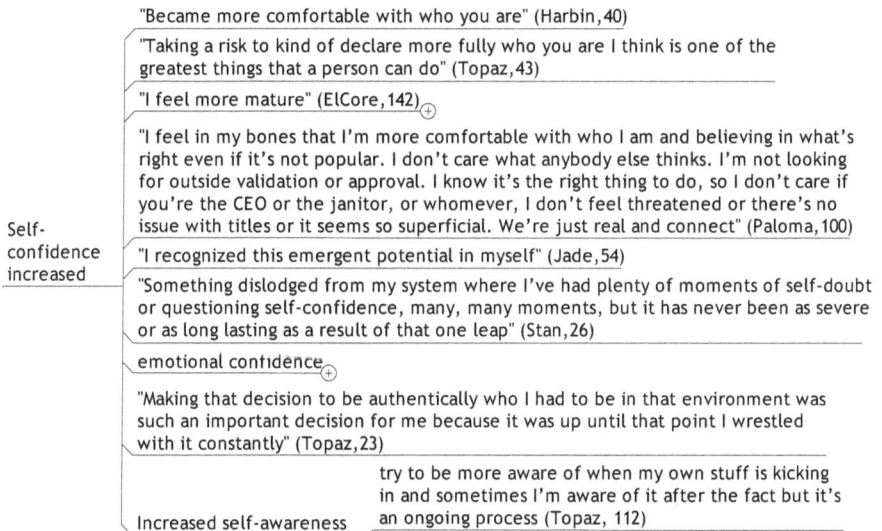

Self-confidence increased	
	"Became more comfortable with who you are" (Harbin, 40)
	"Taking a risk to kind of declare more fully who you are I think is one of the greatest things that a person can do" (Topaz, 43)
	"I feel more mature" (ElCore, 142) ⊕
	"I feel in my bones that I'm more comfortable with who I am and believing in what's right even if it's not popular. I don't care what anybody else thinks. I'm not looking for outside validation or approval. I know it's the right thing to do, so I don't care if you're the CEO or the janitor, or whomever, I don't feel threatened or there's no issue with titles or it seems so superficial. We're just real and connect" (Paloma, 100)
	"I recognized this emergent potential in myself" (Jade, 54)
	"Something dislodged from my system where I've had plenty of moments of self-doubt or questioning self-confidence, many, many moments, but it has never been as severe or as long lasting as a result of that one leap" (Stan, 26)
	emotional confidence ⊕
	"Making that decision to be authentically who I had to be in that environment was such an important decision for me because it was up until that point I wrestled with it constantly" (Topaz, 23)
Increased self-awareness	try to be more aware of when my own stuff is kicking in and sometimes I'm aware of it after the fact but it's an ongoing process (Topaz, 112)

Figure 68. Increased self-confidence.

Furthermore, consciousness leaders have moved beyond the boundaries of their egos by learning how to achieve more with less effort—as described by Star, Chuck, and Stan—releasing their outcome orientation, by letting go of control, accepting what is, changing their material orientation, learning how to be present and open, giving up resistance, being in flow, and taking responsibility.

Achieving more with less effort. After many years of trials, tribulations, and testing, the consciousness leaders researched here have arrived to the realization that they achieve much more when they let go of efforting (see Figure 69). Star, who is a serial high-tech entrepreneur and a self-made multimillionaire, summarized her change in the following way:

There's a true sense of like the divine is acting through this vessel so whatever personal agendas or motivations I had are sort of largely irrelevant. They're kind of goofy. The more I try to do something based on my agenda, the more it becomes constricted and small. The only way to have a big life is to sort of hand over the reigns to the divine creative force that's in charge, and then it can be hugely big. So my life has changed in that I actually do far more stuff with far more ease, and without the sense of trying or doing or efforting. I mean there's still effort, but it's interesting, it comes when I forget When I'm efforting and struggling, or having to exert a lot of willpower, it's mostly because I've taken something on that I think I'm doing. Like my small I-consciousness has sort of taken over.

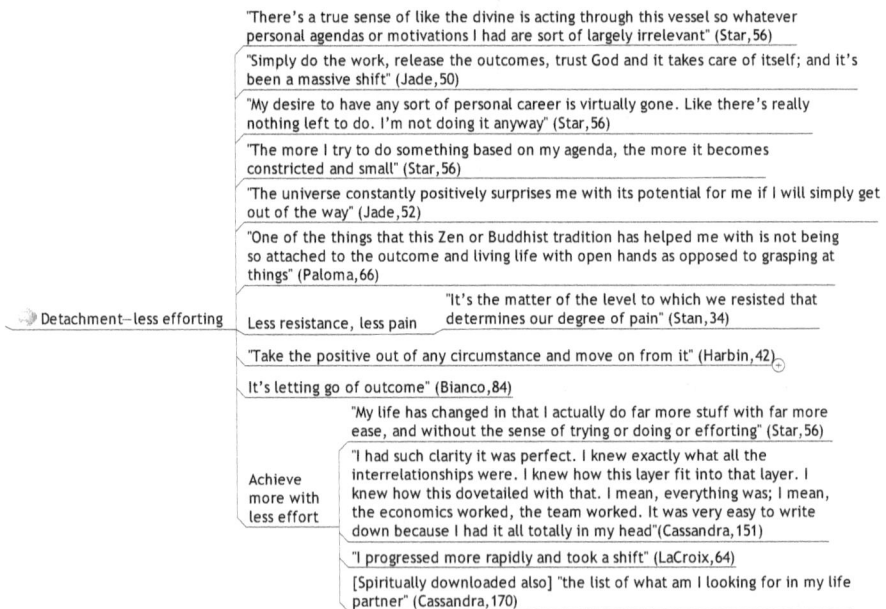

Figure 69. Achieving more with less effort.

Having intentions rather than outcomes. Through their transformation the studied consciousness leaders realized that they became even more successful if they let go of their goals, their need to control people and situations, and stopped working hard. As a result, they have learned to "get rid of" their "outcomes," "life plan," or even "personal career." As they set intentions instead of outcomes, they became more open and were able to "see [more] opportunities" than before. If they "simply get out of the way," "the universe constantly positively surprises" them "with its potential." More verbatim quotes can be found in Figure 70.

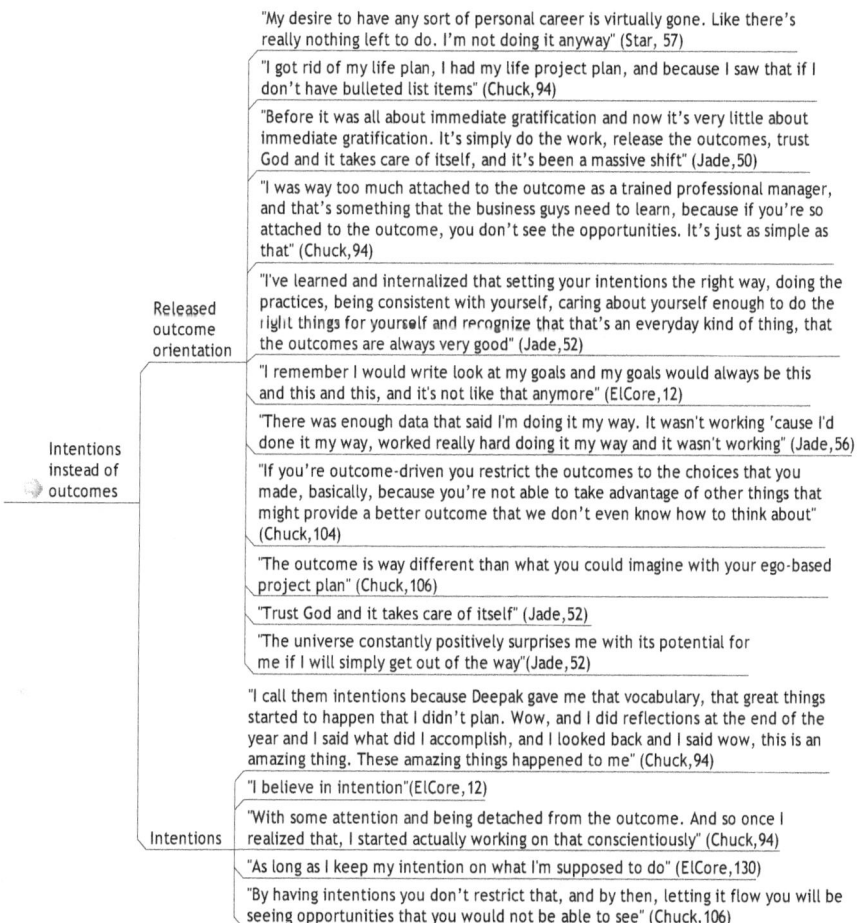

Intentions instead of outcomes

Released outcome orientation

"My desire to have any sort of personal career is virtually gone. Like there's really nothing left to do. I'm not doing it anyway" (Star, 57)

"I got rid of my life plan, I had my life project plan, and because I saw that if I don't have bulleted list items" (Chuck, 94)

"Before it was all about immediate gratification and now it's very little about immediate gratification. It's simply do the work, release the outcomes, trust God and it takes care of itself, and it's been a massive shift" (Jade, 50)

"I was way too much attached to the outcome as a trained professional manager, and that's something that the business guys need to learn, because if you're so attached to the outcome, you don't see the opportunities. It's just as simple as that" (Chuck, 94)

"I've learned and internalized that setting your intentions the right way, doing the practices, being consistent with yourself, caring about yourself enough to do the right things for yourself and recognize that that's an everyday kind of thing, that the outcomes are always very good" (Jade, 52)

"I remember I would write look at my goals and my goals would always be this and this and this, and it's not like that anymore" (ElCore, 12)

"There was enough data that said I'm doing it my way. It wasn't working 'cause I'd done it my way, worked really hard doing it my way and it wasn't working" (Jade, 56)

"If you're outcome-driven you restrict the outcomes to the choices that you made, basically, because you're not able to take advantage of other things that might provide a better outcome that we don't even know how to think about" (Chuck, 104)

"The outcome is way different than what you could imagine with your ego-based project plan" (Chuck, 106)

"Trust God and it takes care of itself" (Jade, 52)

"The universe constantly positively surprises me with its potential for me if I will simply get out of the way" (Jade, 52)

Intentions

"I call them intentions because Deepak gave me that vocabulary, that great things started to happen that I didn't plan. Wow, and I did reflections at the end of the year and I said what did I accomplish, and I looked back and I said wow, this is an amazing thing. These amazing things happened to me" (Chuck, 94)

"I believe in intention" (ElCore, 12)

"With some attention and being detached from the outcome. And so once I realized that, I started actually working on that conscientiously" (Chuck, 94)

"As long as I keep my intention on what I'm supposed to do" (ElCore, 130)

"By having intentions you don't restrict that, and by then, letting it flow you will be seeing opportunities that you would not be able to see" (Chuck, 106)

Figure 70. Consciousness leaders have intentions instead of outcomes.

Letting go of control and accepting what is. The more they were willing to let go of control, the more success they had, and the more accepting they became of themselves and life in general. As they began meeting "people where they are," they had a great sense of "relief," realized that "everything is perfect," and that "there are no tragedies. It's how you look at it."

Changed material orientation. Having enough money and being financially independent is another common topic to all participants in the current study. However, after their transformation, all leaders confirmed that they are "less concerned with material things" as they were before (see Figure 71). They do not "need as many things as" they "used to need. In fact, things sometimes get in the way of what" they are "trying to do." Furthermore, they seem to not "care about showing off" or "accumulating things" anymore.

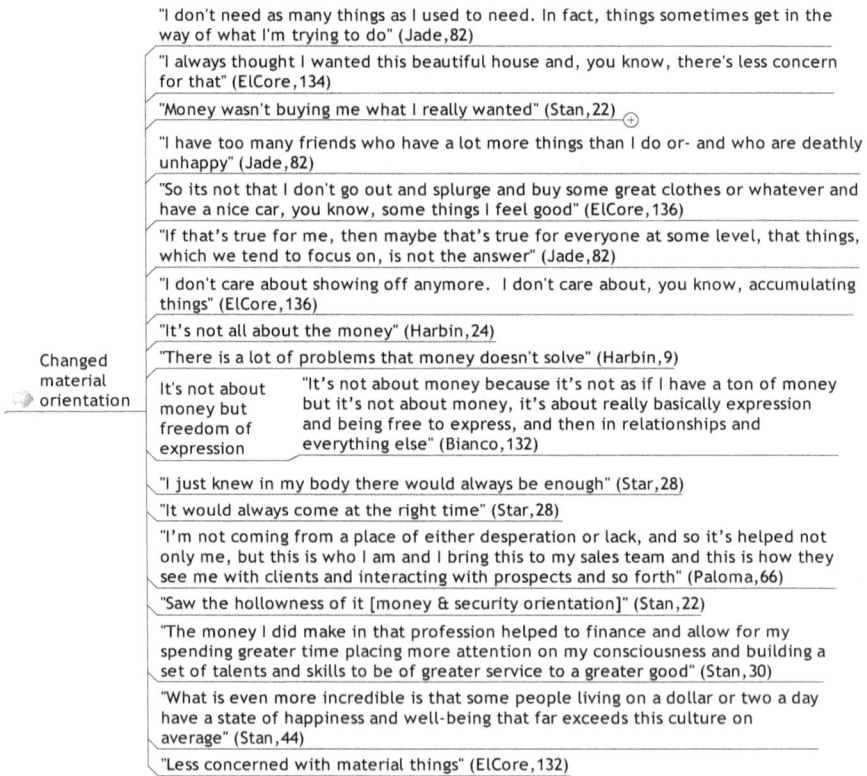

Changed material orientation

"I don't need as many things as I used to need. In fact, things sometimes get in the way of what I'm trying to do" (Jade,82)

"I always thought I wanted this beautiful house and, you know, there's less concern for that" (ElCore,134)

"Money wasn't buying me what I really wanted" (Stan,22)

"I have too many friends who have a lot more things than I do or- and who are deathly unhappy" (Jade,82)

"So its not that I don't go out and splurge and buy some great clothes or whatever and have a nice car, you know, some things I feel good" (ElCore,136)

"If that's true for me, then maybe that's true for everyone at some level, that things, which we tend to focus on, is not the answer" (Jade,82)

"I don't care about showing off anymore. I don't care about, you know, accumulating things" (ElCore,136)

"It's not all about the money" (Harbin,24)

"There is a lot of problems that money doesn't solve" (Harbin,9)

It's not about money but freedom of expression — "It's not about money because it's not as if I have a ton of money but it's not about money, it's about really basically expression and being free to express, and then in relationships and everything else" (Bianco,132)

"I just knew in my body there would always be enough" (Star,28)

"It would always come at the right time" (Star,28)

"I'm not coming from a place of either desperation or lack, and so it's helped not only me, but this is who I am and I bring this to my sales team and this is how they see me with clients and interacting with prospects and so forth" (Paloma,66)

"Saw the hollowness of it [money & security orientation]" (Stan,22)

"The money I did make in that profession helped to finance and allow for my spending greater time placing more attention on my consciousness and building a set of talents and skills to be of greater service to a greater good" (Stan,30)

"What is even more incredible is that some people living on a dollar or two a day have a state of happiness and well-being that far exceeds this culture on average" (Stan,44)

"Less concerned with material things" (ElCore,132)

Figure 71. Changed material orientation.

Through their transformative experiences encountered along their *Hero's Journey*, they also "saw the hollowness" of money and material orientation. They realized there are "a lot of problems that money doesn'tsolve," and that "it's not all about the money" but "freedom of expression and creativity."

Openness and creativity. Being "very curious and very open" is a key characteristic of consciousness leaders in business. All research participants have entrepreneurial spirits and as they became even more open, they were able to see and hone synchronistic events, which they did not notice before. As they realized that "there is no real truth" they became "less dogmatic" and understood that "everything happens" in "a very wonderful way" if they "allow it" (see Figure 72).

	"Synchronicity "was really helpful to me in understanding [that] everything happens if you allow it in a very wonderful way" (Jade,66)
	"I would never be able to accomplish by my own ego or by myself, you know, that then happened, I think. And it's an avalanche of things that I have no control over. Just great things that happened" (Chuck,94)
	"If "you're not open, you don't see" (Chuck,94)
	"I'm going to be open to hearing what people have to say"(Harbin,36)
	"People have to give themselves the freedom to listen to what their emotions are saying, and they have to develop the ear for that" (Harbin,36)
Openness & creativity	"I have a belief that I could start over again, and find joy in life, and would not be devastated as long as the things that I really hold dear to me are there. And even if I lost one of those, because I have lost a spouse equivalent, you pick up your life and you move on, and you can still find joy in life" (Harbin,42)
	"I'm very curious and very open. Very open. I'm a very open person to ideas. Again, I think that's the entrepreneurial ideas, just always open and looking for different things" (LaCroix,88)
	"You just keep reminding yourself that there is no real truth or very few things that are the way we think they are" (Lia,46)
	"Our minds are hard coded in certain ways just because of who raised and what part of society we were born into and all that sort of thing" (Lia,48)
	"There's a distinction in the work we do called fact and interpretation" (Lia,46)
	"I'm much more open to what people need, and not stuck in one [position]" (ElCore,108)
	"Less dogmatic. Less positionality" (ElCore,114)
	"[If] you're not open, you don't see" (Chuck,94)

Figure 72. Openness and creativity.

Cultivating presence. This is another significant structural change of which the participants in the current study were cognizant. Cultivating presence and "being the observer" has become a key transformative practice in the lives of consciousness leaders because it helps them "stay sane" in the stressful business environment in which they live. Presence supports them to become the "vessel" through which the "divine" can "operate."

It helps them connect with nature, their "surroundings," feelings, and their senses. By being present they can stay in the here and now, can get "down into the basic elements of life," and connect with the people in their lives at a much deeper level. Presence helps them "quiet" their minds and in doing that they "feel absolutely grateful and joyful to be alive in this moment." Figure 73 summarizes some verbatim accounts of the research participants regarding their ability to be present. It also indicates the benefits, which they derive from this practice.

All of these newly acquired abilities constitute the foundation of the "unity consciousness" of consciousness leaders. It represented their "one essence" awareness and their deep understanding that "we are all unique representations" of our divine nature. Another significant common characteristic is the emotional component that will be summarized subsequently.

Bridging the Head with the Heart

Figure 66 summarizes the main characteristics of the emotional transformation of consciousness leaders. These are: (a) being driven mostly by positive emotions, (b) willingness and courage to face their shadows, (c) having better emotional skills to transcend suffering, (d) fear transcendence, and (e) higher emotional awareness.

Through their transformation, the researched consciousnesses leaders have been empowered to—and learned how to—face their shadows and their greatest fears. This has been the main focus of the Initiation phase (II) of the *Hero's Journey* (Campbell, 1948/1968). Therefore, the goal here is to present other structural changes related to their emotional mastery.

It could be argued that the most important emotional accomplishment is the realization that they have the power of emotional choice. In Hahm's words, who has spent almost 4 decades of his life in the human potential movement and the last 2 decades researching this subject scientifically, life is

"I was never present in any conversation maybe I was ever in for 35 years" (Jade,46)

"There was always noise in my head, a thousand monkeys, whatever" (Jade,46)

"Presence is about the deepening condition, or the deepening practice of being alert to the arising of those energies and those vibrations within my physical form, and then learning to more consciously create and or de-create" (Star,14)

"Everybody comes from a different family background, so I find that the mindfulness work is helping with the presence to keep me centered in the present moment, and to realize the higher order of what's most important, which is to maintain the peace, sometimes at all costs" (Paloma,58)

"In this moment I feel absolutely grateful and joyful to be alive in this moment" (Stan,44)

"I continue to be present" (Stan,48)

"Let's think about my surroundings. What does it feel like right now? What temperature is it? What am I looking at? What am I hearing? What am I smelling? So taking your senses and focusing on them one at a time" (Harbin,38)

"It feels great, and I can smell the jasmine and just taking yourself into exploring each of your senses, and focusing on that, I find that does quiet your mind" (Harbin,38)

Moment to moment awareness practice	At all times, "I try to stay aware of my mind and my feelings and emotions. I try to keep what we call my pitch up" (Hahm,56)

"Being present and in the moment and enjoying it" (Bianco,84)

"It's just got potential everywhere. That's where I want to be. So that's why I'm attempting to be all the time, but to do that you have to be, like [Eckhard] Tolle says, present" (Bianco,112)

"You've got to get out of the mental stuff and right down into just the basic feeling of it" (Bianco,112)

"It's getting out of the abstract, mostly in getting down into the basic elements of life" (Bianco,112)

Need to be present came from recognizing patterns

"I think that differentiates me maybe from others, and that's I was just always in the weirdest moments, not an out of body experience, but as an observer, you know, observing me doing this high-tech management stuff. And I have to smile sometimes look at this sometimes and say this is funny what you're doing here" (Chuck,152)

Being the observer "helped me stay sane" (Chuck,158)

"The practice that I would say I adopt when I'm in these situations is the naive learner, so trying to approach each time that I go into even the same seminar that I've been through 100 times, I still go into it thinking what is there this time for me" (Lia,42)

"Paying attention to the conscious moment-by-moment evolution of what used to trigger me may no longer trigger me of coming out of being" (Poet,35)

"It's not that I meditate all of the time, you know, it's about the spiritual practicing in every moment. I like to meditate because it helps me relax, you know. But its not that it helps me in spiritual time, I think just living in the moment" (ElCore,86)

"My intention everyday in the moment is to be the witness and to be, you know, strong in your conscious awareness of life and your awareness of yourself, as well as others" (ElCore,12)

"Just being" (ElCore,88)

"It's not that I meditate all of the time, you know, it's about the spiritual practicing in every moment. I like to meditate because it helps me relax, you know. But its not that it helps me in spiritual time, I think just living in the moment" (ElCore,86)

"People have to give themselves the freedom to listen to what their emotions are saying, and they have to develop the ear for that" (Harbin,36)

"I only know how to be that in the moment. So you walk in the door and then you be in the moment. You're in presence and you sort of somehow know. The divine operates and you sort of know what to do next" (Star,82)

"When we get too far into our heads and thinking we know the model, it actually stifles the true freedom which is to be in the presence. So it's almost like we need to go in and teach the presence" (Star,82)

"I think as we each do that as teachers, we carry more and more and more light ourselves, that we will without any sort of conscious knowing of how we did it, because it's not really us, it's not that we're doing anything; but the divine will actually activate" (Star,82)

Cultivating presence

Figure 73. Cultivating presence.

about making emotional choices. Emotions are reactions to some degree and there are emotional triggers, right? So you can instantly feel a lot of things. But then you have a choice immediately after that to feel something else. In many cases, you have a choice to feel before, you know, a certain way. You can choose an emotion more—people can choose an emotion more than they think. Instead of it simply being something of a reactive process.

The ability to choose one's emotional response comes from cultivating awareness, mindfulness, and presence (Damasio, 2006; Goleman, 2000, 2003; McCraty, 2001), a process experienced by consciousness leaders for many decades. Harbin for instance said that her emotional awareness and ability to listen to her inner voice "goes back to being in Michael Ray's class [at Stanford] and learning about 'Is it a yes or is it a no,' learning about 'Listening to your inner voice'" Like Harbin, LaCroix is active in the Venture Capital world and is "using the consciousness and awareness" abilities with his investors. LaCroix summarized the evolution of his awareness ability in the following way:

Because of the program I did 15 years ago and the training, I have an awareness and can put it into intellectual academic terms where I can actually understand what I'm thinking and then through 15 years of experience, implement it and put it into action to help what I'm trying to accomplish in the business world.

Not surprisingly, consciousness leaders "take the positive out of any circumstance and move on from it." As leaders, they cultivate a positive attitude and have developed emotional mastery and intelligence (Csikszentmihalyi & Nakamura, 2002; Goleman, 1995, 2000) around the following main emotions: joy, love, gratitude, compassion and empathy, trust, hope, discernment and humility, as well as humor (see Figure 66). For the scope of this research that focuses on leaders' qualities at the postconventional or later levels of development (Cook-Greuter, 2005; Kegan et al., 1990; Wilber, 2006), the emotions of joy, gratitude, trust, compassion, humility, and humor will be highlighted subsequently.

Joy. After their transformation, consciousness leaders regard the feeling of *joy* along with gratitude as dominating emotions in their lives. Guided by "the joy of being alive at this time" (Poet), the consciousness leader has the belief

> *I could start over again, and find joy in life, and would not be devastated as long as the things that I really hold dear to me are there. And even if I lost one of those, because I have lost a spouse equivalent, you pick up your life and you move on, and you can still find joy in life. (Harbin)*

Harbin expressed eloquently what is a common denominator for everyone else researched in the current study (see Figure 74).

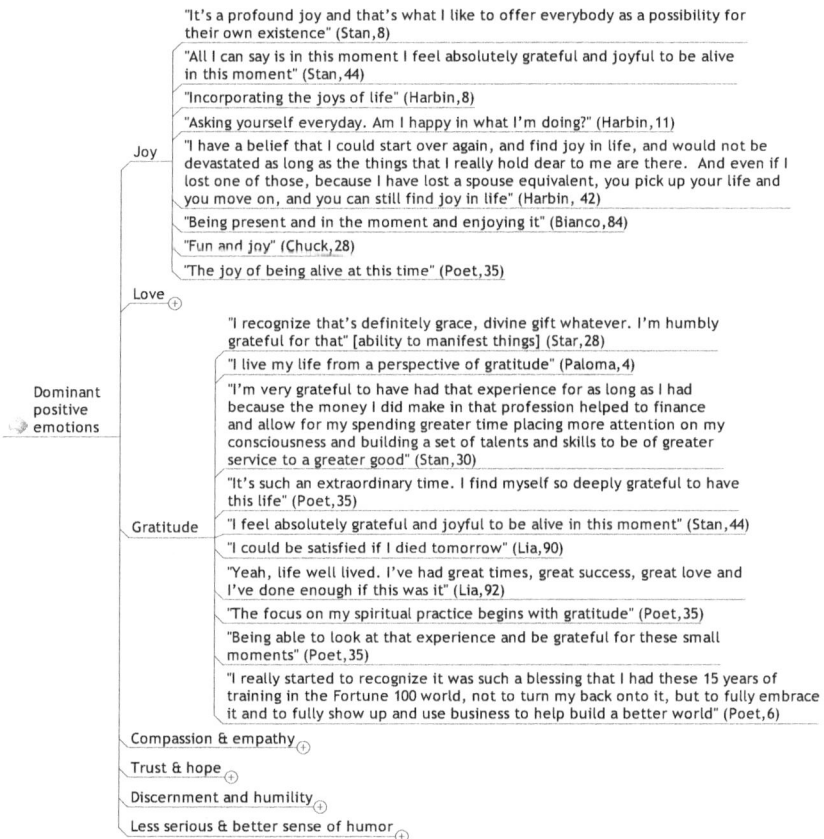

Figure 74. Joy and gratitude as dominant emotions of consciousness leaders.

Gratitude. Gratitude is another common emotion for consciousness leaders who live their lives "from a perspective of gratitude" (Paloma), who find themselves "deeply grateful to have this life" (Poet), and who feel fulfilled because they had a "life well lived . . . had great times, great success, great love" and have "done enough" (Lia; see Figure 74).

Compassion. Their transpersonal experiences enabled consciousness leaders furthermore to develop a deep sense of compassion for their fellow human beings. ElCore, who is a doctor, a renowned author, and a successful entrepreneur in the health-care industry, expressed compassion in the following way:

> *I think if I wasn't given that gift, I don't think I would be as good in what I do, because I have so much compassion for people. When somebody comes and sits there, you know, that's why I like, you know, no one in the room most often, is I immediately become that person. I can feel what they're going through, you know. And it's not that I feel sad about it, it's just that I feel it. I never am resentful, I never get, "Oh, God, I can't listen to it." Because a lot of people, doctors, do that, you know, say, "I can't handle people complaining." I'm not like that. I completely relate. And I think it's because the memory is still very strong and clear what I went through that I have complete empathy.*

Trust. Building trust was "the most difficult element" (Bianco) for all consciousness leaders because they achieved extraordinary successes by believing that they were in control of everything if they worked hard enough. Trusting means to let go of control and of fear, "be present to a much larger entity" (Bianco) and "trust someone other than yourself but inherently you have to trust yourself" (Jade). Poet expressed the process of learning to trust as having "surrendered over to something larger than" himself, and Jade found this to be "the most challenging, difficult, intense kind of way of living there is because you have to take total accountability for yourself in the world." Yet, what convinced all consciousness leaders to trust the "universe," the "divine," also called by some of them "God," were tangible results: "I knew that when I controlled it myself that I didn't get the outcome I wanted" thus he was forced to let go.

Humility. Having gone through the process of transformation was also very humbling for all consciousness leaders researched here. Harbin admitted that "Dealing with failure for sort of the first time in my life, not delivering a success, was very hard" and Star recognized that it is "definitely grace, divine gift whatever [that helped her along]. I'm humbly grateful for that." Stan acknowledged that "in any given moment almost anybody could be more awake than" him, and Poet has decided to let "humility and perseverance" be his guiding emotions from then on.

Humor. Humor, however, seems to top all other emotions and has become part of the regular emotional repertoire of the consciousness leader. Humor helped them all "become a lot softer," be "less serious" (Star), "stay sane as an executive," not "take this circus for reality" (Chuck), and recognize that everything is "a game of consciousness and all I can do is my best" (Stan).

The transformative emotions highlighted above are important because they (a) represent freedom from ego (Cook-Greuter, 2005, pp. 33-35), (b) provide a deep sense of security, (c) lead to differentiated ways of reasoning, (d) provide access to intuitive abilities and sources of wisdom, (e) have more compassion for other human beings, (f) have changed their defense mechanisms, and (g) have enabled consciousness leaders in accepting what "is" individually but also culturally and socially (Beck, 1976; Beck & Cowan, 1996; Beck, 2000; Cook-Greuter, 2008; Goleman, 2000, 2003; Goleman et al., 2002; Pert, 1997; Saron & Davidson, 1997).

Most consciousness leaders believe that their structural changes are irreversible because they recognized that "it's all an illusion" (Chuck), they are "not" their bodies or their emotions and that "underlying that is another reality that's rich and vibrant" (Bianco). However, they also attest to the need for regular practices to help them maintain their new skills. These regular practices provide the integration point between body, mind, and spirit and have been called by Leonard and Murphy (Leonard, 1991; Leonard & Murphy, 1995) *Integral Transformative Practice*, or by Wilber (Wilber, 2006, pp. 201-210) *Integral Life Practice*. Within the context of consciousness leadership in business, it could be called the *Integral Wheel of Life Practice*. Explaining the *Integral Wheel of Life Practices* in detail would go well beyond the scope of this dissertation; however, the spiritual and physical practices identified in this research will be highlighted below.

The Integral Wheel of Life: The Spiritual and the Physical Practices

Figure 75 shows the verbatim accounts and most important aspects regarding the spiritual and physical practices of the consciousness leaders researched in the current study.

Chuck summarized the motivation for such practices by saying: "I have to do that conscientiously because I'm such a driven person. And I've learned to accept that and not say it's bad or good, it's just who I am so I might as well lead it to my advantage, but I need to temper it." All consciousness leaders confirmed that they "would not have survived anything" without their "spiritual life" (DeSiena) and that they "progressed more rapidly and took a shift" (LaCroix) through this kind of conditioning. To their spiritual and physical practices belong meditation, mindfulness work, yogic exercises, communion with nature, gardening, visualization exercises, and even ballroom dancing.

Pioneers of Change

Through the discipline of their integrative practice, the consciousness leaders continue to grow and keep up the *Mastery of the Two Worlds* (Campbell, 1949/1968), the interior and exterior, acquired through the *Hero's Journey*. It provides the internal foundation for and enables the consciousness leaders to share their gifts to the world.

They view "the world in whole terms today," they "integrated the world," and they "no longer overly segmented things." They "started thinking and making much more real-time connections between people, places, things, events" because they "saw the patterns" (Jade) governing the world. Following their transformation, the consciousness leaders real-

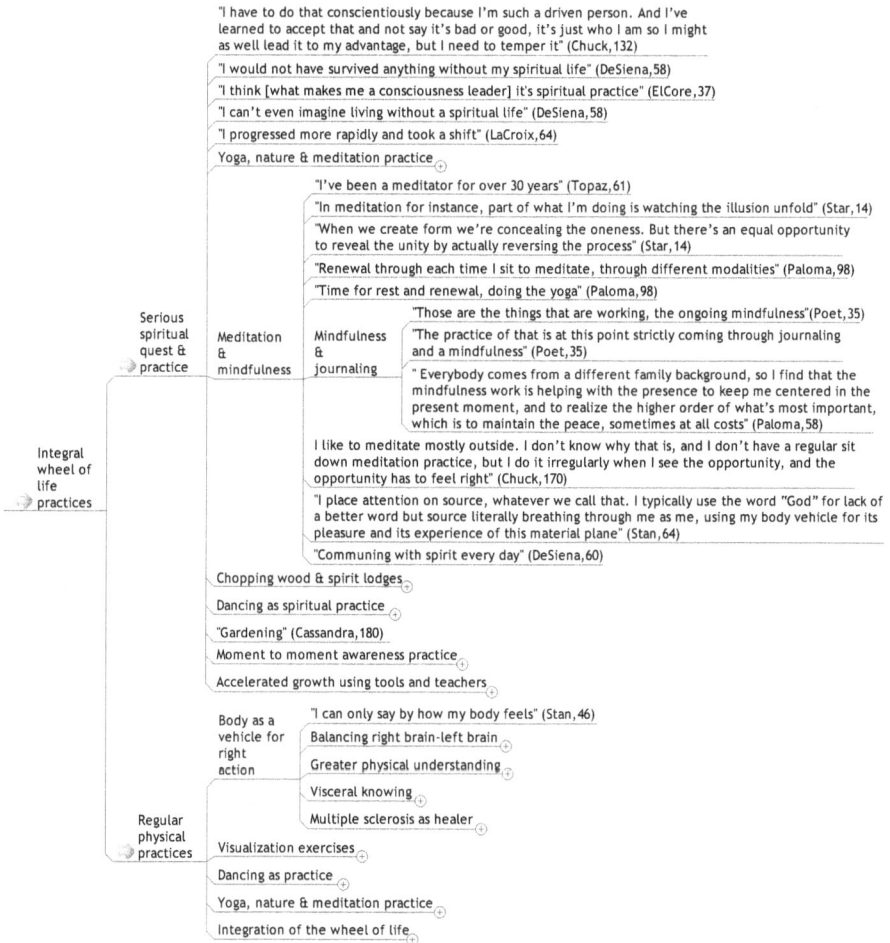

Figure 75. Spiritual and physical practices of consciousness leaders.

ized that "everything is either moving towards that state of expanded consciousness or is retarding it" (Jade). Their consciousness leadership abilities enabled them also to transform both their culture and social environments. They became better relationship people because they are able to build a bridge between the mind and the heart, between the inner and the outer, between having an "enjoyable business as well as make money." They became active with social philanthropy parallel to or alternative with "business as a service" to humanity (see Figure 76).

"Explore and lead and show different ways of creating social enterprises and different financing mechanisms that are behind that" (Chuck, 60)

"We're really about social entrepreneurial philanthropy" (Bianco, 132)

"It's to lead a purposeful life, where I actually work with my talents that are given to me including hopefully consciousness development, to make an impactful contribution to sustainability, holistic sustainability" (Chuck, 60)

"Of serving, of providing value to someone, of serving" (Paloma, 72)

"You're giving of yourself. That's a service, whatever you do. It's however you are aligned with what you find your higher purpose to be, your mission, as I mentioned, my connecting with the source so that I can help others connect as well" (Paloma, 126)

Serving is "rewarding" ⊕

"The element of business or the element of social entrepreneurship" (Bianco, 128)

Social philanthropy & being of service

"I knew even from my own heritage that serving was deeply ingrained in that, in my culture, the culture that I was born in to. You were always encouraged by the parents to do something that would be helpful to other people so- as well as advanced intellectually or academically" (Darlene, 65)

Transforming our understanding of not-for profit businesses ⊕

"I'm much more conscious of the ways in which I might either facilitate or inhibit another person's spiritual growth and I try to really be aware and conscious of that so that I'm not doing anything that isn't of service" (Topaz, 59)

"Creating rural communities" (Chuck, 130)

Philanthropic activism

"I started Women Organization . . . is a not-for-profit but that doesn't mean it's not a business unfortunately because it still takes money and resources and all of that" (Lia, 50)

NGOs are tough businesses ⊕

Creating sustainable organizations ⊕

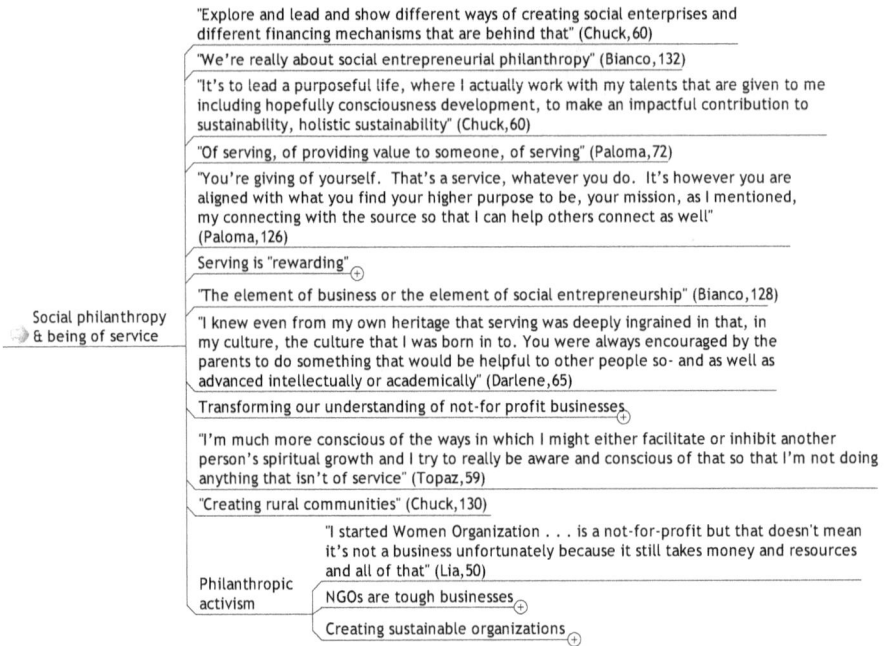

Figure 76. Business as service and social philanthropy.

Furthermore, they became involved with the creation of sustainable businesses (a) by promoting long-term versus short-term thinking, by realizing that it "was not necessarily the shorter term end state you are working towards but the greater good, the greater end state that we all are" (Jade); (b) by "creating social enterprises and different financing mechanisms that are behind that" (Chuck); (c) by "bringing spirit into manifestation" (Jade); (d) by working toward ceasing the "ideology" of "rampant consumerism"; and (e) by creating social justice and seeking appropriate "political leadership" (see Figure 77).

As they evolved spiritually over several decades, some consciousness leaders have developed an understanding of "interconnectedness" and "unity consciousness" through which they "don't care that much about" (Harbin) exceptional human experiences or extraordinary states anymore because they realized that these states are "fingers pointing to

Sustainable Businesses

Conscious Capitalism
- "Move capitalism beyond the pure maximizing of profits" (Chuck, 60)
- "My purpose today is to bring consciousness into the domain of business in a way that creates sustainable change relative to the human beings on the planet and ultimately bringing spirit into manifestation" (Jade, 62)
- "Creating social enterprises and different financing mechanisms that are behind that" (Chuck, 60)

Systemic change through global leadership and activism
- "If we don't change the way that the financial system works, we don't reach sustainability" (Chuck, 60)
- "I launched the Women Organization which is a not-for-profit but that doesn't mean it's not a business unfortunately because it still takes money and resources and all of that. We have I think this false division between for-profits and not-for-profits so I don't think I ever left the business world. Not yet anyway" (Lia, 50)
- "Improve the quality of life while we improve the business outcomes at the same time? The two go together" (Darlene, 65)
- "The local desire to help specific people with specific painful issues is just the local thing. But also conquering world problems, and I don't know if that is any different but I have a definite interest in that" (LaCroix, 71)
- "Bringing spirit into manifestation" (Jade, 62)
- Large systemic change is required now

Creating sustainable social enterprises
- "Explore and lead and show different ways of creating social enterprises and different financing mechanisms that are behind that" (Chuck, 60)
- "Instead of running away from the business world, I found myself running back to say that business has such an amazing framework and foundation to really help re frame, re-imagine, and redesign all of the institutions, all of the systems on this planet" (Poet, 8)
- "It would be total low-integrity and unconscionable for us not to put the financial resources that we have in alignment with helping social enterprises and communities, and making some money by doing that but not only making money" (Chuck, 130)
- "We have so much that can be done through the institution called business" (Poet, 8)
  - Create new value fast
    - "Ability to create new value, to create new concepts, to articulate futures that are very different, and the reason is because the pace of change has accelerated so much" (Jade, 4)
    - "We're out of time" (Jade, 62)
- "A pretty big theme, and it goes back to making a contribution on social enterprises, and different financial models to help conscious businesses if you wish to be more successful in the future. So anything that I do in my life now is aligned around this" (Chuck, 130)
- Creating different distribution systems
- Sustainable businesses through heart-based living

Long term versus short term thinking
- "Understanding the greater purpose of that was not necessarily the shorter term end state you are working towards but the greater good, the greater end state that we all are" (Jade, 12)
- "Short-term market-driven economic realities" (Jade, 74) today

Stop rampant consumerism
- "Is the totality of business making progress in this area of creating sustainable life or not?" I would say no, we're going backwards, the level of consumerism, India, China, Indonesia, Africa" (Jade, 76)
- Matter of survival
- "Rampant consumerism which has grown out of a Western- mostly West but Western culture, the reality that the planet cannot sustain that level of growth, the basic underpinning structures that support that" (Jade, 62)
- "Belief systems that suggest that only happiness can be achieved through that consumerism, these are very deeply held, difficult to break" (Jade, 62)
- "I'm still mystified by the power of the ideology of consumerism. It's astonishing to me how powerful that still has a hold on us. I'm mystified at the extent to which people will act directly against their own best interests based on the power of that ideology" (Topaz, 67)

- Social Justice
- Political leadership is required
- Business as service
- Business is "an incredible laboratory for consciousness research"

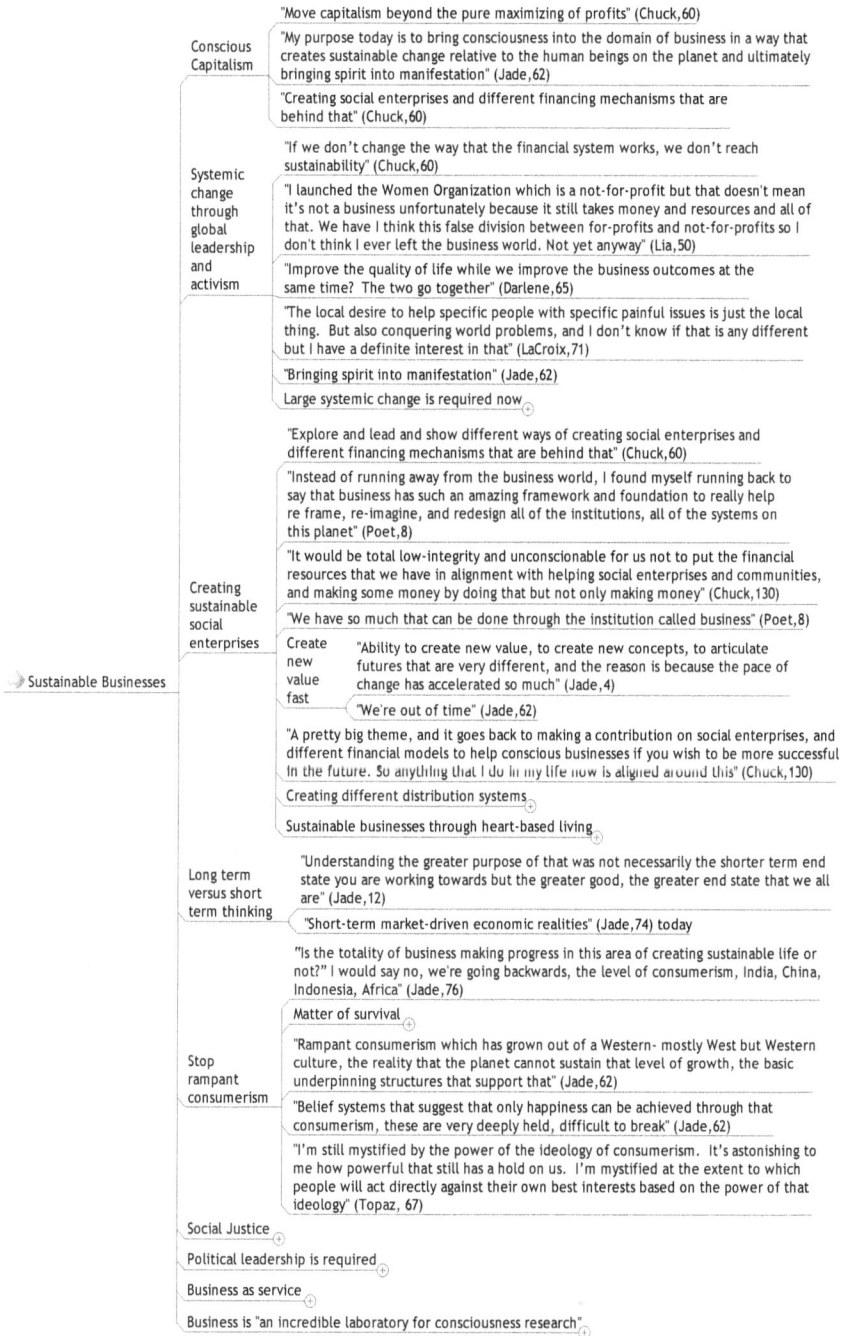

Figure 77. Sustainable business as service to humanity.

the moon and not the moon itself." Thus, in an unassuming way, their mission in life has become more important to them. Star expressed this evolution toward and beyond unity consciousness by explaining how, in her understanding, the process of creation can even be reversed. She said, "When we create form we're concealing the oneness. But there's an equal opportunity to reveal the unity by actually reversing the process" (Star). Through this revelation, the consciousness leader has completed the circle that seems to allow him or her to break through the mind-constructed world (Cook-Greuter, 2008, p.34) and understand the universe even before it was created. In the words of T. S. Eliot (1952), that recognition means

> *We shall not cease from exploration*
> *And the end of all our exploring*
> *Will be to arrive where we started*
> *And know the place for the first time. (p. 145)*

Further research and testing such as the Sentence Completion Test (Cook-Greuter, 2004) or the Leadership Development Profile (Torbert et al., 2004) would have to be performed to be more accurate, however, the research results summarized in phase III of the *Hero's Journey* provide an indication that the research participants in the present study have reached later stages of postconventional development (Alexander et al., 1990; Commons et al., 1084, 1990; Cook-Greuter, 2008; Goleman, 2000, 2002; Torbert et al., 2004, 2008).

In summary, through the *Hero's Journey*, the consciousness leaders researched here appear to (a) have awakened to and embraced non-duality; (b) be able to live with paradoxes and be joyous, fulfilled, and serene; (c) accept reality as "is"; (d) make no separation between their spirituality and their personal or professional lives; (e) cultivate their capacity for compassion, empathy, and unconditional love through integral practices; (f) be able to live in the present and day by day; (g) be humble and display an unassuming presence; (h) have moved beyond emotional and spiritual mastery; (i) be detached from their outcomes and set intentions instead; (j) have transcended money and the material world; (k) live simple lives of global service; (l) experience genuine joy, gratefulness, and have a life-affirming attitude; (m) have the ability to live life in the present moment; and (n) have a sense of interconnectedness with others and the source of life.

An additional observation derived from this research and which would have to be studied further, is that the research participants seem to have also moved beyond the money and material orientation of their original *culture and social environment*. Beck and Cowan (1996) and their Spiral Dynamics model could provide the necessary model for further analysis (pp. 244-287).

Conclusion

This chapter provided a composite depiction and synthesis of the research participants in this dissertation research and has two dimensions. The *first dimension* is the dynamic story line of becoming a consciousness leader and was represented using the three major phases of *Hero's Journey* (Campbell, 1949/1968). The three phases of the consciousness leaders' journey are (a) The Awakening of the Consciousness Leader, (b) The Initiation of the Consciousness Leader, and (c) The Emergence of the Consciousness Leader.

The *second dimension* refers to the *lines* of development involved at each of the three phases of the participants' transformation. This research provides further confirmation that interior transformation occurs along various lines of development, which have been mapped for each research participant (see Appendix D) using the Wilberian (2000a) map of consciousness (AQAL).

In keeping with the heuristic structuralism research method developed for this research, this chapter related furthermore the essence of the transformation toward becoming a consciousness leader not only from the *inside-out* view of the participants themselves but also from the *outside-in* perspective.

Furthermore, phase III of the *Hero's Journey* (Campbell, 1949/1968), *The Emergence of the Consciousness Leader*, attempted to reveal the structural changes that might have occurred through the transpersonal transformation (state stages) of the consciousness leaders studied. Based on the phenomenological observations made in this research, it could be assumed that the center of gravity for most consciousness leaders is located at postconventional levels of egoic development (Alexander et al., 1990; Commons et al., 1984, 1990; Cook-Greuter, 2008; Goleman, 2000, 2002; Torbert et al., 2004, 2008). However, more research and testing would have to be performed to arrive at a more concise assessment. The chapter ended with a call for further research to confirm that assumption.

The next chapter will briefly summarize this dissertation research and present possible implications of the consciousness leadership movement in the light of existing literature, both theoretically and practically.

CHAPTER 6

DISCUSSION, IMPLICATIONS, OUTCOMES, PREDICTIONS

The purpose of this dissertation is to contribute to and explore the phenomenon of becoming a consciousness leader within a business environment. The term consciousness leader in business was chosen intentionally to express the multidimensionality of the interior and exterior aspects of the consciousness evolution that currently seems to occur with some extraordinary leaders in business. In short, consciousness leaders are people who evolve to higher levels of consciousness not only within their own interiorities, but who also help their cultures, societies, and environment do the same.

The original method chosen for the current study was heuristic research (Moustakas, 1990) and the underlying theoretical foundation was Wilber's (2000a) AQAL map of consciousness including its lines, states, stages, and structures. The intention was to keep this complex topic as simple as possible to serve the main purpose of this research. However, during the analysis phase (see chapter 4), certain structural patterns that connected the studied phenomena related by the research participants became obvious. In Wilber's (2006) words, "Phenomenology looks for the *direct experiences and phenomena*, structuralism looks for *the patterns that connect the phenomena*. These patterns or structures actually govern the phenomena, but without the phenomena ever knowing it" (p. 55).

Thus, the term heuristic structuralism was born and with it the multiple dimensions of this research: (a) the Hero's Journey of the consciousness leader, which is represented in three phases; (b) the various lines of development (*cognitive, emotional, physical, ethical, spiritual,* and *egoic*) that are involved in the studied phenomena; and (c) the perceived structural changes that occurred over the course of transformation. The research findings were presented in a composite synthesis (see chapter 5), which indicated that consciousness leaders have evolved through their transpersonal evolution (state stages) from being originally at a conventional stage to being today at postconventional or possibly later levels (Alexander et al., 1990; Commons et al., 1984, 1990; Cook-Greuter, 2005, 2008; Koplowitz, 1984, 1990; Torbert et al., 2004; Wilber, 2000c). However, further research and testing is required to be able to make a more accurate assumption.

Deconstructing the Mind-Body Division

Further research would be required to confirm another significant outcome of this phenomenological research namely that the *cognitive, emotional, ethical,* and *spiritual* evolution must go hand in hand in order to produce a consciousness leader. In other words, this phenomenological research contributed to further deconstructing the division between mind and matter, soul and body, and heart and brain. Like Plato (1938/1961), Descartes (2003) accepted the divine authority of God, which is "to be preferred to our perception" (p. 144), but in his view, mind and body must be separate entities. Descartes argued, "it is very inappropriate for a philosopher to accept anything as true that they never perceived as true; and it is even more inappropriate to trust in the senses" (p. 144). Therefore, the prominence of the mind unencumbered by emotion and body has dominated the scientific evolution in the Western society over the past three centuries since Descartes (1998). With his famous sentence, "I think, therefore I am" (p.18), Descartes has lead humanity out of the dark ages into modernity by emphasizing the logical thinking abilities, the brain, and that which could objectively be verified. In acknowledging "the whole essence of nature . . . is simply to think," (p. 19) Descartes argued, "The soul through which I am what I am, is entirely distinct from the body and is even easier to know than the body, and even if there were no body at all, it would not cease to be all that it is" (p. 19).

Through this "Cartesian dualism" (Schwartz 2000, p. 198) Westerners have begun to "equate their identity with their mind, instead with their whole organism" (Capra, 2000, p. 23). However, it seems obvious today that Descartes committed a "serious error" (Damasio, 2006, p. 249) by separating body from the soul, matter from the mind, and brain from the heart. This division has been since Descartes (Damasio, 2006) at the center of gravity in many parts of modern society, especially in science, business, and politics (Capra, 2000, 2002; Damasio, 2006; Harman & Hormann, 1993; Ray & Rinzler, 1993; Renesch, 2002). It was thought that the mind is superior to matter, which it must control (Capra, 2000, 2002; Damasio, 2006).

As a result, human existence has often been reduced to subjugating matter and emotions (Wilber, 2000). Wilber argued that by exercising control, we have reduced the three value spheres of humanity, the Good, the True, and the Beautiful (see Figure 1) to one, to brain and organisms, to rocks and dirt, to objective Truth. Furthermore, by believing that humans can control the world through the mind and the thereupon-derived scientific method (Descartes, 2003), we have achieved some extraordinary successes in the material world. These include technology advances that simplify the burdens of daily life, progress in medical sciences, flying to the moon, and connecting humanity through the power of the Internet. The one-sided orientation toward the visible world (the True) lead humanity arguably to the imbalanced and life-threatening reality we experience collectively today in our own hearts, economically, geopolitically, and environmentally. The current study confirmed how the emphasis on the mind and intellectual capacity led the consciousness leaders in the beginning of their journey to neglect personal joy, happiness, and true fulfillment.

Through this research, it became obvious that control played a significant role in the lives of the research participants prior to their transpersonal transformations. By exercising control in their own lives, the research participants were reflecting the center of gravity of their own culture and societies that reduced human existence often to the subjugation of matter and emotions (Wilber, 2000).

Yet, the final results of this research give reason for hope, and Kuhn (1996) provided the necessary insights that explain what the next steps out of the current collective crisis might be. In his view, we could (a) "handle the crisis provoking problem" (p. 84) within the existing paradigm; (b) there is no solution, and "the problem resists" (p. 84) despite new approaches; or (c) "a crisis may end with the emergence of a new candidate for paradigm" (p. 84) change. The candidate for a new paradigm could be the emerging consciousness leader.

Wealth Creation versus Money-Making

This dissertation would not be complete without addressing the topic of money and the role of financial independence in the evolution of consciousness leaders. This research indicated that the consciousness leaders have reached a certain level of financial and money transcendence through their transpersonal evolution. Yet, having a full bank account seems to make it relatively easy to state, "Money is not important." However, the results of this dissertation research indicate that security is an illusion and feeling wealthy and abundant is an emotion that is not correlated with having money. This finding seems confirmed by a survey of 800 people with a net worth of more than $500,000 that revealed that 19% of them worry about money (Blanchflower & Oswald, 2004). What was more fascinating is that among the people with a net worth of more than $10 million, 33% worried about money. Moreover, we would suspect that more abundance would make us feel not only more secure but also happier. In the same publication, Blanchflower and Oswald (2004) quoted a research performed by the General Social Survey in the Unites States in the early 1970s that indicated that 34% of people perceived themselves as "very happy" (p. 1366). By the late 1990s, the figure had dropped to 30% although the income nearly tripled after inflation adjustment in the same period.

What can be learned from this is that most people live in fear when it comes to having a sense of security through money. The reason for that must be searched in the way we *think* and how that translates into our *feelings* and *behavior* because only human beings have a notion of security derived from money. No other sentient being on this planet appears to have the same issue. This dissertation research confirmed that money, like time, is a human invention and does not really have any meaning other than the one we attach to it. Money is a means to exchange value between people and we all know that the value of things can be very flexible. In the desert, for instance, water can be more valuable than diamonds, and during war or natural calamities food is more valuable than gold. Knowing all this, we can begin to relax and become more creative about our sense of security and financial matters in general.

What can be learned from the consciousness leaders in the current study is that creating wealth and financial abundance can become effortless once we turn within to identify and unleash our higher potentials. By cultivating our interiorities through meditation, yoga, and other transpersonal practices, we seem to gain a visceral sense of security that we would otherwise expect from money or material gain. In fact, neuroscientific findings deliver additional facts hereto.

For instance, during the Yoga Nidra meditation, which is characterized by a lowered level of desire for action, Kjaer et al. (2002) demonstrated an increase in endogenous dopamine release in the ventral striatum (p. 1). Furthermore, the researchers could also measure a decreased blood flow in prefrontal, cerebellar, and subcortical regions of the brain. Kjaer et al. (2002) derived from their research "that being in the conscious state of meditation causes a suppression of cortico-striatal glutamatergic transmission. To our knowledge this is the first time in vivo evidence has been provided for regulation of conscious states at a synaptic level" (p. 1). On one hand, this means that there is an observable correlation between mystical experiences and brain function, and on the other hand, it means that the brain seems to have a built-in ability to transcend the perception of an individual self. The result is often serenity, inner joy, and calmness, with or without a full bank account, one may add.

In fact, during the past decades, there were numerous neurological studies performed on meditators many of which were critically analyzed by Beauregard and his team at the University de Montreal (Beauregard & O'Leary, 2007). In relating the research performed on Carmelite nuns, Beauregard suggested that religious, spiritual, or mystical experiences are "neurally instantiated by different brain regions involved in a variety of functions, such as self-consciousness, emotion, body representation, visual and motor imagery, and spiritual perception" (p. 274). The meditative state of the researched Carmelite was measured and associated with several brain regions and systems including

> *significant loci of activation in the right medial orbitofrontal cortex, right middle temporal cortex, right inferior and superior parietal lobules, right caudate, left medial prefrontal cortex, left anterior cingulated cortex, left inferior parietal lobule, left insula, left caudate, and left brain stem. (Beauregard & O'Leary, 2007, p. 275)*

The authors' conclusion is that the brain is a mediator but not the originator of the spiritual or mystical experience. Through the transpersonal experiences described by Beauregard (2007), Kjaer et al. (2002), and Newberg and Lee (2005), the brain seems to provide the connection to the ultimate Ground of Being, Kosmic Consciousness (Wilber, 2000), and infinite Spirit (Wilber, 2000). Therefore, it would be fair to assume that this sense of unity with all life is the source of security for people and not a full bank account. The research results in this dissertation corroborate the above neuroscientific findings from a phenomenological perspective. However, much more research would have to be performed in the future to arrive to a greater sense of clarity. Moreover, addressing the question whether there is a correlation between financial abundance and the readiness to embark on the consciousness leadership evolution or not, seems more relevant within the context of the current financial crisis than ever.

The Integral Wheel of Life Practice

From a more pragmatic perspective, all consciousness leaders confirm the need for hands-on tools to help speed up the evolution process of business leaders in particular and humanity in general. Some integral tools that could be derived from this research and that are based on Wilber's AQAL have been summarized in the Integral *Wheel of Life* (see Figure 78).

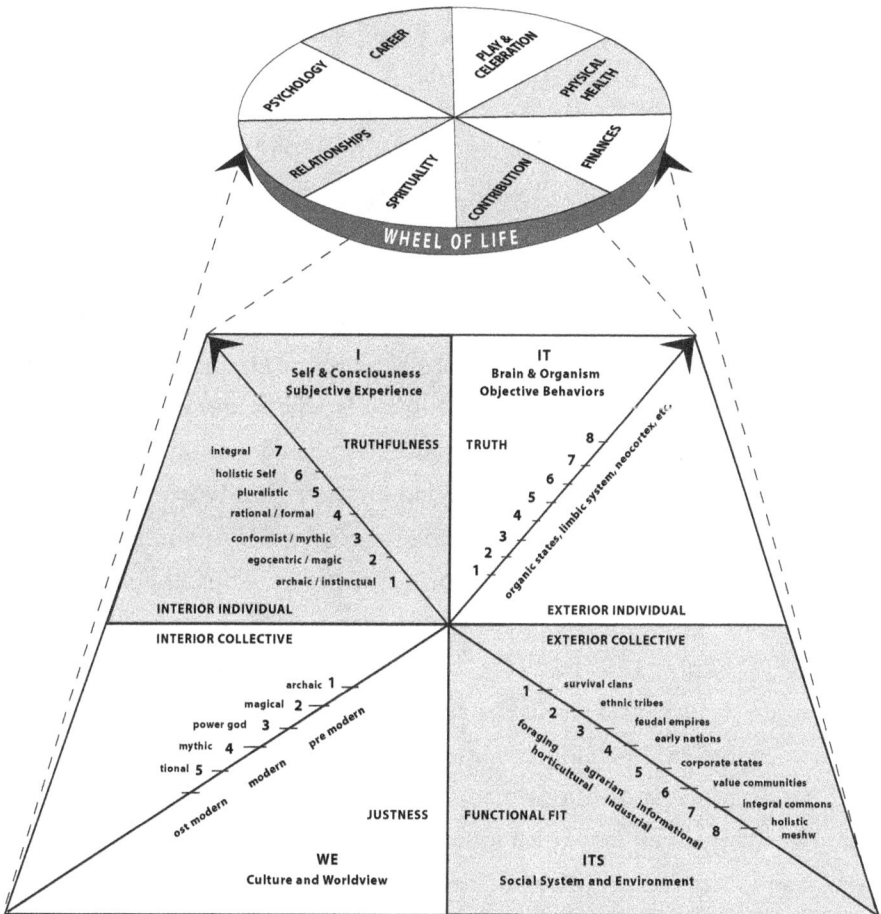

Figure 78. The Integral Wheel of Life Practice adapted after Wilber (2006, p. 22).

The *Wheel of Life* shown in Figure 78 represents in a simplified way the most important aspects in the life of a consciousness leader. These are the interior aspects of the individual (psychology, spirituality, and health), the collective inter-subjective (relationships), the exterior individual (career, finances), and the collective inter-objective (contribution) aspects. Sharing the tools of the consciousness leaders researched in the current study and beyond could become an invaluable resource for future generations of leaders in business and otherwise.

Deconstructing the Business World—Future Predictions

Through the *Hero's Journey*, the consciousness leaders studied have taken advantage of their high levels of cognition to open up, dive into, and be structurally transformed by their transpersonal experiences and their long journey to emotional freedom. Moreover, their consciousness leadership abilities helped them move beyond both the monological awareness of their spiritual practices and the reductionism of the scientific paradigm to come back into the world and address the requirements of postmodern inter-subjectivity and inter-objectivity in a systemic fashion (Wilber, 2000, pp. 774-776). Consciousness leaders are experienced integral thinkers (von Bertalanffy, 1969/2006) who have adapted their worldviews as they grew because they realized that the world is determined by its relationship to the context or the environment (Koplowitz, 1984). Thus, they are able to apply various types of leadership intelligences—inter-personal and intrapersonal (Gardner, 1993, 2004)—as they begin to influence and change the various cultural and social dynamics of the old environment to create the new context for a changed paradigm in business (Beck, 2000).

Based on the observations made in this research, the following exterior systemic changes can be expected as a reaction to the interior transformation of an increasing number of consciousness leaders:

1. *More Professionally Led Non Governmental Organizations (NGOs)*. Some consciousness leaders will leave their old busi-

ness environments to serve existing NGOs or to found new ones that will be based on the new paradigm and changed structures (Yunus, 2007). It is to be expected that these organizations will then be led by the consciousness leaders in a more professional manner. The current conflict and dichotomy between capital and serving a higher cause will be dissolved through the person of the consciousness leader who will be able to bridge the two worlds. In the words of Star, the task lies in knowing

how to integrate the good parts of the lower chakras' performance:
sort of right use of power [of for profit businesses], the right use of
controls and measures and metrics in place that you sort of imag-
ine in the kind of structured survival world of the lower chakras,
but also start to marry that with the relationship-oriented, heart-
oriented human aspects of the higher chakras [of NGOs], and
then the sort of transcendent notions of actually being able to hold
the goodness of the community, the planet, the ecosystem, the en-
vironment, while also trying to maximize the value and the gain
of the individual entity.

2. *The Creation of More Small and Medium Enterprises.* As more consciousness leaders leave their old business environments, we can expect to see them start more for profit organizations that are less capital intensive than large businesses but which have a philanthropic and social mission. Driven by the so-called "cultural creatives" (Ray & Anderson, 2000), this process began already and evolved over the past 4 decades since the beginning of the New Age movement in the late 1960s. The market that has developed since then, but which does not always include companies with a social mission, was in 2006 an U.S. $300 billion market (Howard, 2008). It became known as the LOHAS market (Ray & Anderson, 2000, p. 329). LOHAS is an acronym for Lifestyle of Health and Sustainability and includes five major areas including personal health, eco-tourism, alternative energy, alternative vehicles, green buildings, and nat-

ural lifestyle. Consciousness leaders are participating in a significant fashion in the creation of the next generation of Cultural Creatives that according to Ray and Anderson (2000) represent between 25 and 30% of the Western population.

3. *The Foundation of Capital Intensive Companies Using New Capital Structures.* This is an area in which many of the consciousness leaders researched here—that is Chuck, Bianco, Jade, Darlene, Hahm, Star, and Poet—are spending a vast majority of their time and resources. The financial structures of this new type of company must go well beyond the currently known social responsibility type of businesses. Such new organizations can have many names including Hybrid Social Ventures, Sustainability Enterprises, or Social Entrepreneurships (Ben-Eli & Kleissner, 2008; Yunus, 2007). Explaining in more detail the possible financial structures of such enterprises would go well beyond the scope of this dissertation. However, one aspect must be made clear because it is connected to the topic of money highlighted earlier: The new capital structures must be mission driven and not only profit driven in order to reach their sustainability goals. Therefore, it can be assumed that they will be disconnected from the current profit-oriented organizations traded on Wall Street The reason for that is that old structures are no longer sustainable; a fact that became obvious through the recent financial crisis (Soros, 2008).

4. *Transformation of Old Business Models and Organizations.* All consciousness leaders researched for this dissertation have left their old business environments to pursue one or several of the 3 choices outlined above. Nonetheless, there is a slight chance that some consciousness leaders will be able to change old structures from within old business structures—a tough job. For instance, according to financial experts, the current "bail-out" strategies undertaken by Western governments in an effort to save outdated financial structures may have little or no

chance of survival (B. Lietaer, personal communication, April 26, 2009). Moreover, the research in the current study confirms that change must come not only from without but from within the interiorities of such organizations, namely through the people involved. Miracles happen every day and the human race has shown many times in the past how capable if called upon. Yet, to be sustainable change must be integral (Boyatzis & McKee, 2005; Capra, 1993; Collins, 2001; Sachs, 2008).

In summary, the main lesson learned from consciousness leaders is that we are all looking into a bright and exciting future if we are willing to grow and reinvent ourselves anew every single day. It is a future in which the new emerging paradigm in business is but one significant aspect of the new overall paradigm change in the world today. From the global perspective, businesses, next to politics, are the driving forces of the world economy, because they are at the core of wealth creation. Therefore, those of us who actively participate in the business world in a conscious manner feel not only the need to challenge the way it is currently being performed, but have the responsibility to change it. There could be too much at stake if we do not. In the words of the eminent quantum theorist David Bohm,

> *the most important thing going forward is to break the boundaries between people so we can operate as a single intelligence. Bell's theorem implies that this is the natural state of the human world, separation without separateness. The task is to find ways to break these boundaries, so we can be in our natural state. (Senge et al., 2005, p. 189)*

Along with the shifting worldview in modern science, consciousness leaders in business have the responsibility to define and implement a new worldview that is based on the essence of all existence. This realization is oneness rather than separateness, gratefulness rather than deprivation, abundance rather than scarcity, and love rather than fear. These are essential pillars of a wise humanity that is able to ensure a glorious future for our children and our beautiful planet If we decide to take the step and grow to the next level of our humanity,

> *in the end we will find, I believe, the inherent joy in existence it-self, a joy that stems from the great perfection of this and every mo-ment, a wondrous whole in itself . . . one with the All in this endless awareness that holds the Kosmos together kindly in its hand. And then the true Mystery yields itself, the face of Spirit secretly smiles, the Sun rises in your very own heart and the Earth becomes your very own body, galaxies rush through your veins while the stars light up the neurons of your night, and never again will you search for a mere theory of that which is actually your own Original Face.* (Wilber, 2000a, p. 141)

REFERENCES

Aburdene, P. (2005). *Megatrends* 2010. Charlottesville, VA: Hamptonroads.

Adams, J. D. (Ed.). (2005). *Transforming leadership.* New York: Cosimo on Demand.

Alexander, C. N., Davies, J. L., Dixon, C. A., Dillbeck, M. C., Drucker, S. M., & Oetzel, et al. (1990). Growth of higher stages of consciousness: Maharishi's Vedic psychology of human development. In C. L. Alexander & E. J. Langer (Eds.), *Higher stages of human development: Perspectives on adult growth* (pp. 286-341). New York: Oxford University Press.

Alvarado, C. S. (2000). Out of body experiences. In E. Cardena, S. J. Lynn, & S. Krippner (Eds.), *Varieties of anomalous experience: Examining the scientific evidence* (pp. 183-218). Washington, DC: American Psychological Association.

Andreas, S., & Faulkner, D. (Eds.). (1996). NLP: *The new technology of achievement.* New York: Quill.

Aristotle. (2002). *Nicomachean ethics.* Newburyport, MA: Focus Publishing.

Armstrong, K. (1993). *A history of God: The 4000-year old quest of Judaism, Christianity, and Islam.* New York: Ballantine Books.

Aurobindo, S. (1993). Continuous consciousness. In R. Walsh & F. Vaughan (Eds.), *Paths beyond ego: The transpersonal vision* (pp. 83-84). Los Angeles: Jeremy P. Tarcher.

Barlow, D. H., & Durand, V. M. (2005). *Abnormal psychology: An integrative approach.* Belmont, CA: Thomson Wadsworth.

Beauregard, M., & O'Leary, D. (2007). *The spiritual brain: A neuroscientist's case for the existence of the soul.* New York: HarperCollins.

Beck, A. T. (1976). *Cognitive therapy and the emotional disorders.* London: Penguin Books.

Beck, D. E. (2000, October). *Stages of social development: The cultural dynamics that spark violence, spread prosperity, and shape globaliza-*

tion [Electronic version]. Retrieved December 15, 2008, from http://www.integralworld.net/ beck2.html

Beck, D. E., & Cowan, C. C. (1996). *Spiral dynamics: Mastering values, leadership, and change.* Malden, MA: Blackwell.

Ben-Eli, M., & Kleissner, C. (2008, March 3). *Sustainability Enterprises.* Workshop paper presented at Esalen, CA.

Bertalanffy von, L. (2006). *General systems theory: Foundations, developments, applications.* New York: George Brazillier. (Original work published 1969)

Blanchflower, D. G., & Oswald, A. J. (2004). Well-being over time in Britain and the USA. *Journal of Public Economics, 88,* 1359-1386.

Boorstein, S. (Ed.). (1996). *Transpersonal psychotherapy.* New York: State University of New York Press.

Boyatzis, R., & McKee, A. (2005). *Resonant leadership.* Boston: Harvard Business School.

Braud, W. (1998). An expanded view of validity. In W. Braud & R. Anderson, *Transpersonal research methods for the social sciences: Honoring human experience* (pp. 213-237). Thousand Oaks, CA: Sage.

Braud, W., & Anderson, R. (1998). *Transpersonal research methods for the social sciences: Honoring human experience.* Thousand Oaks, CA: Sage.

Brennan, J. F. (2003). *History and systems of psychology.* Upper Saddle River, NJ: Pearson Education.

Brown, R. B. (2006). *Plan B 2.0: Rescuing a planet under stress and a civilization in trouble.* New York: Earth Policy Institute.

Burkan, T. (2001). *Extreme spirituality.* Hillsboro, OR: Beyond Words.

Buzan, T., & Buzan, B. (1996). *The mind map book: How to use radiant thinking to maximize your brain's untapped potential.* New York: A Plume Book.

Campbell, J. (1968). *The hero with a thousand faces.* New York: Princeton University Press. (Original work published 1949)

Capra, F. (1993). A systems approach to the emerging paradigm. In M. Ray & A. Rinzler (Eds.), *The new paradigm in business: Emerging strategies for leadership and organizational change* (pp. 230-238). New York: Jeremy P. Tarcher/Pedigree.

Capra, F. (2000). *The Tao of physics: An exploration of the parallels between modern physics and Eastern mysticism.* Boston: Shambhala.

Capra, F. (2002). *The hidden connections: Integrating the biological, cognitive, and social dimensions of life into science and sustainability.* New York: Doubleday.

Cardena, E., Lynn S. J., & Krippner, S. (Eds.). (2000). *Varieties of anomalous experience: Examining the scientific evidence.* Washington, DC: American Psychological Association.

Catford, L., & Ray, M. (1991). *The path of the everyday hero: Drawing on the power of myth to meet life's most important challenges.* Los Angeles: J. P. Tarcher.

Collins, J. (2001). *Good to great: Why some companies take the leap and others don't.* New York: HarperCollins.

Collins, J. C. (2005, July–August). Level 5 leadership: The triumph of humility and fierce resolve [Electronic version]. *Harvard Business Review OnPoint Article,* 1-11. Reprint No. R0507M. Retrieved November 8, 2008, from http://harvardbusinessonline.hbsp.harvard.edu/b01/en/common/item_detail.jhtml;jsessionid=T03J355YT5XLMAKRGWDSELQBKE0YIISW?id=R0507M&referral=7855&_requestid=32335

Collins, J. C., & Lazier, W. C. (1992). *Beyond entrepreneurship: Turning our business into an enduring great company.* Englewood Cliffs, NJ: Prentice Hall.

Commons, M. L., Armon, C., Kohlberg, L., Richards, F. A., & Grotzer, T. A. (Eds.). (1990). *Adult development: Models and methods in the study of adolescent and adult thought.* New York: Praeger.

Commons, M. L., Richards, F. A., & Armon, C. (Eds.). (1984). *Beyond formal operations: Late adolescent and adult cognitive development.* New York: Praeger.

Cook-Greuter, S. R. (2004). Making the case for a developmental perspective [Electronic version]. *Journal of Industrial and Commercial Training, 36*(7), 275-281.

Cook-Greuter, S. R. (2005). *Ego development: Nine levels of increasing embrace.* Retrieved October 4, 2008 from www.cookgreuter.com/9%20levels%20of%20increasing%20embrace%20update5201%2007.pdf

Cook-Greuter, S. R. (2008). Mature ego development: A gateway to ego transcendence? [Electronic version]. *Journal of Adult Development, 7*(4), 227-240.

Covey, S. R. (1989). *The seven habits of highly effective people*: Restoring the character ethic. New York: Simon & Schuster.

Csikszentmihalyi, M. (1990). *Flow: The psychology of optimal experience.* New York: Harper Perennial.

Csikszentmihalyi, M., & Nakamura, J. (2002). The concept of flow. In C. R. Snyder & S. J. Lopez (Eds.), *Handbook of positive psychology* (pp. 89-105). New York: Oxford University Press.

Dacey, J. S., & Travers, J. F. (2006). *Human development across the lifespan.* Boston: McGraw-Hill.

Dalai Lama. (1999). *Ethics for the new millennium.* New York: Riverhead Book.

Damasio, A. (2006). *Descartes' error: Emotion, reason and the human brain.* London: Vintage Press.

Descartes, R. (1998). *Discourse on method and meditations on first philosophy.* Indianapolis, IN: Hackett.

Descartes, R. (2003). *Meditations and other metaphysical writings.* New York: Penguin Classics.

Einstein, A. (1954). *Ideas and opinions.* New York: Wings Books.

Eisler, R. (1995). *Sacred pleasures: Sex, myths, and the politics of the body—new paths to power and love.* San Francisco: HarperSanFrancisco.

Eisler, R. (2002). *The power of partnership: Seven relationships that will change your life*. Novato, CA: New World Library.

Eisler, R. (2007). *The real wealth of nations: Creating a caring economics.* San Francisco: Berret Koehler.

Eliot, T. S. (1952). *The complete poems and plays.* New York: Harcourt Brace.

Epstein, M. (1995). *Thoughts without a thinker: Psychotherapy from a Buddhist perspective.* New York: Basic Books.

Erikson, E. (1980). *Identity and the life cycle.* New York: W. W. Norton.

Fadiman, J., & Frager, R. (2002). *Personality and personal growth* (5th ed.). New Jersey: Prentice Hall.

Fowler, J. (1995). *Stages of faith: The psychology of human development and the quest for meaning.* San Francisco: HarperSanFrancisco.

Friedman, T. (2005). *The world is flat: A brief history of the twenty-first century.* New York: Farrar, Stratus & Giroux.

Gandhi, M. K. (1977). *Eine Autobiographie oder die Geschichte meiner Experimente mit der Wahrheit* [Gandhi an autobiography: The story of my experiments with truth]. Gladenbach, Hessen, Germany: Hinder & Deelmann.

Gardner, H. (1993). *Multiple intelligences.* New York: Basic Books.

Gardner, H. (2004). *Changing minds: The art and science of changing our own and other people's minds.* Boston: Harvard Business School Press.

Gebser, J. (1984). *The ever-present origin.* Athens: Ohio University Press. (Original work published 1949)

Gilligan, C. (1993). *In a different voice: Psychological theory and women's development.* Cambridge, MA: Harvard University Press. (Original work published 1982)

Goleman, D. (1995). *Emotional intelligence: Why it can matter more than IQ.* New York: Bantam Books.

Goleman, D. (2000, March–April). Leadership that gets results [Electronic version]. *Harvard Business Review*, 78-91. Reprint No. R00204. Retrieved November 8, 2008, from http://harvardbusinessonline.hbsp.harvard.edu/b01/en/ common/item_detail.jhtml;jsessionid=LOGBEON3PRTE2A KRGWDSELQBKE0YIISW?id=R00204&referral=7855&_ requestid=42039

Goleman, D. (Ed.). (2003). *Healing emotions: Conversations with the Dalai Lama on mindfulness, emotions, and health.* Boston: Shambhala.

Goleman, D., Boyatzis, R., & McKee, A. (2002). *Primal leadership: Realizing the power of emotional intelligence.* Boston: Harvard Business School Press.

Gore, A. (1992). *Earth in the balance: Ecology and the human spirit.* Santa Monica, CA: Dove Audio Cassettes.

Gore, A. (2006). *An inconvenient truth: The planetary emergency of global warming and what we can do about it.* New York: Rodale.

Greenleaf, R. K. (1977). *Servant leadership: A journey into the nature of legitimate power and greatness.* New York: Paulist Press.

Grof, S. (2006). *When the impossible happens: Adventures in non-ordinary realities.* Boulder, CO: Sounds True.

Hansen, D. D. (2003). *The dream: Martin Luther King, Jr. and the speech that inspired a nation.* New York: HarperCollins.

Harman, W., & Hormann, J. (1993). The breakdown of the old paradigm. In M. Ray & A. Rinzler (Eds.), *The new paradigm in business: Emerging strategies for leadership and organizational change* (pp. 16-27). New York: Jeremy P. Tarcher/Pedigree.

Hendricks, G., & Ludeman, K. (1996). *The corporate mystic: A guidebook for visionaries with their feet on the ground.* New York: Bantam Books.

Horibe, K. (2003, Autumn). *Conscious leadership.* Retrieved October 19, 2007, from http://neumann.hec.ca/cme/francais/media_mul-timedia/article_presse/entrevue.pdf

Howard, B. (2008, January 30). *Understanding the LOHAS market* Retrieved January 27, 2009, from http://www.skininc.com/spabusiness/sustainability/14988796 .html

Jacobi, J. (1959). *Complex archetype symbol in the psychology of C. G. Jung.* Princeton, MA: Princeton University Press.

Jaworski, J. (1996). *Synchronicity: The inner path of leadership.* San Francisco: Berret Koehler.

Kegan, R. (1982). *The evolving self: Problem and process in human development.* Cambridge, MA: Harvard University Press.

Kegan, R. (1994). In over our heads. Cambridge, MA: Harvard University Press.

Kegan, R., & Lahey, L. L. (2001). *How the way we talk can change the way we work.* San Francisco: Jossey-Bass.

Kegan, R., Lahey, L. L., & Souvaine, E. (1990). Life after formal operations: Implications for a psychology of the self. In C. N. Alexander & E. J. Langer (Eds.), *Higher stages of human development* (pp. 229-257). New York: Oxford University Press.

Kjaer, T. W., Bertelsen, C., Piccini, P, Brooks, D., Alving J., & Lou, H. C. (2002, April). Increased dopamine tone during meditation-induced change of consciousness. *Cognitive Brain Research,* 13(2), 255-259.

Klein, E., & Izzo, J. (1999). *Awakening corporate soul: Four paths to unleash the power of people at work.* Beverly, MA: Fair Wind Press.

Kofman, F. (2006). *Conscious business: How to build values through value.* Boulder, CO: Sounds True.

Kofman, F. (2007). Conscious leadership [Electronic version]. *Integral Leadership Review,* 2, 25-40.

Kohlberg, L., & Ryncarz, R. A. (1990). Beyond justice reasoning: Moral development and consideration of a seventh stage. In C. N. Alexander & E. J. Langer (Eds.), *Higher stages of human development: Perspectives on adult growth* (pp. 191-207). New York: Oxford University Press.

Kolb, B., & Whishaw, I. Q. (2003). *Fundamentals of human neuropsychology.* New York: Worth.

Kuhn, T. (1996). *The structure of scientific revolutions.* Chicago: The University of Chicago Press.

Kohut, H. (1985). *Self-psychology and the humanities: Reflections on a new psychoanalytic approach.* New York: W.W. Norton.

Koplowitz, H. (1984). A projection beyond Piaget's formal operations stage: A general system stage and a unitary stage. In M. L. Commons, F. A. Richards, & C. Armon (Eds.), *Beyond formal operations: Late adolescent and adult cognitive development* (pp. 272-296). New York: Praeger.

Koplowitz, H. (1990). Unitary consciousness and the highest development of mind: The relationship between spiritual development and cognitive development. In M. L. Commons, C. Armon, L. Kohlberg, F. A. Richards, & T. A. Grotzer (Eds.), *Adult development: Models and methods in the study of adolescent and adult thought* (pp. 105-112). New York: Praeger.

Kouzes, J. M., & Posner, B. Z. (2003). *Encouraging the heart: A leader's guide to rewarding and recognizing others.* San Francisco: Jossey-Bass.

Kouzes, J. M., & Posner, B. Z. (2007). *The leadership challenge.* San Francisco: John Wiley & Sons.

Leonard, G. (1991). *Mastery: The keys to success and long-term fulfillment.* New York: Dutton/Penguin Books.

Leonard, G., & Murphy, M. (1995). *The life we are given: A long-term program for realizing the potential of body, mind, heart, and soul.* New York: Jeremy P. Tarcher/Putnam.

Lewis-Beck, M. S., Bryman, A., & Liao, T. F. (2004). *The Sage encyclopedia of social science research methods.* Thousand Oaks, CA: Sage.

Lietaer, B. (2001). *The future of money: Creating new wealth, work, and a wiser world.* London: Century.

Lincoln, Y. S., & Guba, E. G. (1985). *Naturalistic inquiry.* Newbury Park, CA: Sage.

Lipton, B. (2005). *The biology of belief: Unleashing the power of consciousness, matter, and miracles.* Santa Rosa, CA: Mountain of Love.

Loevinger, J. (1977). *Ego development: Conceptions and theories.* San Francisco: Jossey-Bass.

Lovejoy, A. O. (1942). *The Great Chain of Being: A study of the history of an idea*. Cambridge, MA: Harvard University Press.

Mandala Schlitz, M., Vieten, C., & Amorok, T. (2007). *Living deeply: The art & science of transformation in everyday life*. Oakland, CA: New Harbinger.

Mandela, N. (1994). *Long walk to freedom*. Boston: Little, Brown.

Marques, J., Dhiman, S., & King, R. (2007). *Spirituality in the workplace*. Fawnskin, CA: Personhood Press.

Maslow, A. H. (1999). *Toward a psychology of being*. New York: John Wiley & Sons. (Original work published 1968)

Maslow, A. H., Stephens, D. S., & Heil, G. (1998). *Maslow on management*. New York: John Wiley & Sons.

McCraty, R. (2001). *Science of the heart: Exploring the role of the heart in human performance*. Boulder Creek, CA: Institute of HeartMath.

McCraty, R. (2003). *Heart–brain neurodynamics: The making of emotions*. Boulder Creek, CA: Institute of HeartMath.

McCraty, R. (2003a). *The energetic heart: Electromagnetic interactions within and between people*. Boulder Creek, CA: Institute of HeartMath.

Mertens, D. M. (2005). *Research and evaluation in education and psychology: Integrating diversity with quantitative, qualitative, and mixed methods*. Thousand Oaks, CA: Sage.

Mitroff, I. I., & Denton, E. A. (1999). *A spiritual audit of corporate America: A hard look at spirituality, religion, and values in the workplace*. San Francisco: Jossey-Bass.

Moustakas, C. (1990). *Heuristic research: Design, methodology, and applications*. London: Sage.

Murphy, M. (1993). *The future of the body: Explorations into the further evolution of human nature*. New York: Tarcher Perigee.

Newberg, A. B., & Lee, B. Y. (2005, June). The neuroscientific study of religious and spiritual phenomena: Or why God doesn't use biostatistics. *Zygon, 40*(2), 469-489.

Nicolescu, B., & Volckmann, R. (2007). Transdisciplinarity: Basarab Nicolescu talks with Russ Volckmann [Electronic version]. *Integral*

Review, 4, 73-90. Retrieved January 30, 2009, from http://integral-review.org/documents/Volckmann,% 20Nicolescu%20Interview%20on%20Transdisciplinarity%204,%202007.pdf

O'Connor, J., & Seymour, J. (1990). *Introducing NLP: Psychological skills for understanding and influencing people.* London: Element.

Olson, M. (1982). *The rise and decline of nations: Economic growth, stagflation, and social rigidities.* New Haven, CT: Yale University Press.

Osterberg, R. V. (1993). A new kind of company with a new kind of thinking. In M. Ray & A. Rinzler (Eds.), *The new paradigm in business: Emerging strategies for leadership and organizational change* (pp. 67-71). New York: Jeremy P. Tarcher/Pedigree.

Pauchant, T. C. (Ed.). (2002). *Ethics and spirituality at work: Hopes and pitfalls of the search for meaning in organizations.* Westport, CT: Quorum Books.

Paulson, D. (2002). *Competitive business, caring business.* New York: ParaView Press.

Pert, C. B. (1997). *Molecules of emotion: The science behind mind-body medicine.* New York: Touchstone.

Plato. (1961). *The collected dialogues of Plato: Including the letters.* Princeton, NJ: Princeton University Press. (Original work published 1938)

Porras, J., Emery, S., & Thompson, M. (2007). *Success built to last: Creating a life that matters.* Upper Saddle River, NJ: Wharton School.

Progoff, I. (1973). *Jung, synchronicity, and human destiny.* New York: Julian Press.

Ram Dass. (1989). *A spiritual journey* [2 CDs]. New York: Audio Renaissance.

Ray, M., & Myers, R. (1989). *Creativity in business.* New York: Doubleday.

Ray, M., & Rinzler, A. (Eds.). (1993). *The new paradigm in business: Emerging strategies for leadership and organizational change.* New York: Jeremy P. Tarcher/Pedigree.

Ray, P., & Anderson, S. R. (2000). *The cultural creatives: How 50 million people are changing the world.* New York: Three Rivers Press.

Renesch, J. (Ed.). (2002). *Leadership in a new era: Visionary approaches to the biggest crises of our time.* New York: ParaView Press.

Ricard, M. (2003). *Happiness: A guide to developing life's most important skill.* New York: Little, Brown.

Robbins, A. (1986). *Unlimited power.* New York: Free Press.

Rooke, D., & Torbert, W. (1998). Organizational transformation as a function of CEOs' developmental stage. *Organizational Development Journal,* 16(1), 11-28.

Rooke, D., & Torbert, W. (2005, April). Seven transformations of leadership. *Harvard Business Review* OnPoint Article, 1-11. Reprint No. R0504D.

Sachs, J. D. (2008). *Common wealth: Economics for a crowded planet* New York: The Penguin Press.

Saron, C., & Davidson, R. J. (1997). The brain and emotions. In D. Goleman (Ed.), *Healing emotions: Conversations with the Dalai Lama on mindfulness, emotions, and health* (pp. 68-88). Boston: Shambhala.

Schwartz, S. (2000). *Abnormal psychology: A discovery approach.* Mountain View, CA: Mayfield.

Secretan, L. (2006). *One: The art and practice of conscious leadership.* Caledon, Ontario, Canada: The Secretan Center.

Senge, P., Scharmer, C. O., Jaworski, J., & Flowers, B. S. (2005). *Presence: An exploration of profound change in people, organizations, and society.* New York: Currency Doubleday.

Sogyal Rinpoche. (1994). *The Tibetan book of living and dying.* San Francisco: HarperSanFrancisco.

Soros, G. (2004). *The bubble of American supremacy: Correcting the misuse of American power.* New York: PublicAffairs.

Soros, G. (2008). *The new paradigm for financial markets: The credit crisis of 2008 and what it means.* New York: PublicAffairs.

Stein, M. (2004). *Jung's map of the soul.* Chicago: Open Court.

Taylor, C. (2005). Walking the talk: Building a culture for success. London: Random House.

Thich Nhat Hanh. (2002). *No death, no fear: Comforting wisdom for life.*

New York: Riverhead Books.

Toms, M. (1997). *The soul of business.* Carlsbad, CA: HayHouse.

Torbert, W. R. (1987). *Managing the corporate dream: Restructuring for long-term success.* Homewood, IL: Dow Jones-Irwin.

Torbert, W. R., Cook-Greuter, S., Fisher, D., Foldy, E., Gauthier, A., Keeley, J, et al. (2004). *Action inquiry: The secret of timely and transforming leadership.* San Francisco: Berret Koehler.

Torbert, W. R., Livne-Tarandach, R., Herdman-Barker, E., Nicolaides, A., & McCallum, D. (2008, August 9). *Developmental action inquiry: A distinct integral theory that actually integrates developmental theory, practice, and research.* Paper presented at the 1st Biennial Integral Theory Conference 2008. Retrieved September 25, 2008, from http://www.integraltheoryconference.stirsite.com/page/ page/5863149.htm

Twist, L. (2003). *The soul of money: Transforming your relationship with money and life.* New York: W.W. Norton.

Underhill, E. (2002). *Mysticism: A study in the nature and development of spiritual consciousness.* Mineola, NY: Dover. (Original work published 1911)

Vaughan, F. (2000). *The inward arc: Healing in psychotherapy and spirituality.* Lincoln, NE: IUniverse.

Vaughan, F. (2005). *Shadows of the sacred: Seeing through spiritual illusions.* Lincoln, NE: IUniverse.

Volckmann, R. (2007). *Integral leadership: The 100 book project.* Retrieved October 19, 2007, from http:// www.leadcoach.com/archives/interview/ thierry_pauchant.html

Wade, J. (1996). *Changes of mind: A holonic theory of the evolution of consciousness.* New York: State University of New York Press.

Waldron, J. (1998). The life impact of transcendent experiences with a pronounced quality of noesis. *The Journal of Transpersonal Psychology*, 30(2), 103-134.

Walsh, R. (1999). *Essential spirituality: The 7 central practices to awaken heart and mind.* New York: John Wiley & Sons.

Walsh, R., & Vaughan, F. (1993). Meditation: Royal road to the transpersonal. In R. Walsh & F. Vaughan (Eds.), *Paths beyond ego: The transpersonal vision* (pp. 47-55). Los Angeles: Jeremy P. Tarcher/Pedigree.

Watts, A. (1989). *The book: On the taboo against knowing who you are.* New York: Vintage Books.

Watts, A. (2003). *Become what you are.* Boston: Shambhala.

Welwood, J. (1985). *Awakening the heart: East/West approaches to psychotherapy and the healing relationship.* Boston: Shambhala.

White, R. A. (1998). Becoming more human as we work: The reflexive role of exceptional human experience. In W. Braud & R. Anderson, *Transpersonal research methods for the social sciences* (pp. 128-145). Thousand Oaks: Sage.

Wilber, K. (1996). *The atman project: A transpersonal view of human development.* Wheaton, IL: Quest Books.

Wilber, K. (1997, February). *An integral theory of consciousness.* Journal of Consciousness Studies, 4(1), 71-92.

Wilber, K. (1999). Spirituality and developmental lines: Are there stages? *The Journal of Transpersonal Psychology*, 31(1), 1-10.

Wilber, K. (2000). *Sex, ecology, spirituality: The spirit of evolution.* Boston: Shambhala.

Wilber, K. (2000a). *A brief history of everything.* Boston: Shambhala.

Wilber, K. (2000b). *A theory of everything: An integral vision for business, politics, science, and spirituality.* Boston: Shambhala.

Wilber, K. (2000c). *Integral psychology: Consciousness, spirit, psychology, therapy.* Boston: Shambhala.

Wilber, K. (2001). *Eye to eye: The quest for the new paradigm.* Boston: Shambhala

Wilber, K. (2003). *Kosmic consciousness* [6 CDs]. Boulder, CO: Sounds True.

Wilber, K. (2005). *The integral operating system.* Boulder, CO: Sounds

True.

Wilber, K. (2006). *Integral spirituality: A startling new role for religion in the modern and postmodern world.* Boston: Integral Books.

Williamson, M. (1996). *A return to love: Reflections on the principles of a course in miracles.* New York: HarperCollins.

Yogananda, P. (2002). *Autobiography of a yogi.* Los Angeles: Self-Realization Fellowship.

Yunus, M. (2007). *Creating a world without poverty: Social business and the future of capitalism.* New York: PublicAffairs.

Zweig, J. (2007). *Your money and your brain: How the new science of neuroeconomics can help make you rich.* New York: Simon & Shuster.

APPENDIX A: INFORMED CONSENT FORM

To the Participant in this Research:

You have been identified as a consciousness leader and are invited to participate in a dissertation study designed to explore the transformative experience of becoming a consciousness leader. As a consciousness leader who has made a significant contribution in the world, your involvement in the current study is extremely valuable and I would be honored if you agreed to participate.

Your contribution consists of a single semistructured interview of approximately 60 minutes, the results of which will flow into the overall research evaluation of the proposed study. The interview will occur at a neutral or comfortable and preferred location. There will be no other requirements for your time in the current study. If geographical locations allow, the interview will be performed in person, if not, by phone. The interview will be audio recorded and possibly videotaped. In order to provide an accurate description of your experience, you will be encouraged to keep a reflective attitude regarding the experience of becoming a consciousness leader throughout the length of the interview.

To protect your privacy, your name will remain anonymous at all times and all information received from you will be kept confidential. All written collected data will be kept secure, stored in a locked file cabinet The digital data will be stored in a safe, password-protected place. If there are materials like journals, unpublished work, photographs, video, audio, or other forms of creative expression that you would like to share, please do so. I am asking for permission to study these as well and possibly integrate them into the study without mentioning the source. All materials will be processed anonymously, coded without name identification, and used in relation to this research and the publication of the dissertation only. The only person that will have access to your identity will be the lead researcher on the project: Mariana Bozesan.

Furthermore, the interview will be transcribed through a transcription service that will have signed a confidentiality agreement. Both recordings and transcriptions will be kept strictly confidential. No names will be mentioned within the transcription material. The data may also be used anonymously in future publications pertaining to the experience of becoming a consciousness leader. Moreover, some collected data may not be reported in the dissertation, but it could be processed for future research.

By answering my questions during our interview, you will be contributing to a clearer understanding of how to improve leadership skills both at a personal and professional level, and to reach higher levels of consciousness. Furthermore, through your participation in the current study, you may benefit in the following ways:

1. You could get a better understanding about the hidden determinants (emotionally, mentally, physically, and spiritually) of your own personal and professional success.
2. You might gain a deeper understanding about the origins of your own mind-body health and increase your inner joy and happiness to reach higher levels of fulfillment.
3. You may benefit from the altruistic gesture of sharing your transformative process of becoming a leader in consciousness.

Your participation in the current study is voluntary. By agreeing to be interviewed, you attest that no pressure has been applied to encourage your participation. There are no foreseeable risks associated with this project. However, the current study. like all studies, may also have drawbacks. The recounting of the process of becoming a consciousness leader may also bring back painful memories of personal growth through emotional and spiritual emergencies. This may create discomfort at times and you should know that you can terminate the specific session, if you feel overwhelmed. Names and contact information for counselors in your area can be provided upon request. Additionally, the current study may bring personal change at all levels of your life. Change is not always easy. However, the current study is designed to minimize potential risks to you. The focus of the conversations and interviews will be on the transformative effects of becoming a consciousness leader, rather than on possible traumatic events.

If you have any questions or concerns, please contact me at (650) 856-8388 or through Email at sage@sageera.com. The chairperson of the dissertation committee is Mark McCaslin, Ph.D., who can be contacted at mmccaslin@itp.edu, phone: (970) 881-3407. The chairperson of the Institute of Transpersonal Psychology's Research Ethics Committee, is Kartikeya Patel, Ph.D., who can be contacted at kpatel@itp.edu, phone: (650) 493-4430.

As the potential participant in this research, you may withdraw from the study at any time without penalty or prejudice. A summary of the research findings can be made available to you upon request and by providing your mailing address with your signature. Any transcription of materials will be conducted only after the transcriber has signed the attached Transcriber Confidentiality Agreement.

I attest that I have read and understood this form and had any questions about this research answered to my satisfaction. My participation in this research is entirely voluntary and no pressure has been applied to encourage my participation. My signature indicates my willingness to be a participant in this research.

Participant's Signature   Date

Researcher's Signature   Date

Should you desire a summary of the research findings, please write down below your full name and mailing address:

_____

_____

_____   _____

Researcher's Signature   Date
Phone: (650) 856-8388
Address: SageEra Institute LLC, P.O. Box 1603, Palo Alto, CA 94301

APPENDIX B: TRANSCRIBER CONFIDENTIALITY AGREEMENT

As the transcriber of the recordings submitted to me by researcher Mariana Bozesan, I agree to securely store and to maintain absolute confidentiality with regard to the information from and about the participants. This includes all written materials, audio, and video recordings, possible assessments, and/or any other related material that I come in contact with during this research project. Furthermore, I agree to help aid the researcher, Mariana Bozesan, in protecting the identity of participants to ensure anonymity.

_____   _____
Transcriber's Name and Signature   Date

_____   _____
Researcher's Name and Signature   Date

APPENDIX C: INTERVIEW QUESTIONS

Each research participant in the current study has been asked most of the following questions, if the time permitted it. The questions are structured by themes.

INTRODUCTION

1. To many people around the world, you are a role model for leadership in all areas of live including personal joy, happiness, and true fulfillment, what is the secret to your success?

REQUESTING DEFINITIONS

2. What are the underlying assumptions of your own understanding of leadership and how would you characterize your own leadership competence and practice?

3. What is your understanding of consciousness? In your view, how does consciousness expand and evolve?

SPECIFIC INQUIRY

4. What was the context or circumstances leading to the transformation of your own consciousness? Was there a significant physical/emotional/mental/spiritual or other type of event in your life that lead to your current perspective or did it evolve over time?

5. Could you describe a specific situation or event that led to your particular transformation? At that time what did you sense, feel, see, hear, smell, or touch? What did you think?

IMPACT AND MEANING: (STRUCTURES, STAGES, LINES)

6. What did this experience/process mean to you? How did you FEEL? In what ways did it affect/impact you? Can you give concrete examples?

7. What are other aspects or dimensions of the experience that you think or feel are important and that we have not yet covered? Can you give specific examples?

8. How do you recognize your inner transformation? In what ways have you changed? Could you please illustrate this by concrete, detailed, and specific descriptions?

9. What do you experience (physically, mentally, emotionally, spiritually) now, compared with what you did NOT experience previously?

10. Do you feel your transformation provided you with an increased sense of meaning or purpose in life? Specifically, in which ways?

DIGGING DEEPER

11. In your understanding/view/feeling, what prevented your "awakening" spiritual transformation earlier in your life? Please mention some specific obstacles and hindrances or preventing influences and factors.

12. How have your values, choices, decisions, worldviews have changed?

13. Can you share how your every day life has changed or being impacted?

14. How has your leadership ability been impacted? How do you know that?

15. How has your environment/exterior been impacted through your own change? (other leaders, stake holders) How can you tell?

16. How do you keep it alive - what's your spiritual practice?

IDENTIFYING WHAT'S STILL OPEN/MYSTERY

17. Is there something in your journey that remains a mystery to you and that you still don't understand, that's enigmatic?

18. What sensations, feelings, smells, sounds, and thoughts are coming up with and or generated by this mystery? How do you deal with this and what does it mean for you?

VALIDITY CHECK

19. After each major question, I take five more minutes to summarize what has been said and make sure that my notes accurately reflect the position of the participant.

REQUESTING PERSONAL MATERIAL AND LAST QUESTION

20. Is there any material, photos, or audio-visuals that you would like to share? Can I make copies or keep some of them?
21. How do you want to be remembered?

THANK YOU VERY MUCH FOR YOUR TIME AND WILLINGNESS TO CONTRIBUTE TO A BETTER WORLD

APPENDIX D: MIND MAPS OF PARTICIPANTS

Jade Profile and Core Topics—Mapping Wilber's AQAL

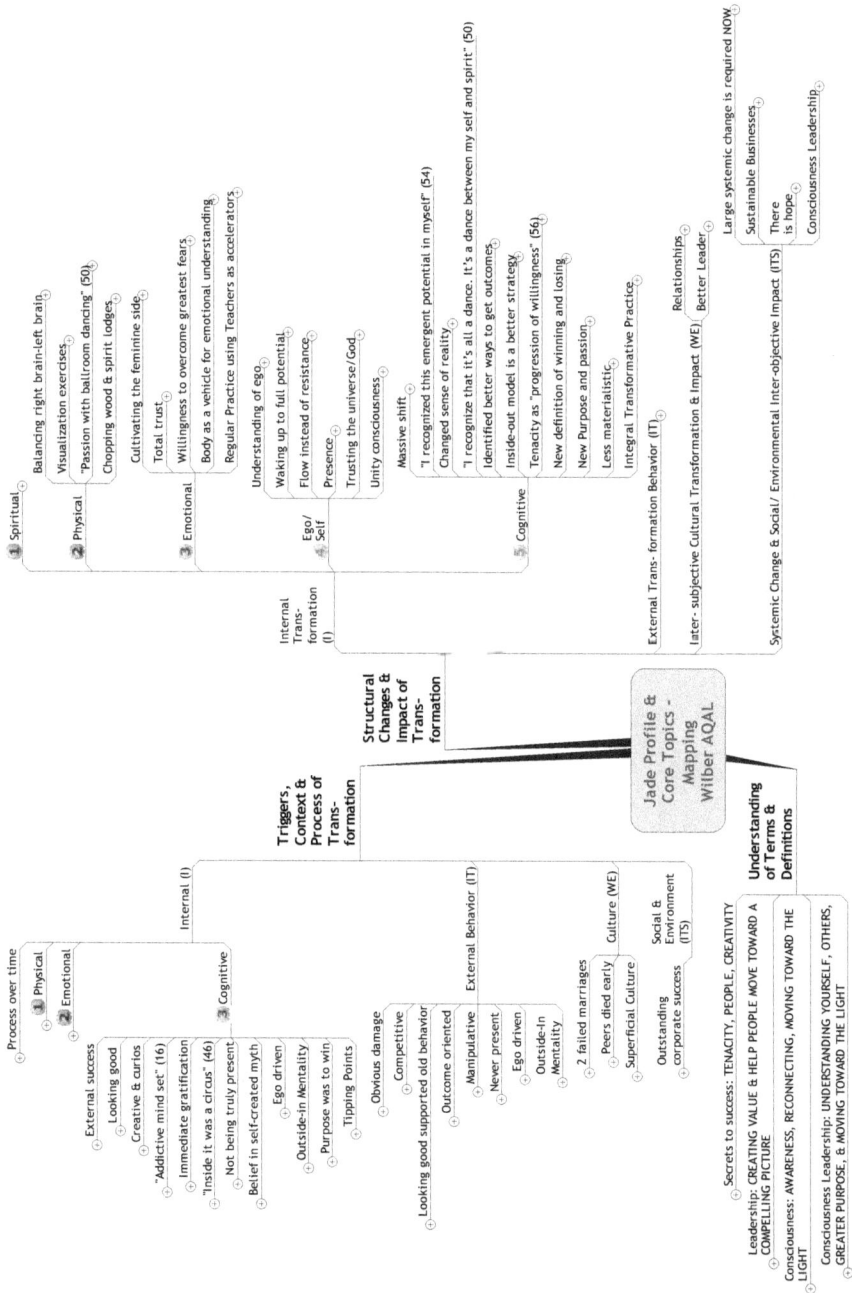

Star Profile and Core Topics—Mapping Wilber's AQAL

Central node:

Star Profile & Core Topics— Mapping Wilber's AQAL

Triggers, Context & Process of Transformation

Internal (I)

① Cognition
- "Peak experiences" (54) & process over time
- Deep desire to evolve intellectually
- Discrepancy: mind and soul
- Aware of natural creative energy
- Ability to manifest
- Curious person
- Cognitive recognition of own personality structure before transformation
- Worry, angst, stress
- Stress & working hard
- Very high intellect
- Loves challenges
- Driven and intense
- Relatively Aggressive
- Major changes "orchestrated by the universe"(30)
- Tipping Points
- Meeting & recognizing the teacher
- Deep desire to grow emotionally

② Emotional
- Difficult relationship with father—painful "emotional abuse and neglect" (24)
- Discrepancy: Everything is fine and feeling of inadequacy
- Conflict: Christian upbringing and inner knowing about divine nature
- Deep desire to grow spiritually
- Meeting & recognizing the teacher
- Pain
- Therapy in mid 20s
- Career stress

③ Spirituality
- Childhood knowingness of divine nature "locked away" (18)
- Exceptional Human Experience
- Embodied / visceral knowing

④ Physical
- Difficult relationship with father, "emotional abuse and neglect" (24)
- Physical challenges
- Body awareness

Culture (WE)
- "I grew up in my early years in a trailer"(28)
- "I've never felt scarcity financially"(28)

Social & Environment (ITS)
- Creating a company right out of business school(28)
- Financial abundance
- Exceptional high-tech career
- Financial & "material mastery"(28)

Consciousness Leadership:
- Secrets to success: Presence, Surrender, Journey not destination
- Consciousness: Sound as the building block creating diversity and collapsing back into unity. Awareness of unity state of duality
- Calling forth the most profound qualities in others

Understanding of Terms & Definitions

Structural Changes & Impact of Transformation

Internal Transformation (I)

④ Spirituality
- Ego transcendence work
- Meditation Practice.
- Becoming a consciousness leader by increasing personal "vibration" (64)
- Softness.
- Less serious.
- Better sense of humor.
- Virtually no personal agenda.

② Emotionally
- Life changed.
- "I actually do far more stuff with far more ease"(56)
- More being less doing.
- Gratitude & humility.
- Blessed & lucky.

③ Physical
- Embodied/visceral knowing
- Conscious creation
- The peak experience "was a major transition for me" (54)
- "I almost think of my life as before and after" [peak experience] (54)
- Deeper Under- standing.
- Aware of natural creative energy.
- Blessed & lucky.
- Abundance thinking.
- Gratitude & humility.
- Ego transcendence work.
- Cognitive recognition of own structural evolution
- Virtually no personal agenda.

① Cognition
- Being rather than doing.
- Softness.
- Less serious.
- Better sense of humor.
- Virtually no personal agenda.
- Less efforting.

External Transformation (IT)
Behavior
- "I actually do far more stuff with far more ease"(56)

Inter-subjective Cultural Transformation & Impact (WE)
- The inside out is important, and the outside in is important"(64)
- "This is a sort of evolutionary process"(66)
- Consciousness "is a vibration" (62)
- Inside out.
- Outside in.

Systemic Change & Environmental Inter-objective Impact (ITS)
- This is a sort of "evolutionary process"(66)
- Consciousness leadership in business.
- Being a consciousness leader.

Paloma Profile and Core Topics—Mapping Wilber's AQAL

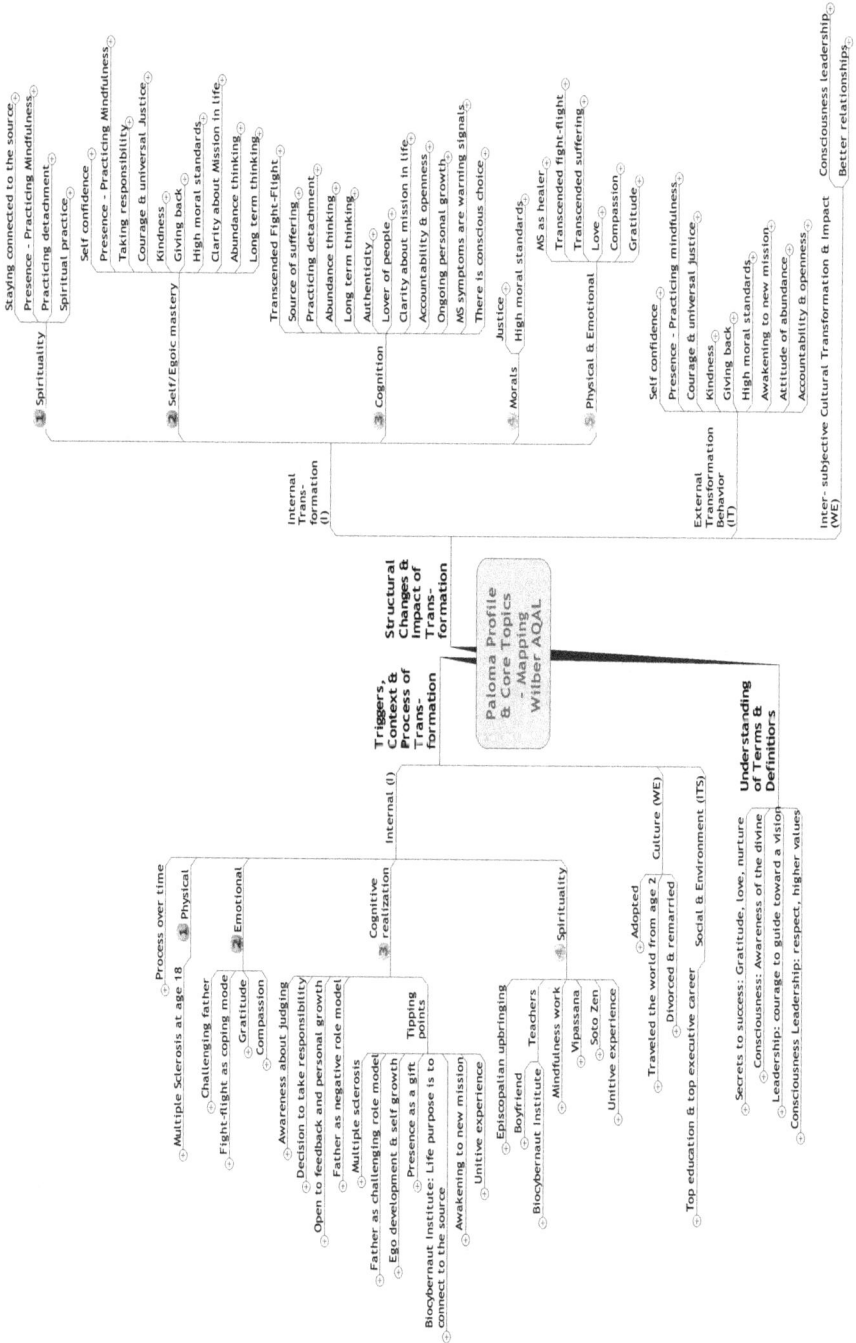

Paloma Profile & Core Topics – Mapping Wilber AQAL

Structural Changes & Impact of Transformation

Internal Transformation (I)

1. Spirituality
- Staying connected to the source
- Presence - Practicing Mindfulness
- Practicing detachment
- Spiritual practice

2. Self/Egoic mastery
- Self confidence
- Presence - Practicing Mindfulness
- Taking responsibility
- Courage & universal Justice
- Kindness
- Giving back
- High moral standards
- Clarity about Mission in life
- Abundance thinking
- Long term thinking
- Transcended Fight-Flight

3. Cognition
- Source of suffering
- Practicing detachment
- Abundance thinking
- Long term thinking
- Authenticity
- Lover of people
- Clarity about mission in life
- Accountability & openness
- Ongoing personal growth
- MS symptoms are warning signals
- There is conscious choice

4. Morals
- Justice
- High moral standards

5. Physical & Emotional
- MS as healer
- Transcended fight-flight
- Transcended suffering
- Love
- Compassion
- Gratitude

External Transformation Behavior (IT)
- Self confidence
- Presence - Practicing mindfulness
- Courage & universal Justice
- Kindness
- Giving back
- High moral standards
- Awakening to new mission
- Attitude of abundance
- Accountability & openness

Inter-subjective Cultural Transformation & impact (WE)
- Consciousness leadership
- Better relationships

Triggers, Context & Process of Transformation

Internal (I)

1. Physical
- Process over time
- Multiple Sclerosis at age 18

2. Emotional
- Challenging father
- Fight-flight as coping mode
- Gratitude
- Compassion

3. Cognitive realization
- Awareness about judging
- Decision to take responsibility
- Open to feedback and personal growth
- Father as negative role model
- Multiple sclerosis
- Father as challenging role model
- Ego development & self growth
- Presence as a gift
- Biocybernaut Institute: Life purpose is to connect to the source
- Awakening to new mission
- Unitive experience
- Tipping points

4. Spirituality
- Episcopalian upbringing
- Boyfriend
- Teachers
- Biocybernaut Institute
- Mindfulness work
- Vipassana
- Soto Zen
- Unitive experience

- Adopted
- Traveled the world from age 2
- Divorced & remarried
- Culture (WE)
- Social & Environment (ITS)
- Top education & top executive career

Understanding of Terms & Definitions
- Secrets to success: Gratitude, love, nurture
- Consciousness: Awareness of the divine
- Leadership: courage to guide toward a vision
- Consciousness Leadership: respect, higher values

Stan Profile and Core Topics—Mapping Wilber's AQAL

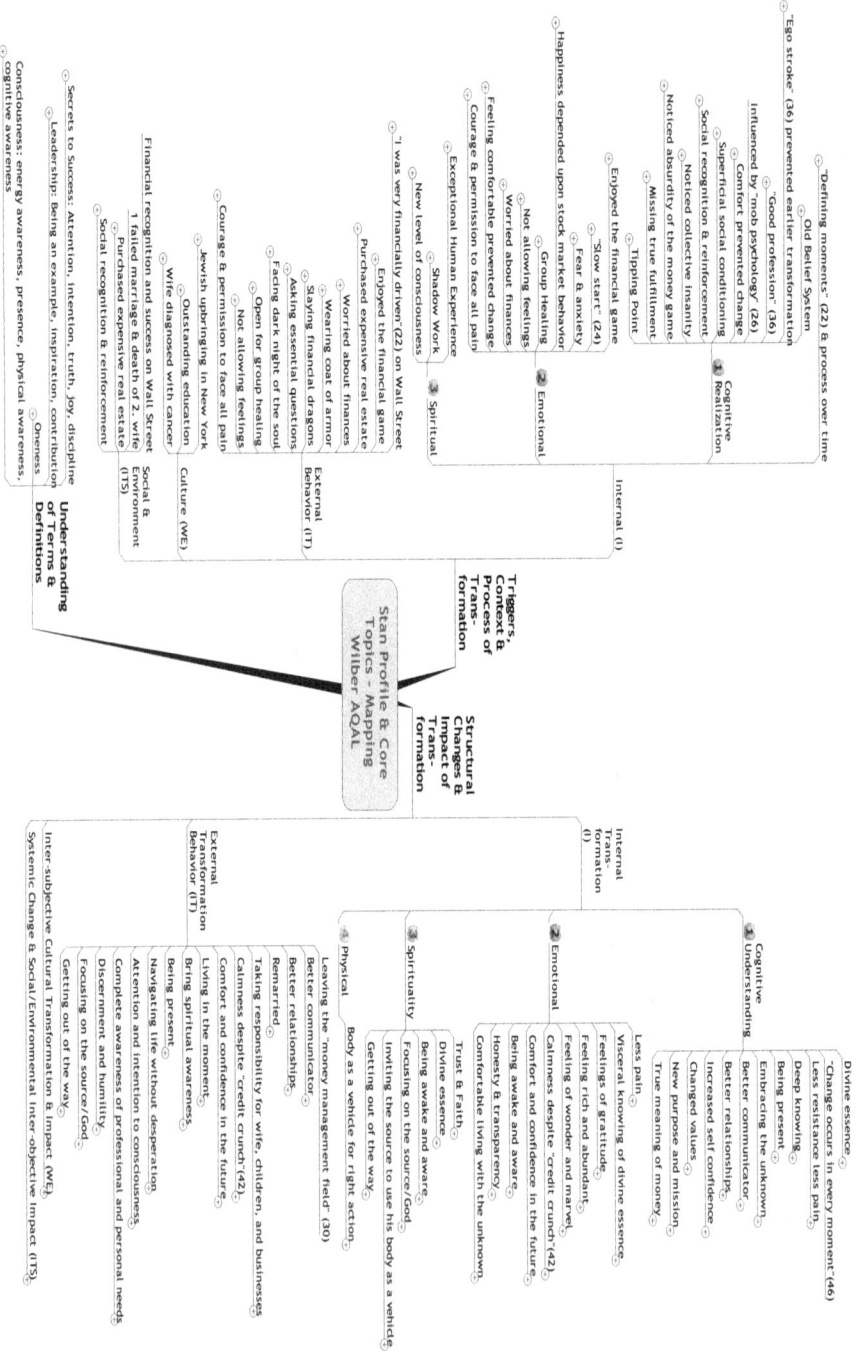

Stan Profile & Core Topics - Mapping Wilber AQAL

Triggers, Context & Process of Trans-formation

Internal (I)

Cognitive Realization
- 'Defining moments' (22) & process over time
- Old Belief System
- 'Ego stroke' (36) prevented earlier transformation
- 'Good profession' (36)
- Influenced by 'mob psychology' (26)
- Superficial social conditioning
- Comfort prevented change
- Social recognition & reinforcement
- Noticed absurdity of the money game
- Noticed collective insanity
- Missing true fulfillment

Emotional
- Happiness depended upon stock market behavior
- Tipping Point
- Enjoyed the financial game
- 'Slow start' (24)
- Fear & anxiety
- Group Healing
- Not allowing feelings
- Worried about finances
- Feeling comfortable prevented change
- Courage & permission to face all pain

Spiritual
- Exceptional Human Experience
- Shadow Work
- New level of consciousness
- 'I was very financially driven (22) on Wall Street
- Enjoyed the financial game
- Purchased expensive real estate

External Behavior (IT)
- Worried about finances
- Wearing coat of armor
- Slaying financial dragons
- Asking essential questions
- Facing dark night of the soul
- Open for group healing
- Not allowing feelings
- Courage & permission to face all pain

Culture (WE)
- Jewish upbringing in New York
- Outstanding education
- Wife diagnosed with cancer
- Financial recognition and success on Wall Street
- 1 failed marriage & death of 2. wife
- Purchased expensive real estate
- Social recognition & reinforcement

Social & Environment (ITS)

Understanding of Terms & Definitions
- Secrets to Success: Attention, intention, truth, joy, discipline
- Leadership: Being an example, inspiration, contribution
- Oneness
- Consciousness: energy awareness, presence, physical awareness, cognitive awareness

Structural Changes & Impact of Trans-formation

Internal Trans-formation (I)

Cognitive Understanding
- Divine essence
- 'Change occurs in every moment' (46)
- Less resistance less pain
- Deep knowing
- Being present
- Embracing the unknown
- Better communicator
- Better relationships
- Increased self confidence
- Changed values
- New purpose and mission
- True meaning of money

Emotional
- Less pain
- Visceral knowing of divine essence
- Feelings of gratitude
- Feeling rich and abundant
- Feeling of wonder and marvel
- Calmness despite 'credit crunch' (42)
- Comfort and confidence in the future
- Being awake and aware
- Honesty & transparency
- Comfortable living with the unknown

Spirituality
- Trust & Faith
- Divine essence
- Being awake and aware
- Focusing on the source/God
- Inviting the source to use his body as a vehicle
- Getting out of the way

Physical
- Body as a vehicle for right action
- Leaving the 'money management field' (30)

External Transformation Behavior (IT)
- Better communicator
- Better relationships
- Remarried
- Taking responsibility for wife, children, and businesses
- Calmness despite 'credit crunch' (42)
- Comfort and confidence in the future
- Living in the moment
- Bring spiritual awareness
- Being present
- Navigating life without desperation
- Attention and intention to consciousness
- Complete awareness of professional and personal needs
- Discernment and humility
- Focusing on the source/God
- Getting out of the way

Inter-subjective Cultural Transformation & Impact (WE)

Systemic Change & Social/Environmental Inter-objective Impact (ITS)

Topaz Profile and Core Topics—Mapping Wilber's AQAL

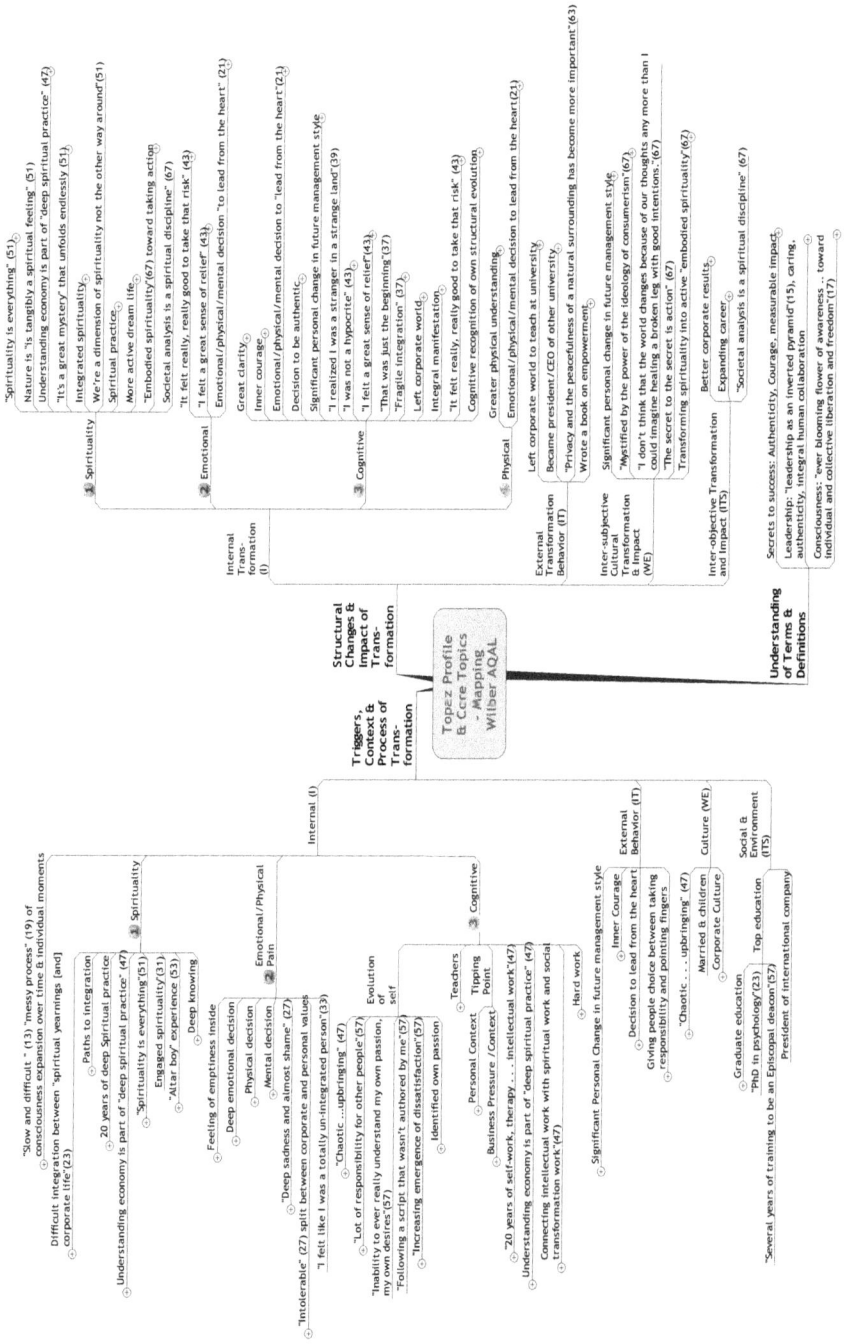

Structural Changes & Impact of Trans-formation

Internal Trans-formation (I)

Spirituality
- "Spirituality is everything" (51)
- Nature is "is tangibly a spiritual feeling" (51)
- Understanding economy is part of "deep spiritual practice" (47)
- "It's a great mystery" that unfolds endlessly (51)
- Integrated spirituality
- We're a dimension of spirituality not the other way around"(51)
- Spiritual practice
- More active dream life
- "Embodied spirituality"(67) toward taking action
- Societal analysis is a spiritual discipline" (67)
- "It felt really, really good to take that risk" (43)

Emotional
- "I felt a great sense of relief" (43)
- Emotional/physical/mental decision "to lead from the heart" (21)
- Great clarity
- Inner courage
- Emotional/physical/mental decision to "lead from the heart"(21)
- Decision to be authentic
- Significant personal change in future management style

Cognitive
- "I realized I was a stranger in a strange land"(39)
- "I was not a hypocrite" (43)
- "I felt a great sense of relief"(43)
- That was just the beginning"(37)
- "Fragile integration" (37)
- Left corporate world
- Integral manifestation
- "It felt really, really good to take that risk" (43)
- Cognitive recognition of own structural evolution

Physical
- Greater physical understanding
- Emotional/physical/mental decision to lead from the heart (21)

External Transformation Behavior (IT)
- Left corporate world to teach at university
- Became president/CEO of other university
- "Privacy and the peacefulness of a natural surrounding has become more important"(63)
- Wrote a book on empowerment

Inter-subjective Cultural Transformation & Impact (WE)
- Significant personal change in future management style
- "Mystified by the power of the ideology of consumerism"(67)
- "I don't think that the world changes because of our thoughts any more than I could imagine healing a broken leg with good intentions."(67)
- "The secret to the secret is action" (67)
- Transforming spirituality into active "embodied spirituality"(62)

Inter-objective Transformation and Impact (ITs)
- Better corporate results
- Expanding career
- "Societal analysis is a spiritual discipline" (67)

Understanding of Terms & Definitions
- Secrets to success: Authenticity, Courage, measurable impact,
- Leadership: "Leadership as an inverted pyramid"(15), caring, authenticity, integral human collaboration
- Consciousness: "ever blooming flower of awareness ... toward individual and collective liberation and freedom"(17)

Topaz Profile & Core Topics – Mapping Wilber AQAL

Triggers, Context & Process of Trans-formation

Internal (I)

Spirituality
- "Slow and difficult " (13) "messy process" (19) of consciousness expansion over time & individual moments
- Difficult integration between "spiritual yearnings [and] corporate life"(23)
- Paths to integration
- 20 years of deep Spiritual practice
- Understanding economy is part of "deep spiritual practice" (47)
- "Spirituality is everything"(51)
- Engaged spirituality(31)
- "Altar boy" experience (31)
- Deep knowing

Emotional/Physical Pain
- Feeling of emptiness inside
- Deep emotional decision
- Physical decision
- Mental decision
- "Deep sadness and almost shame" (27)
- "Intolerable" (27) split between corporate and personal values

Cognitive
- "I felt like I was a totally un-integrated person"(33)
- "Chaotic ...upbringing" (47)
- "Lot of responsibility for other people"(57)
- "Inability to ever really understand my own passion, my own desires"(57)
- "Following a script that wasn't authored by me"(57)
- "Increasing emergence of dissatisfaction"(57)
- Identified own passion
- Evolution of self
- Teachers
- Tipping Point
- Personal Context / Context
- Business Pressure / Context
- "20 years of self-work, therapy . . . intellectual work"(47)
- Understanding economy is part of "deep spiritual practice" (47)
- Connecting intellectual work with spiritual work and social transformation work"(47)
- Hard work

External Behavior (IT)
- Significant Personal Change in future management style
- Inner Courage
- Decision to lead from the heart
- Giving people choice between taking responsibility and pointing fingers

Culture (WE)
- "Chaotic . . . upbringing" (47)
- Married & children
- Corporate Culture

Social & Environment (ITs)
- Graduate education
- PhD in psychology(23)
- Top education
- "Several years of training to be an Episcopal deacon"(57)
- President of international company

Harbin Profile and Core Topics—Mapping Wilber's AQAL

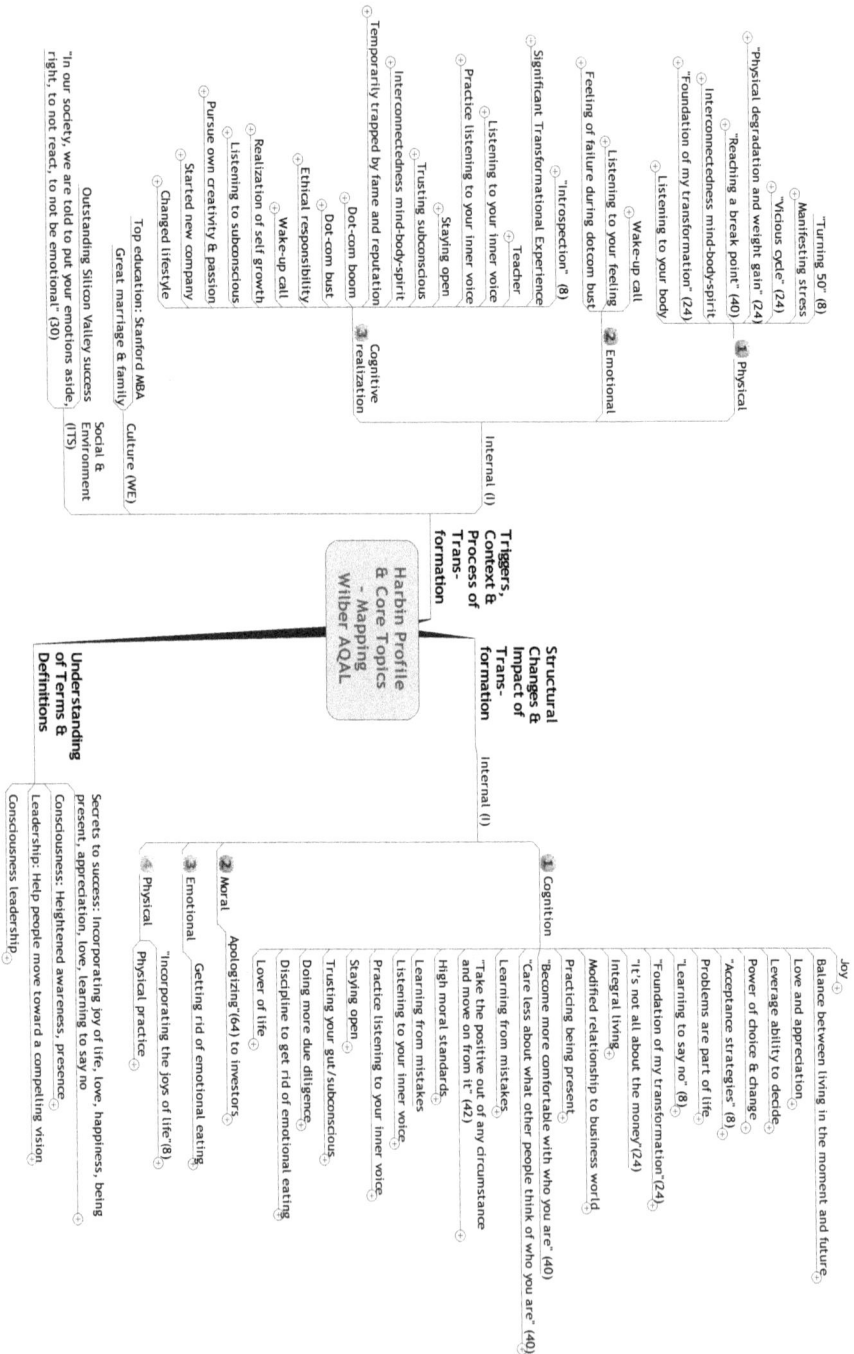

Harbin Profile & Core Topics - Mapping Wilber AQAL

Triggers, Context & Process of Trans-formation — Internal (I)

- "In our society, we are told to put your emotions aside, right, to not react, to not be emotional" (30)
- Outstanding Silicon Valley success
- Great marriage & family
- Top education: Stanford MBA
- Changed lifestyle
- Started new company
- Pursue own creativity & passion
- Realization of self growth
- Listening to subconscious
- Wake-up call
- Ethical responsibility
- Dot-com bust
- Dot-com boom
- Interconnectedness mind-body-spirit
- Trusting subconscious
- Staying open
- Temporarily trapped by fame and reputation
- Cognitive realization
- **Significant Transformational Experience**
  - Teacher
  - Listening to your inner voice
  - Practice listening to your inner voice
  - "Introspection" (8)
- Feeling of failure during dotcom bust
- Listening to your feeling
- Wake-up call
- **1 Physical**
  - "Physical degradation and weight gain" (24)
  - "Reaching a break point" (24)
  - Interconnectedness mind-body-spirit
  - "Foundation of my transformation" (24)
  - Listening to your body
- **2 Emotional**
  - Turning 50" (8)
  - Manifesting stress
  - "Vicious cycle" (24)

Culture (WE)
Social & Environment (ITS)

Structural Changes & Impact of Trans-formation — Internal (I)

Understanding of Terms & Definitions

- Consciousness leadership
- Leadership: Help people move toward a competing vision
- Consciousness: Heightened awareness, presence
- Consciousness: Incorporating joy of life, love, happiness, being present, appreciation, love, learning to say no
- Secrets to success: Incorporating joy of life, love, happiness, being present, appreciation, love, learning to say no
- **4 Physical**
  - Physical practice
  - "Incorporating the joys of life"(8)
- **3 Emotional**
  - Getting rid of emotional eating
  - "Incorporating the joys of life"(8)
- **2 Moral**
  - Apologizing"(64) to investors
  - Lover of life
  - Discipline to get rid of emotional eating
  - Doing more due diligence
  - Trusting your gut/subconscious
  - Staying open
  - Practice listening to your inner voice
  - Listening to your inner voice
  - Learning from mistakes
  - High moral standards.
  - Take the positive out of any circumstance and move on from it" (42)
- **1 Cognition**
  - "Become more comfortable with who you are" (40)
  - "Care less about what other people think of who you are" (40)
  - Learning from mistakes
  - Practicing being present
  - Modified relationship to business world
  - Integral living
  - "It's not all about the money"(24)
  - "Foundation of my transformation"(24).
  - "Learning to say no" (8).
  - Problems are part of life
  - "Acceptance strategies" (8)
  - Power of choice & change
  - Leverage ability to decide
  - Love and appreciation
  - Balance between living in the moment and future.
  - Joy

282

Hahm Profile and Core Topics—Mapping Wilber's AQAL

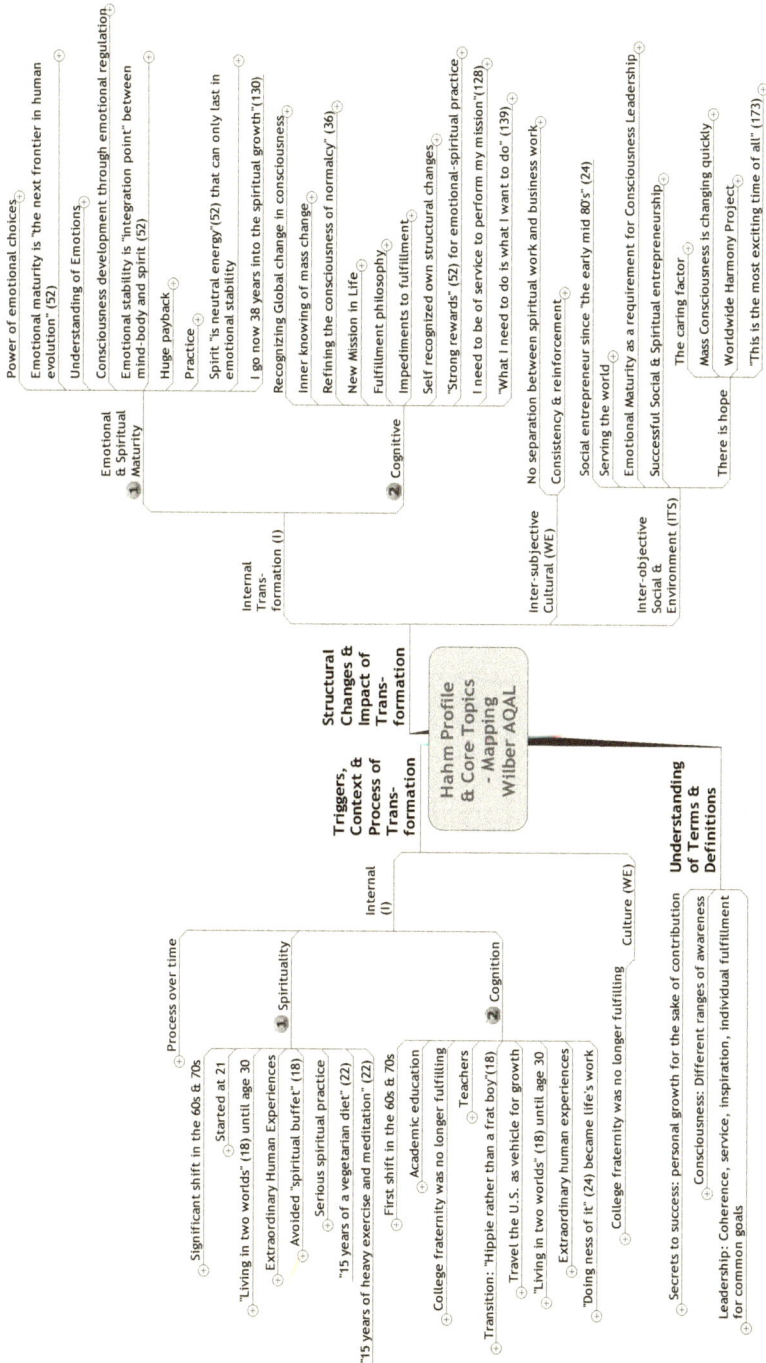

Hahm Profile & Core Topics - Mapping Wilber AQAL

Structural Changes & Impact of Transformation

Internal Transformation (I)

Emotional & Spiritual Maturity
- Power of emotional choices
- Emotional maturity is "the next frontier in human evolution" (52)
- Understanding of Emotions
- Consciousness development through emotional regulation
- Emotional stability is "integration point" between mind-body and spirit (52)
- Huge payback
- Practice
- Spirit "is neutral energy"(52) that can only last in emotional stability

Cognitive
- I go now 38 years into the spiritual growth"(130)
- Recognizing Global change in consciousness
- Inner knowing of mass change
- Refining the consciousness of normalcy" (36)
- New Mission in Life
- Fulfillment philosophy
- Impediments to fulfillment
- Self recognized own structural changes
- "Strong rewards" (52) for emotional-spiritual practice
- I need to be of service to perform my mission"(128)
- "What I need to do is what I want to do" (139)

Inter-subjective Cultural (WE)
- No separation between spiritual work and business work
- Consistency & reinforcement

Inter-objective Social & Environment (ITS)
- Social entrepreneur since "the early mid 80's" (24)
- Serving the world
- Emotional Maturity as a requirement for Consciousness Leadership
- Successful Social & Spiritual entrepreneurship

There is hope
- The caring factor
- Mass Consciousness is changing quickly
- Worldwide Harmony Project
- "This is the most exciting time of all" (173)

Triggers, Context & Process of Transformation

Internal (I)

Spirituality
- Process over time
- Significant shift in the 60s & 70s
- Started at 21
- "Living in two worlds" (18) until age 30
- Extraordinary Human Experiences
- Avoided 'spiritual buffet' (18)
- Serious spiritual practice
- "15 years of a vegetarian diet" (22)
- "15 years of heavy exercise and meditation" (22)
- First shift in the 60s & 70s
- Academic education
- Teachers

Cognition
- College fraternity was no longer fulfilling
- Transition: "Hippie rather than a frat boy"(18)
- Travel the U.S. as vehicle for growth
- "Living in two worlds" (18) until age 30
- Extraordinary human experiences
- "Doing ness of it" (24) became life's work
- College fraternity was no longer fulfilling

Culture (WE)

Understanding of Terms & Definitions
- Secrets to success: personal growth for the sake of contribution
- Consciousness: Different ranges of awareness
- Leadership: Coherence, service, inspiration, individual fulfillment for common goals

Cassandra Profile and Core Topics—Mapping Wilber's AQAL

Cassandra Profile & Core Topics - Mapping Wilber AQAL

Triggers, Context & Process of Transformation

Process

Internal (I)

- Cognitive
  - Mismatch personal versus professional relationships
    - "I'm missing out" (112)
    - Recognized high barriers prevented love too
    - "I didn't have the life I wanted" (74)
    - High Barriers should prevent being hurt again
  - No intimate relationship
    - "Overcoming period of denial" (96)
    - "Not meeting full potential" (96)
    - Financial independence enabled transformation
    - Needed time to look within
    - Stop old pattern
    - Chaos preceded clarity
    - Out of balance
    - Major changes
    - Extraordinary family
    - Painful divorce
    - "Peak economic" (38) success
    - "Really messed up my life" (38)
  - No children
    - Role models
    - Core principles
    - Controlling
    - "Wasn't hurt" and "wasn't loved" (134)
    - Conscious action
    - Subconscious action
    - Tipping Point

- Emotional
  - Unrest
  - Unhappiness
  - Feeling empty

- Physical
  - Painful divorce
  - Being somewhat Ok
  - Overweight
  - High Barriers should prevent being hurt again

External Behavior (IT)
- Extensive traveling
- Competitive
- Outcome oriented
- Outside-in nature
- Stop old pattern
- Failed marriage
- Closed down the business
- Parents as role models

Culture (WE)

Social & Environment (ITS)
- Entrepreneur - 2 companies

Structural Changes & Impact of Transformation

Internal Transformation (I)

- Cognition
  - "Human dynamics" (204)
    - Finding soul mate
      - Intention to meet soul mate materialized personally
      - Inner knowing
      - Clairaudience
    - Preparation
    - Personally
    - Professionally
  - Perfect Clarity
    - New definition of winning and losing
    - Conscious action
    - The universe responded
    - Spiritual downloading of personal & professional plan

- Physical
  - "I lost weight" (174)
    - Regular exercise
    - Plan for life revealed
    - Decided to take care of body

- Spirituality
  - Perfect Clarity
  - Clairaudience
  - Quiet time

External Transformation Behavior (IT)
- "Golfing" (174)
- "Gardening" (180)
- Perfect Clarity
- Quiet time

Inter-subjective Cultural Transformation & Impact (WE)
- Leveraging larger groups
- Focus on organizational development
- Philanthropic involvement
- Traveling around the world for global change
- Honoring diversity

Systemic Change & Social/Environmental Inter-objective Impact (ITS)

Understanding of Terms & Definitions

- Secrets to success: being blessed, drive, focus, intention, competitiveness, taking action, great family support
- Leadership: Vision, intent, process, empowerment, communication, collaboration, sacrifice, winning
- Consciousness: Awareness
  - Awareness
  - Looking within for answers

LaCroix Profile and Core Topics—Mapping Wilber's AQAL

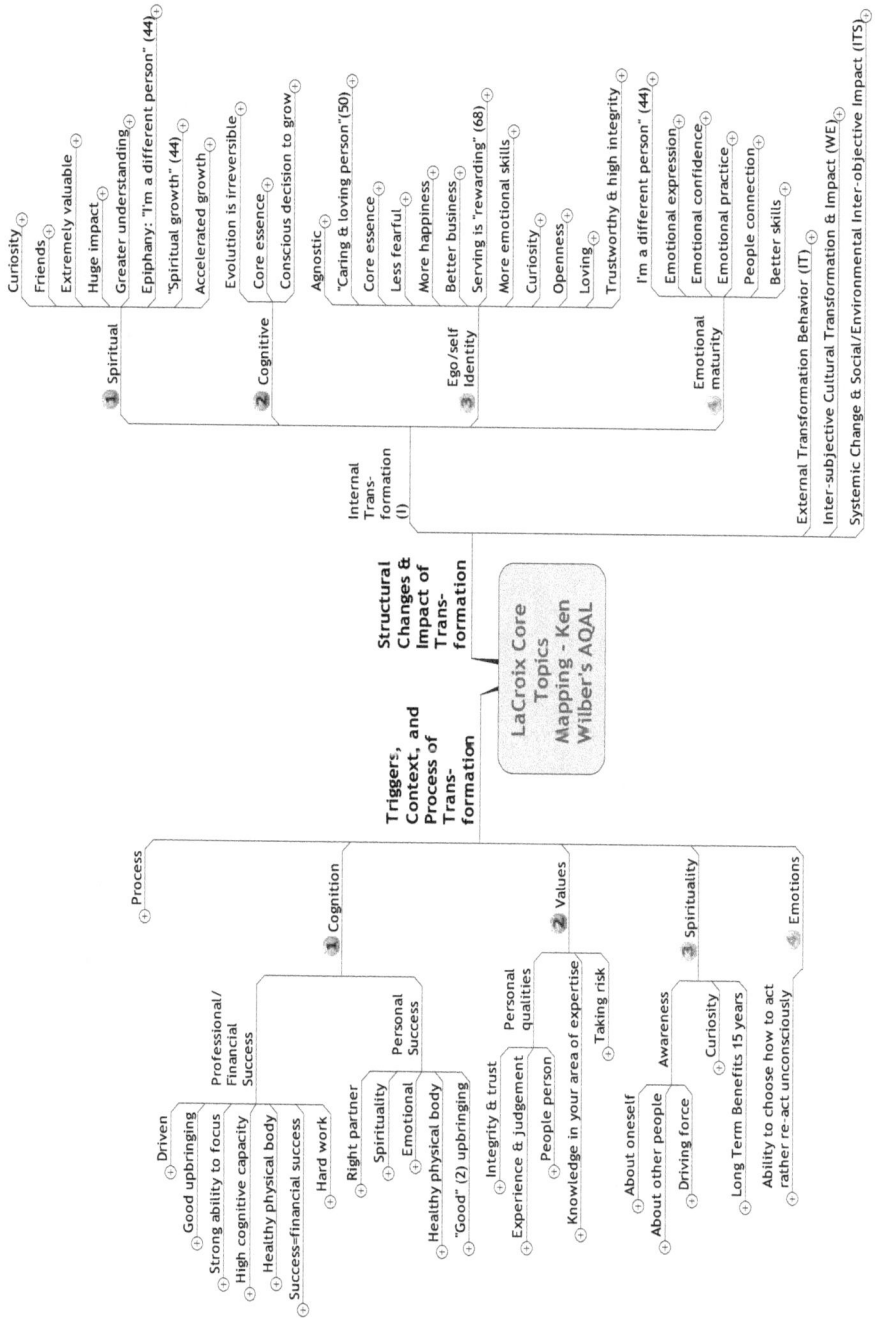

LaCroix Core Topics Mapping - Ken Wilber's AQAL

Structural Changes & Impact of Transformation

Internal Transformation (I)

1 Spiritual
- Curiosity
- Friends
- Extremely valuable
- Huge impact
- Greater understanding
- Epiphany: "I'm a different person" (44)
- "Spiritual growth" (44)
- Accelerated growth
- Evolution is irreversible
- Core essence
- Conscious decision to grow

2 Cognitive
- Agnostic
- "Caring & loving person"(50)
- Core essence
- Less fearful
- More happiness
- Better business
- Serving is "rewarding" (68)
- More emotional skills
- Curiosity
- Openness
- Loving
- Trustworthy & high integrity

3 Ego/self Identity

4 Emotional maturity
- I'm a different person" (44)
- Emotional expression
- Emotional confidence
- Emotional practice
- People connection
- Better skills

External Transformation Behavior (IT)

Inter-subjective Cultural Transformation & Impact (WE)

Systemic Change & Social/Environmental Inter-objective Impact (ITS)

Triggers, Context, and Process of Transformation

Process

1 Cognition
- Driven
- Good upbringing
- Strong ability to focus
- High cognitive capacity
- Healthy physical body
- Success=financial success
- Hard work
- Professional/Financial Success
- Personal Success
- Right partner
- Spirituality
- Emotional
- Healthy physical body
- "Good" (2) upbringing
- Personal qualities
- Integrity & trust
- Experience & judgement
- People person
- Knowledge in your area of expertise
- Taking risk

2 Values

3 Spirituality
- Awareness
- About oneself
- About other people
- Driving force
- Curiosity
- Long Term Benefits 15 years

4 Emotions
- Ability to choose how to act rather re-act unconsciously

Darlene Profile and Core Topics—Mapping Wilber's AQAL

Darlene Profile & Core Topics - Mapping Wilber AQAL

Triggers, Context & Process of Trans-formation

Internal (I)

1 Spirituality
- Process over time & Exceptional human experiences
- Wanted to get enlightened
- 30- years on the path
- Grand Spiritual Openings
- Inner knowing at 5
- Apparition of Christ at 9
- Mystical experience-Apparition
  - Exceptional Human Experiences
- Chakras opening
  - Teachers
- Heart-centered spiritual practice after 20 years of meditation practice
- Triggered support from higher intelligence & intuition
- Real awakening to subtle thoughts and feelings
- Moment to moment,
- Spiritual attunement,
- Higher Awareness & intelligence

2 Cognition
- Excellent education
- Always wanted to be a teacher
- Life's Purpose is to be of service
- Transformed field of psychology
- Wrote several books
- Recognized the importance of direct insight for consciousness evolution
- Major shift in perspective: Transformative power & intelligence of the heart
- Real awakening to subtle thoughts and feelings
- Decision to "filter living life through the heart" (8)
- Conscious decision to connect with intuitive clarity
- Gaining clear perspective through intelligence of the heart.
- Putting out love, appreciation, compassion, and care
- Radical life change through heart-brain-mind coherence
- Heart-based living as a habit,
- Building a bridge to higher self
- Being of Service
- No family background in business

Cultural Inter-subjective(WE)
- Listening to the heart all day long
- Getting out of the head
  - Secrets to success: Listening to the heart
- Consciousness: alignment of mental, physical, emotional, spiritual consciousness to allow spirit to come in and access creative forces that permeate but are beyond cognition

Understanding of Terms & Definitions

Structural Changes & Impact of Trans-formation

Internal Trans-formation (I)

1 Spirituality
- Heart-centered spiritual practice,
- Triggered support from higher intelligence & intuition
- Moment to moment,
- Real awakening to subtle thoughts and feelings
- Spiritual attunement,
- Higher awareness & intelligence
- Business as a spiritual path
- "Awakening put me on track" (33)

2 Cognition
- Major shift in perspective: Transformative power & intelligence of the heart,
- Real awakening to subtle thoughts and feelings
- Decision to "filter living life through the heart" (8)
- Conscious decision to connect with intuitive clarity,
- Gaining clear perspective through intelligence of the heart,
- Putting out love, appreciation, compassion, and care.
- Heart-brain-mind coherence.
- Habit of heart-based living,
- Building a bridge to Higher Self,
- Integration of the wheel of life.
- "Good values" (25)
- "It's all inspiring" (85)
- Business as service
- Business as a spiritual path.
- Business is "an incredible laboratory for consciousness research"
- Problem in business,
- Became a serial entrepreneur & managed two non-profit organizations

External Transformation Behavior (IT)
- Harmonize private and professional in business
- Psychophysiological coherence practice.
- Psychophysiological coherence as cultural tool,
- Stress reducing tools,
- Empowering heart-based living,

Inter-subjective Cultural Transformation & Impact (WE)
- "Promote interactivity and community building" (85)
- Taking Spirituality into the business world using heart-based tools
- Global harmony project

Systemic Change & Social/Environmental Inter-objective Impact (ITS)
- Directing heart energy toward social & ecological change
- Sustainable businesses through heart-based living,
- Reducing health care costs

286

DeSiena Profile and Core Topics—Mapping Wilber's AQAL

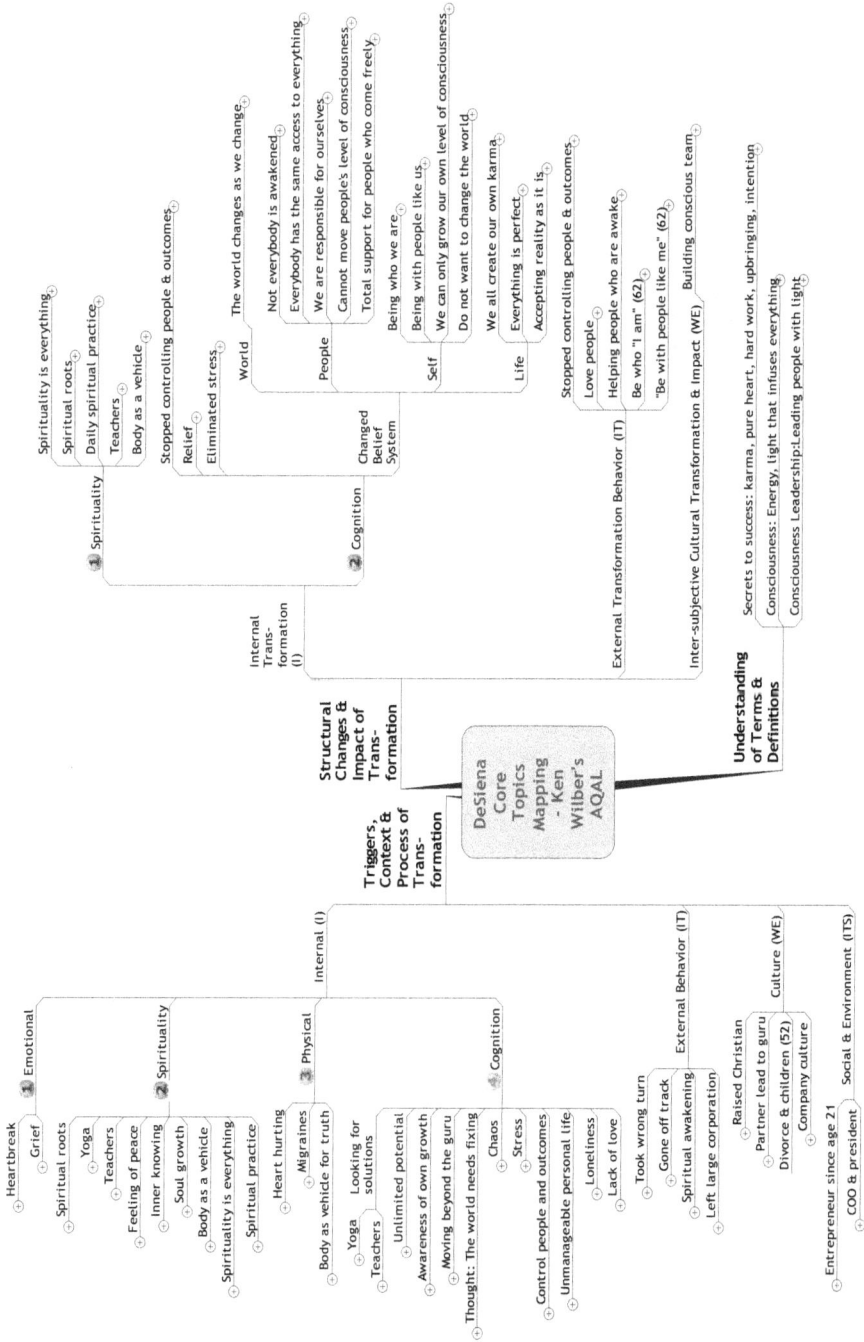

DeSiena Core Topics Mapping - Ken Wilber's AQAL

Structural Changes & Impact of Transformation

Internal Transformation (I)

1 Spirituality
- Spirituality is everything
- Spiritual roots
- Daily spiritual practice
- Teachers
- Body as a vehicle
- Stopped controlling people & outcomes
- Relief
- Eliminated stress

2 Cognition — Changed Belief System

World
- The world changes as we change
- Not everybody is awakened
- Everybody has the same access to everything

People
- We are responsible for ourselves
- Cannot move people's level of consciousness
- Total support for people who come freely

Self
- Being who we are
- Being with people like us
- We can only grow our own level of consciousness
- Do not want to change the world

Life
- We all create our own karma
- Everything is perfect
- Accepting reality as it is
- Stopped controlling people & outcomes

External Transformation Behavior (IT)
- Love people
- Helping people who are awake
- Be who "I am" (62)
- "Be with people like me" (62)
- Building conscious team

Inter-subjective Cultural Transformation & Impact (WE)

Understanding of Terms & Definitions
- Secrets to success: karma, pure heart, hard work, upbringing, intention
- Consciousness: Energy, light that infuses everything
- Consciousness Leadership: Leading people with light

Triggers, Context & Process of Transformation

Internal (I)

1 Emotional
- Heartbreak
- Grief
- Spiritual roots
- Yoga
- Teachers
- Feeling of peace
- Inner knowing
- Soul growth

2 Spirituality
- Body as a vehicle
- Spirituality is everything
- Spiritual practice

3 Physical
- Heart hurting
- Migraines
- Body as vehicle for truth

4 Cognition
- Yoga
- Teachers
- Looking for solutions
- Unlimited potential
- Awareness of own growth
- Moving beyond the guru
- Thought: The world needs fixing
- Chaos
- Stress
- Control people and outcomes
- Unmanageable personal life
- Loneliness
- Lack of love
- Took wrong turn
- Gone off track
- Spiritual awakening

External Behavior (IT)
- Left large corporation
- Raised Christian
- Partner lead to guru
- Divorce & children (52)
- Company culture

Culture (WE)

Social & Environment (ITS)
- Entrepreneur since age 21
- COO & president

Bianco Profile and Core Topics—Mapping Wilber's AQAL

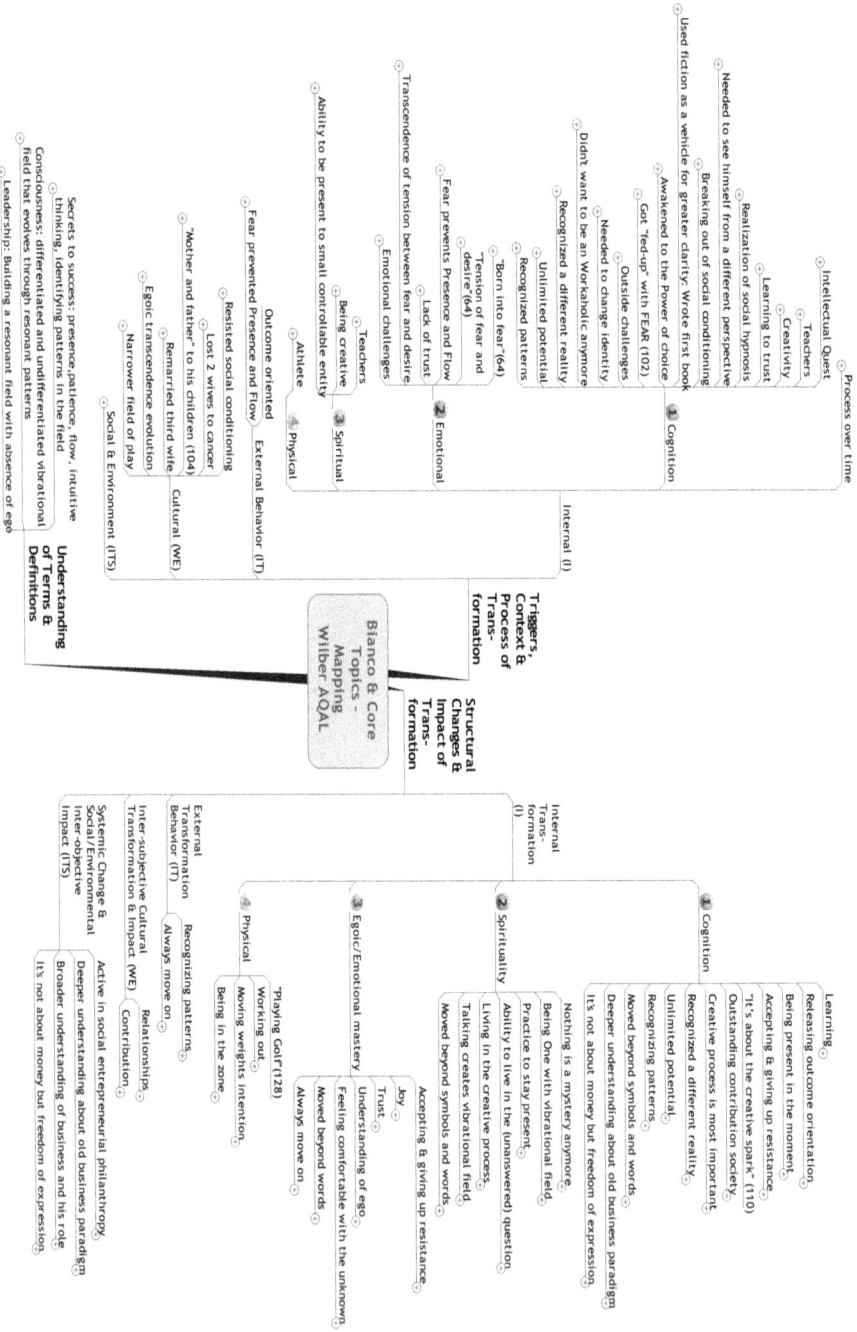

Bianco & Core Topics - Mapping Wilber AQAL

Understanding of Terms & Definitions

- Leadership: Building a resonant field with absence of ego
- Consciousness: differentiated and undifferentiated vibrational field that evolves through resonant patterns
- Secrets to success: presence, patience, flow, intuitive thinking, identifying patterns in the field

Triggers, Context & Process of Trans-formation

Internal (I)

Process over time

- Intellectual Quest
  - Teachers
  - Creativity
  - Learning to trust
- Realization of social hypnosis
- Needed to see himself from a different perspective
- Breaking out of social conditioning
- Used fiction as a vehicle for greater clarity; Wrote first book
- Awakened to the Power of choice
- Got 'fed-up' with FEAR (102)
- Needed to change identity
- Outside challenges
- Didn't want to be an Workaholic anymore
- Recognized a different reality

Cognition
- Recognized a different reality
- Recognized patterns
- Unlimited potential

- Transcendence of tension between fear and desire
- Ability to be present to small controllable entity

Emotional
- Fear prevents Presence and Flow
  - 'Born into fear' (64)
  - Tension of fear and desire (64)
  - Lack of trust
- Emotional challenges
- Teachers
- Being creative

Spiritual

Athlete / Physical
- Outcome oriented

External Behavior (IT)
- Fear prevented Presence and Flow
- Resisted social conditioning
- "Mother and father" to his children (104)
- Lost 2 wives to cancer

Cultural (WE)
- Egoic transcendence evolution
- Remarried third wife
- Narrower field of play

Social & Environment (ITS)

Structural Changes & Impact of Trans-formation

Internal Trans-formation (I)

Cognition
- Learning
- Releasing outcome orientation
- Being present in the moment
- Accepting & giving up resistance
- "It's about the creative spark" (110)
- Outstanding contribution society.
- Creative process is most important.
- Recognized a different reality.
- Unlimited potential.
- Recognizing patterns
- Moved beyond symbols and words.
- Deeper understanding about old business paradigm
- It's not about money but freedom of expression.

Spirituality
- Nothing is a mystery anymore
- Being One with vibrational field.
- Practice to stay present.
- Ability to live in the (unanswered) question.
- Living in the creative process.
- Talking creates vibrational field.
- Moved beyond symbols and words
- Accepting & giving up resistance
- Joy.
- Trust.
- Understanding of ego.
- Feeling comfortable with the unknown.
- Moved beyond words
- Always move on

Egoic/Emotional mastery

Physical
- "Playing Golf (128)
- Working out.
- Moving weights intention.
- Being in the zone.

External Transformation Behavior (IT)
- Recognizing patterns.
- Always move on.

Inter-subjective Cultural Transformation & Impact (WE)
- Relationships.
- Contribution.

Systemic Change & Social/Environmental Inter-objective Impact (ITS)
- Active in social entrepreneurial philanthropy.
- Deeper understanding about old business paradigm
- Broader understanding of business and his role
- It's not about money but freedom of expression.

Poet Profile and Core Topics—Mapping Wilber's AQAL

Poet Profile & Core Topics - Mapping Wilber AQAL

Structural Changes & Impact of Transformation

Internal Transformation (I)

- 1 Spirituality — Daily Practices
  - Joy of being alive
  - Gratitude
  - Compassion
  - Humility
- 2 Emotions
  - Integration of authentic leadership skills
  - "Re-imagined the possibility of business" (8)
  - Re-framing the business world
  - Greater appreciation for own gifts and talents
  - Teachers
  - Creative Capitalism: "Powerful time" (8) in business
  - New Passion—integrating social mission with profit & capital
  - Doing rather than telling
- 3 Cognition
  - Learnings
    - Gratitude
    - Humility
  - Ability to meet people at their own levels of consciousness
  - "All is necessary" (26)
  - Living the miracle
  - "Stage of conscious competence"(26)
  - "Full shift in language"(24) and re-integration in the world
  - Embracing paradoxes
  - "Integrating heart and mind" (26)
  - Joy of being alive
  - Being present
  - Mindfulness
  - Acknowledging growth progress
  - Humility
- 4 Ego
  - Creative Capitalism = "Powerful time" (8) in business
  - New Passion: Integrating social mission with profit & capital
  - "Re-imagined the possibility of business" (8)
  - Sustainable businesses
  - Re-framing the business world
  - Made Movie

Systemic Change & Social/Environmental Inter-objective Impact (ITS)
- Consciousness: awareness
  - Individual consciousness
  - Collective consciousness

Understanding of Terms & Definitions

Triggers, Context & Process of Transformation

Internal (I)

- 1 Cognitive
  - "A slow and painful process, incredibly painful" (14) process over time
  - Dream career fulfilled at 31
  - "Completely unhappy" (2)
  - "Silent voice" (2) was screaming
  - Kept busy not to think or feel
  - "Hit rock bottom"(2) at 34
  - Old conditioning: "me, me, me" (4)
  - Shift from ME to US
  - Maximizing share holder value was no longer fulfilling
  - Lack of depth within business context
  - Unique gifts were not appreciated
  - Tipping Points
  - Natural leadership style: Servant Leadership
  - Interim State: Transcend and reject
  - "Incredibly painful" (14) process

- 2 Emotions & Spirituality
  - Challenges
    - Compassion
    - Empathy
    - Understanding
  - Sources of Pain
    - Fear
    - Need to be taken seriously
    - Need to live integrally and trust gut along with facts (after rewiring)
    - Insecurity about inner shift
    - Difficulties bringing higher consciousness within the business world
    - Lack of understanding of other people
  - Experience of love & joy
  - Bold spiritual transformation
  - Hero's journey as "divine love" (24)
  - Transition process was "mostly emotional and spiritual"(24)
  - Frustration when confronted with the world outside the spiritual one
  - Judgement about other people's levels of consciousness
  - "Bold proclamation" (22) regarding new philanthropic mission

External Behavior (IT)
Culture (WE)
Social & Environment (ITS)

- Marriage & children (39)
- Great education
- Top executive position

ElCore Profile and Core Topics—Mapping Wilber's AQAL

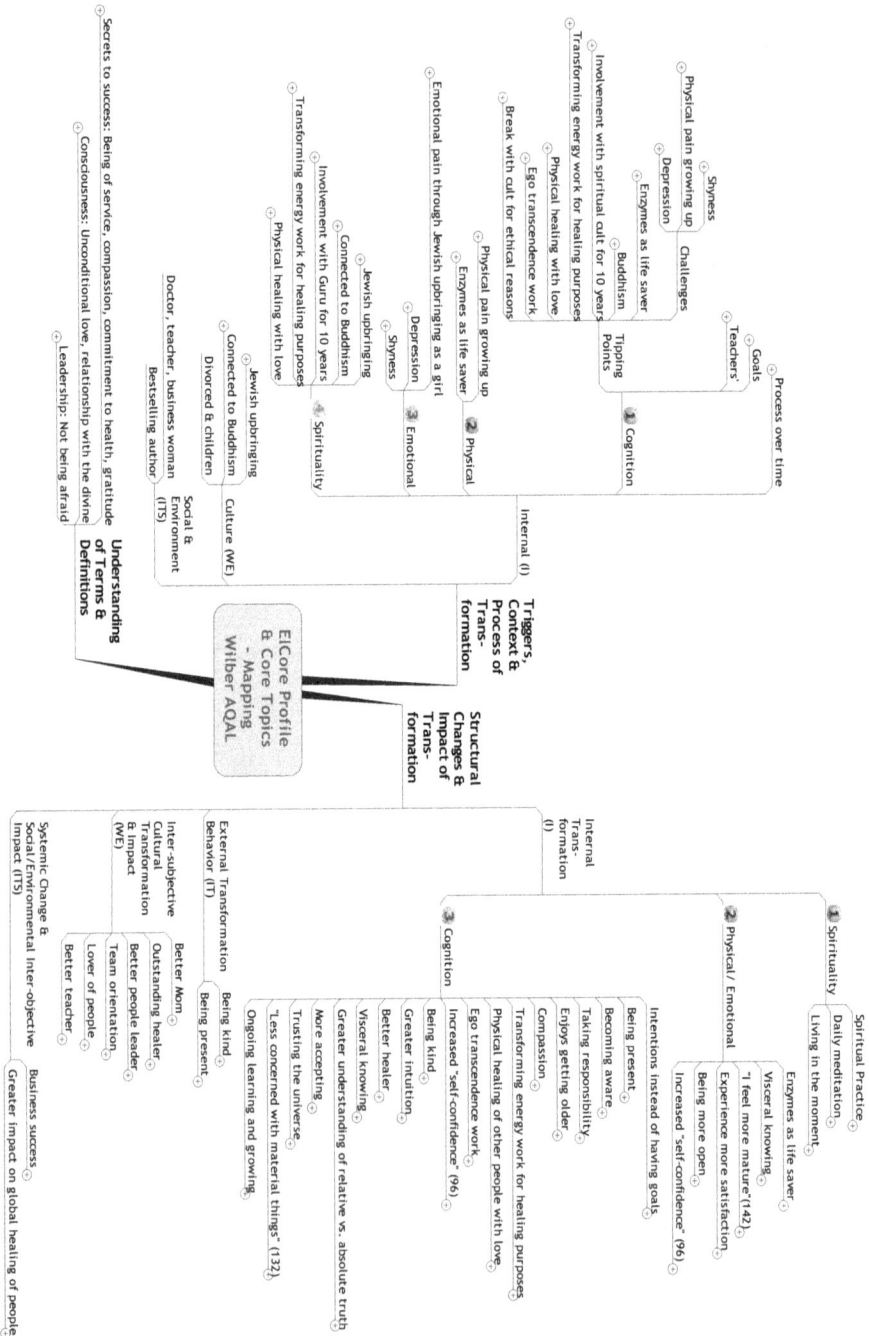

Secrets to success: Being of service, compassion, commitment to health, gratitude

Consciousness: Unconditional love, relationship with the divine

Leadership: Not being afraid

Physical pain growing up

Shyness

Depression

Involvement with spiritual cult for 10 years

Transforming energy work for healing purposes

Physical healing with love

Ego transcendence work

Break with cult for ethical reasons

Emotional pain through Jewish upbringing as a girl

Transforming energy work for healing purposes

Involvement with Guru for 10 years

Physical healing with love

Doctor, teacher, business woman

Bestselling author

Divorced & children

Connected to Buddhism

Jewish upbringing

Goals

Challenges

Teachers'

Enzymes as life saver

Buddhism

Physical healing with love

Physical pain growing up

Enzymes as life saver

Depression

Shyness

Connected to Buddhism

Jewish upbringing

Spirituality

Tipping
Points

Tipping
Points

Cognition

① Physical

② Emotional

✿ Spirituality

Culture (WE)

Social &
Environment
(ITS)

Process over time

Internal (I)

**Triggers,
Context &
Process of
Trans-
formation**

**Understanding
of Terms &
Definitions**

**ElCore Profile
& Core Topics
- Mapping
Wilber AQAL**

**Structural
Changes &
Impact of
Trans-
formation**

Internal
Trans-
formation
(I)

External Transformation
Behavior (IT)

Inter-subjective
Cultural
Transformation
& Impact
(WE)

Systemic Change &
Social/Environmental Inter-objective
Impact (ITS)

① Spirituality

② Physical / Emotional

③ Cognition

Spiritual Practice

Daily meditation

Living in the moment

Enzymes as life saver

Visceral knowing

"I feel more mature"(142)

Experience more satisfaction

Being more open

Increased "self-confidence" (96)

Intentions instead of having goals

Being present

Becoming aware

Taking responsibility

Enjoys getting older

Compassion

Transforming energy work for healing purposes

Physical healing of other people with love

Ego transcendence work

Increased "self-confidence" (96)

Being kind

Greater intuition

Better healer

Visceral knowing

Greater understanding of relative vs. absolute truth

More accepting

Trusting the universe

"Less concerned with material things" (132)

Ongoing learning and growing

Being kind

Being present

Better Mom

Outstanding healer

Better people leader

Team orientation

Lover of people

Better teacher

Business success

Greater impact on global healing of people

Chuck Profile and Core Topics—Mapping Wilber's AQAL

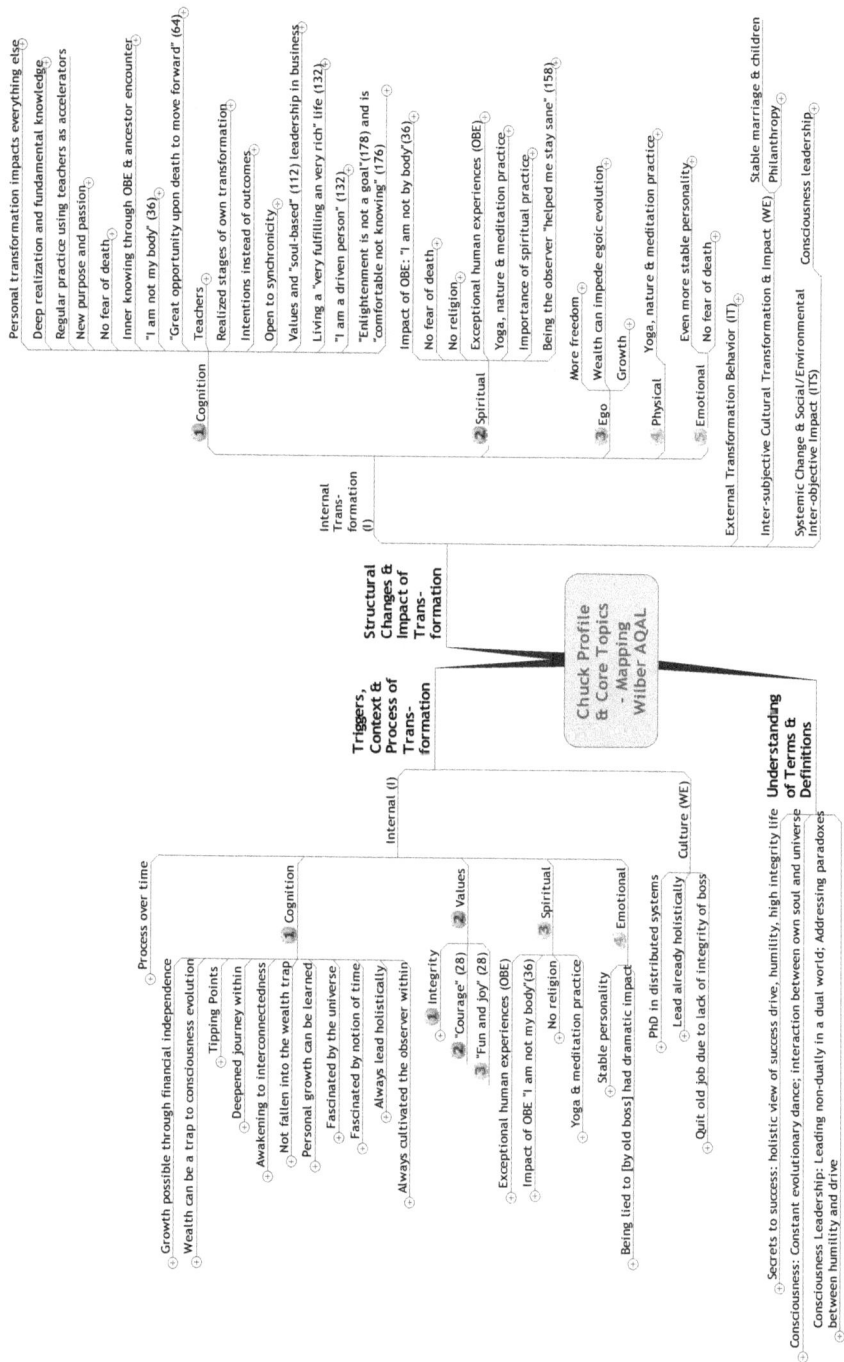

Chuck Profile & Core Topics - Mapping Wilber AQAL

Structural Changes & Impact of Transformation

Internal Transformation (I)

1. **Cognition**
   - Personal transformation impacts everything else
   - Deep realization and fundamental knowledge
   - Regular practice using teachers as accelerators
   - New purpose and passion
   - No fear of death
   - Inner knowing through OBE & ancestor encounter
   - "I am not my body" (36)
   - "Great opportunity upon death to move forward" (64)
   - Teachers
   - Realized stages of own transformation
   - Intentions instead of outcomes
   - Open to synchronicity
   - Values and "soul-based" (112) leadership in business
   - Living a "very fulfilling an very rich" life (132)
   - "I am a driven person" (132)
   - "Enlightenment is not a goal" (178) and is "comfortable not knowing" (176)
   - Impact of OBE: "I am not by body" (36)

2. **Spiritual**
   - No fear of death
   - No religion
   - Exceptional human experiences (OBE)
   - Yoga, nature & meditation practice
   - Importance of spiritual practice
   - Being the observer "helped me stay sane" (158)

3. **Ego**
   - More freedom
   - Wealth can impede egoic evolution
   - Growth

4. **Physical**
   - Yoga, nature & meditation practice

5. **Emotional**
   - Even more stable personality
   - No fear of death

External Transformation Behavior (IT)

Inter-subjective Cultural Transformation & Impact (WE)
- Stable marriage & children
- Philanthropy
- Consciousness leadership

Systemic Change & Social/Environmental Inter-objective Impact (ITS)

Triggers, Context & Process of Transformation

Internal (I)

- **Process over time**
  - Growth possible through financial independence
  - Wealth can be a trap to consciousness evolution
  - Tipping Points
  - Deepened journey within
  - Awakening to interconnectedness

1. **Cognition**
   - Not fallen into the wealth trap
   - Personal growth can be learned
   - Fascinated by the universe
   - Fascinated by notion of time
   - Always lead holistically
   - Always cultivated the observer within

2. **Values**
   - Integrity
   - "Courage" (28)
   - "Fun and Joy" (28)

3. **Spiritual**
   - Exceptional human experiences (OBE)
   - Impact of OBE "I am not my body" (36)
   - No religion
   - Yoga & meditation practice

4. **Emotional**
   - Stable personality
   - Being lied to [by old boss] had dramatic impact

Culture (WE)
- PhD in distributed systems
- Lead already holistically
- Quit old job due to lack of integrity of boss

Understanding of Terms & Definitions

- Secrets to success: holistic view of success drive, humility, high integrity life
- Consciousness: Constant evolutionary dance; interaction between own soul and universe
- Consciousness Leadership: Leading non-dually in a dual world; Addressing paradoxes between humility and drive

Lia Profile and Core Topics—Mapping Wilber's AQAL

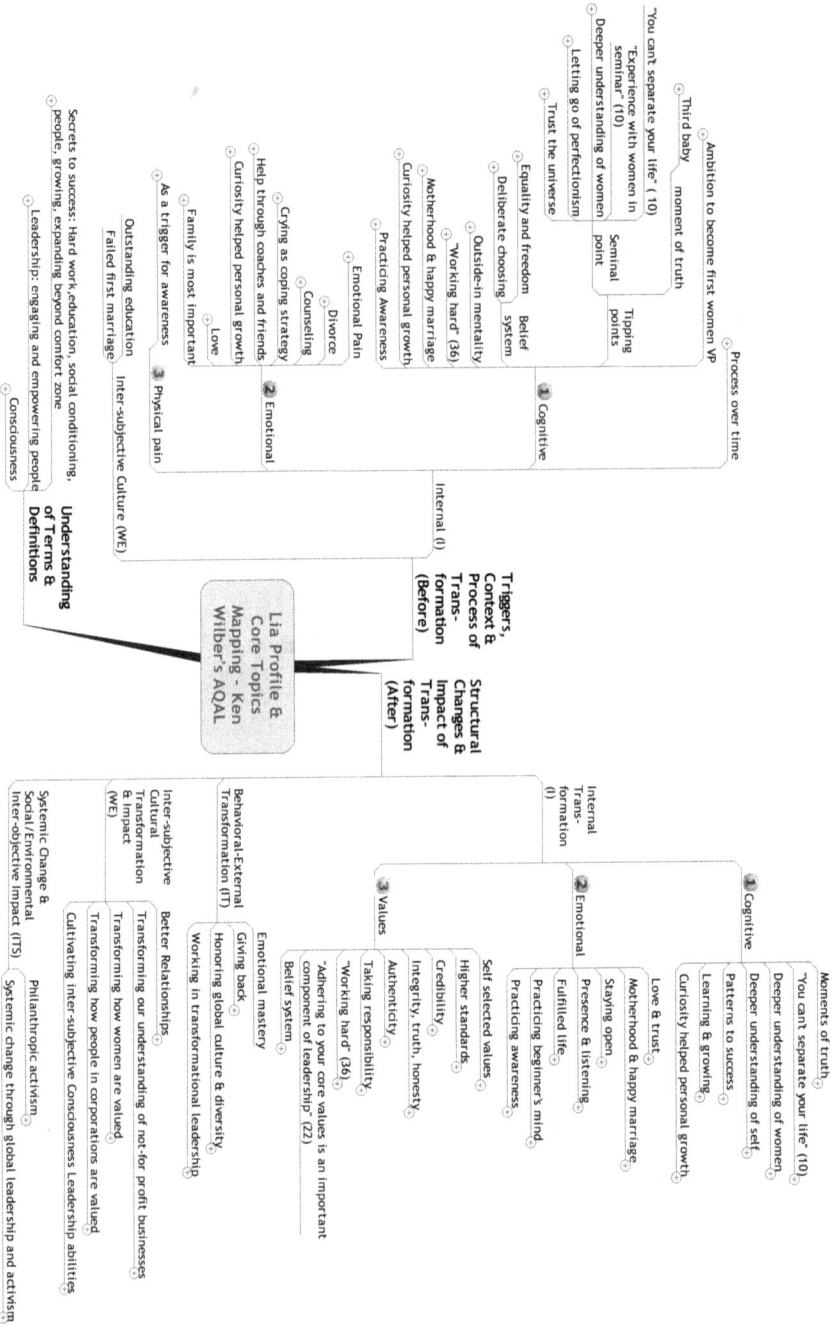

Lia Profile & Core Topics Mapping - Ken Wilber's AQAL

Triggers, Context & Process of Transformation (Before)

Internal (I)

1 Cognitive
- Ambition to become first women VP
- Process over time
- Third baby moment of truth
- "You can't separate your life' (10)
- "Experience with women in seminar" (10)
- Deeper understanding of women
- Letting go of perfectionism
- Trust the universe
  - Seminal point
  - Tipping points
- Equality and freedom
- Deliberate choosing
- Outside-in mentality
- Working hard (36)
- Motherhood & happy marriage
- Curiosity helped personal growth
- Practicing Awareness
- Belief system

2 Emotional
- Help through coaches and friends
- Curiosity helped personal growth
- Crying as coping strategy
- Emotional Pain
- Divorce
- Counseling
- Love

3 Physical pain
- As a trigger for awareness
- Family is most important
- Outstanding education
- Failed first marriage

Inter-subjective Culture (WE)
- Secrets to success: Hard work, education, social conditioning, people, growing, expanding beyond comfort zone
- Leadership: engaging and empowering people
- Consciousness

Understanding of Terms & Definitions

Structural Changes & Impact of Transformation (After)

Internal Transformation (I)

1 Cognitive
- Moments of truth
- "You can't separate your life' (10)
- Deeper understanding of women
- Deeper understanding of self
- Patterns to success
- Learning & growing
- Curiosity helped personal growth

2 Emotional
- Love & trust
- Motherhood & happy marriage
- Staying open
- Presence & listening
- Fulfilled life
- Practicing beginners mind
- Practicing awareness
- Emotional mastery
- Giving back

3 Values
- Self selected values
- Higher standards
- Credibility
- Integrity, truth, honesty
- Authenticity
- Taking responsibility
- "Working hard" (36)
- "Adhering to your core values is an important component of leadership" (22)
- Belief system

Behavioral-External Transformation (IT)
- Better Relationships
- Honoring global culture & diversity
- Working in transformational leadership

Inter-subjective Cultural Transformation & Impact (WE)
- Transforming our understanding of not-for profit businesses
- Transforming how women are valued
- Transforming how people in corporations are valued
- Cultivating inter-subjective Consciousness Leadership abilities

Systemic Change & Social/Environmental Inter-objective Impact (ITS)
- Philanthropic activism
- Systemic change through global leadership and activism